Rome Rules the Waves

Rome Rules the Waves

A Naval Staff Appreciation of Ancient Rome's Maritime Strategy 300 BC – 500 CE

James J. Bloom

Pen & Sword
MILITARY

First published in Great Britain in 2019 by
Pen & Sword Military
An imprint of
Pen & Sword Books Ltd
47 Church Street
Barnsley
South Yorkshire
S70 2AS

ISBN 978 1 78159 024 9

A CIP catalogue record for this book is
available from the British Library.

Printed and bound in England
By TJ International Ltd, Padstow, Cornwall

Pen & Sword Books Limited incorporates the imprints of Atlas,
Archaeology, Aviation, Discovery, Family History, Fiction, History,
Maritime, Military, Military Classics, Politics, Select, Transport, True Crime,
Air World, Frontline Publishing, Leo Cooper, Remember When,
Seaforth Publishing, The Praetorian Press, Wharncliffe Local History,
Wharncliffe Transport, Wharncliffe True Crime and White Owl.

For a complete list of Pen & Sword titles please contact
PEN & SWORD BOOKS LIMITED
47 Church Street, Barnsley, South Yorkshire, S70 2AS, England
E-mail: enquiries@pen-and-sword.co.uk
Website: www.pen-and-sword.co.uk

Contents

Illustrations

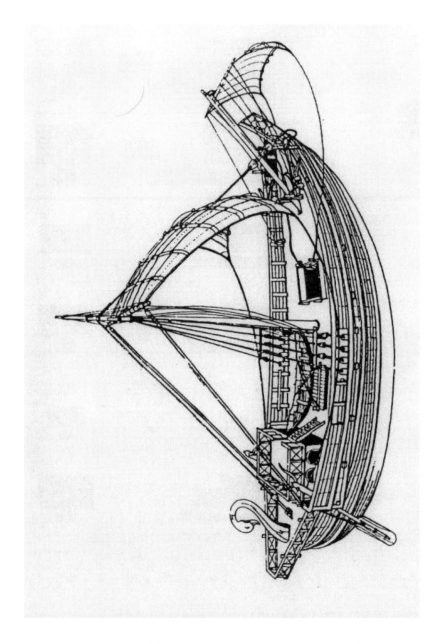

Roman medium-sized Corbita freighter circa second century AD.
These vessels were adapted for use as troop ships.

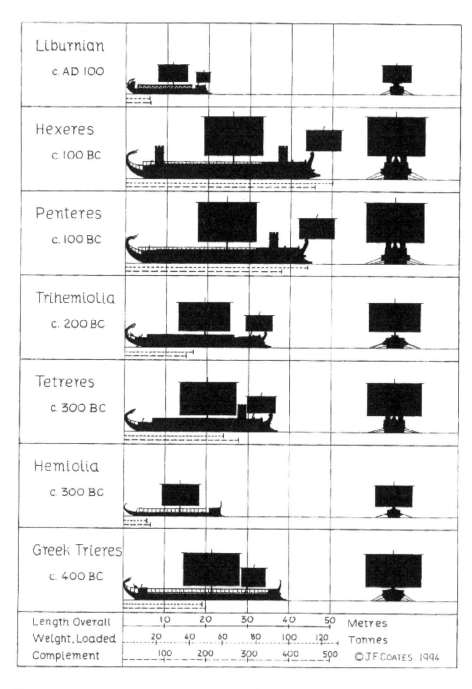

Liburnian c. AD 100					
Hexeres c. 100 BC					
Penteres c. 100 BC					
Trihemiolia c. 200 BC					
Tetreres c. 300 BC					
Hemiolia c. 300 BC					
Greek Trieres c. 400 BC					

Length Overall	10	20	30	40	50 Metres
Weight, Loaded	20 40	60	80	100	120 Tonnes
Complement	100	200	300	400	500 ©J F COATES 1994

Comparative size and configuration of ancient warships.

Maps

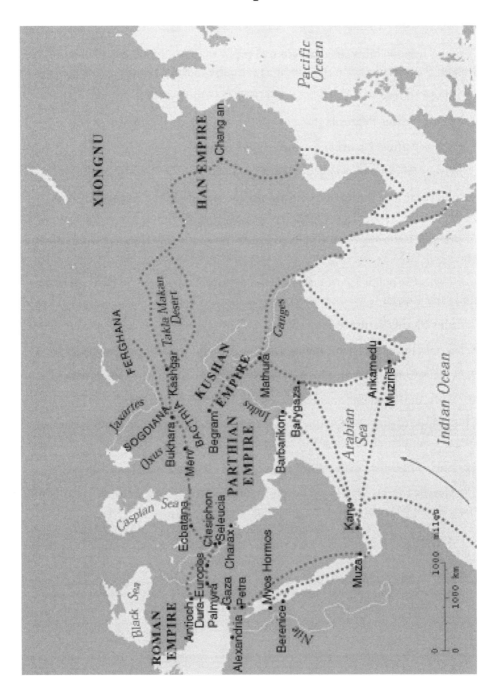

Trade routes of the Roman Empire.

Areas of responsibility assigned from Pompey to the commanders in chief of the Roman fleets deployed in the Mediterranean Sea against the pirates.

COMMANDERS IN CHIEF OF THE ROMAN FLEETS

1. Lucius Gellius Poplicola (former consul, in 72 BC): Tyrrhenian sea

2. Publius Atilius: Ligurian sea and sea of Corsica

3. Marcus Pomponius: Gallicum sea (Gulf of Lion)

4. Aulus Manlius Torquatus: Balearic sea and waters off the Spanish eastern coasts

5. Tiberius Claudius Nero: straits of Cadiz (presently 'of Gibraltar') and Alboran sea

6. Gnaeus Cornelius Lentulus Marcellinus (future consul, in 56 BC): sea of Sardinia and Libyan sea

7. Aulus Plotius Varus: sea of Sicily

8. Marcus Terentius Varro: Ionian sea, low Adriatic and low Aegean until Delos

9. Gnaeus Cornelius Lentulus Clodianus (former consul, in 72 BC): Adriatic sea

10. Sons Aulus and Quintus Pompeius Bitinicus: Egyptian sea

11. Quintus Caecilius Metellus Nepos (future consul, in 57 BC): south-eastern Aegean sea, Pamphylian sea and sea of Cyprus

12. Lucius Lollius: northern Aegean until the Hellespontum (Dardanels)

13. Marcus Pupius Piso Frugi Calpurnianus (future consul, in 61 BC): Propontis (now Sea of Marmara) and the Bosphorus Strait

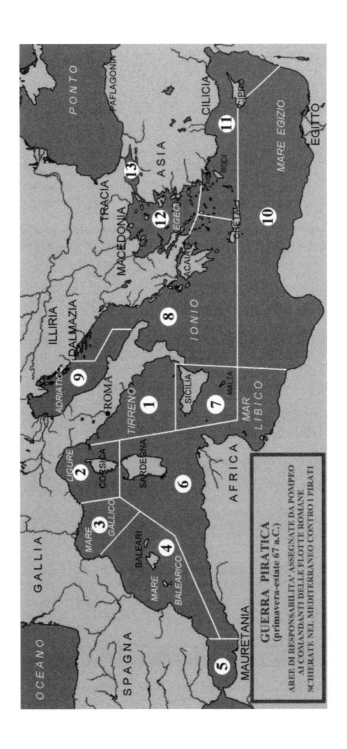

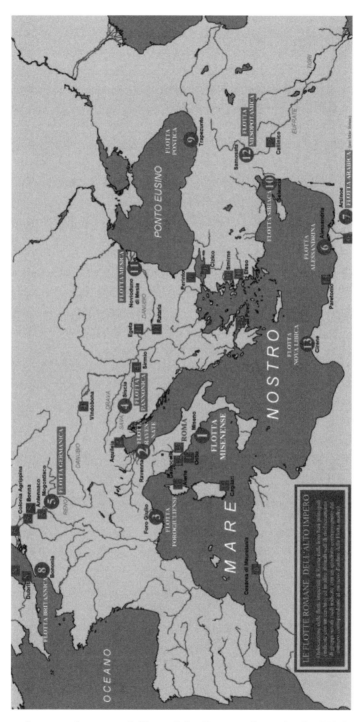

Location and areas of responsibility of the Roman fleets in the High Empire Period.

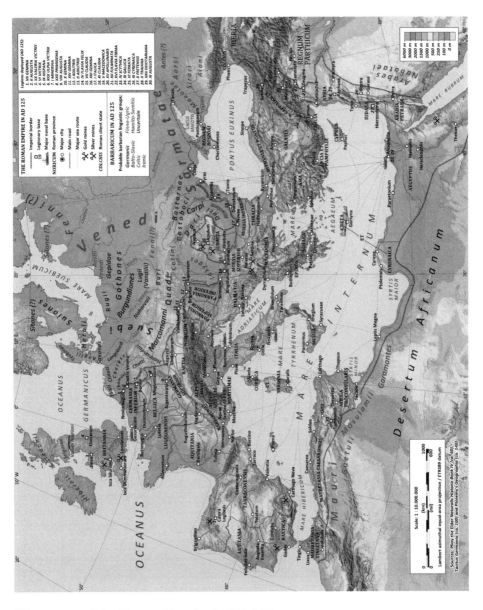

The extent of the Roman Empire in AD 125.

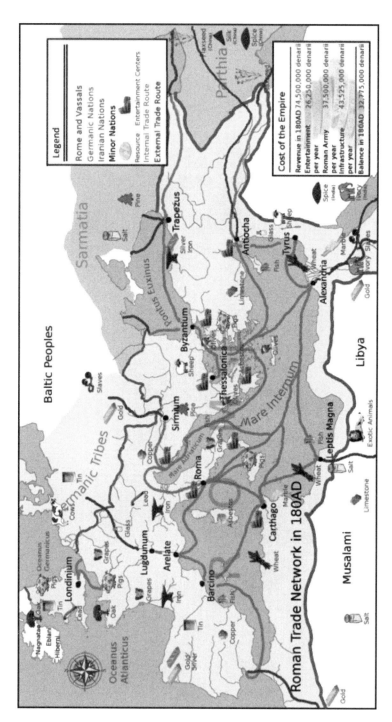

Trade networks, second century AD. Note that the overland routes debouch at maritime *entrépots.*

Roman Arrival and Neutralization of Syracuse; Consolidation 264-2

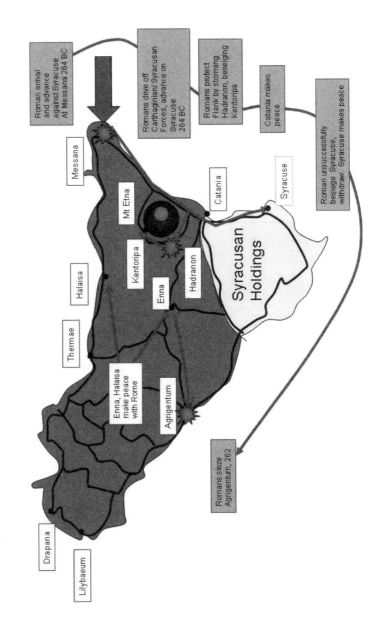

Roman arrival and advance against Syracuse At Messana 264 BC

Romans drive off Carthaginian/Syracusan Forces, advance on Syracuse 264 BC

Romans protect Flank by storming Hadranon, beseiging Kentoripa

Catania makes peace

Roman unsuccessfully beseige Syracuse, withdraw. Syracuse makes peace

Messana

Mt Etna

Catania

Syracuse

Halaisa

Kentoripa

Enna

Hadranon

Syracusan Holdings

Thermae

Enna, Halaisa make peace with Rome

Agrigentum

Romans sieze Agrigentum, 262

Drapana

Lilybaeum

Opening phase of the First Punic War focusing on Carthaginian control of Sicily.

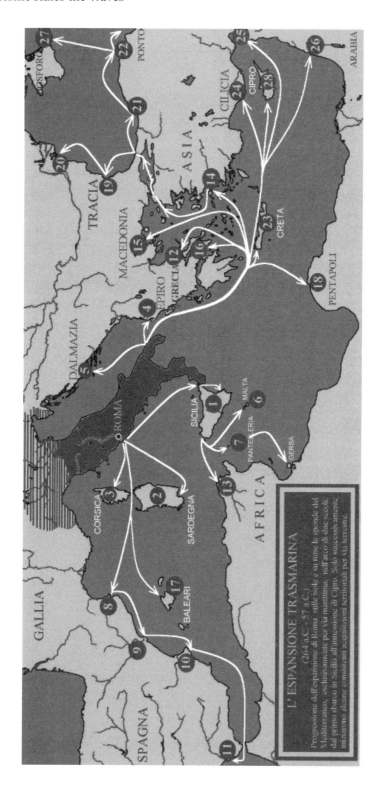

L'ESPANSIONE TRASMARINA
(264 a.C. - 57 a.C.)

Progressione dell'espansione di Roma sulle sedi e su tutte le sponde del
Mediterraneo, esclusivamente per via marittima, nell'arco di due secoli
dal primo sbarco in Sicilia all'annessione di Cipro. Solo successivamente
inizieranno alcune consistenti acquisizioni territoriali per via terrestre.

Progression of the Roman expansion on the islands and on all the coasts of the Mediterranean Sea, exclusively by sea in a period of two centuries: from the first landing in Sicily until the annexation of Cyprus. Thereafter, the Romans began to carry out some significant territorial acquisitions, also by land.

1. Landing in Sicily at the beginning of the First Punic War (264 BC)

2–3. Landing in Sardinia and Corsica (259 BC)

4–5. Landings a Corfu, in Epiro e nelle isole della Dalmazia (229 BC)

6–7. Conquest of the islands of Malta, Pantelleria and Gerba at the beginning of the Second Punic War (218–217 BC)

8–11. Conquest of eastern and southern coasts of Spain (218–206 BC)

12. Landing on the island of Eubea (207 BC)

13. Landing in Africa led by Scipio Africanus (204 BC)

14. Landing in Asia minor led by Scipio Asiaticus (190 BC)

15. Landings in Macedonia and on the island of Samotracia (169–168 BC)

16. Landing in Acaia led by Lucius Mummius Achaicus (146 BC)

17. Conquest of the Balearic Islands by Quintus Caecilius Metellus Balearicus (123–122 BC)

18. Taking possession of the Cyrenaica, or Pentapolis Libya (86 BC)

19–20. Landings on the western coasts of the Black Sea, until the Danube (77–71 BC)

21–22. Landings on the southern coasts of the Black Sea, from Heraclea Pontica to oppidum Cerasus (72–70 BC)

23. Conquest of Crete Island by Quintus Caecilius Metellus Creticus (69–67 BC)

24. Landing in Cilicia at the conclusion of the Piratic War (67 BC)

25–26. Landings on the eastern coasts of the Mediterranean Sea (64–63 BC)

27. Naval blockade and subsequent control of the Bosphorus Cimmerius (64–63 BC)

28. Annexation of Cyprus (57 BC)

Foreword

My title's reference to a 'Naval Staff Appreciation' may seem unusual. I don't suggest that there were official administrative bodies to draft postmortems on Rome's maritime endeavours, as was done commendably by the British Admiralty and related bodies in the late nineteenth and twentieth centuries. The phrase emphasizes my unconventional treatment. It is emblematic of what I call a 'sea power' rather than a narrow 'naval history' approach. Essentially, my book is not so much about battles as it is their maritime context.

In writing these chapters, I have tried to envisage a Roman Mahan or Corbett appraising hand-picked significant naval events (campaigns, wars, conjunct operations with the legions or anti-piracy sweeps) as a demonstration of sea power in action. Vegetius, in his epitome of military matters, *De Re Militari*, written in the fourth or fifth century CE, briefly considers the inventory and personnel of the Roman navy at that time. His comments on naval concerns are more confusing than illuminating. My emphasis is less on the tactical details – except as they bear upon strategy – and more on the maritime implications. I invite those interested in ancient empires and naval affairs to consider my autopsy of the way in which a nautical novice projected naval strength throughout the known ancient world within a fifty-year period, and maintained it for another 500.

Given my approach, this volume doesn't aspire to be a comprehensive history of the fleets and shipboard battles of ancient Rome. Instead, I am introducing something different and, I believe, innovative: a study of the conceivable strategy guiding the stationing, dispatch and operations of these fleets, their freestanding squadrons and legionary naval contingents, with observations on both merits and defects in planning and execution. The assessment is outlined, to the extent possible, using modern-day sea power thought.

This strategy is chiefly discernible in retrospect. It may be inferred from the employment of ships both independently and in conjunction with military campaigns on land. I've mined the ancient sources and modern studies for indicants of a plan of action guiding the commissioning, financing, construction, positioning and dispatch of war vessels, transports and supply ships. In essence, I apply nineteenth and twentieth-century assessment methodology and naval ideas to Rome's intermittent yet tenacious relationship with Neptune. I've endeavoured to do so in a general way, without importing rigid doctrinal tenets and guidelines.

Having initially decided to focus on the reign of the emperors, when engagements between war fleets were rare, I soon realized that nothing had been done in this vein for the preceding period of the late Republic, when Rome was adapting itself to expeditionary conflicts outside of the Italian peninsula. So I expanded the project to a full examination of Roman sea power, from the Pyrrhic war (late third century BC) forward to the fall of the Western Empire in the sixth century AD. Accordingly, analyses of naval operations under the emperors occupy only about a third of the book. This is not because they were less significant; it merely reflects the sparsity of sources for the later period.

To be sure, there are plentiful histories of the Punic Wars, and other naval struggles from the time when Rome was painfully learning to wade, then swim. But, with a few minor exceptions, none of these works employ doctrines derived from studies of relatively modern navies. Using a broad-brush notion of 'sea power' to evaluate Rome's maritime undertakings is a worthwhile exercise. It provides a sort of corrective to those who minimize the role of ships in Rome's growth and sustenance.

The dean of modern sea power theory, Alfred Mahan, wrote eight pages about the Second Punic War in 1890, and Frederick Clark wrote his much-neglected doctoral dissertation for the University of Chicago in 1915, viewing the late Republic's wars through a Mahanian lens. But for the most part ancient navies were studied by academics more concerned with specific details of ship construction, cargoes and shoreside facilities than with their broad sea power implications. Others narrated blow-by-blow reviews of the significant sea battles, neglecting the connective tissue of a strategical framework. So my chapters covering from 300-30 BC developed from an introductory prelude into a more thoroughgoing integral part of the whole book. There have been a few good books on the naval wars of the Roman Republic, notably several from Pen & Sword, in the past year. While they are respectable reviews of the battles, where strategy is mentioned it is confined to brief asides.

As for the ensuing period, few have even bothered to chronicle the naval undertakings of the Empire, holding them to be perfunctory mundane tasks unworthy of distinct comment; they're treated as mere adjuncts to the fundamental activities of the legions on land. As such, they are scarcely referenced. It is difficult to see how the imperial legions could have consummated their operations lacking substantial naval support. The US and Coalition forces have been fighting a 'war on terror' under various headings since the beginning of this century. People writing histories of these campaigns – in Iraq, Syria, Afghanistan and Yemen – do not describe any sea battles. It could not be so, given the lack of an adversary with a navy of any note. However, if the US and NATO, not to mention Russia, were devoid of maritime potency, the outcome might be far different. In evaluating this epoch, when the naval units comprised, in effect, a 'silent service', my broad 'sea power' angle is quite advantageous.

As the pre-eminent naval theoreticians of the twentieth century, Alfred Mahan and Sir Julian Corbett, demonstrated, sea power is not merely about naval engagements between capital ships. In its deeper sense, sea power is the steadfast exertion of command of the sea lanes to conduct trade unmolested, suppress piracy, transport troops and supplies, protect coastal cities from enemy incursions, sustain land-based military garrisons on a hostile shore and mount waterborne raids against enemy coasts. Battles may be won at sea, but wars are won on land. The famous naval battle of Trafalgar in 1805 delivered a crushing blow to Napoleon's fleet, but the war dragged on for another ten years until the French armies were defeated at Waterloo. It's up to armies to utilize opportunities opened by navies.

While there are scant traces in the fragmentary ancient sources of discussions that may have prompted the deployments of fleets and attached naval squadrons, it is nonetheless possible to reason out a maritime strategy from such records as have come down to us. Of all the ancient sources narrating Rome's rise, Polybius is the fullest with respect to naval warfare, but his main thrust is descriptive rather than proscriptive. His perspective from the Roman (actually Greco-Roman) vantage might be expected to gloss over Roman errors and inflate those of Carthage; given his inherent partiality, his remarks are surprisingly even-handed. He utilized both a Phoenician and a Roman source, for a decidedly modern approach.

Chroniclers of the deeds of ancient kingdoms and empires did not theorize about how their rulers saw the role of their sea forces; Rome did not even consider its fleets as being distinct from its land forces. Apart from some puzzling references to a sea power concept labelled 'thalassocracy', the ancient sources didn't reflect upon why their warships and merchant vessels plied the seas. Consequently, in analyzing the sea power of ancient Rome, I apply today's sea power model retroactively. I attempt to surmise how sea power theorists Alfred Mahan, Sir Julian Corbett and some of their contemporary maritime intellectuals might have tackled this project. I devote a few pages to explicating the term 'thalassocracy' as it evolved over time, since it may help bridge the contextual gap from antiquity to today.

I believe that, had the above-noted naval scientists not been compelled to deal with more pressing topics, they would have found time to examine illustrations preceding the Britannic maritime epoch for insights. However, they were perforce focused on historical lessons applicable to the rise and role of the British and American navies in the nascent steel and steam maritime era. This was an urgent matter for national defence planning staffs in the run-up to the First World War, when proliferating unprecedented naval technologies forced a reappraisal of what navies are for and how they might prevail under the new conditions. The naval arms race created a sense of urgency, mandating utilitarian historical research. My book envisions a more antiquarian focus of their studies, nevertheless one which may resonate with today's naval planners in the post-Cold War environment.

My interest in the Roman Empire's sea power was sparked by my search for information about the waterborne engagements of Rome's Judaean campaigns of the first and second centuries AD. I devoted a few pages to the naval actions in the first revolt, and the naval facets of the second and third revolts, in my book about the Jewish uprisings (*The Jewish Revolts Against Rome, AD 66-135: A Military Analysis*, McFarland, 2010). In my hunt for modern references, I was surprised by the paucity of data on naval warfare involving the Roman fleets within my designated timeframe.

In the few monographs covering the military side of the revolts, there was some passing reference to the maritime features as sideshows to the primary struggle on land. The fact is that the Roman commanders, Vespasian and his son Titus, were troubled enough by the threat to their land operations posed by Judaean naval interdiction to divert troops to drive out pirates from their base at Joppa and fight a naval battle on the Sea of Galilee. Later, they deployed their own naval assets to threaten the grain supply of Rome and thereby weaken rival claimants to the purple. This wasn't merely an incidental consideration, but one that loomed large in their calculations.

No doubt due to lack of information, the modern works I consulted referenced this challenging topic in a brief comment; but they lacked a strategic context for these naval activities. How did the future Flavian emperors on campaign in Judaea envision the need for seaborne assistance? How did the Roman emperors and their staffs customarily regard the naval component of their military capability? Did they even regard warships, transports and freighters as having unique roles to play? If so, did they craft a strategy incorporating warships, troop conveyances and supply vessels? The more I searched, the more perplexed I became.

I examined sundry academic articles on narrow topics, analyzing underwater archaeological discoveries such as the Athlit ram and various cargo vessel debris fields. They suggested their implications for the presumptive configuration of ancient warships and their weapons emplacements. This information is quite crucial as raw data, but it leaves out the 'big picture'. The latter is the essence of the present study. General surveys of ancient naval history appeared to assume that naval history was in abeyance from 31 BC to the rise of Islamic naval power in the eighth century AD. Further, their recaps of the Punic Wars and Rome's power projection into the Eastern Mediterranean were prosaic retreads of the events, with insufficient explanation of the presumptive naval strategies directing the contending fleets. J.H. Thiel is the exception, but his treatises are over sixty years old. Interspersed among his data on commanders, fleet composition and tactical replays of battles are valuable, bold observations on likely strategical choices of the contenders.

After researching and writing the pages on the naval features of the revolts, I decided to fill the gaps and create my own critique of the Roman Empire's sea power. The germ of this study was formulated in a couple of articles I contributed on the subject to *Strategy & Tactics* magazine in the early 2000s and a paper presented at the New York Military Affairs Symposium in June 2004, 'The Influence of Sea Power on Ancient History', a rebuttal to Chester Starr's booklet by that name, published in a shorter format online at The Roman History Reading Group website (http://romanhistorybooksandmore.freeservers.com/r_bloomsea2.htm).

What is more, having grown up on an Atlantic Ocean coast and knocked about in boats as a boy, I've always been a nautical enthusiast; so maritime history is a particular interest of mine. I've contributed dozens of articles on ships, sea power and maritime history to various journals over a twenty-year period. This project proved to be a more challenging – and fascinating – task than I at first envisioned.

I was compelled to change course in the midst of writing a manuscript. After compiling a sizeable rough draft giving a straightforward chronological recounting of wars, campaigns and battles, and codas reviewing the strategic 'sea power' underpinnings, I found that Michael Pitassi had recently written detailed, comprehensive, workmanlike volumes on the topic, encompassing the entire span of the Republic's and the Empire's naval enterprises from the founding to the fall. I didn't aspire to 'one up' his fine studies.

In order to distinguish my project, I condensed the elaborated recaps of the wars, campaigns etc. and expanded the codas on the sea power aspect to comprise the main body of text. My conceptualization is appropriate, inasmuch as Admiral Mahan was initially inspired by Rome's contemporary (late nineteenth-century) relevance in terms of sea power. The admiral briefly applied his ideas about the assessment of sea power to the Second Punic War and the earlier Athenian expedition to Syracuse in a most informative way. He declared that it was his study of the Second Punic War that started him on his naval history-writing path before he turned his full attention to the Royal Navy in the age of sail.

I accordingly refashioned my manuscript from a detailed review of fleet composition, naval campaigns and battles (thoroughly delineated in Dr Pitassi's books) to an operational analysis of Roman maritime strategy from the fourth century BC to AD 500. The battle and fleet details conveniently presented in Pitassi's volumes and elsewhere helped me to elaborate my strategical summaries. My work thereby morphed into a sea power treatise in the manner of the great naval historian-theorists of the past century. My research revealed that nothing like this had been done with respect to the period I studied.

I could not simply reorganize and paraphrase the existing rough draft; I had to reshape the whole narrative afresh. Many of the tactical details of the various campaigns I had compiled needed to be either eliminated or sharply condensed. So, much to the chagrin of the patient, trusting folks at Pen & Sword, the manuscript delivery date slipped until I was over five years late. Health problems and an attractive invitation to present a paper to a seminar on Flavius Josephus and his Jewish War at Oxford University in 2014 delayed completion of the work yet again. I hope the result has repaid their patience.

This book, then, undertakes what I believe is a fresh approach to the naval history of ancient Rome – both the Republic and the Empire. After Octavian became Emperor Augustus at the start of the first millennium of the Common Era, Roman naval predominance was a *fait accompli*. Without a major sea power to challenge her command of the waters through which her economic lifelines flowed, her naval history up to the fall of the Western Empire has conventionally been regarded as irrelevant or, at best, uninteresting, to naval historians and aficionados. This assessment is based on a misconception of what the term 'sea power' implies. Further, its explication is not compatible with traditional naval history favouring colourful recaps of decisive sea engagements such as occurred in the Republic's prime.

With respect to recent history, this narrow reading is illustrated by surveys that suggest that American and British naval history, in effect, ended with the Japanese surrender in 1945. The historian assumes that, since the victorious navies were virtually omnipotent by then, their postwar role was the dull function of passive deterrence, unworthy of recounting, because it was unfit fare for gripping prose. As anyone might see, this is far from the case.

There was plenty for warships and merchant fleets to do in coping with the postwar 'anti-colonial' turmoil and the Soviet exploitation of this trend. Much of it was under-the-radar type containment/deterrence missions forestalling open hostilities, while others involved peripheral wars in which the big capital ships traditionally conspicuous in high seas drama were mostly superfluous overkill. At most, they were the 'big sticks' that kept the Soviet Bloc navies at bay. This departure in roles from naval engagements between fleets becomes even more pronounced as we consider the evolution of 'irregular warfare' since the Vietnam War of the 1960s. My approach to the subject is accordingly tailored to a broad 'sea power', rather than a narrow traditional 'naval history', formulation, as I will explain.

I frame the history of the *Pax Romana* at sea in terms of modern naval strategic theory, something rarely done with the ancient eras and not at all with regard to the Roman Empire. It comprises what I consider that the famed sea–power scholar Alfred Mahan might have written had he expanded his eye-opening, albeit brief, notes on the Second Punic War to a full reappraisal of Rome's exercise of sea power. Instead, he centred his two-volume magnum opus upon the British Empire's great age of sail, and consequently emphasized a strategy of seeking out and destroying the enemy's main battle fleet, though he didn't neglect tangential naval actions and minor warship operations along the shoreline. His self-proclaimed disciples ignored the latter. It also suggests what Sir Julian Corbett, applying his broader 'maritime' concept, might have written on the subject. Although Mahan wrote very little on the ancient period, and Corbett nothing, their outlooks inform my survey.

While I touch upon battles, both large and small, the book is not battle-centric. Given my emphasis on the big picture, an elaborate tactical replay of major battles would be incompatible with my purpose. One can provide many examples of so-called decisive battles that failed to determine the outcomes of wars; the war dragged on until one side or the other was either war-weary or simply ran out of the physical resources required to continue the struggle. For example, as will be seen, the lopsided Roman victory of Ecnomus in the First Punic War neither ensured the success of the thwarted direct Roman attack on Carthage itself nor prevented Carthage from reinforcing its besieged garrisons on Sicily to continue the war. The selected engagements featuring ships, seamen and marines are described only to the extent that they reflect the broader topic of Roman 'maritime strategy', as this concept is formulated by notable modern analysts. Besides, in the past few years there have been some excellent studies elaborating on the minutiae of Roman fleets and their combat records. These are discussed a little later in the text.

Although the Roman polity was not in the habit of commissioning 'lessons learned' studies from their military commands, such as have been done by military and naval staffs for the past century-and-a-half, for each conflict, or naval component of a conflict, I attempt to draw up what might pass for a professional critique in a modern formulation.

There were, of course, no Roman naval think-tanks such as the many official and unofficial commissions of professional experts advising the armed forces of maritime states today. It's likely that the emperors and senators did occasionally consult with men experienced in naval matters, but there is no record of these discussions. So here is my attempt to show what such an after-action review might look like for each noteworthy instance of the employment of ships to further Roman foreign policy.

Although I am retrofitting the work of naval strategists whose forte was the Royal Navy from the seventeenth to the early nineteenth centuries, I have tried to abstain from 'presentism'. It's not sensible to minutely utilize their systems to assess naval matters preceding their preferred era by over a thousand years. For example, the modern concept of littoral/expeditionary warfare – a maritime state encountering minor or non-state actors on the oceanic fringes – does not precisely comport with the Roman Empire's near-shore and riverine expeditions. But they are more or less akin in their concentration on backwaters, an environment unsuitable for spectacular clashes between ancient ram-shod or modern big-gun monster warships. These comparatively low-intensity operations primarily embrace constabulary and irregular warfare functions.

While the approximate parallels I draw may be edifying, I refrain from the kind of superficial analogies best confined to science-fictional hypotheticals in which military or naval units with modern weaponry time-travel back to alter the outcome of a famous battle or war. Where modern examples are relevant, I mention them by way of an apt comparison of broad strategical principles, keeping in mind that twenty-first century sea control does not equate with naval effectiveness in antiquity. In many instances, technology trumps analogy.

Modern war-fleets with their over-the-horizon weaponry ranges, high speeds, protracted action radii and omniscient communications and surveillance systems, including shipboard helicopters, are fully capable of dominating sea lanes of commerce and supply in ways unthinkable in the age of Horatio Nelson, much less in ancient Rome. When I say, as my title declares, 'Rome ruled the waves', this connotes that it was the most powerful naval presence in the Mediterranean, not that it swept the seas of all adversaries. It does not correspond to the era when 'Britannia ruled the waves'. Ships that normally proceeded at a walking pace, or at a jog in half-hour spurts, could not descry and overtake all naval challengers.

Such present-day naval tasks as 'access denial' and 'sea control' were plainly unworkable with the short-legged galleys and storm-tossed, tubby cargo/troop carriers of antiquity. The interception of an enemy fleet was very iffy, and had to be facilitated by spies in the enemy camp and lookouts posted at key coastal nodes. They perforce had to engage enemy vessels within one or two day's sailing of a friendly harbour or provisioning depot, and their vision from a low-level crow's nest was limited to a horizon of about 5 or 6 miles. As the narrative will show, the galleys could not stop the occasional warship or troop transport from getting through to a 'blockaded' army on shore. Nonetheless, there *was* such a thing as maritime strategy, in a more limited sense, tailored to the available engineering and navigational skill sets. Even though there are no perfect correlates, I hope to demonstrate that Mahan and Corbett's broad precepts may be judiciously applied to the period between the rise and fall of the Roman Empire.

Conversely, the naval enterprise of the Roman Empire is not without its ramifications for the twenty-first century, when major naval conflicts are unlikely – unless one regards the threat of Chinese expansion to her 'nine-dash-line' perimeter in the western Pacific. A recent (2009) work, *China Goes to Sea: Maritime Transformation in Comparative Historical Perspective*, adduces the relevance of case studies ranging as far back as the Greco-Persian Wars of the fifth century BC to the unexpected achievement of Chinese naval power. 'Rome in the Mediterranean' is the topic of an important chapter in that study.

This survey aims to bring the relevant information on Ancient Roman sea power together in a form that historians and naval professionals should find interesting and informative. Like the Royal Navy in centuries past, and the fleets of the Roman Empire, the United States Navy underwrites the global economic and security order through its forward presence, deterrent power and, ultimately, war-fighting capabilities. Hopefully, this analysis of the employment of sea power under the Roman Republic's leaders and the emperors will provide useful analogies for twenty-first century aspirants to naval predominance.

I am not an academic scholar. Hence, my reading is largely confined to convenient translated editions of the ancient sources, a wide range of modern works in English, plus some extracts of studies accessed via translation software. I don't challenge the work of professional ancient historians or archaeologists, but I do make use of their researches in delineating my sea power analysis. My book doesn't seek to advance our knowledge of the subject in the sense of new interpretations of ancient texts, but I am reshaping the information in the commonly recognized sources to suggest the relevancy of sea power theory. J.H. Thiel made a fine start in his two books, now some sixty-five years old, but his interesting remarks on Rome's strategic grasp of her naval role are dispersed throughout the detailed narrative.

As the annotated bibliography and my discussion of the secondary literature in the Introduction will show, I have read widely on the subject within these criteria. This book is intended as 'popular history', which I trust is not understood as a pejorative term, but rather to connote that it is written for a general audience with a keen interest in ancient naval matters. I have tried to employ reliable references, but the main thrust of this book is to examine the efficacy of Rome's sea power through the lens of modern constructs, not to present new discoveries or scholarly revelations. I hope that my effort might also appeal to those with a professional interest in naval affairs.

Tempting as it was to make protracted comparisons between Rome and, say, the evolution of modern Chinese or Soviet/Russian sea power, this would be a mistake. I make passing mention of some general similarities to the naval events of the past century or so, but a point-by-point analogue would lead to glaring anachronism. I thank sea power scholar Dr Milan Vego, an instructor at the US Naval War College, for gently discouraging me from making any such detailed equivalences in a private email. I trust that my occasional references to other historical cases of what one recent anthology calls 'maritime transformation' in habitually agrarian/continental powers will achieve their purpose in pointing out common threads.

This comparison with ancient examples is not uncommon in modern security studies. For example, Samuel J. Tangredi's naval policy-driven *Anti-Access Warfare: Countering A2/AD Strategies* (Naval Institute Press, 2013) traces this distinctively modern notion back to the Greco-Persian War of the fifth century BC. It demonstrates what an outnumbered fleet can do to forestall and weaken an attacker at the water's edge. The US Joint Chiefs of Staff's studies of combined operations, placing modern doctrine in historical context, have cited examples dating back to Julius Caesar's landings in Britannia.

I am mindful that applying twentieth and twenty-first-century concepts too literally to ancient kingdoms and republics can produce glib anachronistic analogy. Bear in mind, though, that ancient naval warfare was no less complex than modern naval warfare. Many issues that concern contemporary strategists and tacticians were being posed in antiquity. For example, Mahan's and Corbett's notions of protection of trade are certainly based on studies of the sophisticated mercantile networks and comparatively nimble long-range warships of the Renaissance forward to the nineteenth century; they're not so well suited to the relatively rudimentary trade system and rowed and sail-propelled vessels of the first to the sixth centuries. Yet when pirate gangs and rogue nations menaced Rome's vital grain supply, and Rome devised a plan to defeat them, they may as well have taken some pages from Mahan, Corbett, Charles Calwell and Herbert Richmond to heart. Rome's search for forward bases from which to mount retaliatory patrols against restive tribes near coasts or along river systems dotted with legionary forts has a distinctly modern ring, and can be related to what is now called 'expeditionary warfare'. One might also find a review of the strategy of rooting out the bases and logistical depots of the pirate gangs by landing parties – as Pompey did notably in the first century BC – in the 1927 book *The Army and Sea Power* by Major R.B. Pargiter and Major H.G. Eady.

While the contemporary marine landing force with its integral amphibious landing craft and air support cannot bear extended comparisons with, say, Rome's Rhineland campaigns or its expeditions to Carthage, Macedonia, Dacia, Egypt and Britannia, there are nevertheless some similar broad strategical conditions worth noting. Modern frigates and littoral combat vessels certainly cannot be equated point-for-point with the ancient 'small combatants', the *liburnae*, *hemiolae* and *lembi*. However, the decision to switch from the heavy polyremes of Antony and Cleopatra's doomed armada to these lighter ships (originally designed to chase down pirate craft) predominating in Agrippa/Octavian's fleet does bear some resemblance to the modern shift from the capital ship-intensive fleets of 1900-1990 to the twenty-first century's smaller, swifter naval workhorses, or the French *jeune ecole*'s earlier (late nineteenth century) doctrine for a lesser maritime power still smarting from its defeat at Trafalgar, planning a riposte using small torpedo boats and fast commerce raiders. In the following pages, I've tried to demonstrate why, at the strategic level, such generic comparisons are appropriate as a framework for discussion.

I have sparingly employed footnotes to indicate matters of controversy, but my acknowledgment of authorities used in this work is relegated to the critical bibliography at the end of the book. My annotations under each listing will indicate the chapters or episodes of the text to which the reference is germane; where there is a direct quote or paraphrase, I will state the source in the text. As this is an amalgamated work of synthesis, quotes are selectively employed, but where insights or data are derived from a particular source, I will mention this in the main body of the book.

I want to especially thank Admiral Domenico Carro for permission to use his excellent maps and for directing me to his enlightening studies, quite in synch with my own discernment of the roles and operations of the *classis Romana* and the source of many fresh viewpoints which enhanced my understanding. I only hope that my modest book merits his kind indulgence of my requests.

Introduction

'Whosoever commands the sea commands the trade; whosoever commands the trade of the world commands the riches of the world, and consequently the world *itself.*'
Sir Walter Raleigh, *History of the World*, 1616

'As Hannibal left no memoirs, the motives are unknown which determined him to the perilous and almost ruinous march through Gaul and across the Alps. It is certain, however, that his fleet on the coast of Spain was not strong enough to contend with that of Rome. Had it been, he might still have followed the road he actually did, for reasons that weighed with him; but had he gone by the sea, he would not have lost thirty-three thousand out of the sixty thousand veteran soldiers with whom he started.'
Alfred Thayer Mahan, *The Influence of Sea Power Upon History, 1660-1783*

The Scarcity of Recent Ancient Sea Power Analyses

Devotees of maritime history preceding the Medieval period likely know several standard accounts purporting to cover the entire gamut of ancient naval activity. Typically, these works highlight the sea fights of the Greco-Persian, Peloponnesian and First Punic Wars. They perhaps include a brief comment on the naval aspects of the Second Punic War (typically considered as overshadowed by the land combat) and some perfunctory discussion of the preliminaries to and seaborne combats of the civil wars of the late Roman Republic leading up to the climactic Battle of Actium in 31 BC, which is covered in some detail. These purportedly comprehensive works then pass over some 600 years following the Battle of Actium to the seventh and eighth centuries AD, resuming with the so-called Dark Ages and the Muslim effort against Byzantine naval forces. Their coverage of the earlier phase is frequently unremarkable – a recital of battles, data and leaders, without much consideration of the underlying rationale for the described actions (or inaction) – while the later period is dismissed in a page or two when described at all.

In 1994, a professor at the US Naval War College in Newport, Rhode Island, observed that:

> '[T]he current disinterest in ancient naval history contrasts notably with the nineteenth century when Admiral Jurien de la Graviere, Admiral Serre, and Professor Cartault acted as pioneers in the field. Historians of ancient naval wars still appreciate their studies, despite their age.' (John Hattendorf, *Ubi sumus?: The state of naval and maritime history*)

In that same publication, Lionel Casson, author of several fine studies of ancient seafaring, noted the limitations of such studies that existed:

> 'The history of the sea in ancient times is a fledgling discipline. It came into being, strictly speaking, only in the twentieth century. To date, it has dealt almost exclusively with the technical aspects of ships. There are two reasons for this. The first is that, in this century, new disciplines were developed, such as archeology, epigraphy, numismatics, art history, and, most importantly, marine archeology in the latter half of the century, and these have transformed our knowledge of the technical aspects, filling in what hitherto had been black holes. Inevitably, research has concentrated on these. The second reason is that, for the ancient world, we lack information on which to base meaningful exploration of larger historical aspects.'

Because of this inattention (or perhaps contributing to it), there is a general impression that there was a half-millennium hiatus in noteworthy maritime activity from the start of the first millennium. Further, the treatment of the earlier period of Roman naval history suggested that it was not a suitable subject for naval theorists. Any reasonably curious reader might wonder why, during her imperial era, Rome seems to have forsaken those who, in the renowned words of Psalms 107:23, 'go down to the sea in ships, who do business on great waters'. We know that the Roman Empire maintained fleets and naval squadrons, both at its centre and its margins. Was there nothing for these assemblages of ships to do? With the legions stretched thin in order to guard the expanded imperial frontiers, why would Rome squander precious *denarii* on such capital-intensive items as ships, naval bases, crew training, wharfs, breakwaters, light towers, dockyards, mercantile warehouses, ship sheds etc., if they were simply for show? Tens of thousands of would–be legionaries were siphoned off from overextended land forces to serve as oarsmen and shipboard marines. Something more than flag-showing ostentation was in play here.

As indicated above, the emphasis in this century and the last has been upon the technical and structural aspects of ancient maritime history: shipbuilding, harbour construction, naval tactics, fleet organization etc. These subjects had hitherto been either totally or imperfectly known, and the emergence of fresh evidence provided by the newly developed technologies understandably gave them a leading role in scholarly research. This raw data comprises the essential building blocks for ancient naval warfare scholars. But, as I suggested in the Foreword, the 'larger historical aspects' have been overlooked, unless one counts Chester Starr's *The Influence of Sea Power on Ancient History* (Oxford University Press, 1989). A purported rebuttal to Mahan, it covers the field succinctly and usefully, but its touted thesis misses the mark. I will revisit that slim booklet in my discussion of the Second Punic War.

Some students of antiquity have acknowledged the sea's centrality to Roman dominance of the Mediterranean world, but lament the apparent neglect of the subject. This inattention was cogently expressed by a scholar over eighty years ago:

> 'We hear very much about the influence of Roman roads in promoting Roman civilization, but the influence of Roman fleets in bringing about that miracle has been almost entirely ignored. Yet it is demonstrable that the Roman empire depended quite as much on its fleets as on its roads.'
> (J. Holland Rose, *The Mediterranean in Ancient Times*, Cambridge, 1933).

I propose that the principal reasons for the lapse in coverage are twofold:

(1) The 'great battles as spectacle' bias in naval and military history. By this criterion, the Roman Republic's seaborne struggles are depicted as dramatic highlights without context, while the Empire's maritime history merits but a footnote. I hope to demonstrate that this preconception neglects much enlightening history;

(2) The arbitrary geopolitical division of states into 'continental' and 'maritime'. Rome is designated as one of the former, and, as such, its naval efforts were deemed to be atypical, reluctant, unskilled, sporadic and perfunctory; in short, they're not attention-worthy by sea power students and professors alike.

It is important to point out, as both Professor Michael B. Charles and Dr J.H. Thiel astutely observed, that our task is complicated by the fact that troop transport and the attendant supply chain, despite its great importance in Roman military operations of the period, was not of great interest to the ancient sources. They were generally far more concerned with warships designed to sink or disable other warships in set-piece naval encounters. Indeed, there are many occasions where we know how many warships and soldiers a commander had available, but the transports that must have accompanied them are not mentioned. (M.B. Charles, 'Caesar and the Maritime Troop Transport in the Civil War (49-45 BC)' in Carl Deroux (ed.), *Studies in Latin Literature and Roman History, vol. XV. Collection Latomus 323*. Bruxelles: Éditions Latomus, 2010)

Given this disinterest in even bothering to record the presence of transports, it's not surprising that the sources do not give clear indications of the manner in which maritime transport services were acquired and deployed. Along with this lapse, there is a general tendency to ignore the troopships' cousins, the merchant vessels that contributed to Rome's naval power. This information is vital to a detailed assessment of the naval side of the 'combined operations' expeditionary warfare that characterizes much of the period. What is more, if the warships protected the freedom of the seas for the merchant vessels, we should know something of the latter's routes and cargoes.

All of this information about trade and maritime logistics has been pieced together by marine archaeologists and through critical analysis of the ancient records that have come down to us. But the sources are reticent about any naval strategy that may have underpinned the expeditions. As the French maritime expert Jean Pagès has observed:

> 'The only author who could have shed light on the naval thinking of the Roman Republican period was Polybius (200-125 BC), but unfortunately the part of his work which could teach us how, in such a short time, the Romans achieved such superiority is lost at sea.... Strabo (63 BC-19 AD) has coined the concept of thalassocracy (*thalassokratia*. Geography, 48), which term is lately in vogue, but the loss of much of his historical writings leaves us unable to assess the importance he gave this concept. Similarly, Suetonius (69-122 AD) informs us that the Romans, in their prejudices against the Navy felt that the existence of their fleets was a negligible factor for them.'
>
> (Jean Pagès, 'Y a-t-il eu une pensée navale romaine?' 'Was there a Roman Naval Thought?', www.stratisc.org- [the translation is mine])

Dr Pagès goes on to demonstrate that, notwithstanding the lack of ancient sources who have bothered to suggest the 'why' rather than just the 'how' of Roman sea power, one may extrapolate the existence of 'naval thinking' from the decisions of the consuls, the legates, the Senate, the emperors and their delegates regarding the make-up and roles of the various fleets and their outliers. While Dr Pagès did feature these matters in his articles, they are dispersed in various journals and await synthesis in a single volume.

In Italy, the foremost champion of reviving the study of Roman sea power as an essential element in her rise is retired admiral Domenico Carro. My inability to read Italian has unfortunately precluded my use of his printed works, but luckily I found his website, *Rom Aeterna* (http://www.romaeterna.org/roma/tabulae_navales_br.html#p2), and through use of online translation software, I was able to study his most important essays and chapters. It is safe to say that he has revitalized the study of ancient Rome's sea power as a fit subject for modern naval cadets. His enlightening maps have not only enriched my book, but also helped to frame my narrative.

Michel Redde, in his *Mare Nostrum Les infrastructures de la marine romaine en l'epoque imperiale* (Rome: Ecole francaise de Rome, 1987) focused on the Roman imperial navy. This significant work stands out because of a very erudite analysis of the infrastructure of naval bases at the disposal of the Roman navy. On the other hand, it must be noted that his consideration of naval tactics and strategic employment of fleets was somewhat sparse; Redde did not express a keen interest in these important aspects of naval warfare.

Although Redde does not seem particularly interested in the doctrinal issues which may have underpinned Roman naval warfare, his first section, on the various types of vessel and their construction, equipment, manning and armament in itself refutes the notion of Rome's 'landlubberly' lack of aptitude or interest in naval affairs. The typologies are minutely analyzed and indicate a steady progression in technique and size, even during the Empire's relatively quiescent periods. The impression of nonchalance that Thiel, among others, gleaned from Polybius, Livy, Zonaras and others is by and large disproved. The Roman mentality was not restricted to boarding, but developed a whole range of ballistic and incendiary devices as well as markedly increasing the strength of the ram. The boarding bridge was a passing expedient; for how long we do not know. But Rome's adaptation of a whole array of naval warfare techniques is impressive for a tyro sea power wherein seafaring was held in low esteem. Further, as I hope to show, the use of the corvus itself required a high degree of skill at ship-handling. The canard about it converting a sea battle into a land battle is a simplistic formulation.

As I hope to establish, the sparsity of commentaries, especially in modern times, is attributable to the unspectacular, businesslike nature of maritime activity during the Roman imperial epoch and its subordination to land operations rather than its unimportance. The inattention is also due to the exaggerated belief that Rome harboured a natural and abiding distaste towards all things nautical. This attributed mindset has skewed the coverage of Rome's naval activities. In the recent past, this sort of bias was demonstrated by how the principal focus of American defence strategy from the 1960s to the 1980s was on massed Soviet and Warsaw Pact armour, infantry and its protective air umbrella facing NATO's central front, rather than the substantial threat of the sea power of the former Soviet Union. Yet the Russian submarine fleet posed a critical challenge for Western anti-sub warfare technology.

In the Cold War era, under the astute guidance of Admiral Sergei Gorshkov, the USSR had a first-class navy capable of challenging the operations of the US Navy; it had a large merchant marine, one of the leading fishing fleets of the earth, oceanographic and scientific knowledge about the sea of the first order and an impressive shipbuilding industry. Yet the Soviet Union was not considered a sea power; quite the contrary, it was deemed a typical continental power, the very epitome of one – not only, and not even firstly, because of the relationship of the Red Navy to the other services, but because of the continental thought characterizing its political system as well as its political and strategic culture.

Tracing all the way back to the reign of Peter the Great, continental-oriented Russia sought to build up its naval power – but this occurred in fits and starts, waxing and waning as Russia traditionally favoured its land forces. The aristocratic land-owning class frowned upon maritime commerce with the wider world as a subversive intrusion and threat to their power and privilege. The Soviet navy never came to blows with its Cold War enemies, so, like them, it was celebrated only in the 'future war' fiction that proliferated in the waning decades of the USSR. Now that much of Russia's former maritime borders are lined with break-away states, her navy is dwindling and cutting-edge Russian naval technology appears more often in foreign navies than in that of the mother country. Similarly, the Roman naval forces under the emperors were the largest among all those entities surrounding the Mediterranean basin, and yet were seldom viewed as worthy of attention.

As Virgilio Ilari's perceptive essay, 'Roman Seapower: The Emergence of an Historiographical Theme' (2014), frames it:

'The modern-day geopolitical image of Rome is in fact the one forged by the Punic wars: the seeming anomaly of a continental power par excellence that triumphs over a sea power. This idea was rooted in the present-day notion of distinctly continental succeeding empires in the West (Holy Roman Empire) and the East (Byzantine and then the Ottoman Empire), but also by the geopolitical thread which traced the history of the modern West from the sixteenth to the twentieth century.'

This image embraced the antagonism between the continental powers (France, Germany, Russia) and the maritime powers (England, USA). The continental versus seaward-oriented formulation is thus an amalgam of modern geopolitical and sea power theories. It dismisses any naval superiority achieved by continental powers as uncharacteristic and transient, merely an adjunct to their land (and latterly air) forces. While twentieth century geopolitics stressed geographical influences on national strategy, the economic model regards the continental/ maritime dichotomy as depending on whether a state had adequate agricultural resources to feed its population or had to look both to the seas and across the seas for its sustenance. Thus, Ancient Greece with its largely rocky soil, unsuitable for farming, and myriad small islands looked seaward, while Rome – at least in the early Republic – had a very fertile agrarian hinterland to the south of the Tiber and thus was not initially drawn (or impelled) to the sea for sustenance.

The Roman Empire, however, was wrapped around the Mediterranean Sea, as Socrates said of Athens with respect to the Aegean, 'like frogs around a pond'. This meant that naval power was necessary for complete mastery of the area. Loss of naval predominance might not be fatal, as it was for Athens, but it would be a serious blow to Roman potency. Where naval supremacy was lost, as to the Vandals in the fifth century or the Arabs in the ninth, the state was doomed to retreat to an attenuated continental redoubt. Not the least of these difficulties was the interruption of imports vital to the provision of 'bread and circuses' to mollify the restive populace. The maintenance of order at home and abroad was another key Roman priority sustained by its sea power.

Conforming with the 'continental' model described above, Rome's maritime endeavours are by and large regarded as unworthy of distinct treatment. They are customarily relegated to mere sidebars or codas in articles and books dealing with the general military history of the empire. Rome's naval undertakings are widely misunderstood as being reluctantly initiated – as if that were a relevant or even ascertainable factor – superficial, short-lived and amateurish.

For reasons I will explain below, I believe that modern naval theory, specifically that formulated by Alfred Thayer Mahan and Sir Julian Corbett at the turn of the nineteenth and twentieth centuries, is an apt tool with which to reassess Rome's neglected sea power component in the period commencing with the the reign of Augustus and the precedent naval expeditionary campaigns of the late Republic. In the case of the Mahan, his ideas are not accurately represented by the lopsided version that some of his followers in the navy have adopted, but rather by the actual substance of his texts.

Are Mahan's Precepts Applicable to Aniquity?

At this point it is apropos to review what Mahan wrote about sea power in the ancient period. Actually, his discussion was confined to eight discerning pages about Hannibal's Italian campaign in the introduction to his *Influence of Sea Power on History: 1660–1783* (1890). Also, in his collected Naval War College lectures, titled *Naval Strategy, Compared and Contrasted with the Principles and Practice of Military Operations on Land*, published in 1911, Mahan devoted several pages to the Athenians in Syracuse (the Sicilian Expedition, 415-413 BC). He characterized this expedition as an example of a failed conjunct sea-land operation, a notion ahead of its time. These two brief treatments comprise the extent of his commentary on ancient naval matters.

Importantly, Mahan maintains that the epiphany that sparked his influential books and lectures about British naval primacy of the seventeenth to nineteenth centuries was produced by reading eminent German ancient historian Theodor Mommsen's statement that Hanniba's strategy was a consequence of his lack of sea command in the Second Punic War (*Römische Geschichte*, 1856). Mahan didn't attempt to make a direct correlation between the *Pax Romana* (first to sixth centuries AD) and the *Pax Britannica* (late seventeenth to early nineteenth centuries). In fact, in his commentary on the Second Punic War he suggested that the paucity of reliable sources for the naval actions in that conflict recommended a more cautious assessment. Nonetheless, he fashioned an astute critique of the naval side of that struggle. As to why he passed over the First Punic War – a decidedly more naval case than the Second – I will consider below.

Mahan had been stationed in Peru in command of a US warship protecting American interests during the War of the Pacific (1879-1883) and read Mommsen's *The History of Rome* at the English Club in Lima. On reaching the chapter on the Second Punic War, he was struck by the historian's observations on the unappreciated role of the Roman fleets in that conflict. Mahan's take-away from reading Mommsen was that the success of the Roman Empire against Hannibal had been shaped by its sea control that was established in the First Punic War, and that the Second Punic War, although relatively deficient in decisive, discrete naval actions on the high seas, was more emblematic of *bona fide* sea power than was the predominantly naval preceding conflict. I will discuss Chester Starr's curious strictures about Mahan's Second Punic War analysis in my chapter covering that struggle.

The central thesis of Mahan's landmark studies is derived from the experience of the sail-powered Royal Navy from the mid-1600s to the early nineteenth century. In the 1890s, Mahan wrote that the best use of a navy is to find and defeat an opponent's fleet, but from the earliest history of the American republic the US Navy had been involved in operations *other than* fleet-on-fleet engagements. It has been kept quite busy in relatively shallow constricted zones of water, usually within a couple of hundred miles of a coastline. Mahan himself notes this distinction in his book *Gulf and Inland Waters* (1883), No.3 in Scribner's 'Navy in the Civil War' series. The chief task of the Union navy was the close blockading of Confederate shipping, much of which managed to elude the Northern blockading fleets. The events chronicled in that book are more in line with the naval situation in the Roman Empire than are his later works, which nonetheless may likewise be utilized profitably in assessing this epoch.

I've observed that the few significant pages of his first *Influence of Seapower* book concerned with Rome are devoted to the low-key and diffuse naval excursions of the Second Punic War. In all of Mahan's further writings, there is no mention of Rome and in fact just one other reference to ancient naval affairs – that being the Sicilian expedition of the Peloponnesian War. It seems odd then, that a noted authority on ancient empires, the late Chester Starr, was motivated to write a pamphlet, the imputed purpose of which was to debunk Mahan's supposed exaggeration of sea-power's role in antiquity. I don't mean to minimize the contributions of Starr to the study of ancient naval history, specifically that of the Romans, but he sparred with a chimerical Mahanian apparition.

Starr's earlier work, *The Imperial Roman Navy, 31 BC – AD 324* (1941, reprinted 1960), was helpful in researching my project. It is an anatomy of the various fleets; as such, it doesn't tie these separate mini-biographies together. The overarching imperial strategy directing their campaigns has to be extrapolated from each and stitched together. In the preface to the reprint, he admitted that had he had the chance to revise the work, he would have provided a strategical overview – a task which I am attempting in the present work.

My problems are with Starr's 1989 tract (of only eighty-four pages of text) titled *The Influence of Sea Power on Ancient History* mentioned in the foregoing section. Its title is a pointed paraphrase of the title of Mahan's masterworks. In it, according to the publisher's promotional literature, Starr demonstrates that sea-power's influence on the rise and fall of ancient empires is highly exaggerated – and that it was Mahan and his (unnamed) disciples who did the exaggerating.

It appears that the principal reason for the publication of Starr's booklet was to exploit the centennial of Mahan's landmark book and the then fashionable anti-colonialist trend, the admiral being regarded as an arch-imperialist. By 1989, Vietnam War repudiation was in vogue and 'American Imperialism' was in the dock. There's no denying Mahan's affinity for America's 'manifest destiny' in his various articles on its merited primacy in the Pacific Ocean. However, there is nothing in Mahan's sparse comments on ancient naval combat to suggest an exaggerated claim for its importance in that epoch.

I don't mean to belittle the work of Professor Starr. He did an excellent job in his first book on ancient naval warfare mentioned above. The later pamphlet's ill-conceived swipes at the admiral seem to be attributable to the publisher's marketing folks rather than the author. The difficulty seems to be that its disparagement of Mahan relies on retrofitting a Mahanian concept of thalassocracy (an ancient

Greek term denoting 'rule from the sea') back to the ancient era, when the term had a much more modest connotation in its historical context. I will explain my understanding of the word in a coda to the first chapter. It was not the equivalent of Mahan's 'sea power', applicable to the seventeenth to the nineteenth centuries, which Starr seems to believe. Nor did Mahan make this analogy. In fact, apart from the promotional material by the publishers, there is hardly a word about this theme in Starr's text itself.

Several naval historical conferences in the late 1990s at the US Naval War College in Newport, Rhode Island, have examined why the works of Mahan, Corbett and Richmond (and others) are not mutually contradictory but should be viewed in concert to provide a rich tapestry of ways to gauge sea power's influence on a people's history, and vice-versa. Significantly, these discussions are chiefly devoted to fleet policy matters affecting modern (i.e. since the 1890s) navies.

It's safe to say that before the end of the nineteenth century, historians didn't treat sea power apart from the general military strength of a political entity, and that it was Mahan who set the pattern of carving a niche for an explicitly naval history. My references to the modern theorists in my text are not point-by-point examples of specific principles, but application of the general content as a whole. I note that in Mahan's two-volume masterwork, he limited his delineation of theory to the introductory chapter, letting the ensuing narration of historical events speak for themselves for the most part.

Battle Books versus Strategic Surveys

The reason for this inattention has been suggested above as being attributable to the continental/maritime dichotomy, as well as the hold that the 'great battle' or 'decisive battle' approach has on authors of 'popular' military histories. Beginning with Sir Edward Creasy's *The Fifteen Decisive Battles of the World*, published in 1851, this paradigm has guided the writing of military and naval history. This is what Nelson sought in 1805 as he chased the combined Franco-Spanish squadron, and it is what Yamamoto sought in 1942 at Midway. Within the 800-year scope of this book, there were perhaps a handful: two or three during the First Punic War, one each in the Macedonian, Illyrian, Mithridatic and Syrian campaigns, one for the Civil War at the close of the first century BC and perhaps one during the reign of Constantine.

In today's world there is little or no chance of such an engagement, except possibly among two smaller navies. The anticipated big naval battles between China and the US is the stuff of techno-thrillers and war college think-pieces, but seems unlikely in the real world. The criterion that worthy battles need to have changed the direction of history (i.e., be 'decisive') seems to preclude the relative naval doldrums of the Roman imperial period. Further, ancient history is, well, antiquarian.

Histories of the American or British navies 'in action', accenting heroic sea fights, certainly are more popularly appealing than studies about the preventive presence of navies in peacetime or under threat from crudely equipped war-bands in outlying regions. These latter include works demonstrating how the United States and Britain employed the relatively low-key deterrent effects of 'naval presence' to maintain the long peace following the defeat of Napoleon in the nineteenth century, in the British case, or shadow box with the Soviet surface and submarine fleets during the forty-five-year Cold War era when US naval power was dominant, albeit contested. Although the Korean and Vietnam wars are not regarded as naval conflicts, the US Navy's Inchon landings of 1950 and its Operation Market Time interdiction of the North Vietnamese maritime resupply effort are equally deserving of attention as those occurrences highlighted in 'Great Battles' surveys.

The ancient period has, in contrast to the modern and contemporary eras, largely been the province of compartmentalized scholarly treatments of narrow technical aspects, founded on archeological discoveries. Those academics venturing to write about sea warfare prior to the dramatic naval confrontations between, say, the English and Dutch in the sixteenth century, the English and French from the seventeenth to early nineteenth centuries, the Russians and Japanese (1904-05) and the twentieth century's world wars, tend to write for other scholars. The policy-driven strategical inferences of sea-bed finds are rarely addressed.

Much of the relevant information regarding ancient maritime activity, specifically that of the Roman Empire, is dispersed among various learned specialist monographs dealing piecemeal with archaeological, numismatic or epigraphical relics. These essential volumes document the fieldwork that provides the raw data for naval historians to interpret. The information gleaned from seabed debris fields, ship shed and seawall ruins, funerary inscriptions etc. is critical as the building blocks for more general studies. But thus far, few of these field reports have been incorporated into bird's-eye surveys of the Roman Empire's maritime endeavours. The sparse references I could find about Roman sea power were routine rundowns of Rome's ascent to sea power and skimpy on the imperial period.

About sixty years ago, military historians began to modify their 'decisive battle' approach and ushered in a concern for logistics – civilian infrastructure, organizational systems, manufacturing, agriculture, trade, technology, research, supply bases, fuelling/re-provisioning depots and transport. These are the vital strategical 'sinews of war'; but their depiction is unexciting compared with rousing battle vignettes. Authors of these industry-and-supply monographs usually pitch them at other experts, unless their writing style is sufficiently robust to attract a general readership. The same applies to accounts narrating relatively minor naval activities: supporting the legionary outposts in skirmishing with local tribes upon sheltered waters on the periphery of the empire. This policing the peace role was brought to the fore by the anti-colonial conflicts of the 1950s and 1960s.

The maritime might of the mature Roman Empire has more to do with the 'dull' logistical aspect and colonial patrolling type of sideshows than with theatrical major naval encounters upon the briny deep depicted in novels, cinema and digital wargames. Archaeological fieldwork has uncovered extensive naval support facilities, ports and bases along Rome's various sea lines of communication. These were not just safe anchorages, for the main Roman squadrons did not patrol but, except on major operations, exercised their influences as fleets-in-being. Like the US Navy asserting 'freedom of navigation' presence along contested archipelagos of the western Pacific Ocean today, the fleets of ancient Rome had a deterrent value as well. A case in point will be illustrated in my discussion of the Macedonian Wars.

In this connection, the most impressive study concerning Roman maritime history was presented by Michel Redde, *Mare Nostrum Les infrastructures de la marine romaine en l'epoque imperiale* (Rome: Ecole francaise de Rome, 1987) and focussed on the Roman imperial navy. This monumental work stands out because of a very erudite analysis of the infrastructure of naval bases at the disposal of the Roman navy. On the other hand, it must be noted that his consideration of naval tactics and strategic employment of fleets was somewhat thin; Redde did not take a keen interest in these important aspects of naval warfare.

A navy predominately manifests its authority in conjunction with land operations and objectives, and, with a necessarily higher level of manning, is the more dependent on abundant supplies. The discovered Roman naval structures were centres for supply from the hinterland, the housing of personnel and construction of field fortifications. In modern strategical parlance, these facilities supported 'peripheral conflict', 'protection of trade', 'police actions', 'military operations other than war', 'naval presence', 'low intensity combat' and the all-embracing 'littoral warfare'. Clearly, there are important planning considerations underlying the preparations for these relatively low-key activities, but such books and essays that are written about them are usually of interest to the naval professional rather than the naval enthusiast.

Histories which include naval contributions to campaigns customarily concentrate on the sea battles and the tactics so employed rather than on the guiding maritime strategy of the warring camps, a policy-planning concept that embraces logistics and operational calculations. Maritime strategy and its cousin naval strategy slowly developed as separate disciplines from military strategy, but it was not until the end of the nineteenth century that historians started to write on the specific value and influence maritime policies had on the overall strategy of countries and empires. The two fathers of this discipline were Alfred Thayer Mahan, an American naval officer, and Sir Julian Stafford Corbett, an English naval historian. I'll describe their varying perspectives momentarily.

Maintaining order along the wet flanks of the Empire and guarding the mercantile sea lanes is not suitable fare for stirring 'drum and trumpet' military history. Nevertheless, economic/logistical planning, conducting combined operations along coasts and rivers and 'gunboat diplomacy' characterizes the heyday of Rome's maritime dominance. It warrants an analysis tailored to its traits. Much of it would be described today as 'littoral warfare' and constabulary patrols against non-state adversaries. Such maritime police work has become the latest trend in naval thinking as the Cold War morphed into the Great War On Terror. Think Somali pirates or the 1980s tanker war in the Persian Gulf rather than the epic clashes of Trafalgar, Leyte Gulf, Midway and Jutland.

A few more modern examples should suffice. In 1839, during the Second Seminole War, the 'Mosquito Fleet', under the command of Lieutenant John McLaughlin, conducted joint counterinsurgency operations in the Florida Everglades, working with army units. In 2015, Iran sent munitions to Hamas and Islamic Jihad groups operating in the Gaza Strip and the Sinai, and the cargo vessels were interdicted by the Israeli Navy. Somalia-based pirate craft ambushed US- and allied-flagged merchantmen off the Horn of Africa from 2008-2014, and were frequently driven off by a few well-placed salvos from frigates or corvettes. Iranian 'boghammer' speedboats buzzed around a Liberian-flagged tanker and were driven off by the approach of a US frigate. Chinese and Indian vessels were also active in this struggle against rogue-state actors, which resembled the British Royal Navy's gunboats in protecting the Empire's mercantile outposts in the nineteenth century.

This type of policing is classified in the US military lexicon as Low Intensity Combat. However, the moniker doesn't signify that the various skirmishes with 'irregulars' are insignificant actions. It's only in comparison to the 'Big War' battles that they are so categorized. They usually don't grab the headlines unless they escalate, but are no less worthy of attention by naval professionals.

The Relevance Of Modern-Day Sea Power Debates to Ancient Maritime History

To glean apropos examples from the beginning of the first millennium might seem a bit of a stretch to some aficionados of modern naval affairs. But a few examples from recent literature might help explain what I am trying to accomplish.

A US Army War College study, 'Mahan Goes to War: Effects of World War I on the US Navy's Force Structure and Operational Planning', demonstrates how Mahan's 'lessons' were misapplied in light of the Navy's experiences in the Great War. Of course Rome did not critique such lessons as she might apply to future operations, but the War College study does attest to the timeless tendency for service lobbyists to selectively interpret the past in order to tout their favoured weapon.

The Roman rulers were cognizant enough of how smaller, swifter and more manoeuvrable liburni defeated the clumsy huge polyremes of Antony and Cleopatra at Actium. Augustus discarded most of the captured 'battleships' when he built up his home fleets, concentrating on the smaller vessels that won him his crown. There is certainly evidence of the continued use of the 'heavies' in subsequent galley warfare, but as potential and actual enemies with massive warships dwindled, the lighter, swifter ships became predominant.

Reference is heard in contemporary naval circles to three metaphorical 'colours' of water: blue, green and brown. They denote generally the proximity of land: 'blue'water, the oceanic, reaches farthest from land; 'green' water is the oceanic littoral (coastal sea-land interface); and 'brown' water comprises rivers, bays and estuaries. The ancient Romans formulated no such compartmentalization (the navy was essentially the wet flank of the legions), although these concepts are useful in making some modest modern correlates.

To return to the present situation of the modern US Navy, there is a vigorous debate over the utility of the Cyclone-class patrol craft and the Littoral Combat Ship, and the necessity for a small surface combatant optimally designed for operations in the littoral. Questioning the mission overkill of deploying the capital ships of today (e.g., Aegis cruisers and destroyers as well as aircraft carriers) for such low- to mid-intensity conflict, contemporary theorists hold that the Navy is sorely missing a littoral-capable patrol craft that can operate on 'presence' missions in the South China Sea, Persian Gulf, Caribbean and Mediterranean. Critics of the troubled LCS project have fastened on an alternate, more robustly armed and longer-range 'light patrol frigate' design. The debate is highly contentious and reflects the hold of the capital ship lobby (formerly known as the 'big gun club') on US naval thinking.

Frank Uhlig, former editor of the *US Naval War College Review*, conducted an exhaustive study of the actual employment of naval forces in his recent book, *How Navies Fight: The U.S. Navy and Its Allies* (US Naval Institute, Annapolis, Maryland, 1994). Through extensive historical analysis, he concluded that the most common employment of these forces was the support of operations ashore, the landing of forces and the protection of shipping at sea. Most of the actions and reactions of the Roman fleets and flotillas described in this book may be similarly characterized.

Much as the leading naval powers found their large capital ship inventories of the twenty-first century ill-suited to conduct green- and brown-water operations, the Roman Empire gradually discarded its monster war galleys (the towering polyremes of the late Hellenic world), with multiple tiers of oarsmen last utilized at Actium and concentrated on the *liburnium*, *hemiola* and *lembus*, smaller, shallow-draft yet seaworthy craft better suited to handling policing tasks in coastal and riverine areas in conjunction with land-based legions and embarked marines. These craft are roughly equivalent to the littoral combat ships, light frigates and corvettes of today. They were adapted from ships captured from Aegean pirate and north European indigenous fleets.

Popular naval histories of Britain customarily skip from the campaign of Trafalgar (1805) to the Crimean War (1856), omitting the Opium Wars of 1839–42 and 1856–60, in which the Royal Navy brought diminutive gunboats and marines to bear in order to take out fortified Chinese blocking positions along the riverbanks – the Taku Forts. It is only in recent decades that these relatively minor engagements have received attention. Similarly, the American exercise of 'gunboat diplomacy' – positioning warships so as to influence events ashore without actually opening fire – during the Soviet-American Cold War (1950s to 1990) has been receiving more attention in the past few years, as too the flag-showing 'Yangpat' patrols along China's Yangtze River and its tributaries and branches during the warlord era of the 1920s and 1930s.

In the post-Cold War environment, these mundane tasks are typically the constabulary responsibilities of a world-class navy. The permanent attributes of genuine sea power as it is now understood encompass precisely those functions so offhandedly characterized by popular historians as secondary roles: patrolling to pre-empt lurking threats to maritime trade on or near choke points; guarding the routes of merchant vessels on the high seas against lawless predators; attacking sea raiders in their coastal lairs; facilitating the safe movement of troops, munitions and provisions to outlying posts; transporting officials, diplomatic envoys and dispatches to sustain the vital communications network of a global empire, intercepting smuggler vessels and policing episodic eruptions of tribal unrest on the realm's fringes.

As I hope to demonstrate in my review of Mahan's analysis of the Second Punic War, he had a more nuanced notion of sea power than he is generally credited with by pundits who vilify his supposed imperialist programme and penchant for big battles between main fleets. These critics, in addition to rebuking his imperialist tendencies, accuse him of being obsessed with decisive sea battles as the *sine qua non* of sea power. Had this been the case, he would have not neglected the First

Punic War in favour of the later conflict, in which there were no such melees upon the high seas. He did not advocate fighting decisive battles for their own sake, but asserted that nations must have a strategic objective beyond tactical victory, because 'unless the position won is strategically decisive … the battle might as well, or better, never have been fought'. As he demonstrates, with respect to the Second Punic War, Rome had, by virtue of her success at sea in the First Punic War, already set herself up in 'strategically decisive' positions by the start of the second conflict and further enhanced her strategic posture during that later war.

The doyen of modern sea power theorists, Geoffrey Till, in his book *Maritime Strategy and the Nuclear Age*, has noted that the nearest thing to an ancient 'philosopher of sea power' was Thucydides in his *History of the Peloponnesian War*. Thucydides rarely generalized about warfare at sea, but instead 'provided illustrations of the importance of maritime strength and the various uses to which it could be put'. It was up to more recent authors to draw such conclusions, such as Admiral Sir Reginald Custance, who, in his analysis of the Athenian expedition to Syracuse, derived some lessons applicable to the early twentieth century, when he wrote *War at Sea: Modern Theory and Ancient Practice* (1919). Mahan had discussed this same operation in his collected Naval War College lectures, published in 1911 as *Naval strategy compared and contrasted with the principles and practice of military operations on land*, as well as his above-noted section on the Second Punic War in his 1890 treatise.

The Limitations And Possibilities of Ancient Sea Power

We need to broaden our perspective concerning what was important and feasible in ancient warfare at sea. As is the case today, practical matters in seafaring had implications for naval strategy. There was no room for much, if any, water or food in ancient warships. Crews needed access to a coast to get water, food and rest after each voyage; thus control of safe landing places and ports was essential. The Romans were well aware of this. Therefore, when evaluating the role of the Roman navy, the number of sea battles is not the most important thing. The navy had other vital functions. It worked in cooperation with the army, and the organization of supply routes, depots and landing places enabled the Romans to wage war overseas. In addition, during the period of the Republic, the Roman navy operated at sea independently, participating in the contest for thalassocracy in the western and eastern Mediterranean by challenging and defeating the Punic, Macedonian and Seleucid fleets. By the accession of Augustus, practically all challengers possessing credible war fleets had been tamed.

The record of Rome during her imperial ascendance – the five centuries or so of the *Pax Romana*, or Roman Peace – warrants the scrutiny of those readers who appreciate both the enforcement and deterrent value of naval mastery. Sea power's deeper significance connotes domination of the vital sea lanes (today called 'command of the sea'), essential to sustaining economic/military strength, as opposed to one-off encounters between major warships.

While there is little in the way of exciting war-fleet clashes during these stretches of great power naval control, there's much that should interest the student of sea power in its profounder sense. It is the message propounded by modern theorists such as Mahan, Corbett, Philip Colomb, Raoul Castex, Wolfgang Wegener, Curt von Maltzahn, C.E. Calwell, George Furse and Herbert Richmond, based on their analyses of post-Renaissance maritime empires. Of these, only Mahan took any special note – and that very brief – of pre-Renaissance occurrences, but the Roman Peace is pertinent to the various theories of all. As I hope to demonstrate here, these pundits of sea power would find much food for thought pondering why and how so many of these battles took place around islands or in narrow channels and shallow waters, and what this meant to the character of naval dominance.

The emergence of Roman sea power, as it defined its make-up and function, was nurtured through the sequence of power projection and frontier defence endeavours spanning from the conclusion of the Second Punic War to the Battle of Actium. Hence I devote more space than most studies of Roman sea power to these antecedent operations, known as the Illyrian, Macedonian, Mithridatic and Syrian (aka Asiatic) conflicts, occurring in the closing decades of the Republic. I similarly also pay more attention to the naval side of the Second Punic War as a template for this more muted kind of naval activity.

Here Mahan's observation is to the point:

> 'At the beginning of the war, Mommsen says, Rome controlled the seas. To whatever cause, or combination of causes, it be attributed, this essentially non-maritime state had in the first Punic War established over its sea-faring rival a naval supremacy, which still lasted. In the second war there was no naval battle of importance, a circumstance which in itself, and still more in connection with other well-ascertained facts, indicates a superiority analogous to that which at other epochs has been marked by the same feature.'

Mahan did not insist that fleets must always mass their ships in permanent battle formation, but rather that they should remain close enough to concentrate if necessary. Nonetheless, the balance of his *Influence* books did appear to feature decisive battles between the opposing navies' heavy warships, since there were ample examples of this throughout his featured time period. Even so, he didn't neglect the tangible effects of such victories upon freedom of navigation. It is for this alleged concentration on big battles between line-of-battle ships that he is sometimes compared unfavourably with Corbett.

In the early sections of his major work, Mahan writes of ancient Rome during the Carthaginian wars, discussing how the Roman fleet was positioned to 'check' Macedonia, an ally of Hannibal, and was so successful in doing so that 'not a soldier of the phalanx ever set foot in Italy'. The principle employed by this threatening naval force was one of prevention and deterrence. Similarly, he goes on to assert, coercion through overt presence and demonstrations of omnipotence was applied when 'Roman fleets … visited the coasts of Africa'. The deterrent effects of Rome's sea power in the Second Punic War will be outlined in my section on that conflict.

The Logistical, Policing Aspect versus the Battle-Centric View

The introduction to *Beans, Bullets and Black Oil*, a study of US naval logistics in the Second World War, explains the unsung key role of naval logistics thus:

> 'From 7 December1941, when the Japanese attacked Pearl Harbor, until they admitted defeat in August 1945, our fleet continuously grew. During those stirring and difficult times, the accounts of ship actions, air strikes, and amphibious operations make up the thrilling combat history of the Pacific theater. Linked inseparably with combat is naval logistic support, the support which makes available to the fleet such essentials as ammunition, fuel, food, repair services – in short, all the necessities, at the proper time and place and in adequate amounts.'

There is the concept of 'sea control', a relatively modern notion, which in its familiar interpretation entails destroying the enemy forces by a decisive action, driving his most powerful warships from the ocean. This rarely happened during the period of the Roman Republic and later in the Principate, in which the desired status was usually achieved by destroying enemy forces over time (attrition), containing the enemy fleet (a form of blockade – though not in the modern sense), 'choke point' (straits) control in which sorties could be made from convenient headlands along nodal islets, and capturing important enemy positions for use as forward basing areas. Again, these are notions that failed to grab the attention of the ancient authors whose chronicles of Rome's martial laurels have come down to us. They have to do with the passage of ships through hostile waters and, absent of a high-seas encounter, are in the logistical rather than combat vein.

The 'great naval battles' collections typically ignore such modern-era episodes as shallow-draft gunboats intimidating rough-and-tumble aboriginals along the rivers, inlets, bays and estuaries of the British Empire's 'barbarian' coasts, American patrol vessels quelling dissent by native labourers protesting harsh treatment by the United Fruit Company in Central America in the 1920s, gunboats fending off forays by pirates in the South China Sea from the nineteenth to twenty-first centuries or ambushes by warlords along the perilous reaches of the great Yangtze waterway in the interwar period. Political science professors and 'War and Society' researchers are more apt to study these bush warfare conflicts than are military historians.

This type of waterborne threat is more typical of the situation facing Rome's fleets and naval squadrons during the *Pax Romana* than the swarms of manoeuvring and ramming quadriremes and triremes favoured by 'sword and sandal' films. Further, the depiction of the fleet-to-fleet engagements gives scant consideration to the underlying plans of battle and pre-battle positioning of the warships and their seagoing supply caravans.

Benito Mussolini, in the 1920s, invoked a vision of sea power 'before men whose lives and thoughts are among mountains'. Il Duce derided the supposed contempt for Roman naval power in the days before the First Punic War, epitomized in a catchphrase attributed to the ancient arch-enemy, that 'Romans could not even wash their hands in the Mediterranean without permission from the Carthaginians.' In politicking to build up a powerful Italian Navy to confront the British, he recalled the glorious days when the Mediterranean was a 'Roman lake'. It has been said that he saw his government under the Fascists as a regeneration of the old Roman Empire, and embraced anything connected to it.

In lectures and pseudo-scholarly papers, Mussolini emphasized how in modern times, as in ancient, a powerful Roman fleet was the key to uniting an empire running from Gibraltar to the Indian Ocean. See especially his thirty-two-page pamphlet *Roma Antica sul Mare*, derived from his lecture at the *Università per Stranieri* of Perugia delivered on 5 October 1926. Oddly, for someone who was touting the great accomplishments of Roman sea power in the Punic Wars, the pamphlet repeats some of the late nineteenth-century canards about Rome being a fundamentally landlubberly state and the unflattering observation that the employment of the boarding bridge simply converted a sea contest to a land battle. This was by way of demonstrating the obstacles confronting and the perseverance of the ancient Roman seafarers, echoing in a way the later works of J.H. Thiel, who commended Rome on her dogged determination to build and man ships in the face of her predilection for farming and land warfare.

The study of naval history and sea power in the ancient world has been left to a somewhat eclectic group of scholars operating on the very fringes of the naval history discipline. Much of the scholarship on sea power in antiquity has been undertaken by classical specialists and ancient historians, whose works are rarely if ever referred to by modern naval practitioners, naval historians and theorists, or students of maritime affairs.

A Brief Survey Of Popular Naval Books on Sea War In the Galley Age

Among most of those few naval historians who pay attention, the maintenance of the *Pax Romana* at sea comprises, at best, a footnote to the Punic and Civil Wars. In fact, prior to the 1950s, there were hardly any authors who bothered to reflect on the modern parallels that might be derived from naval conflicts preceding the sixteenth century. I did find four older books that correspond with my endeavour to transmogrify 'sea power' as exhibited in the nine centuries bracketing the notional birth of Christ to what the term signifies during the past three centuries.

In 1919, retired British admiral Sir Reginald Custance wrote *War at Sea: Modern Theory and Ancient Practice*, which targeted naval history buffs as well as policy-makers interested in the sea power lessons of the just-concluded Great War, as illustrated by the naval operations of the ancient Greeks in the Persian and Peloponnesian wars. His 'modern theory', however, does not engage with the extant (as of 1918) authorities on sea warfare, but seems to draw from Clausewitz and Jomini. In evident contradistinction to Mahan, and concurrence with Corbett, he did emphasize how neither land power nor sea power alone had won wars, but rather both operated in agreement.

Consider Arthur McCartney Shepard's *Sea Power in Ancient History: The Story of the Navies of Classic Greece and Rome* (1924), in which the foreword by US Rear Admiral William A. Moffett, Chief of the US Navy's fledgling Bureau of Aeronautics, stressed the significance of the ancient material in underscoring sea power's role as an arbiter of national standing. Shepard made good use of the ancient sources to survey the naval wars around the Mediterranean basin prior to the accession of Augustus. As usual, both this book and that of Custance noted above skip the military efforts of the Empire as lacking both significance and intrinsic naval interest.

John van Duyn Southworth in Book One (*The Ancient Fleets*) of his popular *War at Sea* through the ages trilogy cuts from Actium to the Crusades, dismissing all naval history in between with the brusque observation: 'No naval power raised its head to challenge Rome. The early centuries of the Christian era provide little to interest a chronicler of naval history.' Of course, that depends on your definition of naval history, which to Southworth would seem to be limited to major battles and campaigns. I do not mean to single out Shepard and Southworth, as they were, after all, writing for a general audience who liked its history packaged in dramatic vignettes. And their coverage of the major naval conflicts of the Republic was respectable enough.

Helmut Pemsel, in his well-regarded *A History of War at Sea*, similarly, after a brief note on the establishment of permanent fleets under Augustus, skips from

Actium to the accession of Constantine and the Battle of the Hellespont in AD 323. He at least details the role of ships during the Empire's decline. Here is his parenthetical comment after his analysis of Actium:

'Agrippa's command of the sea had been the deciding factor in this campaign – which featured raids, blockades and, an eminently suitable weapon, the fire-arrow. As in the sea war against Sextus Pompey, the careful training of the crews paid handsome dividends. The Civil Wars and the Republic were thus ended, and the Imperial Age began. *For the next five hundred years, Rome would command the whole of the Mediterranean, and the fleet's main tasks would be those of police force and transport medium for numerous armies.*' [author's emphasis]

He does not bother to describe these policing and transport activities, presumably because they constitute legionary, as opposed to naval, history. Yet ships and sailors had significant, if supporting, roles in these activities.

Here's another dismissive passage from a text used at the US Naval Academy in the 1920s, *A History of Sea Power* by William Oliver Stevens:

'After the battle of Actium and the establishment of a powerful Roman empire without a rival in the world, there follows a long period in which the Mediterranean, and indeed all the waterways known to the civilized nations, belonged without challenge to the galleys of Rome. Naval stations were established to assist in the one activity left to the ships of war, the pursuit of pirates, but otherwise there was little or nothing to do. And during this long period, indeed, down to the Middle Ages, practically nothing is known of the development in naval types until the emergence of the low, one- or two-banked galley of the wars between the Christian and the Mohammedan. The first definite description we have of warships after the period of Actium comes at the end of the ninth century.

'There was some futile naval fighting against the Vandals in the days when Rome was crumbling. Finally, by a curious freak of history, Genseric the Vandal took a fleet out from Carthage against Rome, and swept the Mediterranean. In the year 455, some six centuries after Rome had wreaked her vengeance on Carthage, this Vandal fleet anchored unopposed in the Tiber and landed an army.'

In this case, five centuries of naval history are summed up in two paragraphs. Apparently the 'great battle' syndrome still held sway among sea power advocates.

A 1960 US Naval Institute publication, *Sea Power: a naval history* by Elmer Potter and Henry Adams, a follow-on to the Stevens casebook, which also served as a textbook at the US Naval Academy, has even less to say about the subject:

> 'For five centuries after Actium, commercial vessels moved from the Black Sea to the Atlantic, protected only by small fleets of police vessels to keep down piracy. The entire Mediterranean and its tributary waters had become a closed sea, with all coasts and naval bases controlled by Rome. On land and sea, the Pax Romana was established, the longest period of comparative peace in history.'

This brief remark acknowledging the attainment of naval mastery suffices to address the 500-year span of the Roman imperial sea power at its pinnacle. The next section following this paragraph jumps to the close of the fifth century AD, as if there was no notable naval activity during that long interval.

During the concluding four centuries of the millennial span under consideration, the main functions of the *classes* or fleets was to contend with piracy, provide the vital grain convoys (and shipments of other goods) with unmolested sea passages, and support the far-flung operations of the legions in stemming the incursions of unruly tribes in the march-lands, as well as tipping the balance in the endemic civil unrest at the heart of the Empire. This unspectacular though nonetheless critical role simply reflects the fact that there was no opponent capable of seriously challenging Roman sea power during this period. It corresponds with the tasks envisioned by modern analysts of maritime strength.

The imperial navy maintained two larger fleets based in the Mediterranean, with smaller squadrons and transient naval detachments operating on the North Sea, Black Sea and the major rivers and co-located with legionary riverine or coastal forts. Ravenna and Misenum, on opposite sides of the Italian peninsula, were the main naval bases in *mare nostrum* ('Our Sea', as Roman writers referred to it, designating the Mediterranean as a Roman lake), though ships were regularly dispatched to peripheral theatres and squadrons were positioned there on a more or less ad hoc basis as emergencies dictated. There existed some dedicated fleet installations along the River Rhine and Danube, but most were attached to bases of the frontier armies. There can be no tidy table of organization with respect to the various naval stations – they shifted, expanded or contracted, from crisis to crisis. My chapter on fleets and their functions should make this clear.

The ships used by the imperial navy comprised oared warships, most of them adapted to fighting swift pirate vessels and the similar craft of hostile ethnic tribes on the maritime periphery, and transports as well as sailing craft used mainly for logistical support, chiefly merchant vessels adapted to the purpose. Some galleys mounting rams and missile weapons (catapults and ballistae) used auxiliary sails to allow the oarsmen to rest enroute to and from sea battles, particularly those more distant than a day's journey from port, while the troop transports, merchantmen and supply ships were mainly sail-borne, with oars utilized during calms or during manoeuvring to enter or leave a port.

Rowing, needless to say, was extremely strenuous, not to mention that in the warm weather sailing seasons it required a lot of drinking water and nourishment. Both of these considerations limited sustained oar-propelled transits to a few hours, rarely more than a day at a stretch, in calm seas. The slender galleys, packed with rowers and marines, had little room for stores in any case. This meant that war galleys generally had to keep within sight of land when on patrol. Of course, when engaging the enemy, the intense exertion meant that the seamen and any embarked marines would become exhausted and parched even more rapidly. However, this didn't mean that they were incapable of hoisting makeshift sailing rigs to accompany troop and supply ships on extended expeditions, as will be demonstrated at several points in the text. When possible, the masts, sails and rigging were stowed ashore preparatory to naval engagements, as they clogged the decks and obstructed the marines and rowers.

Some pundits allege that Rome habitually delegated its naval function to associates with maritime expertise, and thus its claim to wielding sea power was indirect. While this is true to some extent, it's hard to imagine how Rome could have met the challenges confronting its authority at sea exclusively by relying upon the volatile friendship of naval-minded allies. Though the ships were often manned by naval associates, their efforts were supervised by Roman patricians and the ships were built in Roman shipyards, albeit to foreign designs. Rome was especially adept at ingesting and employing foreign expertise. It is this ability to incorporate the skill and assets of more experienced naval allies that characterizes Rome's judicious approach to maritime affairs.

The Roman navy, although somewhat overshadowed by the legions, played an important role for the Roman Empire. For the army to conquer and rule its vast territories, control of the sea lanes was essential. The navy fleets needed to be capably structured and powerful in order to dominate the trade routes, transport the legions unimpeded and defend and attack against pirates and other predatory enemies. Under Augustus in 31 BC, the navy consisted of 800 warships, with many being sent to Ravenna and Misenus in Italy, and smaller squadrons to the external coasts (e.g. Gaul, Spain and Britain) and to the major rivers, to support land operations (e.g. Rhine, Danube and Seine). When Roman coasts came under attack from Teutonic raiders in the third and fourth centuries, the navy played a key part in the defence of the Empire.

This then is neither an institutional history of the various ancient Roman navies nor an all-inclusive narration of naval battles, but a study of the sea power, writ broadly, of ancient Rome. Undramatic 'naval presence', 'sea control' and coastal/littoral and fluvial operations are all important factors, while spectacular sea battles are not treated as isolated manifestations of naval presence and deterrence but are subsumed within an overall maritime framework. Such large-scale fleet-to-fleet combat that I describe is done within a strategical overview of the conflict or episode being discussed; tactical details may be sketched in subordinate to that aim.

Outside of the novels of Tom Clancy and kindred techno-thriller projections of the Third World War that never happened, the confrontation between the Soviet and US navies was very much a matter of sea power in its broader, more subtle application. In fact, Clancy visualizes just one 'big war' scenario, that of *Red Storm Rising*. The preponderance of his works (esp. *The Hunt for Red October* and others of that ilk) describe geopolitical cat-and-mouse encounters short of war. So too with the exercise of Roman naval supremacy in the 500-600 years after Actium. Ships were the silent partners of the glorious legions in enforcing the *Pax Romana*. Sea power was an unspectacular, though vital, component of imperial mastery.

A run-down of the existing modern studies of ancient sea power shows that, apart from the abbreviated treatment of the subject in Chester Starr's slim 1989 pamphlet, there has been virtually nothing written that is dedicated to the formation and implementation of Roman naval policy in the imperial epoch. Starr's earlier book, *The Roman Imperial Navy, 31 BC – AD 324* (1941), is a guidebook, sketching separate accounts of the several fleets, rather than a cohesive analysis of Roman naval power in that time frame. It furnishes the raw material from which a sea power analysis of the Empire might be fashioned, but which the author failed to fully realize in his 1989 survey.

There are a number of pathbreaking studies of the naval aspects of the Republic that helped me in my analysis of the sea power of the Empire. For example, there is some important German scholarship tucked away in several erudite journals of the 1890s, notably that of Professor Johannes Kromayer, '*Die Entwicklung der romischen Flotte vom. Seerauberkriege des Pompeius bis zur Schlacht von Actium*', which, although written in 1897, is one of the more noteworthy early examinations of the foundations of the Roman fleets in the late Republican period, between Pompey the Great's anti-pirate campaign in the 80s BC and the Battle of Actium. Typically, the author concludes with Actium. Kromayer's insights were anticipated by Theodor Mommsen's volumes on the Roman provinces dating from the 1880s – which have been mentioned in connection with the germination of Mahan's theories. H.D.L. Viereck's *Die römische Flotte. Classis romana* (1975) was useful as well, providing a good, short synopsis of the activities of the various fleets.

Viereck is especially good on the design of the ancient warships. His maps were particularly helpful.

Much of the early research was carried forward in the fundamental works of the Dutch historian Johannes H. Thiel, published in the late 1940s and early 1950s. Thiel's two books are devoted to the naval activities of the Republic and are valuable in furnishing critical background. His *Studies on the History of Roman Sea-Power in Republican Times* (1946) and *Roman Sea-Power Before The Second Punic War* (1954) are, after over half a century, still very helpful in analyzing the prelude to Rome's abrupt and unexpected victory over Carthage in the First Punic War, as well as the naval actions of that conflict and those of the second war, which may be considered as laying the foundation for the relatively uncontested Roman naval mastery during the ascendance of the Empire. Despite the existence of more recent scholarship, I found that Professor Thiel had treated the topic amply and sensibly. He makes some bold inferences from reticent literary sources, but they are always stimulating and challenging, even where not entirely convincing. His works have been of much help in filling out some blanks in the ancient accounts.

On the face of it, Thiel clings to the questionable notion that the Romans were by temperament landlubbers innately averse to maritime endeavours. However, on further examination, he did not suggest that they were timid seafarers. He modifies his seeming disparagement somewhat by the observation that having at last recognized its importance to them, the Roman leaders provided for sea trade and its protection with their typical thoroughness and organizational skills. Further, his characterization of the Romans as landlubbers is not as condemnatory as it might seem at first. His cardinal point was not that they feared, hated and thus shunned the sea. Rather, he says that they were overly bold and impetuous in their naval ventures, amateurishly putting out to sea under conditions when a nautically vigilant people would have kept to the harbour or at least have prepared their vessels accordingly. In other words, they lacked natural sea-savvy, and were thereby slow to appreciate and cope with the hazards of seafaring.

Speaking of the origins of Roman sea power, I have found a rather obscure doctoral dissertation from 1915 by Frederick William Clark, 'The Influence of Sea-Power on the History of the Roman Republic', which, despite its age, was useful in supplementing Thiel's works, particularly with respect to the naval aspects of the period between the end of the First Punic War and Actium. Clark specifically references Mahan in his analysis and, as demonstrated by the title of his thesis, emulates him. His analytical tract bristles with insights derived from his reading of Mahan's masterworks, though he cites only the ancient sources, with some critical Mahanian analysis of these.

Likewise, Christa Steinby's 2007 thesis, 'The Roman Republican Navy: From the Sixth Century to 167 BC', published in Finland, was of some value in tracing the roots of Roman seafaring. Even though Dr Steinby may have overstated her rejection of Thiel's doubts about Rome's sea-mindedness, and sometimes makes rather creative use of the ambiguous sources, her research offers a counter-argument to the prevalent view of Rome as a complete naval novice in the period prior to the First Punic War. Again, while my study concentrates on the imperial era, roughly 150 BC to the sixth century AD, it is nonetheless necessary to correct the notion that Rome's victory over Carthage in the First Punic War was a bolt from the blue. Dr. Steinby's later book, *Rome Versus Carthage: The War at Sea* (2014), elaborating upon her dissertation, is also quite useful, advancing her ideas in a more cohesive framework.

Similarly, Peter Grant's 2010 masters thesis for the University of Cape Coast, Ghana, 'The Navy in Rome's Rise to Empire, 264-146 BC', was helpful in framing my argument regarding the minor campaigns during this preliminary period. Even though Grant's study is at the masters level, it contains some keen observations as well as handy summaries of naval campaigns. Some other earlier works are interesting for their reflection of the time when they were composed rather than for any helpful insights.

A US Army War College Strategy Research Project, 'Comparing Strategies of the 2d Punic War: Rome's Strategic Victory Over the Tactical/Operational Genius, Hannibal Barca' (2001), by Lieutenant Colonel James Parker, while naturally concentrating on the land campaigns, also has much useful discussion of the effect of sea control upon them. Early in this paper, he comments:

'Central to Roman strategy was the critical advantage of Roman sea supremacy. Their ability to control the sea lines of communication of central and western Mediterranean enabled them to move and resupply large forces at will. The Romans maintained this advantage throughout the war and they were quickly able to respond to problems arising in distant areas. This stands in marked contrast with Carthaginian naval efforts. Carthage possessed a potent naval force but never successfully deployed it against the Romans.'

Roman Naval Power – Some Traditional and Modern Views

This observation in the British newspaper *The Standard*, from May 1912, is instructive as to the Edwardian era take on Roman sea power: 'Because of that formidable and threatening Armada across the North Sea [i.e., Germany's fleet], we have almost abandoned the waters of the Outer Oceans. We are in the position of Imperial Rome when the Barbarians were thundering at the frontiers. The ominous word has gone forth. We have called home the legions.'

An 1899 lecture at Britain's prestigious Royal United Services Institution, 'The Importanceof Sea Power in the Growth of the Roman Empire and the Lesson Taught to Great Britain', concludes, as usual, with the Battle of Actium; once again, this time frame reflects the prevailing notion that since Rome's mastery of the Mediterranean was achieved by that time, the rest is merely a coda. Only the 'growth' (pre-Actium) of the Empire was deemed worthy of study to mine lessons germane to Britain's sea force at the end of Victoria's long reign.

The analogy of Rome's climb to naval pre-eminence with Great Britain's situation at the beginning of the twentieth century is inapt. Britain had already built up its naval expertise over a period of four centuries when the lecturer spoke. He might have instead profitably discussed the period from the first century BC to the sixth century AD. But this oversight is understandable; the speaker lacked the reference materials, and what few there were, as usual, implied that naval power was irrelevant between Actium and the rise of the Byzantine fleets.

Interestingly, the author of the above RUSI lecture reflects upon why he chose the navy of Rome for his subject, rather than that of Minoan Crete, Mycenae, Athens, etc. The first reason is that, unlike the ephemeral powers preceding it, Rome had solidity and permanence; yet he slights the naval sinews of this staying power during its peak in the half millennium following the death of Christ. Another reason is that Rome's principle effort was vested in her legions, and it was instructive 'to prove the value of Sea Power even to a nation whose strength was in her soldiers and in the genius of her generals'.

I selectively consulted Vice-Admiral William Ledyard Rodgers' oft-reprinted *Greek and Roman Naval Warfare; A Study of Strategy, Tactics, and Ship Design from Salamis (480 BC) to Actium (31 BC)*, and, to a lesser extent, his *Naval Warfare under Oars: 4th to 16th Centuries*. Both works initially appeared in the late 1930s, and the scholarship employed is thus somewhat dated. As the titles indicate, the time periods for both books don't coincide precisely with my research interest. Rodgers seems to have relied more upon his experiences with the modern US Navy than early twentieth-century scholarship on ancient fleets. He is mainly useful on surmising the strategies employed by the opposing fleets, but his scholarship is obsolete with regard to the characteristics of the warships. His salty perspective is nonetheless helpful and his battle narratives are detailed, though, as usual, with more than a dash of informed speculation.

Herman Wallinga's 1956 analysis, *The Boarding-bridge of the Romans*, although naturally mainly concerned with the mechanics of that device, is useful as well in correcting the crude formulation that the only way that the Romans in the First Punic War could prevail upon the sea was by converting sea battles to land battles. Wallinga explains the intricate seamanship required to exploit the potential of the *corvus*. This expertise is not indicative of a hopelessly land-minded folk that feared and hated sea voyaging. But the *corvus* was largely abandoned after that conflict, and so was the ephemeral tactic for its use. His more recent book, *Ships and Sea-power before the Great Persian War: the Ancestry of the Ancient Trireme*, although covering the period just before the rise of Rome, provides important background on why and how that iconic warship evolved.

Jorit Wintjes, who has written widely and wisely on ancient Roman sea power, punctures the 'land warfare afloat' image of the Roman fleets, often inaptly compared to the cavalry flank of a land army, in his 'Command at Sea – The Roman Perspective', *Mars & Clio* No. 22, Summer 2008, a perceptive analysis of several Roman naval battles of the Republican epoch.

My minor reservations nothwithstanding, my study of Roman naval activity was facilitated by Chester Starr's *The Influence of Sea Power on Ancient History*. I have discussed this work passim above. While its presumed message was askew, it does provide a useful summary of maritime events.

Since so much of Roman naval activity was closely tied to land-based campaigns – what in today's lexicon is called 'littoral warfare' – Valentine J. Belfiglio's *A Study Of Ancient Roman Amphibious And Offensive Sea-ground Task Force Operations* proved to be a useful guide. It helpfully illustrates how the fleet worked in close harmony with its shipboard marines in making both unopposed and contested strategical shore lodgments and seizure of harbours on which to forward-base war galleys and to unload supply and troopships. His unorthodox approach, employing the US Joint Chiefs of Staff's 'Doctine for Landing Force Operations' to assess ancient amphibious actions, pointed the way that I might likewise make use of current doctrine derived from Mahan, Corbett and several others. He uses a select few campaigns to illustrate his thesis; however, these are by no means the whole story. As is the case with most of the few references on ancient Roman naval operations, his book ends shortly after the accession of Augustus, as attested by the subtitle 'from the assault against Carthage in 204 BC to the invasion of Britain in 43 AD'. Nonetheless, it was useful to me in developing a perspective on later 'conjunct operations' of the Roman fleets.

Although over a half-century old, Alfred Vagts' massive study, *Landing Operations*, is quite useful. Over 120 pages are devoted to ancient and medieval examples and were written in the aftermath of perhaps the most successful amphibious campaign in history, the US war in the Pacific, 1941-45. Another useful reference, this one from the standpoint of how armies have furthered sea power over the ages, is Charles Calwell's two volumes mentioned below. Even though focusing on British examples since the sixteenth century, it is nonetheless useful in gauging the efficacy of sea-land coordination throughout history.

Interestingly, a recent US Joint Chiefs of Staff publication, *Joint Military Operations Historical Collection*, in *Military Incident* #3, 'The Price of Poor

Planning: Caesar Lands in Britain' discusses how, similarly to MacArthur's Inchon Landing in the Korean War, what might have been a near disaster was salvaged by clever improvisation. The data was extracted from Caesar's *The Conquest of Gaul*. I suggest that there were many more such episodes that might today be classified as 'joint operations', also known as 'combined operations', in the record of ancient Roman naval history, to include both coastal and riverine (in modern naval parlance, 'green' and 'brown' water) campaigns in close conjunction with the legions.

The Sea Power Centre in Canberra, Australia, an institution run by the Australian Navy, publishes a newsletter, *Semaphore*. While most of the historical articles deal with modern naval campaigns, two issues are devoted to ancient topics in the manner in which I am attempting here. The issue for 16 August 2006 is devoted to 'Ancient Egyptian Joint Operations in the Lebanon Under Thutmose III (1451-1438 BC)', and that for 2014 is devoted to 'Maritime Strategy in Action – Sea Power in Antiquity'. Both are worthwhile consulting and are fertile with ideas regarding enduring lessons for modern sea-power historians without indulging in jarring analogies.

I have already mentioned Michael Pitassi's recent works on the Roman navies. He has provided a great service to students of the Empire's sea power, but, as indicated, my book is distinguishable in that it employs the broad-brush concept of sea-power analysts Mahan, Corbett and Herbert Richmond, the last-named notably in his *Amphibious Warfare in British History* (1941). My emphasis on the authentic exercise of sea power, as opposed to merely engaging in disjunctive, epic naval conflicts, is in synch with the works of these modern naval theorists. Given my somewhat different approach, I trust that my study doesn't overlap Dr Pitassi's estimable, meticulously researched volumes.

The books, articles and theses I consulted while preparing this text are discussed more fully in the critical bibliography at the end of the book, that may also provide a guide to what has been written that has some relevance to my theme. In my search, I found nothing that attempted to apply sea power theory to the Roman Empire.

Continental versus Maritime Powers – A Misleading Distinction

The impulse that has routinely compelled inherently 'continental' powers to develop a home-bred maritime outlook is the broader context in which the Roman Empire's sea power should be properly evaluated. One does not have to completely rebut Johannes Thiel's 'landlubber' pejorative in acknowledging that Rome did not show an early proclivity for plying the briny deep; it was abruptly forced upon her, and in her typical technocratic fashion, she developed a unique style in naval warfare, imbued with her engineering talent. In ancient times, superpowers with continental mindsets include: Persia, under Cambyses II (late sixth century BC), Darius and Xerxes (early fifth century BC); Sparta contra the Athenians; and Rome, the latter especially in the imperial epoch. Several backward looks at these early examples have been taken in works trying to understand the modern maritime breakout of another erstwhile continental power, China, in the twentieth and twenty-first centuries. Hence, I likewise include some reference to the corresponding pivot towards the sea by these other traditional land powers.

I also cite modern Israel as an example of a nation that, unlike Rome, does not have a traditional 'continental' (agrarian) outlook, but which, similarly to Rome, has excelled in the training and deployment of her army (and its modern adjunct, air forces) to repel multiple threats across her vulnerable land perimeters, and in which sea power has accordingly been downplayed. It's only since the late 1970s that the modern Jewish nation has been devoting major planning and resources to her sea service. The Israeli Navy, like the Roman Navy, has willy-nilly evolved from the purely defensive role of repelling naval raids on its coastal dwellings and industrial installations to the strategic missions of deterring the ultimate enemy, Iran, from direct attacks by utilizing nuclear missile-bearing sub patrols and protecting offshore oilfields from strikes by Iran's cat's-paws to its north and south.

Sea power was indisputably a significant, if not always determinative, component in the growth and defence of the great empires of antiquity. Like much of the world's history, economic and social influences affected the prestige and power of the *imperium* more than the passing land battle or sea fight. That said, the ability to safely navigate estuarine, coastal and offshore waters in order to carry trade goods and essential commodities upon them was a vital component of imperial power. To protect such mercantile traffic in time became indispensable to the fiscal well-being of any claimants to rule over territories flanking the Mediterranean rim. Moreover, the combat capability of the land forces of ancient Mediterranean-based powers increasingly relied upon seaborne transport, reinforcement, replenishment and security. The stirring decisive battles of the Roman Republic's naval highlights are stitched together by an invisible strategic thread tying the naval action to the wars as a whole. This inter-relatedness is particularly applicable to Rome in the imperial epoch, roughly spanning from the time of Pompey the Great's anti-piracy sweep in the first century BC to the Fall of the Western Empire in the sixth century AD.

To the end, the Empire remained capable of major naval operations: that of AD 468 from Constantinople against the Vandals of North Africa may have numbered over 1,000 ships; Belisarius' successful duplication of this feat in AD 533 used 500 transports and 100 warships, with more than 30,000 sailors; in AD 610, Heraclius was able to transport two armies from North Africa to Egypt and Constantinople, to take the imperial crown. However, such major operations as occurred when the

Western Empire unravelled were not characteristic of the period encompassed by this study, during which imperial ships mostly followed the legions.

Command of the Mediterranean, monopoly of the sea – for that is what the famous Roman word picture 'mare nostrum' implies – was more characteristic of the Empire than the winning or losing of frontier provinces, for which the legions are everlastingly celebrated or cursed. The early twentieth-century British liked to recall the 'silent pressure' applied to world affairs by their battle fleets, and they gloried in it. The Roman fleet, more successful for far longer, was largely unsung and no tradition emerged.

As regards the function of the navy after 31 BC, the remarks of Richard Gabriel are apposite in his online essay 'The Roman Navy: Masters of the Mediterranean' on The History Net (http://www.historynet.com/the-roman-navy-masters-of-the-mediterranean.htm):

> 'The navy's role changed over time, from active combat fleet to multipurpose military service and finally to a smaller, mobile force. Once rival navies were no longer a concern, the river fleets (Rhine, Danube and Nile) came into being to support ground operations and secure the imperial borders …
>
> 'The fleets became vitally important to the defense and survival of the empire, as they patrolled its waterways and borders, safeguarding regional trade routes. In times of crisis, the navy switched roles to transport troops and supplies, but even then its light combatants could be brought into play in direct support of ground operations.'

What of Rome's alleged aversion to and neglect of waterborne warfare? Alfred Mahan's acute observation on the Roman attitude is quite pertinent:

> 'The Romans disliked the sea, but so too the early Greeks were equally distrustful of open waters; the enthusiasm of Athenian thalassocrats was not necessarily the norm, and true celebration of the challenge of the sea was to come only in modern Portuguese, Dutch and English poetry. Yet when it became necessary for the Romans to provide fleets and utilize them for the ends of Roman policy, they simply did so.'

Bear in mind that Sparta, like Rome, was considered to be incapable of and indifferent to exerting naval power. Then, in the Peloponnesian Wars against Athens – the foremost sea power of the known world at that time – Sparta built, manned and trained a newly created, large naval fleet. This was the major factor contributing to Sparta's victory. Previously, Athens had been as strong in its navy as Sparta had been weak. Although pretty much all of Greece had the sea to one side, Sparta fronted a particularly dangerous stretch of the Mediterranean – actually, a situation that had prevented her earlier from becoming a sea power. During the First Peloponnesian War, Athens had kept Sparta at bay by blockading the Peloponnesus with its navy. During the Second Peloponnesian War, Darius of Persia supplied the Spartans with the capital to build a capable naval fleet.

It has been argued that despite the Spartan commander Lysander's naval victories, Athens actually possessed the better navy. This observation is immaterial and misleading. Consider a modern analogy. Many authorities hold that notwithstanding the Allies winning the Battle of the Atlantic in late 1943, Germany possessed superior undersea boats and its capital ships were arguably better-designed than those of Britain and the US. Also, it is said that the Italian fleet had newer and better quality ships than the British in the Mediterranean. While this notion is to a large extent true, it is also irrelevant. By the way, the chestnut about the antiquity of the alleged inherent German aversion to seafaring is also a spurious gauge of her capability – witness the Roman need to devote substantial naval assets to combat native craft along the Rhinelands and the Germanic coast early in the first century AD. Bear in mind, as well, that the Carthaginians built the best warships during the later Roman Republican period, while those of Rome were comparatively poorly built and unwieldy. Yet the Romans in the end prevailed on the sea.

During both the Republican and Imperial periods, nearly all of the provinces had extensive coasts alongside the Mediterranean, Black Sea or Atlantic Ocean. Rome controlled expansive river systems linking these seaways. These interconnected ocean highways gave the Romans a distinct advantage over their adversaries around the perimeter, who generally had to utilize coasts adjacent to or interdicted by Roman maritime control. Notwithstanding the risk of loss from storms or poor navigation, movement of bulky military equipment and supplies by sea was much more efficient – and labour-saving – than arduously lugging the stuff around a circuitous perimeter through territory of varied terrain more or less controlled by unreliable allies, quirky neutrals or hostiles. Many pack animals and men otherwise subtracted from the fighting fronts to cart supplies were freed up by utilizing sea transport.

The quote from Putarch at the head of this section illustrates the importance of the navy to Rome. According to Plutarch, in 56 BC, the Roman Senate awarded Pompeius Magnus (Pompey the Great) a vital special responsibility, designated *curator annonae*. It was Pompey's duty to supervise the transport of the critical grain supply from the Egyptian breadbasket to Rome. There were storms brewing and the sailors in the cereal convoy were reluctant to sail homeward from Alexandria. Pompey took command of the leading ship in the procession and curtly advised his apprehensive seamen, '*Navigare necesse est, vivere non est necesse*' ('we have to sail, we don't have to live'). Pompey's imputed quip was made in the wake of his comprehensive, wide-ranging victory, a decade earlier, over the piracy that had threatened to strangle Roman sea communications in the years preceding the Civil Wars. Hence, he was acutely aware of the importance of shipping the grain to Rome, as well as the dangers besetting any vessel that ventured beyond the sight of land.

The cited Latin expression attributed to Pompey has been employed several times since to underscore the importance of sea power. It adorned the gate of the Marine Building in Bremen, Germany, during the Middle Ages as a guiding motto of the maritime Hanseatic League. The saying is likewise displayed in the Central Hall of Rotterdam, whose designer wanted the building to betoken the importance of his city as a world port and centre of marine trade. Ironically, while the sentiments seem natural with reference to the Hanse and to the Dutch mercantile empire, it is not so readily associated with its source, Rome at the dawn of its imperial phase. The phrase is emblematic of the Roman Empire's largely unacknowledged dependency upon ships and seamanship to sustain its might.

In connection with my emphasis on a grand strategy perspective, it is curious that an important modern study, *Roman Imperial Grand Strategy* by Arther Ferrill (1991), avers that, 'Indeed, naval power was not terribly important in Roman imperial grand strategy. In some ways the riverine squadrons of the Rhine and the Danube, and later the squads operating in the English Channel, served a more urgent military need than the two Mediterranean fleets.' But regardless whether it is the two home fleets or the outlying squadrons, the point is that naval power *did* have an important role to play in what passed for Roman imperial grand strategy. The implication that naval operations in rivers and straits did not connote 'naval power' requiring strategic direction is erroneous. It is emblematic of the downgrading of low-intensity naval combat and littoral engagements as being tantamount to land warfare with wading boots.

In order to explore this continental versus maritime geopolitical schism, the final chapter of this book will incorporate a comparison with Rome's achievement of some other empires and nations that are deemed to be continental powers, and who have nonetheless achieved what the book on China's return to the sea referenced above calls a 'maritime transformation'. The main focus will be modern China, but I will also consider Russia and Germany, regarded as land powers through most of their histories.

Temporal Focus of This Book

A word about the time frame of this book is in order. Most authorities agree that the Roman Empire began, portentously enough, with a naval battle – that of Actium in 31 BC. Although that event marks the consolidation of power under the first emperor, Caesar Augustus, the roots of Rome's involvement in the world beyond the Italian heartland can be traced back to the Pyrrhic War, commencing in 281 BC, when a powerful foreign invader gained a lodgment on the Italian peninsula by traversing a body of water. As this episode also coincides with the germination of the Republic's 'naval awareness', I will devote several chapters to the maritime aspects of the Republic's foreign and military policy from shortly before the Pyrrhic War to the First Punic War, the latter deserving an extended coda discussing the sea power implications of that conflict in some detail. The ensuing chapter is devoted to the Second Punic War, which for reasons already mentioned has direct significance to an assessment of the sea power of the Empire. Likewise, there is a separate chapter covering the naval lessons of the Illyrian, Macedonian and Syrian (or Asiatic) wars. These conflicts are all prior to the formation of permanent fleets by Augustus; however, they are harbingers of the maritime situation post-Actium.

Although the conflicts covered in these early chapters have been amply reviewed in other books on Roman naval history, I am specifically treating them here as being instrumental in forming the naval outlook of the Empire. Thus my discussion of the wars of the Roman Republic aims to cast them in terms of how modern theorists might perceive them; old wine in new bottles. The balance of the book discusses the sea strategy of Rome from the reign of Augustus down to the campaigns of Heraclius and Belisarius in the Empire's closing years, as shown by its employment of ships and marines. As might be expected, my selection of examples is governed by the availability of ancient records. Thus, for example, the campaigns of Gallus in the Red Sea, Drusus the Elder in Germania and the maritime features of the Dacian Wars occupy a larger space than their significance to the security of the Empire may warrant. But they are emblematic of the employment of ships on campaigns in which the naval components are not so well attested.

Further Regarding Mahan, Corbett and Similar Modern Naval Theorists

Mahan

Being as I am using the approach that I presume that these two eminent sea-power theorists might have taken in surveying the naval strategy of Rome between 100 BC and AD 600, a brief comparison of their respective conceptualizations about sea power is pertinent. In retrospect, their traditionally imputed differences in mindset may have been exaggerated. In passing, I will consider some other relatively recent authors whose works may have some bearing.

In the past two decades or so, some have disparaged Alfred Mahan's supposed emphasis on great naval battles as comprising a puerile approach to naval theory.

As can be seen from his brief, cogent analysis of the Second Punic War, a conflict patently lacking in noteworthy sea battles, this characterization of his works is too sweeping. At least in the eight pages on the Second Punic War he eschewed the decisive battle approach employing powerful capital ships. His chief works devoted to British sea power during the eighteenth and nineteenth centuries for certain analyze naval campaigns and battles, but they also embrace the broader implications of sea power underlying the protection of maritime commerce and seaborne military logistics. All in all, he did derive an emphasis upon decisive naval engagements from his study of the British Empire. However, this statement, taken from *The Influence of Sea Power Upon History, 1660–1783*, presents a more discriminating definition:

> 'It is not the taking of individual ships or convoys, be they few or many, that strikes down the money power of a nation; it is the possession of that overbearing power on the sea which drives the enemy's flag from it, or allows it to appear only as a fugitive; and which, by controlling the great common, closes the highways by which commerce moves to and from the enemy's shores. This overbearing power can only be exercised by great navies.'

This explanation of the term is more nuanced than the paragon of determinative fights between powerful capital ships. It takes into account that sea power may be exerted without necessarily achieving a *coup de main* against the enemy's main battle fleet. In fact, Mahan's later studies of the American War of Independence and the War of 1812 paid more attention to 'conjunct operations', as joint warfare (naval and marines) was then known, but he did not draw conclusions as to the importance of such amphibious attacks applicable to the then-current conditions. In fact, he played down this facet of naval power projection as 'a diversion' from the primary task of defending the principal maritime routes against enemy threats.

Mahan pointed out that during the French Revolution and the Napoleonic Wars, the French strategy of *guerre de course* (commerce raiding) failed to defeat the British. It was decisive fleet actions such as Trafalgar and the Nile which enabled the British to control the oceans by destroying the enemy fleets. The French had a long tradition of using commerce raiders in the wars with Britain in the eighteenth century. Though Mahan's beloved battleships have given way to the massive aircraft carriers and their associated 'carrier battle group', his concept of controlling the seas with big fleets is still with us today.

Mahan's concept of an ample American battlefleet replacing the commerce-raiding cruisers and gunboats changed the emphasis of American naval policy. Mahan recognized that control of maritime commerce through command of the seas is the primary function of the navy. But he expected command of the sea to be gained by fleet battles which would drive the enemy from the sea. He felt that commerce raiding itself was not sufficient to crush an enemy, though he acknowledged that it could harass and interfere with its trade. The problem was that though the submarine was evolving from a coastal or harbour defence boat best suited for slowing down or crippling naval forces approaching one's shore, he failed to foresee its primary role as an elusive undersea pirate ship that it assumed in 1914. It was during the First World War that the Germans began to perfect their commerce-raiding tactics and strategy, and the Royal Navy adapted to this new threat. Mahan's fixation on the decisive battle between fleets and his aversion to *guerre de course* led to the United States Navy being unprepared to counter commerce raiding in the Second World War.

I have previously stressed how, in the introduction to *Sea Power 1660-1783* (pp.13-21), Mahan illustrated the importance of command of the sea through a superb analysis of the impact of Rome's command of the western Mediterranean Sea upon the course of the Second Punic War. Being as this command had already been won in the preceding conflict with Carthage, this analysis is a more rounded and subtle demonstration of sea power than the 'big battle' emphasis in his following examination of the Anglo-Dutch Wars of the seventeenth century and the Anglo-French wars of the eighteenth century. Again, it is this section which inspired my own appraisal of Rome's exercise of thalassocracy in the period from roughly 200 BC to AD 500. Thus, I devote more space to it than the other sea wars of the Republican period. In *The Second Punic War – A Reappraisal* (1996), Boris Rankov's nine-page chapter, 'The Second Punic War at Sea', provides an excellent and knowledgeable resumé on how the limitations of warships and troop transports of the day affected the Roman and Carthaginian strategies in that war. It jibes with Mahan's view of Roman naval strategy in that conflict.

Mahan ended the main narrative of the second volume of *The Influence of Sea Power upon History* with an account of the British defeat at Yorktown in 1781. The outcome of this battle was determined by the reinforcement of American and French armies by sea and French naval control of surrounding waters, which prevented a British fleet from relieving the besieged British army. The Yorktown disaster prompted negotiations that ultimately ended the war and established American independence. So, while the naval Battle of the Virginia Capes, in which a French fleet under Admiral compte de Grasse defeated a British fleet under Admiral Thomas Graves, was an unquestionably decisive naval encounter, Mahan emphasized that the import of this battle was its effect on the outcome in the land battle at Yorktown, a conclusion with which Corbett would agree.

As American historian R.B. Watts has pointed out in his recent study *American Sea Power and the Obsolescence of Capital Ship Theory*, the so-called disciples of

Mahan stressed his alleged advocacy of a navy predominantly consisting of big-gun capital ships and ignored his caveats written shortly before his death in 1914, in which he stressed that a fleet should be balanced between dreadnoughts and lesser vessels engaging more or less in independent, as opposed to fleet, actions. These advocates for an all big-gun capital fleet continued to ignore technological challenges to their perspective throughout the interim between the two world wars. The Battle of Jutland in May 1916, in which the two Mahanian fleets of Germany and Britain conducted an indecisive slugfest in the North Sea, was ignored by American navalists of the 1920s and 1930s, who continued to stress the primacy of the big-gun battleship in future naval conflicts. Watts notes how the lessons of submarine attacks on shipping from 1914–1918, as well as naval raids and blockades, were ignored due to a failure to keep abreast of the advances in the undersea weapon and cruiser warfare concepts between the wars. In particular, the Germans had improved the endurance, weapon load, torpedo efficacy and stealth of their U–boats, and the Italians developed naval commando techniques enabling small craft to sink or disable capital ships.

Today, the 'big gun' enthusiasts' emphasis on battleships has been replaced by the centrality of the aircraft carrier and the ballistic missile nuclear sub, and their nemeses, the attack sub. Even the inclusion of 'littoral warfare' in the doctrinal mix is often inaptly tacked onto a carrier task force strategic scheme. Mahan, in his *Naval Strategy: Compared and Contrasted with the Principles and Practice of Military Operations on Land* (1911), explained in some detail many aspects of what would be considered today operational-level warfare in the littorals, a dimension missing or muted in his earlier books.

Mahan's own recognition of the limitations of ancient fleets was aptly described in his Second Punic War analysis: 'The control of the sea, however real, does not imply that an enemy's single ships or small squadrons cannot steal out of port, cannot cross more or less frequented tracts of ocean, make harassing descents upon unprotected points of a long coast-line, enter blockaded harbors.' Given these limitations, he wonders that Carthage didn't accomplish more in evading Roman naval forces to support their own troops on land.

In 1901, Mahan wrote an essay for the British journal *National Review* entitled 'Considerations Governing the Dispositions of Navies'. It was a study of why, where and how a nation should exercise their naval forces in times of relative peace, 'for the dispositions of peace should bear a close relation to the contingency of war'. While the essay is little-known compared to his seminal book, Herbert Rosinki, the noted strategist of the 1930s and 1940s, wrote that it was probably some of Mahan's best work. It gets directly to the heart of the questions that early twenty-first-century naval planners must answer: what are the ideas which govern how to deploy and use the fleet today? On the website of the US Naval Institute, creators of the professional journal for American naval advocates, Lieutenant Commander Benjamin 'B.J.' Armstrong advocated utilizing the wisdom contained in the 1901 essay in lieu of the classic misinterpretations of Mahan's earlier studies ('A New Sea Power Strategy: What Would Alfred Thayer Mahan Do?', July 2014).

One idea from this essay that might resonate with Rome's senators is Mahan's discussion of forward-deployed naval forces. He suggested that the locations for overseas bases are critical and must be selected with strategic elements in mind. He touches on the maintenance of allies and partners, as well as the facilities needed to repair and resupply ships in theatre, rather than always having to bring them back to the homeland. This notion would be learned by the Roman consuls when Carthage was able to use forward bases in Sicily to overcome naval defeats on the island, and when, in the Second Punic War, Rome deprived her of the same while securing its own for operations in Spain and the invasion of Africa, forging alliances with restive local tribal leaders, as well as being poised to thwart any attempt by Philip V of Macedon to capitalize on Hannibal's invasion.

Influenced by Jomini's geometrical principles of strategy, Mahan argued that in the coming wars (looking forward from 1890), control of the sea would grant the power to control the trade and resources needed to wage war. Mahan's premise was that in the contests between France and Britain in the eighteenth century, domination of the sea through naval power was the deciding factor in the outcome, and therefore, that the resulting control of seaborne commerce was critical to domination in war. This seems like a commonplace today, but up to the time when Mahan published his landmark studies, no one had attempted such a sea-power interpretation of history.

In Mahan's view, a country obtained 'command of the sea' by concentrating its naval forces at the decisive point to destroy or otherwise master the enemy's battle fleet; blockade of enemy ports and disruption of the enemy's maritime communications would follow. Accordingly, Mahan believed that the true objective in a naval war was always the enemy fleet, *not necessarily to destroy it in major knockout blows* but to overcome its dominance of the sea lines of communication. Mahan's writings were highly influential. His best-known books, *The Influence of Sea Power upon History, 1660-1783* and *The Influence of Sea Power upon the French Revolution and Empire, 1793-1812*, were published in 1890 and 1892 respectively, and his theories are believed to have contributed to the naval arms race between 1898 and 1914.

Mahan disliked amphibious operations, declaring that they were 'harder to sustain than to make'. He judged them dangerous to those forces extended ashore, and that this danger outweighed their potential benefit. In Mahan's cost-benefit analysis of amphibious operations, they were a waste of resources. Mahan viewed the sea power side of the equation as decisive. In a paper published by the Joint

Military Operations Department of the US Naval War College, Dr Milan Vego has expressed the following caveats about Mahan's 'lessons':

> 'Mahan's neglect of the importance of the navy's support of friendly troops on the coast had a negative influence on generations of U.S. naval officers. In fact, Mahan warned his readers that if the fleet is reduced merely to guarding one or more positions ashore, the navy becomes simply a branch of the army, whereas the true end of naval war is to preponderate over the enemy army and so control the sea by assailing enemy ships and fleets on all occasions. Mahan's neglect of the need for cooperation between the navy and the army was surprising because his study of England's rise as a sea power should have convinced him of the importance of such cooperation. Mahan was cautious in treating maritime expeditions in remote waters or what is now called power projection. He wrote that as a rule a major operation of war across the sea should not be attempted, unless naval superiority for an adequate period is probable. He was also dubious about any employment of naval forces against land. Supposedly, the experience of the Union ships' bombardments of Confederate fortifications during the Civil War (1861–1865) made Mahan skeptical as to the effectiveness of naval gunnery against coastal artillery positions and fortifications. Mahan mostly disregarded power projection as the navy's mission. He also gave only passing attention to amphibious warfare and its place in naval warfare. This is somewhat surprising because Jomini devoted an entire chapter in his *The Art of War* on what he calls descents onto hostile shores. Also, Mahan was surely well aware of the role amphibious landings played in the British conduct of war at sea.' (*Naval Classical Thinkers and Operational Art*, NWC 1005, US Naval War College, 2009)

In his memoirs, Mahan recalled that his writing career was launched when he discovered that the Roman Empire owed its prominence primarily to its sea power. In 1885, he had chanced upon Theodore Mommsen's history of ancient Rome. While reading this book, Mahan was struck by the thought that the outcome of the second war between Rome and Carthage would have been different had the latter possessed the ability, as did the former, of using the sea as an avenue of invasion, instead of moving its armies over land – witness Hannibal's famous march, which was primarily, though not solely, chosen because of Rome's ability to interdict the more direct, albeit risky, waterborne route to the Italian heartland.

After some reflection, Mahan decided to apply the example of the victory of a state that could use naval force effectively over one that could not to the history of European wars in the late seventeenth and eighteenth centuries. But it was the Roman transformation that provided the insight to sea command's importance, describing how the Romans, a continental/agrarian culture, defeated the Carthaginians by their ability to maintain sea lines of communication to transport troops timely and in enough strength to the locations where they were needed to win battles. His insightful thoughts on the maritime root of Hannibal's dilemma was limited to a few pages by way of an introduction. His switch from portraying an ancient conflict in which sea power was utilized in a sense that would resonate with readers at the beginning of the twentieth century, to focusing on more recent conflicts in which high-seas main-fleet engagements dominated, has tended to obscure his more nuanced thoughts on applying sea control.

One aspect of Mahan's writing that is widely ignored or misunderstood is his focus on deterrence. Mahan's world was characterized by the existence of great powers overseas that had navies capable of conducting operations in the Western Hemisphere. Mahan worried about the US defence of the soon-to-be opened Panama Canal and about the challenge of European adventurism in Latin America. His prescription for a strong battle fleet and its deployment was based as much on deterring outside intervention in the Americas as it was on protecting American interests overseas. An analogous value also resonated with the early Roman Empire.

Having touched upon joint or combined (amphibious) operations in his discussion of the Second Punic War, it is somewhat surprising that Mahan practically ignored them in the balance of his two volumes of the *Influence of Sea Power* books. However, the subjects of his two later books, *The Major Operations of the Navies in the War of American Independence* (1913) and *Sea Power in its Relation to the War of 1812* (1903), did entail to some extent the role of amphibious raids and maritime troop insertions. It is somewhat perplexing then that he neglected the importance of the navy's support of friendly troops on the coast. In fact, Mahan warned his readers that if the fleet is reduced merely to guarding one or more positions ashore, the navy becomes simply a branch of the army, whereas the true end of naval war is to 'preponderate' over the enemy army and so control the sea by assailing enemy ships and fleets on all occasions.

Mahan's neglect of the need for cooperation between the navy and the army was surprising because his study of England's rise as a sea power should have convinced him of the importance of such cooperation. Corbett's study of the Seven Years' War, in contrast, was practically dedicated to the subject.

As noted above, Mahan's chronicle of major fleet-to-fleet actions have led some to conclude that he was obsessed with the decisive naval battle as the true objective in a naval war. A more balanced consideration of his works shows this to be an oversimplification. For Mahan, the battles were a necessary, though not central, component in creating the sea control necessary to sustain a nation's role as a great power.

As an example of Mahan's approach, later in this book I will review his insightful synopsis of the seagoing aspects of the Second Punic War, in which he demonstrates how, while there were few ship-to-ship engagements, sea power was nevertheless crucial. It is clear that Mahan and Corbett are not polar opposites; Mahan's decisive naval battles simply comprise one means among several to achieve the ends of Corbett's command of the sea.

Corbett

For his part, Sir Julian Corbett focusses unambiguously on the use of sea power in a larger context – not especially on great naval battles. Like Mahan, Corbett did not *specifically* ally his principles to operations other than war; indeed, his work has been described as 'weak on law and order at sea in peacetime'. Instead, he preferred to develop his ideas as the principles which govern a war in which the sea is a substantial factor. However, he did discuss 'limited war' at some length; it could be argued that his theories on blockade, both naval and commercial, and on the strategy of a 'fleet in being' could be applied at different points on the spectrum of conflict, and thus be effectively used as tools of coercive naval diplomacy. The larger context of his thinking is the strategy suited to a maritime power, which expresses itself in amphibious warfare directed at a continental enemy's vulnerable peripheries.

Corbett's two-volume history, *England in the Seven Years' War*, is probably the deepest study of amphibious warfare ever written. The thrust of this work indicates that, had he dealt with the sea power of the ancient world to any extent, he might have found the study of the period commencing with the establishment of Augustus' standing fleets more suitable than the preliminary skirmishes of the Republican era. However, he is principally concerned, as is Mahan, with the British navy from the seventeenth to nineteenth centuries. While it is clear that Mahan and Corbett are not polar opposites, Mahan's decisive naval battles are simply ways to achieve the ends of Corbett's command of the sea

For example, in *England in the Mediterranean* (an expansion of Corbett's War Course lectures), the underlying theme, which only dealt with England's entry into the Mediterranean and the growth of her influence there, was the power of a naval presence in the absence of any great battles. The ability of England to maintain a fleet year-round in the Mediterranean interposed herself on the French sea communications between France's two seats of maritime power. This act of positioning the fleet, rather than engaging the enemy vessels, in Corbett's formulation, 'proved that with a dominant sea power well placed in the Straits, her

[France's] Mediterranean Frontier was useless to her for offence, and that neither for her nor for any other power could the dream of the Roman Empire be revived'. This showed the strategic significance of sea communications, which would be a major part of Corbett's theories on 'command of the sea'.

Unlike Mahan, Corbett saw the possibility of a limited maritime war, where complete destruction was unnecessary. A belligerent would only have to set the conditions that it would cost his opponent more to win than it would be worth. Commerce raiding could easily fall within the parameters of either limited or unlimited war, depending on the means available. In any case, it is a legitimate alternative approach to gaining command of the seas without a big fleet.

Had Corbett and Mahan written more extensively about sea power in antiquity, they would have likely found more contemporaneously applicable illustrations in my time frame, approximately 300 BC – AD 600. In fact, as suggested, Mahan's few pages devoted to the Second Punic War are quite applicable to the maritime state of affairs at the high tide of empire occurring several centuries later, a matter that I will address further in Chapter Four. I venture to say that Mahan's interpretation of the Second Punic War is very similar to what Corbett might have written about this conflict.

At first sight, Corbett's theory that military (land) power is necessary for the final successful outcome of war appears to be contradictory to Mahan's advocacy of seeking out and destroying the enemy's most powerful warships. However, in his aforementioned discussion of the Second Punic War, Mahan acknowledged that the issue was decided without a major fleet-to-fleet action. Of course, this had been done in the First Punic War and guaranteed naval predominance in the later conflict. Had Corbett devoted any space to the ancient period, this is pretty much how he might have summed up the Second Punic War, although he would have made more of a direct correlation between the command of the sea and the ability to affect land battles.

Corbett wrote in the same period as did Mahan. He was a meticulous researcher and became a leading maritime strategist to rival Mahan. Corbett counterbalanced Mahan's ideas while presenting a more logical and structured argument. His development of 'maritime strategy' was a necessary complement to Mahan's development of 'naval strategy'. The former embraced not only the combats among warships, but also operations in conjunction with land forces, merchant fleet contributions to the war effort and the actions of diplomats coincident with the exercise of naval power.

Adherents maintain that Corbett was more pragmatic and, therefore, a more effective strategist than Mahan. He had studied Carl von Clausewitz, and adapted the Prussian's military theories – linking war strategy with broader geopolitical objectives – to the maritime environment. Corbett's theories eventually became the accepted way of conducting maritime conflicts. Corbett differed from Mahan in placing much less emphasis on fleet-to-fleet combat on the high seas. Instead, Corbett concentrated on the geopolitical role of sea power, not as a form of self-contained naval warfare, but as the maritime element in a nation's grand strategy.

Corbett stressed the interdependence of naval and land warfare, and tended to concentrate on the importance of opening or maintaining sea communications rather than battle. He held that battle at sea was not an end in itself; the primary objective of the fleet was to secure one's own communications and disrupt those of the enemy, not necessarily to seek out and destroy the enemy's fleet. Ship-to-ship engagements might sometimes be unavoidable in gaining sea control, but they were not to be deliberately sought, nor were they the *sine qua non*. This will be illustrated in my treatment of the Second Punic War and selected examples following that conflict.

To Corbett, command of the sea was a relative, and not an absolute, which could be categorized as general or local, temporary or permanent. Corbett defined the two fundamental methods of obtaining control of the lines of communication as the actual physical destruction or capture of enemy warships *and merchant ships*, and/or a naval blockade. He also stressed coordination of naval forces with land elements in securing forward bases and harbours from which to mount littoral warfare operations. His most famous work, *Some Principles of Maritime Strategy*, remains a classic. As noted, however, this book does not reference ancient naval matters, nor does Corbett address them elsewhere. Nor did his thesis deal with naval operations during relative peacetime; his dicta were all in relation to the conduct of a major conflict.

Corbett holds that, in the context of war, command of the sea means control of passage either over, under or upon the sea. He notes that having possession of the sea is a physical impossibility, since to do so would require the stationing of ships in every square mile of ocean throughout the world, and no nation can do this. Even today, with satellite observation of the entire planet, no state can prevent the passage of enemy vessels upon every ocean. Only control of choke points or of specific areas can be accomplished by those in command of the sea. This was Corbett's idea, and it is still valid today. This dominance of key maritime nodes would force an enemy to take circuitous routes at great expense and loss of time, or in some cases, altogether forgo exerting naval force on a particular seacoast; or at least such force would be limited to small areas. Only when one opponent or the other is militarily defeated can command of the sea be absolute. As Corbett pointed out in *The Campaign of Trafalgar*, though England had command of the sea after 1805, France still was able to disrupt sea commerce and Napoleon was able to achieve some of his greatest military victories. Absolute command of the sea did not exist, and without a military victory, sea power can achieve only limited goals.

According to Corbett, the example of Wellington in Spain was as follows:

> 'in perfect conditions he [Wellington] was applying the limited form to an unlimited war. England's object was unlimited. It was nothing less than the overthrow of Napoleon. Complete success at sea had failed to accomplish it, but that success had given us the power of applying the limited form, which was the most decisive form of offence within our means.'

This statement also brings out Corbett's main strategic thought concerning maritime power. Basically, Corbett said that sea power was limited in what it may accomplish. As powerful and important as maritime power is, it takes military (land) power to finalize and solidify any gains accomplished by sea power.

At first sight, Corbett's theory that military (land-based) power is necessary for the final successful outcome of war appears to refute Mahan's theories of sea power. However, as remarked above, in the introduction to his book *The Influence of Sea Power upon History 1660-1783*, Mahan describes how the Romans defeated the Carthaginians by their ability to maintain sea lines of communication to transport troops timely and in enough strength to where they were needed to win battles *on land*.

Perhaps Corbett's key difference in comparison to Mahan was his realization that command of the sea was neither as easy nor as absolute as Mahan implied. In the reality of limited assets and vast ocean space, a nation can generally only maintain command of the sea locally and for a limited amount of time. Corbett also disagreed with Mahan's premise that the enemy fleet was always the centre of gravity, and he did not advocate the 'big battle' approach. Favouring economy of effort, Corbett preferred lower-risk strategies that enabled maritime states to exploit advantages through the use of force multipliers like joint operations and commerce raiding.

Unlike Mahan, Corbett had absolutely nothing to say about ancient naval affairs, his principal concern being world navies, especially that of England and later Great Britain, from the galleon epoch embodied by Sir Francis Drake (roughly 1550) forward. However, his nuanced emphasis on the effect of sea dominance upon land warfare – besides being in synch with contemporary trends – is particularly germane to the Roman Empire's utilization of the sea to protect and enhance its welfare during a period when no major navy could challenge it on the high seas and when the fleets cooperated closely with the legions' undertakings on land.

It is telling that the United States Navy, in its recent turn towards the littoral warfare (coastal operations against irregular forces) that characterizes the naval challenges of the twenty-first century, has emphasized the writings of the

Englishman Corbett as being a more serviceable guide than the American Mahan. It is a reversal of the situation that prevailed in Great Britain in the 1890s, when Mahan's analyses fostered the naval race between Great Britain and Germany to establish an overpowering battlefleet. Corbett had a tough time convincing his own country's Royal Navy to adopt his theories of sea power. In fact, he was roundly criticized as a meddling amateur for his suggestion that the Royal Navy was overemphasizing the need for and effectiveness of its high priority capital ship programme.

Although, as noted, Corbett did not discuss ancient sea power, his emphasis on littoral/amphibious roles and projecting power ashore is as applicable to the *Pax Romana* at sea as to the situation confronting the major power navies today. Corbett never tired of saying that the real point of sea power is not so much what happens at sea, but how that influences the outcome of events on land. The Roman emperors and their legionary commanders would agree.

Sea power in the ancient world, in terms of its diplomatic and constabulary roles, had much in common with modern thinking. Its military role in supporting land forces is in synch with present-day naval thinkers. Early battles at sea, nevertheless, in effect comprise a continuation of land warfare by other means. Galleys provided the means to transport soldiers to a place where they would meet similar vessels containing their opponents, and would then proceed to engage in hand-to-hand combat between embarked marines of the ships as they grappled close together. This changed with the development of the ram as a naval weapon in its own right. Once the ram was perfected, maritime warfare was sufficiently differentiated from its land counterpart, and the weapons and methods of land warfare were largely discarded from the warship. However, note that during its opening engagements with Carthaginian warships during the First Punic War, Rome at first used a particular development of the earlier grapple-and-board technique – the *corvus*.

Here, the remarks of the important late nineteenth-century German military historian Hans Delbruck regarding the First Punic War in *Warfare in Antiquity* are enlightening:

> 'It is incorrect, as has long been recognized, to see in this war [First Punic War], the struggle of a purely land power against a sea power. Rome was itself a very old trading city, the market of Latium, and had as its crest the galleon [*sic*]. The alliance, moreover, of which it was the head, included the seafaring cities of Greater Greece from Cumaea and Naples to Tarentum. If up to that time Rome had used all of its power for land warfare, that was because its opponents were land powers. And to the extent that such was not the case, as in the oldest times with the other Latin sea powers [e.g., the Etruscans], or finally Tarentum, Rome had waged these battles

in league with no other than Carthage, which spared her the trouble of creating a stronger sea power. Not until the struggle against Carthage herself was it necessary to develop further in this direction. Rome built herself the fleet of five-rowed galleys [or penteremes] that she did not yet possess, a feat that, with her rich variety of materials needed for shipbuilding, she was able to accomplish without great difficulty. It will be useful to note that the famous account that the Romans had understood absolutely nothing of seafaring, had built their ships on the model of a stranded Carthaginian pentereme, and had trained their oarsmen on scaffoldings on land stems from Polybius, who here clearly fell victim to a monstrous rhetorical exaggeration. The counterpart to this is that the Carthaginians had to have themselves instructed in the art of land warfare by the Spartan Xanthippus. Mommsen considers this account, too, to be the echo of Greek guard house tales.'

In contrast to Mahan but similarly to Corbett, French Vice Admiral Raoul Castex (in *Strategic Theories*) firmly believed in the need for close cooperation between the navy and army. He explained that the relationship between the army and navy must be as between infantry and artillery. As infantry is the queen of battle, so the army is the queen of general strategy. Everything has to be subordinated to it because its success means the success of the general strategy. The navy is often to the army as the artillery is to the infantry; an indispensable support that allows it to accomplish its objectives. He correctly stressed that the success of land operations is, after all, what matters the most. Only victory on land permits the occupation of the enemy territory and convinces the enemy that he is defeated. For Castex, the importance of sea power is directly related to its contribution to the victory on land. Only in exceptional cases can sea power achieve complete victory by itself.

George Furse, in his 1897 publication *Military Expeditions Beyond the Seas*, devotes the first thirty-eight pages in the second volume to conjunct operations in the Punic Wars and in the civil war between Pompey and Julius Caesar, which was very helpful to me in furnishing a template for my own investigation. His early chapters deal with ancient and medieval examples. Sir Charles Calwell, in *Military Operations and Maritime Preponderance, Their Relations and Interdependence* (1905) and his earlier *The Effect of Maritime Command on Land Campaigns since Waterloo* (1897), similarly provides a broad-brush treatment of an aspect of 'expeditionary warfare' that received scant attention from Mahan's advocates in the United States Navy, notwithstanding the admiral's references to shoreline and riverine operations in his aforementioned later publications.

These studies likewise proved helpful to my project at the level of theory and relevant examples through time.

Application of Current Sea Power Theories and Problems Adapted to Conditions In Antiquity

While I don't prescribe specific remedies for current naval problems based on Roman precedent, I believe it is not irrelevant to suggest some parallels. After all, the prestigious Naval Institute Press in Annapolis, Maryland, in *China Goes to Sea: Maritime Transformation in Comparative Historical Perspective* (2009), evoked Persia, Sparta, Rome, the medieval Chinese Song and Qing empires and the Ottoman Empire among others to give some perspective on 'continental' China's aspirations to achieve Mahanian sea power.

Finally, it is important to tell what this book is NOT. In 2008, Indiana University Press published John A. Adams' *If Mahan Ran the Great Pacific War: An Analysis of World Two Naval Strategy*. This book's purported method was to examine the American and Japanese operations in the Pacific as if Mahan would have critiqued them had he been around (he died in 1914). It was an ill-suited 'score card' approach as proposed. Reviewers have noted that the author's reliance on Mahan's prescriptions leads Adams into contradictions and conundrums which fail to take into account the personalities of the commanders and the blind spots caused by inadequate intelligence of the enemy's situation and intentions. Further, the war occurred under conditions which rendered most of Mahan's rhetorical devices obsolete. While the book is a useful review of decision-making in the Pacific campaign, the book's reliance on Mahan's obsolescent criteria as a critical template is misleading.

Obviously, such a treatment is even less appropriate with regard to sea warfare and strategies of over a millennium and a half ago. Rather than undertake a tally of how ancient naval administrators either heeded or ignored modern maxims point by point, I employ a method which entails imagining how a contemporary sea-power analyst might portray the operations of the various Roman fleets in campaigns. Once more, with reference to the title of this study, it is written in the manner of modern assessments such as the British Admiralty's notable 'staff appreciations' written up in the aftermath of the First World War and the analogous post-mortems on British naval operations shortly after the Second World War, as well as the US Naval War College's war games held in the aftermath of the Second World War, applying such lessons from after-action reports that seemed pertinent.

I have earlier referred to the interesting notion by the French maritime historian Jean Pages that it is possible, even desirable, to comprehend the working of a Roman naval thought through a critical examination of the chronologies that have come down to us. The studies by Pages on presumptive naval thinking, armament, tactics and thalassocracies are dispersed in different publications. They provide materials for application in future publications. Hopefully Monsieur Pages will provide readers with a full account soon. Meanwhile, I hope my modest effort will fill some gaps.

Dr Pages has observed that historians have advanced our knowledge of ancient navies but that their approach is usually archaeological/technical (debris fields, artifacts, etc.) or institutional (organization theory). His studies are the work of one who is not only an historian but a sailor as well. They seek to understand the mechanisms of naval warfare from a traditional viewpoint that has been wrongly neglected. After all, the navies are designed to fight and too many recent studies have lost sight of this basic truth. As I have noted above, this goes beyond the mere recital of battle highlights. The technical study of weapons and ships, tactical study of the convoys and their escorts, and strategic and political study of disarmament and rearmament allows us to better understand the essence of ancient fleets. They show that ancient naval warfare was no less complex than modern naval warfare, and that many issues that concern contemporary strategists and tacticians were being posed in antiquity. This book aims to be a contribution to naval history and to tactical and strategic theory.

The current disinterest in ancient naval history contrasts notably with the nineteenth century, when Admiral Jurien de la Graviere, Admiral Serre and Professor Cartault acted as pioneers in the field. Historians of ancient naval wars still appreciate their studies, despite their age. One must also note that there is a recent work (1987) in French on ancient ships, *Le Musee imaginaire de la marine antique*, written by Lucien Basch, a Belgian specialist, that tries to augment our understanding of battle tactics and operations by use of ancient boat and ship models.

Did Imperial Rome have a Grand Strategy?

Since my treatment of Roman naval affairs to some extent depends on the use of fleets in enforcing foreign policy, I will explain my use of the term 'grand strategy' here. The issue of whether the Empire indeed formulated, or even implemented, a grand strategy as we understand the concept, has been hotly debated. The two chief antagonists in this debate are Edward Luttwak (*The Grand Strategy of the Roman Empire*) and Benjamin Isaac (*The Limits of Empire*). Perhaps Isaac's comment on Luttwak's work might provide a handle on this ongoing dispute:

> 'Luttwak has described Roman strategy in a systematic manner. He assumes that there was a coherent system built up with an inner logic and that it is possible to describe the coherence and dynamics of this system. We can admire his lucid analysis, but we must still ask whether

the system analysed did in fact exist. If we do ask this question it is thanks to Luttwak's own admirable synthesis. However, his central assumption, that there existed a system whose object was to defend and enhance the security of the empire is a hypothesis based on analogies with modern army organization. It is not based on an independent analysis of the ancient literary sources or archaeological materials, but derives from a lucid perusal of modern literature, and naturally the result is an approach already implicit in the writings of most specialists on Roman frontiers.'

In a sense, my book takes a maritime slant on the eternal controversy over whether or not the Roman Empire really had a grand strategy. I won't attempt to answer that larger question here, but I hope to at least suggest how the fleets, sailors and marines may have furthered such imperial policy goals as hindsight can glean, whether or not one can label it 'grand strategy' in the modern sense. For example, as I have noted above, Arther Ferril (*Roman Imperial Grand Strategy*, 1991) didn't feel that the principal Italianate fleets – the Misenian and Ravennate – were employed in pursuit of any such grand strategy; but I don't think that this rules out that ships were utilized to implement such ad hoc designs as were contemplated in response to challenges with an implicit maritime dimension. I believe that Rome's response to the various threats at sea, along seacoasts, on inland waterways and riverine systems went beyond being merely reactive; there was some degree of planning involved, and planning entailed some kind of strategical vision, regardless of whether it equates to modern long-term planning.

The modern field of strategic studies defines 'grand strategy' as the allocation of a state's resources to meet its major objectives. A grand strategy, contrasted to a strategy plain and simple, is a matter of comprehensiveness. Formulating and implementing a grand strategy would entail a high-level coordination of all the assets of a nation – military, diplomatic, political, economic and social – to further long-term international national goals. Surviving sources regarding the patterns of troop movements in the Roman Empire show that emperors decided how to allocate resources empire-wide to meet objectives, and thus thought about grand-strategic issues even if they did not recognize the concept or engage in long-term planning. There were no defence appropriation panels, preparedness commission hearings, budget oversight reports, etc. But threats were long-festering – much more so than today, with the seeming rush from crisis to crisis – and the emperor and the senators had their advisors and experts with whom to consult.

Much as is the case with the road network and the chain of fortified camps along the frontiers with hostile or non-aligned kingdoms, there was an underlying concept of operations governing the construction of warships and merchantmen. This scheme may seem even less apparent than the imperative driving the building of defensive outposts along the Empire's frontiers and linking them with traversible roadsteads. But much as road, outpost and fortress-building entailed military planning of a sort, so too did the design, construction, siting, commissioning and command of fleets. Until the Battle of Actium, the fleets waxed and waned, usually being abandoned after each emergency compelling their construction.

The underlying issue is whether Rome had some kind of deliberate imperialist programme. Between 241-197 BC, although Rome had defeated Carthage, taken over her dominions, controlled the Illyrian coasts and a good deal of that piratical tribe's hinterland, she annexed only four provinces during this period. Next, even though there was a period of intense warfare, with Rome beating Macedonia in three successive wars and pacifying Greece, she annexed only four further provinces during that period, spanning from 146-121 BC.

F.B. Marsh, in *The Founding of the Roman Empire* and *A History of the Roman World: From 146-30 BC*, asserts that Rome's *provinciae* were acquired merely in response to crises and not by design; otherwise she would have grabbed more in this period. But a more judicious analysis of Rome's expansion during the late Republic will show that far from being a mere defensive reaction to the aggressions (or ambitions) of other state actors, Rome had generally acted in an imperialistic and aggressive manner. It is hard to see just what Rome may have been 'defending' against when she warred against Tarentum from 282-272 BC, and against Carthage in the Punic Wars. However, as Arthur M. Eckstein has observed in his chapter 'Rome Dominates the Mediterranean' in the book *China Goes to Sea: Maritime Transformation in Comparative Historical Perspective* (Naval Institute Press, 2009), Rome was no more aggressive and imperialistic than the other regional actors, and her actions were shaped by living in a tough neighbourhood. To fail to react harshly to provocations would be to invite predators to strip her of allies and possessions.

The fact is that whether willing or unwilling, her pattern of behaviour was incrementally hegemonic, though not necessarily imperialistic in the sense of the colonizing great powers at the turn of the nineteenth and twentieth centuries. There is no coherent programme of acquiring territories by conquest or intimidation, as could be seen with respect to Persia, Athens, or eighteenth-century Britain, Wilhelmine Germany or Soviet Russia in more recent times. However, it is a mistake to infer from this apparent lack of a 'grand strategy of conquest', as it were, that Rome's Empire sprang, willy-nilly, from external pressures beyond her control. In short, she demonstrated a pattern of arrogance and stiff-necked unwillingness to compromise or make reasonable accommodation with those whose interests came into contention with her own. She was cognizant of her growing military and naval prowess and knew how to use it.

Arther Ferrill has examined this question at some length in his above-referenced 1991 paper for the Association of Ancient Historians, 'Roman Imperial

Grand Strategy'. He has weighed the arguments *pro* and *con*. In the chapter titled 'Preclusive Security' (a term denoting reliance on defensive barriers such as Hadrian's Wall in Britain), he argues that even though there are no traces of any such bodies as imperial planning staffs, the emperors likely had military (to include naval) advisors who served that function. Alas, there was no wikileaks or Pentagon Papers to reveal their counsels to posterity, so I use my own mole in the ancient Roman planning counsels to bring this 'intel' to you. His/her names have been withheld to protect confidentiality of sources.

With the foregoing caveats in mind, I have endeavoured to show the part of sea power in attaining and securing imperial objectives, regardless of whether they rise to the level of what we now call grand strategy. After the close of the second century AD in particular, much of this strategy will be seen to be reactive and improvised – staving off the increasing threats to the imperial periphery – rather than proactively expanding the perimeter of the Empire.

A Note on the Organization of the Book

While my emphasis is upon the period encompassed by the rise, rule and fall of Rome, I devote a chapter to earlier naval history as laying important foundations. Since Rome drew upon the traditions and technology of its naval-minded predecessor states, the first chapter covers the rise and fall of naval empires prior to Rome's inception, with a coda on 'thalassocracy', as that term may apply to ancient fleets (the context for a 'command of the sea' construct) and another on the speed and endurance of merchant and war craft, limits that dictated the deployment of these vessels in support of military campaigns.

The chapters relating the salient features of the Republican naval wars cover what is elsewhere handled in a straight chronological recounting. Sufficient tactical detail is provided to illustrate the lesson taught, whether or not it was learned.

The second chapter discusses the onset of Rome's sea-mindedness and her early experiences up to the First Punic War, whose salient features are covered in Chapter Three. The fourth chapter is devoted to my resumé of Mahan's take on the Second Punic War, since it underlies much of the ensuing argument, while I provide separate chapters on the naval aspects of the Macedonian, Illyrian and Syrian (Asiatic) Wars, as well as Pompey's anti-piracy campaign, and a brief overview of the naval campaigns in the Civil Wars leading to the accession of Augustus.

While these topics have been amply covered elsewhere, as has the First Punic War, I seek to provide a strategic overview of these conflicts in modern terms. I direct the reader to books, articles and monographs cited in my introduction and critical bibliography if he or she needs more in-depth coverage of a particular war or campaign. My surveys are intended to convey only sufficient information to illustrate my points. Similarly, I discuss Julius Caesar's amphibious assaults on Britannia in some detail, since they were a prelude of sorts to Claudius' much larger operation of the following century.

The chapter on fleets is not intended to provide a comprehensive snapshot of the status of the stations and bases harbouring the Empire's central and outlying naval units at various points in time. This data is fluid and evolved as contingencies arose and subsided. The sources are not consistent or informative as to the possible beginning and end dates of these fleets. I have striven to cover all the fleets as well as provide an idea of their probable status through time. I have also included in this chapter a run-down of the various ship types, both war-like and merchant vessels. Illustration number two comprises a graphic depiction of these ships and their characteristics, with essential data so far as this can be gleaned. A separate chapter covers maritime commerce, including trade routes, weather and currents affecting maritime trade, ports, commodities, etc.

Following this, the chapters are arranged in rough chronological order to discuss the selected operations of the fleets chosen to illustrate aspects of modern naval theory. In order to maintain same cohesion in covering regional campaigns, there is necessarily same chronological backtracking in the various subchapters. When I get to the naval operations of Augustus' fleet and afterward, there are few wars and campaigns illustrating war fleets engaging on the high seas and more joint operations combining land and naval forces. The material for a full-blown 'naval history' in the traditional sense is quite sparse here. I utilize the selected campaigns and episodes such as the sources support, so the selections are concentrated in just about half of the five-century imperial period. As the ancient chroniclers, lacking colourful fleet-to-fleet engagements, made only passing reference to how ships were employed in support of the various campaigns and police actions, the raw material is thin here. The exception is the famous Trajan's Column, which vividly depicts all manner of vessels supporting the Dacian Wars.

Chapter One

The Origins: The Rise of Rome and Evolution of Sea-Faring, Maritime Commerce Preceding the Rise of Rome and the Question of 'Thalassocracy'

From Tranquil Streams and Ponds to Fast-Flowing Rivers and the Open Sea

The sea was dangerous and difficult to predict – a fearsome and hostile presence in ancient sacred texts – but from at least the Middle Palaeolithic epoch, circa 300,000-30,000 BC, people sought its resources and attempted to move upon or beneath its surface. The evolution of primitive watercraft facilitated coastal foraging, fishing, hunting and travel, and the later development of sailing allowed long offshore passages, fundamental to all other sea-borne activities and interests. Increasing maritime exploration, migration, trade and colonialism together stimulated the integrating effects of 'globalization', describing a developing reach and complexity in human affairs that is comparable with, and in various ways holds up a mirror to, the course of terrestrial prehistory across the late Quaternary Era, about 14,000 to 15,000 years ago.

Dugout canoes roughly fashioned from tree trunks, with burnt and excavated hollowed spaces for passengers and cargo, are traced back to the Stone Age. No doubt the accidental discovery of water-borne transport was made across a wide geographical area by virtue of noticing how stream-side trees uprooted by storms and floods floated along effortlessly with the current. It is difficult to determine when these unwieldy craft, as well as rafts made of lashed twigs and reeds, or yoked arrays of buoyant gourds or pots, progressed from merely fording streams, carrying goods along rivers and tributaries or upon placid landlocked lakes, to the ability to follow estuaries into the sea and navigate large, exposed, churning bodies of water.

It would have been apparent very early that in order to get from point A to point B one would often have to traverse water that was too deep for wading and too extensive for one to swim, or to swim carrying any trade goods for barter with neighbouring tribes. The alternative was often to take a long, circuitous route through dense forest or hilly terrain, making transportation of commodities prolonged and gruelling. Prehistoric man would naturally have observed that flotsam strewn on streams and rivers was borne along by currents.

So flotation devices, whether hollowed tree trunks (the hollowing necessary to securely accommodate people and their cargoes) or rafts, were the way to go. At first these were paddled, depending upon brute arm power, then, when the lever principle was discovered, through more energy-efficient hull-mounted oars which could utilize the larger, stronger muscles of the back and torso as stern-facing oarsmen exploited this lever principle to efficiently propel the craft. It was not merely the imposition of water as an obstacle to travel that spurred these insights, but the realization that the conveyance of bulky, heavy goods upon it was much more efficient than tiresome, roundabout land portages, even where watercourses entailed more protracted passages.

Gradually, shipwrights learned to fasten boards to the sides of the dugouts to prevent swamping of the little craft in a strong current and provide for some necessary dry carriage of supplies and/or trade goods. Sails attached to a crude mast were next, possibly when observing how a favouring wind could propel the paddled or rowed craft along much faster and longer than unaided muscle power. Or perhaps some astute observer noted how fallen trees were sped on their downstream journey by breezes acting upon foliage-laden branches. These primal mariners would have also discovered early how the bow, or entry point, of the vessel should be somewhat arrow-shaped, while the main body could be widened for stability. The dugout log core was next fashioned into a sort of keel so that, once sails were fitted, the craft had some lateral stability on the water and didn't drift too much from a true course. Stays were fastened from mast and yard to various points on the hull to both steady the masts, yards and sails, and later to twist them so they could take best advantage of following winds on the quarters or abeam.

The earliest seaworthy boats capable of open-water passages may have been developed as early as 45,000 years ago, according to one hypothesis explaining the settlement of Australia, New Guinea, as well as Melanesia and Micronesia along the south-western Pacific stepping-stone route. However, Stone-Age Polynesian or Asian-Pacific voyages, impressive as they were, could not affect the development of seafaring in the Mediterranean basin. The Polynesians utilized unique celestial 'star maps' and an acute sense of ocean currents, wind patterns, sea-life migrations and land-signs that were not ascertained by Western mariners until well into the Medieval period – likely by the Viking navigators.

Humans began whaling in prehistoric times, enticed by the carcasses that washed up on the shore to pursue the resource-rich mammals further out to sea. It is believed that the art of fishing followed a similar path. The first fishermen used spear and net to snare what could be gathered as far out as wading depth, but it was obvious that some kind of float-borne method would yield the richest edible sea-life harvest farther from the shore.

The utility of the rafts and dugouts as cargo-carriers was contemporary with the discovery, likely around 40,000 BC, that surplus goods produced by one tribe or extended clan could be traded for items that were available in quantities to another group, likely across an unfordable stream or river, or many miles downstream. It entailed a long learning curve of several thousand years before these unwieldy rafts and dugouts evolved into seaworthy, manoeuvrable craft capable of ranging beyond inland streams, rivers and lakes. This story has been told in terms of reports of excavations of ancient vessels, nautical artifacts, etc., and the details are beyond the scope of an examination of Roman imperial sea power. I have listed several works in the bibliography covering the early evolution of water craft if an interested reader wants to pursue it. Thus, I begin this prelude with the watermen lining the Nile delta and river.

Ancient Egypt: The First Sea-Conscious Civilization?

In describing the relationship of Pharaonic Egypt to the sea, I use the term 'sea-conscious' rather than thalassocratic; the ancient Egyptians were more of a river-going and coast-hugging people who, step by step, undertook some short open-water journeys along the Eastern Mediterranean terminus. Even their celebrated long hauls down to the Red Sea trading depot at Punt and back were combined overland, riverine and shore-wise expeditions. Nevertheless, an argument can be made that Ancient Egypt was not merely a riverine culture, but that, in the applicable ancient context, it was a maritime nation.

The Egyptian Nile operates as a natural communications link between the cities, towns and villages of Egypt, and as a conduit for communications between the regions bordering the Upper Nile, Mediterranean Sea and Red Sea. Goods, people and ideas from Nubia, the Sudan and even Central Africa entered Egypt from the south along the Nubian Nile. After negotiating the First Cataract at Aswan, ships could travel almost anywhere along the Egyptian Nile.

To the north, ships travelled downstream, along one of the then seven branches of the Nile, into the Eastern Mediterranean. The Eastern Mediterranean was also a natural communications link between the major cultural centres of Syria-Canaan/Palestine, Cyprus, Crete, Greece and Libya. A third communications link travelled parallel to the Nile, south along the Red Sea. This route included a short trip to the Sinai peninsula, and also led to the ancient region of Punt, located somewhere near the horn of Africa.

The Red Sea route grew into one of the main trade routes to the Persian Gulf, South Asia and beyond. As it was not possible to navigate directly from the Egyptian Nile to the Red Sea, some means of overland transportation was required, mostly over the Wadi Tumulat in Lower Egypt or the Wadi Hammamat in Upper Egypt. Ships were dismantled for transportation by donkey pack, sledge or wagon, and then reassembled on the Red Sea coast before continuing their journey along the Red Sea. These sea lines of communication helped to blend Egyptian civilization into a cultural mixture of Middle Eastern and African influences.

The first recorded appearance of warships as such is on the Nile River, where Egypt's history has centred since antiquity. These boats were built of bundles of reeds lashed together to form a narrow, sharp-ended hull, upturned at the extremities and coated with pitch. They were hardly suitable for tempestuous seas. By 3000 BC, larger wooden seagoing versions of the reed craft sailed for distant cruising, trade and conquest. The shape of the wooden craft simply copied that dictated by the earlier bundled-reed construction. Egypt was limited in the size of these vessels by the lack of forested areas. The only trees available were small, and hence construction was by a complex series of short boards held together by linen scarves and wooden pegs, end-to-end. Bound by tradition, the wooden vessels parroted the crescent shape of the reed boats. This did not make for a craft capable of handling rough waters. Sometimes the Egyptians commissioned Lebanese shipwrights (Lebanon had an abundance of tall cedar) to build the ships, or the Egyptians bartered for the cedar timber so they could build their own seaworthy ships.

Whether impelled by fishing needs, cargo-hauling or migratory urges in search of better hunting grounds, by the advent of Pharaonic Egypt the frail riverine and inshore craft evolved into vessels capable of travelling along hundreds of miles of coast, or even across short stretches of open waters. Queen Hatsepshut's famous obelisk ships on the expedition to Punt (modern Somalia) circa 1480 BC are an example of early vessels fitted out for hauling cumbersome cargoes over long distances. However, their route did not take them over large stretches of unsheltered seas, and it is unlikely that they could have undertaken the expedition had it not primarily entailed riverine, inland, coastwise travel and land-bridge portages throughout.

Most likely the first craft fitted purposely to make war were adaptations of the dugouts, yoked inflatable bladders, papyrus rafts or hide boats used in everyday transport. It is probable that the conversion at first consisted simply of a concentration of weapons in the hands of a raiding party. In time, the modifications added offensive and defensive powers to the craft itself. As vessels became more seaworthy and more numerous, warships designed as such developed both as marauders and as defences against marauders. The first craft designed and built especially for combat may have sailed in the fleets of Crete and Egypt 5,000 years ago.

The concept of 'sea power' in connection with the civilizations of Egypt and Crete (Minos) is a complex and contentious one. Rather than becoming mired in this issue, perhaps it is best to briefly revisit our earlier discussion of just what is intended by the ancient term 'thalassocracy' and then, without making a definite conclusion (best left to scholars specializing in ancient Egypt and Crete), we can briefly consider the contributions of these two civilizations towards seafaring in general. So to not interrupt the narrative, the reader is directed to the brief consideration of the meaning of thalassocracy appended to the end of this chapter.

The Egyptians were adept sailors and navigators. They had extensive experience with the Nile River, canals, lakes and the sea. Their earliest boats were likely papyrus skiffs for Nile haulage, but even in pre-dynastic times, they were building elaborate ships with oars (controlled using the lever principle, in sockets rather than inefficient hand-wielded paddles) and rudimentary cabins. By this time there was an established maritime trade with other lands, notably Lebanon's Sidon and Tyre (Byblos), Crete and the Red Sea Horn of Africa. There is evidence that the Egyptians developed a variety of craft for diverse purposes. They had squat transport ships, which were inwardly curved at the prow and stern, long ships, funerary barks to figuratively convey the dead across the Nile to the city of the dead (necropolis) or to make a journey to Abydos, the sacred city of Osiris, or to sail the heavens. They also had barges in which to transport animals, corn or stone.

By the epoch of the New Kingdom (circa 1570-1070 BC), specialist warships were built and several innovations were introduced. After that time, the fleet did not alter much until Dynasty 26 (c.600 BC) when new features were introduced by the Greek and Phoenician mercenaries whom the Egyptians employed. In the New Kingdom, however, the so-called 'Knpwt' (Byblos, that is Phoenician) and 'Keftiu'(Cretan) ships played their part in the Egyptian navy. Copies of the alleged Byblos ships may have been specially constructed in Egypt to travel to Byblos or other Syrian coastal towns. On the other hand, this term may simply refer to vessels that were built at Byblos for the use of Egypt. Another possibility is that the ships were simply modelled on ships that were captured by Thutmose III during his Syrian campaigns and thereafter used as a prototype vessel for the nucleus of his navy.

There is evidence that the Egyptians had been sailing along the Red Sea to a land they called Punt (the coast of the Horn of Africa in what is today Eritrea and eastern Sudan) before Hatshepsut's reign, as early as 2500 BC. Adjacent to Cheops's pyramid at Giza, a funerary pit has been opened and the contents carefully removed and reconstructed by staff from the Cairo Museum. The pit contained a boat, dismantled into pieces for burial in antiquity that is now housed in a glass museum alongside the Great Pyramid. The ship is over 130ft long and made of carved pieces of cedar bonded with small cords, the complete vessel providing evidence of great skill in shipbuilding techniques early in the Old Kingdom.

Within Egypt and Nubia, the Egyptian troops were transported by boat. In Egypt's relations with its northern neighbours, the Syrian coastal town of Byblos was of great importance, and Egypt's close association with its inhabitants from Dynasty 2 down to the Ptolemaic Period was only interrupted when Egypt faced internal problems. Coniferous woods were imported from Byblos and environs (sea pine and parasol pine), and also from northern Lebanon (firs and cedars). The rulers of Byblos not only traded with the Egyptians, but provided them with support and ships for their military campaigns.

Sea journeys were also undertaken to the land of Punt. This district, known as the 'Terraces of Incense' or the 'God's Land', was where the Egyptians sought incense for use in their temples. Egypt's relations with Punt, which probably go back to the early dynastic period, may have involved some military coercion on the part of the Egyptians rather than reflecting a true trading partnership between equals. Punt is now generally identified as Somalia – the notorious Horn of Africa, latterly haven to dangerous modern-day pirate gangs.

The Egyptians were clearly excellent sailors, both on the Nile and when they travelled to other lands on sea coasts. Their greatest naval victories over their enemies occurred not abroad, however, but when they were forced to protect the mouths of the Delta against the Sea Peoples and their allies in the late New Kingdom. Temple carvings attest to one battle where the Sea Peoples were attempting an amphibious landing opposed by Egyptian marines and warships.

Egypt's Nile boats were built of bundles of reeds lashed together to form a narrow, sharp-ended hull, and coated with pitch; they were hardly suited for tempestuous seas. By 3000 BC, larger wooden seagoing versions of the reed craft sailed for distant cruising, trade and conquest.

Egyptian wooden ships had both oars and sails, being fitted with a bipod (inverted V) mast and a single, large, square sail. The whole mast could be lowered when under oars. Large Egyptian ships had more than twenty oars to a side, with two or more steering oars. The war galley was built to the same pattern, but was of stouter construction. Modifications that could be easily incorporated in a merchant ship's hull under construction included elevated decks fore and aft for archers and spearmen, planks fitted to the gunwales to protect the rowers and a small fighting top high on the mast to accommodate several archers. Some galleys had a projecting ram, well above the waterline, which may have been designed to crash through the gunwale of a foe, ride up on deck and swamp or capsize him, unlike the underwater rams on later war vessels, designed to puncture the enemy hull below the waterline and flood it.

Thus, while not a truly seafaring people, as later understood in terms of the Athenian and Phoenician thalassocracies, it is clear that the Egyptians were capable of some remarkable trading and warlike expeditions in the Eastern Mediterranean and along the Red Sea coast. Their voyages were not as bold as those undertaken by the Phoenicians, Mycenaeans, Greeks and Romans, but it is clear that they were no mere waders. By the later Pharaonic dynasties, they had been in contact with the seafarers of Minos/Crete, Phoenicia and Mycenaean Greece, and so were introduced to what today we would call 'short sea trading', as contrasted to mere coastal navigating.

Minoan Crete – A Quasi-Thalassocracy?

Although the Egyptians built the first sea-going ships, the Minoans of Crete were said to be the first great seafarers of the Mediterranean Sea. Little is known of their ships, but they reportedly traded pottery as far west as Sicily, and their legendary King Minos conquered the islands of the Aegean (according to Thucydides). As to whether one ought to hold with Thucydides that this monopoly of sea trade constituted a *bona fide* thalassocracy, the jury is still out. Much of pre-Greek historiography is shrouded in myth and legend.

While we remain in the dark about many aspects of Minoan civilization, it is still maintained by some scholars that the Cretans 'ruled' the Aegean Sea, in the context of the limitations of ships and seafaring of that era. According to the 'pro' school of thinking, this thalassocracy, if we may call it such, usually placed in the late Minoan I-II Period (c.1570-1400 BC), permitted the Cretan overlords of Knossos to live in an unfortified palace, since no trans-oceanic expedition could get through to them, encouraged the expansion of Cretan trade to the mainland of Greece and generally fostered peaceful conditions in the Aegean.

Given the ambiguity of the evidence, it is fair to ask whether there really was a Minoan sea empire, or genuine thalassocracy. This is an open question. The idea that the Minoans created a thalassocracy in the Aegean derives from traditions passed on by fifth-century Greek historians. Thucydides' account is very straightforward and acknowledges that it rests 'on tradition'. (I will revisit the meaning of thalassocracy in the ancient context at the end of this chapter.)

According to this tradition, Minos (the god-king) was the first person to organize a navy. He controlled the greater part of what is now the Aegean Sea and ruled over the Grecian outer ring of islets, the Cyclades, in most of which he founded the first colonies, installing his sons as governors after having driven out the native Carians. It is reasonable to suppose that he did his best to put down piracy in order to secure his own revenues. One doesn't have to accept this mythology verbatim, but only as emblematic of some underlying factual situation.

Note that Thucydides doesn't identify Minos' ethnicity, nor does he place Minos chronologically. Herodotus has more information regarding Minos and Minoan sea power, but his account is problematic. Without historical refinement, he says that the tyrant Polycrates of Samos was 'the first Greek we know of to plan a dominion of the sea, unless we count Minos of Knossos'. This hedges the question. What he meant by 'dominion of the sea' is not elaborated, and one is obliged to infer that it was something less than that exercised by, say, Athens centuries later.

It is evident that what Thucydides passes on about Minos and Crete is strongly coloured by myth and legend. Herodotus says that in ancient times, Crete was inhabited by non-Greek peoples, and that the two sons of Europa – Sarpedon and Minos – fought for the throne, a struggle that Minos won, after which he expelled Sarpedon and his followers (*Histories*, 1.174).

So while Thucydides suggested that a Minoan thalassocracy under King Minos may have existed at around this time, this label is only partially supported by the evidence. Although Minoan cities did have some ability to assemble maritime forces and were particularly involved in Eastern Mediterranean trade, the evidence suggests that they did not have sufficient naval power to challenge the Egyptian fleet for maritime supremacy along the eastern terminus of the Mediterranean Sea – sea control in the Mahanian sense.

Elsewhere in the *Histories*, Herodotus describes a massive Cretan naval expedition against the town of Camicus in Sicily, which led to the destruction of the Cretan fleet in a storm, as a result of which the shipwrecked Cretans settled in Sicily, leaving Crete depopulated – after which it was settled by the Greeks (7.171f.).

Furthermore, Herodotus' chronology is badly confused. Herodotus dates Minos to three generations before the Trojan War (7.172) – in other words, in the mid- to late fourteenth century BC, which places Minos 100 years after the Greek conquest of Crete by our reckoning, and would, therefore, make him a Greek, not a pre-Greek Minoan. But disagreements over details need not shroud the whole idea of Minoan sea power in fanciful tales and fantasy.

Scholarly opinion on the question of the Minoan thalassocracy is much divided. Some scholars flatly dismiss the existence of *any* Minoan sea empire of whatever character. In the mid-1950s, Chester Starr said the Minoan thalassocracy was myth, pure and simple (Chester G. Starr, 'The Myth of the Minoan Thalassocracy', *Historia: Zeitschrift für Alte Geschicthe*, Vol.3, No.3, 1955). But his total rejection of the idea is not commonly accepted.

Other scholars are less sceptical and try to distill useful historical information from the accounts of the fifth-century historians in combination with archeological discoveries. Thucydides' information is very circumstantial, and clearly the oral traditions from which he gleaned his information both remembered the existence of a Minoan sea realm and offered detail about it. It is uncertain whether that detail was as factual as what Thucydides relates, or whether he distilled the detail from imaginary fabled material. We will likely never know.

Archaeology has indicated that the Minoans had established a significant mercantile presence in the Cyclades, but this doesn't prove Thucydides' implication that it comprised a colony. It is also clear that Minoan trade routes extended throughout the Aegean and the Eastern Mediterranean. Herodotus' material seems less valuable, and few historians base their evaluation of the likelihood of a Minoan naval empire on Herodotus' account. Herodotus was quite infatuated with myth and fable, and wasn't careful to separate these tales from observed fact in his literary reconstructions.

Aside from claiming Minos' organization of the first navy and creation of an Aegean thalassocracy, Thucydides' information has nothing in common with Herodotus' colourful material. They were possibly working from contrasting threads of a common ancient folklore tradition.

Thus, despite all the circumstantial evidence, there is no escaping the fact that the existence of any pre-Greek sea empire based on Crete needs further corroboration. I emphasize 'sea empire', which term does not rule out some kind of maritime mercantile arrangement. As we have just seen, Herodotus describes Minos as a pre-Greek figure, but his chronology places Minos after the Greek conquest of Crete. Thucydides provides neither a chronological framework for his statements, nor any indication of Minos' ethnicity. In other words, in Thucydides' account, Minos could just as well have been a Greek ruler of Crete as a pre-Greek Minoan.

The Minoan settlements on the Cyclades need not have been colonial possessions of Crete; they might just as well have been independent, as were later Greek and Phoenician colonies which, nonetheless, maintained ties to the mother country. Minoan political authority need not have accompanied Minoan trade goods as they spread throughout the islands of the Aegean. Such was the case with the Phoenicians much later. The best way to describe these outliers is 'trading posts', with some resident representatives and facilities. The earliest Spanish, Portuguese and Dutch outposts in the age of exploration were likewise mere trading posts; imperial domination followed.

On balance, the existence of some degree of Minoan thalassocracy cannot be proven unequivocally, but clearly, the Minoans were a sea-faring people; in fact, theirs was the first civilized society in all of history to be based upon an island. This means that the Minoans were dependent on maritime trade not only for their prosperity, but for many of the raw materials from which life's necessities were made, especially copper and tin, the constituent elements of bronze.

As a people dependent on maritime trade, the Minoans had a particular need to secure the sea routes over which goods travelled to and from their island. To protect their trade against piracy, the Minoans would have needed to build not just a navy, but also to extend some degree of political control away from Crete. This notion requires further clarification.

In order to suppress piracy more than temporarily, the Minoans would have needed to deprive the pirates of bases. As evidenced by the Egyptian heiroglyphs, the piracy of the sea-raiders was rampant in the Eastern Mediterranean by the time of Minoan ascendancy. This meant capturing and occupying the islands that pirates used. Yet since ancient warships of that period had little ability to remain at sea, it also meant acquiring bases throughout the Aegean, where Cretan anti-piracy squadrons could be based. But does it prove that, in turn, it meant doing as Thucydides says Minos did – ruling over the Cyclades and 'colonizing' its islands?

In other words, direct rule, or political hegemony, was not the only way that history's first island civilization could protect its maritime lifeline. But, in the limited capacity of the shipping of that time, it would have to do what Thucydides' 'tradition' says it did – create a thalassocracy – here implying outlying bases. However, this logical inference neither proves nor disproves Minoan naval power.

Having weighed the pros and cons of the tradition, we must concede that most of the details about the history of a Minoan thalassocracy are lost. We don't know when it was created. We don't know how it was run (aside from Thucydides' 'tradition' statement that royal princes were used as governors). We don't know what types of ships it used (apart from ambiguous hints on schematically rendered frescoes from a possible secondary harbour – Santorini) and we don't know where its bases were located.

The fall of the imputed Minoan thalassocracy is as obscure as everything else about the Minoans. All we know for sure is that Greeks from the mainland (the Mycenaean, or Bronze Age, Greeks) replaced native Minoans in control of the palace at Knossos in the middle of the fifteenth century BC. This transition was accompanied by the destruction of the other palaces, showing that the replacement was violent, whether from a volcanic tsunami, as some believe, or conquest.

Some scholars use this very fact *against* the existence of Minoan thalassocracy. They hold that if the Minoans had command of the sea, it is hard to imagine how the Greeks could have mounted a successful invasion and conquest of Crete. It is possible that thalassocracy in her case signifies only that she was the principal carrier of trade goods by sea in the Mediterranean during her period of ascendancy, rather than ruling the seas in the manner of Greece, Rome or Great Britain in the respective heydays of these sea powers.

Now the Greeks had certainly become wealthy. Mainland culture had blossomed after the eruption of the volcano on Thera, with large palaces appearing at numerous locations, and rich grave goods testifying to the wealth of their rulers – a wealth probably derived from trade, perhaps made possible by the dislocation of Minoan trade after the eruption of the aforesaid volcano.

One possibility sometimes raised is that the Minoans employed skilled Greek soldiers as mercenaries, and these mercenaries rebelled, expelling their former masters from power. Or perhaps the Minoans' control of the sea was crippled by some great defeat, like Herodotus' legend of the failed Sicilian expedition, and then the Greeks saw their chance and launched a great raid to eliminate their Minoan trading rivals.

There is no evidence that the Minoans engaged in warfare, or acted aggressively with other cultures. Like the Phoenicians, whose mercantile system matured during the height of the Minoan commercial network, they were a trading culture. The sea was critical to their prosperity and survival. The Minoans were involved in the tin trade, critical in the Bronze Age. Tin, alloyed with copper which may have come from Cyprus, was used to make bronze. They were quite prepared to enforce and protect their trade monopoly, but since they were supreme upon the sea by virtue of the lack of seafaring rivals, this hardly called for the creation of a navy.

In summation, the Minoan fleet appears to have been essentially a trading fleet, but with weapons for defence from pirates. There is nothing in our knowledge of the Minoans to suggest that they were ever an aggressive military power, but with a large fleet they apparently felt safe enough to leave their cities unfortified in a world where warfare was constant.

The ships depicted on the frieze excavated on the Greek island of Santorini (Akrotiri), widely believed to be the site of a Bronze Age Minoan trading post, provides what is most likely the best depiction we will have of the likely configuration of the vessels of Minoan Crete, albeit in a stylized, schematic format. They don't seem to be mere coastal craft, meant to putter about around safe anchorages. These appear to be seagoing ships, and the scenes render indications of a maritime commerce well beyond the sight of land. But, as noted, the iconography is somewhat crude, so this aspect is a little speculative.

The simple truth is that, like so much else about the Minoans, we just don't know. But it was not with the people of Crete, whether Minoan or Greeks, that the future lay. The future lay on the mainland, with the people of Greece itself – who, as the Minoans sank into obscurity, began their own ascent to power and, ultimately, to empire. Suffice it to say that the Minoan mercantile base on Crete had established a trading network throughout the Aegean and the Eastern Mediterranean. Whether or not this constituted a thalasoccracy is a moot point. Although Egypt would challenge the Minoan 'reach' along the Levant and in North Africa, the Minoans were apparently a vigorous seaborne trading entity in the Mediterranean during the period of their activity, and this is sufficient to demonstrate their maritime dominance.

Phoenicia: Merchant Seamen, but not Sea Warriors

The Phoenicians, who exercised mastery of the world's known seas for a period of six or seven centuries, are still somewhat of a mystery as well. Their 'reign' spanned the rise and fall of the Egyptian and Minoan civilizations and overlapped the rise of Athenian sea power. We have seen that they interacted with the naval forces of Pharaonic Egypt and were active from approximately 1500 BC to around the time of the Greco-Persian Wars, a time period spanning well over a millennium, after which their Carthaginian branch in North Africa took over and reigned as the Mediterranean sea lords until the Punic Wars.

We know a bit more about the Phoenicians than we do the mysterious Minoans of Crete, but still not enough to appreciate the actual deployment of their naval power. There is no written record from Phoenician scribes. What is more, Phoenicia was never politically unified, was often under foreign rule, did not effectively retain control of its colonies and never used colonies as footholds of conquest. The greatest Phoenician colony, Carthage, itself came rather closer to a thalassocracy, retaining control of colonies in the Western Mediterranean and then, under Hamilcar Barca, undertaking the conquest and development of Spain as a Carthaginian imperial possession. But why did the primal Phoenicians turn seawards?

First, ancient Phoenicia, modern-day Lebanon, was a hilly coastal area whose rough terrain made it hard to unite. As a result, independent city-states such as Byblos, Ugarit, Tyre and Sidon emerged along the coast. Secondly, the Phoenicians did not have the sort of rich soil that one found in Egypt and Mesopotamia. In fact, they had only two major natural resources that were useful for trading: timber and snails. Their timber, the fabled cedars of Lebanon, was highly prized for use on the building projects and navies of the ancient Near East, witness King Solomon's famous partnership with King Hiram of Tyre. The third and final geopolitical factor of Phoenicia was its position between the two great civilizations of the time: Egypt and Mesopotamia. This brought a lot of trade their way, but also left Phoenicia caught in wars between its powerful neighbours, a situation that modern Lebanon still faces today.

Initially, the Phoenicians were based in northern Canaan (later Judaea-Palestine) and important centres are identified with modern Sidon, Sarafand and Tyre in Lebanon. Like ancient Greece, they were a loose confederation of city-states rather than a unified entity. As will be seen under the discussion about Greece below, each city-state was an independent unit politically, at times they fought among themselves, and one city could be dominated by another city-state. They would frequently collaborate in leagues or alliances. Rather than characterize Phoenicia as a national or ethnic entity, then, the most we can say is that the Phoenician civilization was an enterprising maritime trading culture.

The Phoneicians are credited with conducting some prodigious exploration journeys, venturing into the Atlantic at a time when that body of water was largely cloaked in myth and rumour. Since they jealously guarded their maritime routes lest competitors break their trading monopoly, we have no written records attributed directly to Phoenicians, only second- and third-hand accounts largely from Greek and Latin sources. The invention of the trireme, that supreme warship of antiquity, is alleged to be a Phoenician project, as H.T. Wallinga attests in *Ships and Sea-Power Before the Great Persian War: The Ancestry of the Ancient Trireme* (Mnemosyne, Bibliotheca Classica Batava, 1992).

The height of Phoenician trade was around the seventh and eighth centuries BC. There is a dispersal of imports (ceramic, stone and faience) from the Levant that traces a Phoenician commercial channel to the Greek mainland via the central Aegean. Athens shows little evidence of this trade, with few eastern imports, but other Greek coastal cities are rich with them, which evidence this maritime commerce. The famed Tarshish or Tarsus on the south–western coast of Spain shows evidence of being established by Phoenician traders, as well as another Spanish harbour opening to the Atlantic, Gades (later Cadiz).

Al Mina is a specific example of the trade that took place between the Greeks and the Phoenicians. It has been theorized that by the eighth century BC, Euboean traders established a commercial enterprise with the Levantine coast and were using Al Mina (in Syria) as a base for this. There is still some question about the veracity of these claims.

The Phoenicians even got their name from the Greeks due to their trade. Besides cedar timber, their most famous trading product was purple dye, very important to the tincture of garments for royalty and the aristocracy. The Greek word for this die is *phoenos*. It is also the root of the Latin term Punic.

Late in their history, the Phoenicians established a large trading centre at Carthage, in what is now Libya, which was to become the successor to the original trading network based on the eastern terminus of the Mediterranean. It was inevitable that sooner or later the mercantile reach of the Phoenicians would run afoul of Rome's increasing overseas ambitions.

Given their extensive development of sea trading networks throughout the Mediterranean and beyond, one may ask whether this mercantile people maintained a thalassocracy. For all their dependency on control over maritime trade routes, there is no indication that the Phoenicians were fundamentally martial. That they built and crewed warships is not doubted. King Xerxes of Persia famously employed Phoenician biremes and triremes in his attempted invasion of Greece. Being as the Phoenicians left no discernible written records, it is difficult to assess the extent to which the Phoenicians engaged in combat with other naval powers, such as the Egyptians or Mycenaeans.

The indications are that the Phoenicians primarily employed warships to combat the uncontrolled piracy in the Eastern Mediterranean rather than in naval warfare. As they coveted trade more than territory, they avoided combat against other entities that maintained war fleets in the Mediterranean. Nonetheless, their ability to deter potential rival trading states from encroaching on their sources of raw materials and wares shows that Phoenician warships were not to be trifled with. They jealously guarded their trade routes and commodity sources, and for this task powerful warships were required.

Greece: An Intermittent Maritime Confederacy

By the time the Phoenicians' Carthaginian successor trading network was established, a major bona fide thalassocracy had already arrived. In general, Greece exhibited the same characteristics as Phoenicia. Greek city-states founded colonies but then retained little or no control over them. With the rise of the city-state, or *polis*, of Athens, we got something different.

Unlike Rome, with its rich farmlands on the Italian peninsula, Greece had no extensive flat tracts of fertile land. The myriad islets were largely rocky outcroppings, whereon productive agricultural parcels and livestock grazing lands were sparse. Apart from vineyards and olive groves, agricultural products for the most part had to be imported by sea, and fishing became an important food source. As Mahan would agree, their geo-strategic circumstances compelled them to look seaward.

The power of Athens began with the League of Delos, or Delian League, a defensive confederation formed to oppose the Persian invasion of Greece in 480 BC. All members made proportional contributions to the common defence, which were kept at the Temple of Apollo on the Island of Delos: hence the name. With the Persians defeated, the League continued. But the status of Athens as the predominant member became overbearing to the other members. Pericles wanted to move the Treasury of the League from Delos to Athens. He did this even though none of the other members of the League agreed. Athens then began spending the money for its own purposes, and the contributions of League members became in effect tribute paid to Athens.

The League became what historians now like to call the Athenian Empire, although such terminology is rather anachronistic. Nor is it apt. The 'empire' of Athens, with more or less unwilling participants, depended wholly on the ability of Athens to maintain naval supremacy in the Aegean Sea. If that were lost or disrupted, Athens would be powerless. This fits the ancient notion of 'thalassocracy', which does not comport with modern empires such as Tsarist Russia, Great Britain or Austro-Hungary.

Contrary to common belief, most archaic navies (and a number into the Classical period) depended largely upon privately owned vessels pressed into service on behalf of the *polis* (roughly, the city-state, centred on a metropolis not bound to any central governing power), one important exception being Corinth. It follows that most of these fleets would be without the costly triremes unless and until the *polis per se*, rather than individual citizens, took a leading role in the fitting out of the navy. In the case of Athens, this was not actually accomplished until Themistocles' naval bill in 483 BC. That event may properly be considered the commencement of the thalassocracy of Athens. It would last for only a generation.

The Persian Wars of the fifth century BC were the first to feature large-scale naval operations, both sophisticated fleet-to-fleet engagements with dozens of triremes on each side, as well as combined land-sea operations. It is highly unlikely that this burst of high-tech naval activity was the product of a single mind or even of a unique generation. It seems to represent the flowering of an unrecorded long period of evolution and experimentation. For its part, Persia, not an inherent sea power, made use of Phoenician ships and crews, either mercenaries or co-opted from captive regions.

After they had succeeded in subjugating the Greeks on the Ionian coast in a series of battles, the Persians set out to invade Greece proper. In 483 BC, the Athenian politician and general, Themistocles, figured that the Persians would outnumber the Greeks on land, but Athens could safeguard its population by building a fleet of 200 triremes, to become famous as the 'wooden walls', financed from the proceeds of the silver mines at Laurium. In the event, the first Persian campaign set for 492 BC was aborted due to the ravages of a storm on the Persian fleet, but a second effort two years later succeeded in capturing islands in the Aegean Sea before making a landing on the Greek mainland near Marathon. This assault was driven back by the Greek army in the celebrated land battle bearing that name.

Persia did not easily forgo its ambition of assimilating the stubborn naval thorn in its side, and under Xerxes I, repeated the pattern of the first campaign in a third (480 BC) by first dispatching the army via the Hellespont while the fleet guarded the foot soldiers' wet flank. In the narrow channel between the mainland and Euboea, near Artemesium, the Greek fleet repelled multiple onslaughts by the Persians. The latter succeeded in breaching the first line of Greek ships, but were then flanked by a second line of vessels. This momentary naval victory was squandered when the Persian success on land at Thermopylae forced the Greeks to withdraw, and the Athenian population, now exposed to the Persian advance, was evacuated to nearby Salamis island, this setback being commemorated in Aeschylus' famous play, *The Persians*, performed around 477 BC – the oldest known surviving play.

The subsequent naval Battle of Salamis is celebrated as one of history's most decisive engagements. Themistocles trapped the Persians in a channel too narrow for them to bring their greater numbers to bear, and attacked them smartly, in the end causing the loss of 200 Persian ships against just forty Greek. After the battle, Xerxes still had a fleet stronger than the Greeks, but withdrew nevertheless, and after losing on land at Plataea in the following year, returned to Asia Minor, leaving the Greeks to enjoy their freedom. All the same, the Athenians and Spartans attacked and burned the laid-up Persian fleet at Mycale, and freed many of the Ionian towns.

During the fifty years following their victory at Salamis, the Greeks commanded the Aegean, but were wracked with internal squabbles. After several minor wars, about which we know little, tensions exploded into the Peloponnesian War in 431 BC between Athens' Delian League and the Spartan Peloponnese. Naval strategy was critical; Athens walled itself off from the rest of Greece, leaving only the port at Piraeus open, trusting in its navy to keep supplies flowing while the Spartan army besieged it. This strategy worked, although the close quarters likely contributed to the plague that killed many Athenians in 429.

The breaking of the Athenian thalassocracy occurred in the war with Sparta, the Peloponnesian War (431-404 BC). Sparta had an invincible army, so the best that Athens could do was avoid it – relatively easy in a land of peninsulas and islands. If some Spartans could be trapped on an island, as did happen, then they could even be defeated and captured. This all worked fine until the Spartans began building their own navy. Once that happened, Athenian allies had an easier time defecting, since they were no longer entirely at the mercy of Athens. The Spartans could now support even island friends. And if Sparta could wipe out the Athenian fleet in a great battle, it would win the war in one day. The great battle came in 405 at Aegospotami in the Hellespont, where the Athenians had drawn up their fleet on the beach, and were surprised by the Spartan fleet, who landed and burned all the ships. Athens surrendered to Sparta in the following year. Destroying the Athenian fleet, the Spartans proceeded at once to the siege of Athens, which surrendered in 404. The Athenian thalassocracy burst like a bubble. However, the preceding Persian Wars are more representative in that they mark the full flowering of the sea power of Athens.

Navies next played a major role in the complicated wars of the successors of Alexander the Great. It would take more room than is available in this book on Roman sea power to fully describe the various naval campaigns of the successor wars. Suffice it to say that during this epoch, the upper limits of ship size was attained as each claimant to Alexander's legacy tried to out-build his rivals in terms of both numbers of vessels and the power of the individual warships, reflected in their great girth. This marks what Chester Starr and Lionel Casson have termed 'the age of the monster fleets'.

The next state heavily dependent on sea power was the Phoenecian successor power, Carthage. Carthage itself came rather closer to a thalassocracy, retaining control of colonies in the Western Mediterranean and then, under Hamilcar Barca, undertaking the conquest and development of Spain as a Carthaginian imperial possession. The confrontation between the pre-eminent sea power, Carthage, and the naval upstart Rome marks the debut of the Roman 'blue sword'. It will be discussed more fully in Chapter Three.

This is a good place to review what 'thalassocracy' might signify in the context of the period described by Thucydides.

Thalassocracy and the Limitations of Ancient Ships

'Thalassocracy' is the phonetic adaptation of a noun which has sometimes been interpreted as meaning 'sea power' in Greek. However, this conflates the Mahanian concept of the late nineteenth century with a term that actually connotes rule by those who *control* the sea, or alternatively command of the sea. The key to a state being a thalassocracy is if its power, even its political existence, would collapse completely with the annihilation of its navy. One such ideal example is provided by Plato's Atlantis, a notional sea power that he invented to demonstrate what he perceived to be the corrupting effects of maritime trade on an erstwhile virtuous civilization – primeval Athens. Ancient Greek historians – and, as I've indicated, particularly Thucydides – used the concept of thalassocracy as an analytical tool in investigating the past.

Obviously, they did not contemplate the ability of eighteenth-century sailing men-of-war, much less steam-powered steel dreadnoughts of Mahan's time, to cripple a weaker naval enemy's capacity to inhibit trade or threaten the transport of armies to critical theatres. Thus, it is a very time-dependent term, indicating simply a national entity which largely relied on the passage of trade goods by sea and possessed the capability to protect this commerce.

The Odyssey gives an account of a naval power in its description of the Phaeacians: they delight in ships rather than in war; their fault is isolation, rather than promiscuity in their foreign relations, the usual later criticism of maritime cities epitomized by Plato's Atlantean hypothetical. But Homer was essentially describing fairylands beyond the ken of mere mortals, although a hint of the notion of sea power in his time creeps in.

Thalassocracy, as is well known, becomes a clear-cut idea in Herodotus. According to him, Polycrates, the Tyrant of Samos, was the first who conceived the design of gaining the empire of the sea, 'unless it were Minos the Cnossian, and those (if there were any such) who had the mastery of the Aegean at an earlier time' (Herod., iii, 122). A period of thalassocracy is attributed also to Aegina (v.

83), located some 17 miles from Athens. During ancient times, Aegina was a rival of Athens, the great sea power of the era. Clearly her naval power was exercised not to dominate other poleis but to control trade.

In the alleged debate at the court of Gelo, the dictator of Syracuse in Sicily, where the Spartan and Athenian ambassadors are supposed to have come for help (Herod., vii, 157ff.), Gelo asks for the supreme command in exchange for his generous offer of ships and men, but concedes that he would remain content with the command of the fleet. The Athenians indignantly refuse to yield it: if the Spartans do not want to have it, the Athenians, who have 'raised up a navy greater than that of any other Greek people', are the only ones entitled to the succession. This is a typical piece of Athenian ex post facto inflation written at the time of the Delian League.

The Greek church father Eusebius (circa 325 AD) famously compiled a list of thalassocracies in his *Chronikon*, allegedly derived from Diodorus (Book VII). Diodorus' contemporary, Castor of Rhodes, is known to have composed a treatise on thalassocracies, now lost. It is possible that Castor and, in general, the scholars of the Alexandrian tradition were able to utilize fifth-century BC studies on that theme besides Herodotus and Thucydides, but there are no traces of such.

Thucydides saw early Greek history as a succession of thalassocracies, starting with, as we have seen, the mythical figure of Minos in Crete. As noted earlier in this chapter, some effort has been put into seeing Minoan thalassocracy in the archaeological remains of Minoan Crete and the Cyclades Islands, but it is now accepted that this is largely a fifth-century historical construction rather than an accurate reflection of Minoan realities. Nonetheless, there can be no doubt about considerable Minoan seafaring and mercantile reach. Most scholars allow that, at most, the term as used in relation to the Minoans should be modified to indicate a maritime trading network without much control over the foreign trade depots, not dissimilar to the early Phoenician system. It was not a 'sea-based empire' in the sense of operating from an organized structure of naval bases from which to dominate the shipment of trade goods, above all in the narrow passages such as channels and the short gaps among archipelagos. There was nothing analogous to 'task force' armadas constantly patrolling open waters or conducting naval blockades, so typical of the nineteenth and twentieth centuries and which forms the basis for much of the analysis in Mahan and Corbett.

The opportunity for such limited control as there was presents itself often in the maze of islands, straits and inlets on the north Mediterranean coast, and that opportunity arose more often in antiquity because of the ancient mariners' aversion to losing sight of land. Additionally, the ships were not capable of sustained maritime patrol in the modern sense – they had 'short legs'. The relatively large portion of oarsmen, plus the complement of marines, combined with the slender hull forms needed to achieve speed and power (for ramming purposes), meant that there was little room for food and water. In any event, no matter how fit the rowers were, they couldn't sustain a brisk pace for longer than it took for a feverish close-in sortie. But, as indicated above, the geography of the Mediterranean, Tyrrhenian and Adriatic Seas did not preclude the use of these ships to dominate the trade routes.

The oared galleys, which have been aptly described as large racing sculls, were thus incapable of much else than positioning at chokepoints and key positions on the coast. They were too slow to catch sailing ships with a good wind in their favour, whose speed they could match only in short bursts. They could not carry much of anything except rowers. They carried too few marines to secure a landing on a hostile coast and too few provisions to stay at sea for long periods, so normally they were beached every night. They could not prevent a fleet from crossing the open sea, nor could they blockade any long stretch of coast or operate at all without a friendly shore that could be reached in a few hours' rowing time. But they were independent of the wind and, over a short distance, were faster and more manoeuvrable than any sailing ship. Their range could be extended somewhat by a sail rig, the masts, sails and tackle of which could be stowed or, if possible, deposited ashore prior to engaging the enemy. The sailing apparatus would have taken up too much room on the ship, making ramming or boarding manoeuvres difficult. However, on longer expeditions, they still needed periodically to seek inlets or coves where they could beach for reprovisioning the crew.

They could attack or defend the supply lines of a large army. The Persians used them for this when they invaded Greece in 480 BC, for so huge an army had to be supplied by sea. In 415 BC, the Athenians landed another huge amphibious force against Sicily, and again the real function of the galleys was to protect the supply lines of the army. Likewise, galleys could attack or defend the supply routes of a large city. In the fifth century, a major function of the Athenian fleet was to guard the grain route from the Black Sea, which ran through the Hellespont, a passage highly vulnerable to the galleys.

The galleys were most effective against small islands or other exposed points easily cut off by sea; their ideal theatre was the island-studded Aegean, the inmost arm of the inland sea. Even in the Aegean, the galleys could command the sea only to a limited extent. For an apt modern parallel, one only has to look at the US Navy's quest and strategy for deploying a swift, manoeuvrable Littoral Combat Ship at the beginning of the twenty-first century. While these little ships may be able to undertake lengthy ocean passages to a theatre of operations assisted by underway replenishment oilers and victualling/ammo supply vessels, they are not designed to conduct combat on the high seas; they are best suited to operate in conjunction with naval or marine commando forces operating on the shoreline.

During the Peloponnesian War, when the Athenians moved to take over the little island of Melos, they warned the Melians that they should expect no help from Sparta, as the Athenian ships controlled the sea. The Melians replied that on the west they were separated from the mainland by a 70-mile stretch of open water, where the Athenians could never be sure of intercepting ships. The Melians were grasping at straws: Spartan help never came, and if it had, the Athenians would have done their intercepting not on the open sea, but at Melos harbour. Nevertheless, this exchange shows the common assumptions about the strategic reach of galleys.

On the other hand, the reader may find that the modern 'sea power' model has introduced features that demonstrably did not exist in the past. An example would be A.W. Gomme's demonstration that it is invalid to employ a modern naval operations concept to ancient naval warfare because ancient warships could not stay at sea for longer than a couple of days (Gomme, A.W., 'A Forgotten Factor of Greek Naval Strategy', *Journal of Hellenic Studies* 53, 1933, 16-24, quoted in Josiah Ober's study, *The Athenian Revolution*).

It has been seen that navies originated in the Mediterranean, with its access to three continents and favourable climatic conditions. Although the first recorded naval battle was about 1200 BC between the Egyptians and the so-called Sea People (possibly proto-Phoenicians), ships were probably used to transport and supply armies much earlier. Ancient warships usually relied on ramming, although sometimes catapults were used to fire missiles or incendiaries, and their crews fought as infantry, most notably in the opening naval battles of the First Punic War with the aid of the *corvus*, or grappling and boarding ramp. Later, the invention of the catapult-launched harpago filled this function. Galleys dominated the Mediterranean at least until the Battle of Lepanto (AD 1571) between Christians and Muslims.

In China, junks (high-poop-decked ships with battened sails) were used as fighting platforms for sea battles and for invasion fleets, such as the Mongol attempt to take Japan in AD 1281. In northern Europe, the Norsemen perfected oared Viking ships with square sails and strong keels that were used to transport raiders or for boarding at sea, but they could not ram or carry as many fighters as a galley. They were organized into small but effective fleets. It was to meet their attacks that Alfred the Great, in the ninth century AD, organized a royal fleet and became the first to realize that a navy was essential to England's security. But all this takes us beyond our period of interest.

It may well be that thallasocracies are merely historical constructs, more useful for categorizing historical trends than true determinations of absolute maritime sovereignty. In his 1989 book *The Influence of Sea Power on Ancient History*, Chester Starr wrestles with the idea of retrofitting Mahan's late nineteenth-century notion of sea power, derived from his study of the British navy from the late seventeenth to early nineteenth centuries, back to the ancient epoch. In doing so, Starr exaggerates Thucydides' much more modest idea of thalassocracy. His text in fact illustrates how the ancient naval powers that he discusses depended on their ships and fleets, even though this factor may not have been a constant nor equally important in all civilizations. In applying the term 'thalassocracy' to the ancient fleets, it is well to keep the more modest conceptualization described above in mind.

The foregoing discussion of thalassocracy entails estimates of the seaworthiness and reach of both warships and merchantmen in antiquity. This factor warrants some further consideration.

The Speed and Endurance/Range of Ancient War Fleets

A good deal of attention has been given to how fast ancient warfleets could travel under oars and for how long (time and distance) they could maintain flank speed. This calculation goes directly to the issue of the capabilities of warships in action, since it has been established that they rarely if ever utlilzed sail while engaging the enemy. Lionel Casson has given this factor much thought. The following paragraphs summarize his findings as spelled out in two of his books, *The Ancient Mariners* and *Ships and Seamanship in the Ancient World*.

The record 8-knot dash from Brindisi to Corcyra – a distance of 90 nautical miles – cited by Aemilius Paulus in 168 BC during the last Macedonian War is frequently quoted. But it was undoubtedly achieved with very favourable strong winds and assisted by spells of hard rowing. Yet fleets did not travel sustained distances under oars – when they did, it could not have been often nor for long distances that they made 8 knots.

Modern reconstructions of ancient galleys confirm the obvious: flank speeds of 8 knots taxed crews' endurance such that only dashes of several scores of miles were possible, lasting perhaps as much as ten or twelve hours at most. During a journey of any extent to the theatre of operations, they hoisted sail and depended on the wind. Here we come to a problem that has never been touched: how fast could a fleet sail under wind power? Lionel Casson, in the works mentioned above, has put together a credible table of likely speeds of fleets under sail.

In gathering the evidence to answer this question we must be very selective. We must not include voyages where it is likely that oars played a part. We may use those in which supply ships participated, for a fleet's speed is determined by its slowest members and the swift triremes would have no occasion to run out their oars when they had to dawdle alongside slow-sailing transports. We may also use voyages that lasted several days or more. On such occasions, oars were rarely used, if at all, since rowing was a short-lived power, to be held in reserve for battle or emergencies.

Casson's reliable data shows that before a favourable wind, a fleet could log between 2-3 knots. With unfavorable winds, a fleet could usually do no better than 1-1.5 knots. So optimally, the fleets could manage between 65-75 miles per day, and on exceptionally favourable journeys, as much as 85 miles. The discussion of trade and cargoes later in the book will treat the specifics of the various routes as far as can be determined from the literary, epigraphical and archaeological evidence.

A remarkable yet mostly obscure part of the Roman naval story concerns the fleets of the inland frontier. There is no well-known other case in history where a large-scale power deployed a navy for the control of rivers. By accident or design, the northern boundary of the Empire would be marked by the great rivers of Europe – the Rhine and the Danube – so a naval force was required to act in support of the army. The Rhine was the western boundary of the Empire from the time of Julius Caesar, with the Danube following during the time of Augustus, who sought to move the boundary north to avoid attacks emanating from the Alps. Augustus had Drusus and his brother Tiberius push east from the Rhine as far as the Elbe, but following reverses like the massacre at the Battle of the Teutoburg Forest in AD 9 , Rome retreated to its old boundary on the Rhine.

With rivers as a physical boundary, Rome needed a naval force to protect it: to protect merchant traffic, quickly ferry the army to vulnerable locations and control any adversarial movement on the waterways. Today, such operations are classified under the rubric 'brown water operations', or, if they are in estuaries or along sea coasts, 'littoral warfare', otherwise known as 'green water operations', essential components of modern sea power. The various Roman fleets will be referenced in the chapter covering that topic, while the operations of the riverine fleets and naval detachments accompanying the legions are discussed in the several chapters summarizing the maritime events of the Late Empire.

Rather than arbitrarily assign dates and sequential ordering to the gradual evolution of ship types that were employed by the various Roman fleets when the Republic, then the Empire, was establishing sea control, I thought it would be more helpful to readers to set out the various types of warships and merchant vessels (not always clearly distinguishable) employed by Rome during the span of the six centuries or so covered by this study. This is not such a problem as it might seem at first sight, since the evolution of naval technology proceeded glacially during ancient times, especially in comparison to the rapid changes we are accustomed to since the end of the eighteenth century. Rather than interrupt the text with asides detailing the characteristics of these vessels, illustration number two contains a tabular pictorial guide to the ship types and their characteristics, a handy guide, in graphic form, to the types of ships utilized by the Late Roman

Republic and the Empire in asserting control of the Mediterranean Sea and its outlying maritime frontiers. I next will consider the inception of Roman naval awareness.

Review of Naval Developments in the Western Mediterranean

At the risk of some repetition, I thought it would help to set the scene for the Punic Wars by briefly reviewing the relevant maritime events that prepared the arena for the great naval contest that launched Roman sea power and eclipsed that of Carthage.

Beginning around 1200 BC, the Phoenicians, from their base in what is now modern Lebanon, explored westward and founded trading colonies in the Western Mediterranean. Around 814 BC, Phoenicians from Tyre founded Carthage (near Tunis), and when the Assyrians overran the Phoenician homeland along the Levantine coast, Carthage became the protector of all the other Phoenician colonies. In 540 BC, in an early display of her naval prowess, the Carthaginians, allied with the Etruscans, recently united on the Italian peninsula, stopped Greek penetration of the Western Mediterranean by defeating the Phocians at the Battle of Alalia off Corsica. Since the Etruscans had limited themselves to coastal trade, the Western Mediterranean became an exclusive Carthaginian trading area, save for the Greek colony of Massilia (Marseilles) in southern France, which, in 530 BC, defeated a Carthaginian squadron offshore, assuring the survival of the trading colony.

In 510 BC, Carthaginian forces destroyed, then occupied, Tartessus (Tarshish) in southern Spain, extending Punic trade westward via Gades (Cadiz), and her trading vessels reached the North Sea (monopolizing the tin trade) and southward to the West African coast, which, in 480 BC, the Carthaginian explorer Hanno reconnoitred as far south as the present-day Cameroon.

Meanwhile, the Etruscans attempted to extend their reach southward to expand their trading area, but in 474 BC ran up against Syracuse in eastern Sicily, which by now had become the most powerful city in the Greek sphere of influence. At the Battle of Cumae, the Syracusan fleet defeated that of the Etruscans, halting the latter's southward expansion.

Carthage, sensing the value of establishing control of Sicily, secured the western coast of the island by establishing several possessions there. As Syracusan ambitions grew, Dionysus I attacked those colonies in 398 BC, inaugurating a two-year war. In 398, he captured the Carthaginian town of Motya with the aid of heavy siege equipment and beat off an attempted relief of the siege by the Punic fleet. In the 397 Battle of Catania, the Carthaginian fleet defeated that of Syracuse, destroying half of the latter's fleet, whereafter Syracuse was placed under siege. However, after Dionysius I mounted a combined land-sea night raid on the besieging force, the Carthaginians, already weakened by plague, concluded a peace.

In 356, civil war broke out in Syracuse, with the Democrat faction gaining control of the sea in a battle outside the city's harbour, thereby winning the civil war. Carthage, in firm control of the western areas of the island, made repeated assaults on the Greek half of Sicily in 312-306. Finally, the tyrant of Syracuse, Agathocles, landed with an army at Aspis (Clupea) in Africa, attacking Carthage in her heartland, forcing her to sue for peace. The lesson of this overseas excursion would not be lost on Rome, half a century later, in its own war with Carthage.

Chapter Two

Neptune Rising: The Measured Beginnings of Roman Sea Power

Clash with Tarentum, Invasion of Pyyrhus: Rome's Maritime Baptism

While it isn't strictly true that the Romans had not built a warship before the First Punic War, they were unquestionably neophytes at the practice of naval power. Expansion throughout, and conquest of, the Italian peninsula required little by way of maritime activity. With its lack of islands, and inlets and bays forming natural harbours in comparison to, say, the myriad islets and archipelagos of Greece that kept eyes always pointed seaward, sea-borne military activity would have offered far more inherent risk than reward for a budding power whose experience up to that point had always been on land. Though there was little demand at the time for attention to naval efforts, it may not be wholly accurate to claim that the Romans had not, in some fashion, begun to think about the sea – or, more correctly, the gains to be made in lands beyond the sea – an attitude which set the stage for their eventual ambition to spread power and influence on the far side of Italic shores.

What can we infer from the ancient literary sources' comparative silence about Rome's naval activities in connection with these pre-Punic War conflicts? The scholarship suggests that there are two opposing viewpoints, epitomized on one side by the sceptical sentiments of Johannes Thiel over half a century ago, and on the other by the 1915 dissertation by Frederick William Clark ('The Influence of Sea-Power on the History of the Roman Republic') and the more recent treatise by Christa Steinby (*The Roman Republican Navy: From the Sixth Century to 167 BC*) on Rome's conceivable earliest experiences with naval combat. Upon further examination, the perspectives of Thiel and Clark/Steinby are not all that different.

While Ms Steinby may have exaggerated to an extent in claiming that the Roman naval activity in the Second Samnite conflict, the Tarentian incident and Pyrhhic War was substantive, most can agree that at least these episodes mark the beginnings of 'naval-mindedness' among the Romans. Her Italic neighbours certainly appreciated the uses of the sea, and this was demonstrated to Rome as it tried to expand its domain beyond the plain of Latium. The clash between Rome and Tarentum, the southern Italian pretender to dominance in the toe of the Italian boot, corresponds with Rome's naval awakening, whether reluctant or not.

Although Thiel has been identified with a sceptical attitude towards Rome and the sea, a more thorough examination of Professor Thiel's writings will show that he did not ridicule Roman nautical ineptitude but rather accurately described their matter-of-fact pragmatic, albeit oft-times carelessly rash, attitude towards maritime navigation. He disparaged their nonchalance about approaching violent weather, an indifference that would result in the plurality of ship losses in the First Punic War. He considers her early (pre-Punic Wars) naval encounters to be faltering and inconsequential.

Numismatist Harold Mattingly, in his *Roman Coins from the Earliest to the Fall of the Western Empire*, examines some coins portraying Roman ship prows, likely dating from the late fourth century BC, and has sagely suggested that:

> 'The type obviously originated in a time when Rome's interests were turning towards the sea – probably, as we have seen, in the generation before the Pyrrhic war. The coins suggest that, if we had fuller knowledge of the years preceding the first struggle with Carthage, we might find the miracle of the building of the great Roman fleets in the First Punic War something less than miraculous after all.'

Although Thiel questions the imputed early date (338 BC) of these coins in the Mattingly book, it seems probable that they were at latest contemporaneous with the Pyrrhic War.

In 311 BC, two '*duoviri navales*' were appointed to supervise the equipping and refitting of the fleet, according to Livy. Each of these officials presided over a squadron of about ten ships, which were used to protect the coastal roads connecting Rome with its southern allies from the predations of pirate raids, which were frequent at this time. Many mark this event as the beginning of Roman sea power. Whatever the intended role of this minimal force, by 282 BC, Roman warships operated off the coasts of southern Italy. According to Christa Steinby, this occasion also likely marked the introduction of triremes into the Roman naval inventory, which theretofore consisted largely of biremes and penteconters, comparatively slow and clumsy vessels. As the crews of the modern Greek Navy's trireme replica, *Olympias*, will attest, manoeuvring this slender warship in battle takes a high degree of coordination and training.

Note, however, that with regard to the early part of Roman maritime history, Professor Thiel draws a sharp distinction between a system of state management embodied in the duumviral squadrons of 311 BC and an auxiliary system which originated in the fourth treaty with Carthage of 278 and was reorganized on an

Italian basis in 267 (see his summary on pp.38-39 of *A History of Roman Sea-Power before the Second Punic War*). Before 311, there were the humble beginnings of a state system; the auxiliary system was more recent. Consequently he agrees with those scholars who do not accept the possibility that the Romans in 386 BC dispatched a colony to Sardinia, and likewise he rejects the dating as early as 338 or 311 of the early Roman coins with the ships' prow. While no one could pretend that Rome was, or energetically wanted to be, a strong naval power at this time, Thiel underrates such interest as there was, based on his notion of the Romans' alleged inherent neglect of nautical matters.

That Rome failed throughout these early maritime efforts is undeniable, but failure implies perhaps lack of ability or resources, not necessarily lack of interest. With Steinby and contra Thiel, I stress the positive fact of the very creation of the duumviral squadrons rather than their miserable unfitness to do more than police the Italian coastline. It's unnecessary to give much weight to the supposed Sardinian expedition in 386 BC, but later in the same century we find, in 342, a Roman privateer operating with twelve ships in Sicilian waters (Diod., XVI, 82, cf. Thiel, p.7, and Strabo, v, p.232), in 310 the expedition to Corsica, in 306 the treaty with Carthage, perhaps a little later the treaty with Tarentum and, most important, about 306-305 the first Roman relations with Rhodes (Pol., xx, 5). At this time, Rhodes was a major regional sea power and Rome would have learned much from this relationship. Thiel holds that the terms of the Tarentine and Carthaginian treaties show Rome's weakness, but taken together with the construction of the fleet in 311, they do show a more serious awareness of the possibilities of a maritime future than he allows.

The fourth-century BC treaties between Rome and Carthage regarding spheres of influence shed some light on the former's incipient struggle to establish sea commerce and naval power. In the treaty of 348 BC, Carthage had undertaken to respect all Latin territory and coast towns as a Roman sphere of influence, and granted to Roman traders admission to the ports of her dominions of Africa, Sardinia and Sicily, as well as of Carthage itself. However, Sicily was considered off limits to Rome so far as establishing any permanent naval bases or trading stations.

So too were Roman ships of war to enjoy transitory access to these ports in wars against third parties. The Romans in turn were excluded from settling in Sardinia and Africa, accepted limits of Roman seafaring and recognized the Carthaginian claim to regulate trade in other territories. Carthage was also granted freedom of military action in Italy if attacked by entities or groups taking refuge there.

Roman merchants were accepted into Carthage itself and its possessions in Sicily, and Carthaginian merchants were to have similar access to Rome. Though Greeks are not mentioned, the effect of the treaty was to bind Rome, through commercial concessions, not to interfere with any Carthaginian attacks on the Greek cities of the south. A significant distinction was drawn between the protectorate of Rome and those cities which were merely allied with the Romans by treaty. In particular, if Carthaginians should sack a town in Latium which was not under Roman protection, though captives and loot might be taken away, the site was to revert to Rome. The treaties provide an eye-opening view of what had been going on out of reach of the tyrant Dionysius of Syracuse's warships.

Although the Romans undoubtedly understood the advantages of deploying ships to establish links with potential allies situated across stretches of open water, until the end of the fourth century BC they were totally absorbed in the struggles against rival folk within the Italian peninsula. This effort inevitably entailed land warfare. However, it cannot have escaped their notice that their neighbours to the north, the Etruscans, had exercised some mastery of supply and reinforcement by ship, or at least in utilizing warships to defend coastal logistical nodes against attack. The Etruscans had also enjoyed the benefits of a considerable import-export business conducted over neighbouring waterways in markets that the Romans likely perceived as worthwhile exploiting.

As Roman control of the Italian peninsula spread down through the sole of the boot, domination of Sicily became the *cassus belli* for the lesser conflicts that led up to the first great war with Carthage, as it was for the First Punic War itself. We have seen how Crete's dominating position astride the sea lanes of trade of the Eastern Mediterranean mercantile nations fostered the development of a Minoan thalassocracy, rudimentary though it may have been by current standards of sea power. Similarly, Sicily's guardianship of access to both the Western and Eastern Mediterranean induced the Romans to look upon encroachments upon that appendage just off the toe of the Italian boot as a threat to her very lifeblood. As J. Holland Rose has acutely observed in *The Mediterranean in the Ancient World*:

'But still more was Sicily coveted for its position; for it dominates the narrow waist of the Mediterranean. That island prolongs the mountain system of Italy and so belongs to Europe; but it also stretches out far towards the north-eastern tip of the Atlas Mountains of North Africa. Less than 100 miles separates Sicily from Cape Bon and therefore Sicily renders easy the passage between Europe and North Africa. But besides beckoning the two continents to intercourse it separates the Mediterranean Seas into two not very unequal halves. At the strait between Sicily and Cape Bon an enterprising maritime people, holding both shores, and maintaining a good navy, is able to hamper the intercourse between the two great parts of that sea. If such a people cannot altogether bar the way, it can at least make safe intercourse between East and West precarious. In fact, a sea power, occupying both Sicily and the North of Africa, will go far towards gaining command of the whole of the Mediterranean. And in ancient times to command that sea was to rule the known world.'

The importance of Sicily would first be demonstrated during the Pyrrhic War that ensued from the troubles between Rome and Tarentum (modern Taranto). It was early recognized by Carthage, then Pyrrhus, as the key to maritime dominance of the Western Mediterranean. The prelude to and events of the Tarentine episode constitutes Rome's expansion from a land-based urban and agricultural core to a central Italian power. While not the aquaphobic landlubbers of popular caricature, their immersion into Mediterranean maritime affairs, albeit hesitant and incremental, was ultimately inescapable.

Its position in the south-eastern tip of Italy made Tarentum an important hub for Mediterranean Sea trade and also isolated it from Roman naval activity on the Tyrrhenian Sea, between Rome and the islands of Corsica and Sardinia. Due to its position, and relationship with Greece, Tarentum possessed the most powerful navy of any Italian city at the time

As suggested above, the treaties negotiated with Rome's Carthaginian soon-to-be allies gives some idea of her emerging sea power, both its strengths and limitations. As the treaties are emblematic of Rome's initiation into external maritime enterprise, they bear further scrutiny. In the treaty of 348 BC, for example, Carthage undertook to respect all Latin territory and coast towns as a Roman sphere of influence. Carthage was barred from possession of territory, but not from activity. In particular, if the Carthaginians should sack a town in Latium which was not under Roman protection, captives and loot may be taken away, though the site was thereafter to become a Roman possession. The treaty seems to have made a significant distinction between areas under direct Roman protection and cities who were mere allies of Rome. Cities under Roman rule were to be immune from Carthaginian attack altogether, whereas allies were not. Roman traders and merchants were granted admission to the ports of Africa, Sardinia and Sicily, as well as to Carthage itself. Roman ships of war were to enjoy access to these ports in wars against third parties. Carthaginian merchants were granted access to Rome.

The Romans in turn were excluded from settling in Sardinia and Africa, and accepted limits on Roman seafaring. Importantly, Carthage was granted freedom of military action in Italy. It seems to have been a major Carthaginian concern to prevent Rome interfering in any of its attacks on Greek cities in the south of the latter's home territory. Carthage was evidently aware of Rome's growing military prowess; however, some have taken the terms of this treaty as evidence that Rome was not yet a regional sea power, as she, in effect, conceded Carthaginian veto power over certain naval and mercantile rights while Carthage simply formalized the dominance she already possessed.

Domenico Carro has pointed to the underlying cause of the ensuing war with Tarentum, and, ultimately, that with Pyrrhus (*Le forze navali, strumento essenziale della grande strategia di Roma*, in *L'esercito e La Cultura Militare di Roma Antica* – author's translation):

> 'Between the sixth and fourth centuries BC, the development of maritime trade, which also represented a lucrative source of income for enterprising Roman ship owners, was accompanied by a similar increase in the number of warships. But a very significant increase in the consistency of the naval vessels took place in 338 BC with the capture of the Anzio ships. To that point the Roman Navy had assumed the dimensions such as to allow wider use of the only defence of the commercial traffic. For the fleet, Rome consequently established the new position of command, the *duumviri naval*, while the new missions assigned to it reflects the determination of the Senate to consolidate and expand the maritime power of Rome: management of the safety of its coastal waters and control of adjacent waters down to Campania in the sole of the Italian boot; exploration of other coasts of more immediate interest; obtain overseas missions, as far as Greece; establish a dissuasive naval presence in most remote waters, and to impress the populace of the Greek maritime colonies at home in the Gulf of Taranto. This last mission provoked a hostile reaction of the Tarentines, creating the casus belli of the Tarentine war, the outcome of which allowed the Romans to complete its control over our peninsula.'

In the mid-fourth century BC, Rome established several maritime (Roman) colonies, which were similar to her military (Latin) colonies, except that the *maritime* colonists retained all their rights as Roman citizens, whereas the *military* colonists relinquished these rights and became 'Latins'. Latins (*Latini*) were freeborn residents of Italy (until 89 BC, when they were all granted full citizenship) and of certain other Roman municipalities who had some legal rights but were not full Roman citizens. The first of these colonies was Antium (modern Anzio) in 338 BC; then Tarracína (329 BC), Minturnae and Sinuessa (296 BC) were established. Later several others were founded.

Subsequently, when Antium was changed from a maritime into a military colony, its navy was destroyed, and the beaks (*rostra*) of its ships were taken to Rome and placed as ornaments on the speaker's stand opposite the Senate-House.

Hence the name *Rostra*, the origin of the modern term rostrum, denoting the speaker's podium. This place of honour may indicate that perhaps maritime power was significant even at that early date. On the other hand, the destruction of the vessels rather than their capture and utilization may denote a lesser importance. It seems at this juncture that Rome only had use for a token force of ships, as its army had adequately served to guarantee its hold on the peninsula. Antium had been taken from the landward side by the legions. In just over a decade, this offhanded attitude towards ships was to change.

During the conclusion of the Samnite Wars and that with the Lucanians, Rome had consolidated its position as master of central Italy, extending its dominion down just to the north of the Greek colonial city-states (Magna Graecia). The successful conclusion of the Samnite Wars allowed the Romans to solidify their hold over the coastal strip where the more significant maritime cities of the Tyrrhenian coast were centred. This dictated that Rome took a greater interest in and responsibility towards the Adriatic and Ionian coasts, thereby enhancing their naval capacity and leaving only the sea power of the Greeks of Tarentum to oppose their bid for hegemony on the Italian peninsula.

Given its rising power in the Mediterranean, Rome's conflict with Magna Graecia was inevitable. The Lucanians and Bruttians, in the early third century BC, continued attacks on these Greek colonies, and in 283 BC Thurii appealed to the Roman regional power for help. The most influential city of Magna Graecia at the time was Tarentum. It was the overlap of interests between this maritime mini-power and Rome that caused the latter to recognize that, like it or not, she had to deal with naval challenges on her doorstep. This, in turn, would draw her into her first experience as the target of an overseas expedition, one that would spill over to Sicily.

In response to Thurii's appeal for assistance, in 284 BC a Roman consul mounted a ten-ship exploratory expedition along the southern coast of Italia. Its purpose was ostensibly to reconnoitre and back up, if necessary, Rome's land assault on the Lucanians and Bruttians, but the Tarentines took great offence as this was in violation of a twenty-year-old treaty – similar to those executed with the Carthaginians – that restricted Roman ships from sailing beyond the Lacanian Cape, the western limit of the Bay of Tarentum. Rome did not seek to provoke a naval confrontation at the time, but considered the treaty outdated in view of her expanded role along her eastern shores and the need to buttress her interests there. Convinced that the Romans were up to no good and threatened their own influence with Thurii, the Tarentine navy attacked the Roman squadron, sinking five of the ships, killing the commander and selling the captured sailors into slavery.

Confident of aid from across the Adriatic Sea, the Tarentines rebuffed the Roman request for compensation for the sunken ships. The legions immediately began to march for southern Italy and Calbria. Realizing their land forces were no match for those of Rome, the Tarentines requested King Pyrrhus of Epirus to come to their aid. They had earlier helped Pyrrhus conquer the island of Corcyra, further evidence of their naval prowess.

If their relative weakness at sea hadn't already been made evident by the unequal treaties signed with Carthage and Tarentum, then the trouncing their ships suffered in the Bay of Tarentum would have driven this point home. Now their entanglement with their naval-minded Greek neighbours to the south embroiled Rome in a contest with a power that was soon to demonstrate the meaning of sea control, by its ability to send a large invasion force across an open body of water unmolested.

The Pyrrhic War

Pyrrhus showed no reluctance to heed the Tarentines' request for assistance, as he had been looking for an excuse to make a conquest (he desired an empire to the west, much as his cousin Alexander the Great achieved one to the east) and realized that the rising power of Rome impeded that objective. His real target was most likely Sicily, but the appeal by Tarentum offered him a pretext to obtain a toehold in the proximity of that island. It is likely that he did not anticipate a prolonged war with Rome, but would defend Tarentum rather quickly and then embark the bulk of his forces from Italy to Sicily.

Recognizing that their navy was not up to the task of frustrating Pyrrhus' landing operations, nor of interdicting his seaborne supplies once a beachhead was established, Rome formed an alliance with sea-power-savvy Carthage. In essence, this assistance was required under the latest treaty, but Rome couldn't fail to note her dependency on a more powerful naval ally – one which was soon to famously become her enemy. Carthage naturally rejected Pyrrhus' offer of an anti-Roman pact, even sending a squadron up to the Tiber's mouth to offer Rome aid against Pyrrhus.

Like many other Hellenistic people, Pyrrhus underestimated Rome. In 280 BC, he landed 25,000 troops in Italy, including some 3,000 horsemen, 2,000 archers, and twenty war elephants – the first elephants brought to Italy. The seaborne expedition sailed to Tarentum without interference. It is possible, as when he later reshipped his forces from Italy to Sicily, that the Carthaginians were given the slip. However, the longer open sea passage of a large armada would hardly be overlooked by the Carthaginian naval reconnaissance.

After two campaigns in which, though he always won battles, Pyrrhus was losing more men than he could afford (hence the term 'pyrrhic victory'), he moved on to Sicily (278 BC) to aid the Greeks there, who were being hard-pressed by the Carthaginians; the Romans had little difficulty in dealing with his allies and rearguards posted on the Italian mainland. That the Carthaginians did not interfere with Pyrrhus' crossing from Italy was likely due to their confidence that they could deal with such forces as he would land, which could be thereafter isolated by sea and deprived of a supply chain back to Epirus. Focused on Sicily, Pyrrhus thereby lost an opportunity to make inroads against the Romans, whose armies were as yet unable to cope with his superbly trained and experienced Greek soldiers.

The Carthaginians had not waited to be attacked. When Pyrrhus sailed for Sicily, they were already besieging Syracuse, his indispensable base, and looking for him with their fleet. He evaded their ships, however, and drove off their field army, captured the cities of Panormus and Eryx and refused their offer to surrender everything in Sicily except for Lilybaeum, which they direly needed if they sought to keep their hold on Sardinia. But all the while Pyrrhus' losses had been heavy and his reinforcements few. Tarentum was hard-pressed by the Romans, and between them and the Carthaginian fleet Pyrrhus might have been trapped in Sicily. So in a desperate attempt he returned once more to Italy to fight one more campaign. He faced the Romans at the town of Malventum in southern Italy and was defeated. After the battle, the Romans renamed the town Beneventum in recognition of their victory over Pyrrhus. He then retreated into his temporary base in Tarentum for the duration of the war. Pyrrhus soon left Italy forever, returning to the Greek mainland.

Jean Pages says of this conflict:

> 'Rome's victory over Pyrrhus in 275 and its alliance with Taranto in 272, which was, like Naples, constrained to provide wartime ships and crews, made her a Mediterranean power. The office titled *quaestores Classici* was created in 267; the officials were not intended for a command in a still non-existent fleet, but rather to control the mobilization of squadrons of allied cities of Rome, the *socii navales*.'

This interpretation comports with the pre-Punic Wars Roman inability or unwillingness to establish an indigenous naval force.

After their defeat of Pyrrhus, Rome was recognized as a major power in the Mediterranean, though their effectiveness at sea had as yet been untested, being that their ally of convenience, Carthage, had underwritten this component of military strength. Nothing makes this new esteem clearer than the opening of a permanent embassy of amity by the Macedonian king of Egypt in Rome in 273 BC. The Sicilian campaign and Carthage's effective use of sea power should have pointed out how Rome needed to develop self-sufficiency at sea if they were to maintain their status as a rising star in the Mediterranean Sea. But they were dilatory in recognizing this need so long as they still had the assistance of the *socii navales* ('naval allies') and Carthage.

New Roman colonies were founded in the south to further secure the territory to Roman domination. In the north, the last free Etruscan city, Volsinii, revolted and was destroyed in 264 BC. There, too, new colonies were founded to cement Roman rule. Rome was now mistress of all the peninsula from the Straits of Messana to the Apennine frontier with the Gauls along the Arnus and Rubicon rivers. But what of her maritime flanks?

We've seen how, from 282-267 BC, Rome had entered into agreements with Carthage to police her waters and to supply ships to assist Rome in the case of any naval operations. However, because of the mutual distrust that grew between these powers soon after the war with King Pyrrhus, Rome transferred the task of policing her waters and the provision of naval transports to her *socii navale,* the coastal Greek colonies in the sole and heel of the Italian boot, whose obligation was to provide either partly or fully crewed warships to the Roman fleet. With the defeat of Pyrrhus, the few holdouts among these colonies cleaved to Rome. Thus, beginning in 267, these Italian allies operated what was equivalent to an auxiliary naval system for Rome.

In the conflict with Pyrrhus, it was apparent that Rome was not strong enough on the sea to prevent the enemy from landing in Italy. Later, when Pyrrhus had crossed to Sicily, the Carthaginians defeated him again in a naval battle in which Pyrrhus lost seventy of his ships. The chief lesson of this war, albeit not fully realized at the time, was that Rome had needed an ally proficient on the sea in order to defeat a maritime expedition against the vulnerable seaboard of the Italian homeland. They had found such an associate in Carthage; but the very fact that Rome had to rely upon Carthaginian naval expertise came back to haunt them a little over a decade later when their erstwhile ally, in turn, blocked Rome's mercantile ambitions along the maritime trade routes converging on the Sicilian hub.

Thus, the next lesson to be learned – a hard one – was the necessity of naval self-sufficiency. As will be seen, this lesson ran counter to Rome's landward orientation, and within a few generations of victory was forgotten. When the crisis arose requiring such a Roman-built armada, Rome proved equal to the task. The way in which they created a first-class naval force nearly from scratch as a wartime emergency shipbuilding programme is comparable to the United States' Liberty Ship emergency effort of the Second World War; as distinguished from Rome, the US had already embarked on a warship expansion programme in the decade prior to the outbreak of hostiliies. Similarly, her employment of this naval force, after the opening of hostilities, was part of a painful, though urgent, learning process.

It was but a step from the Greek cities of Italy to the Greek cities of Sicily. But when Rome ventured to cross the Sicilian Strait, they were drawn into a struggle which was not ended until they were mistress of the Mediterranean. In passing beyond the limits of their own peninsula, they became one of the great world powers. The strength which they had acquired in their wars with the Latins, Etruscans and Samnites was now to be used in the greater conflicts with Carthage and Macedonia and Syria.

Chapter Three

Roman Sea Power Triumphant: The First Punic War and the Recognition of the Meaning of Sea Power

The First Punic War: A Crash Course for 'Landlubbers'?

The First Punic War is long-recognized as the pivot to the achievement of Roman maritime dominance; for the purpose of this book, which is to delineate the naval strategy of the Republic and the Empire, it will suffice to trace the salient attributes of that conflict with only that tactical information necessary to underpin these traits. Mahan, in the preface to his coverage of the Second Punic War, passes lightly over the first conflict thus: 'To whatever cause, or combination of causes, it be attributed, this essentially non-maritime state had in the first Punic War established over its sea-faring rival a naval supremacy, which still lasted.' His cursory reference to that conflict is perhaps attributable to his emphasis upon the ensuing war as illustrating the *effects* of the sea power achieved in the earlier conflict. In any case, it has been well-covered in detail elsewhere, (e.g., in J.E. Lazenby's excellent *The First Punic War* and Christa Steinby's *Rome versus Carthage: The War at Sea*).

The First Punic War is sometimes emphasized under the dubious assumption that it marks the acme of Roman naval power – or at least until the next high-water mark at Actium, whereafter it supposedly lapsed into irrelevance due to lack of a credible maritime challenger. What follows is a survey featuring the significant highlights of this naval contest. Key battles are briefly described, but only as necessary to assess lessons 'taught'; as to whether they were 'learned', I will address this question in my discussion of the Second Punic War.

The Strategical Setting

With Rome and Carthage separated by the sea, and Sicily – the main theatre for land operations – only accessible by sea for both opponents, naval power was set to play a crucial role in the conflict. The First Punic War was ultimately fought to establish control over the strategic islands of Corsica and Sicily. The war not only saw both sides undertaking large-scale operations on a strategic level; enormous amounts of manpower, materiel and not the least money were poured into the construction of large fleets, replacing recurrent huge losses. Indeed, going by the vast numbers of naval personnel involved, the First Punic War probably has to rank among the largest naval conflicts in history. Although it marks the ascent of Rome to become a world-class sea power, so far as serving as an exemplar of its exercise of this supremacy during the imperial epoch is concerned, it was a unique case, particularly considering how Rome some sixty years thereafter regressed to its earlier perfunctory attitude towards maintaining a fleet. This attitude prevailed until the sweeping pirate-quashing campaign of Pompeius Magnus and the ensuing Civil War, marking the demise of the Republic, when sea power conclusively demonstrated its importance to the well-being of Rome.

The distance from Carthage (near Tunis) to present-day Calabria, at the toe of Italy, is only 280 miles, of which 160 miles are formed by the island of Sicily. This leaves about 120 miles of open-sea passage to reach the Carthaginian principal base of operations in Africa from the nearest jump-off point not controlled by Carthage or sympathetic to her. While the Greeks and Phoenicians had been achieving such unsheltered water transits for centuries, it would be an especially bold and risky move for the comparative seafaring neophytes of Rome. Thus, their sights remained fixed on land warfare in Sicily until, after three years of inconclusive combat, they had to concede that they must contest command of the sea from Carthage to loosen the latter's grip on their western Sicilian strongholds sustaining the lifeblood of the land forces.

The objectives of the opposing sides might be summed up as follows. The Carthaginians wanted to protect and preserve their important commercial presence on Sicily, and likely contemplated that Rome would not persist in trying to dislodge them once they realized that Carthaginian sea power was a formidable obstacle. The Romans bit by bit recognized that they could/would not compromise in sharing Sicily with Carthage, as it was an intolerable check on their own expanding mercantile interests in the Western Mediterranean.

Rome did not recognize the need for independent command of the sea until the war had raged for three years on Sicily. This contradicts some historians, who presuppose a Roman hegemonic plan from the start of the war. The goal of driving Carthage totally out of Sicily, then from the sea altogether, evolved gradually during the first three years of the war. The strategic value of Sicily was forcefully stated in the paragraph from J. Holland Rose cited in the previous chapter. Its position was as critical to trade between the eastern and western sectors of the Mediterranean as was Gibraltar to Atlantic-Mediterranean maritime communications some 1,800 years hence. Up to the Mammertine/ Syracuse episode, Rome was content to share access to Sicily with Carthage. The importance that ridding Sicily of Carthaginian influence was to assume is a measure of the economic value that Rome's export-import trade had assumed by this time.

In Frederick W. Clark's doctoral thesis of 1915, 'The Influence of Sea Power on the History of the Roman Republic', the author notes three occasions when the determination of Rome to persevere with her pursuit of sea command survived demoralizing disasters. Her full appreciation of the need to control Sicily and Italy's maritime approaches was gradual and intermittent, thanks in large part to the negative impact of the naval defeats noted below as well as the temporary encouragement of progress in the land campaign, which Rome naively expected might eliminate the expensive and arduous task of naval rebuilding. These three maritime reverses are described below. Clark perhaps lays undue emphasis on repeated assertions attributed to Polybius regarding Rome's awareness of the need to overcome Carthaginian naval supremacy in order to prevail in the conflict. He devotes two pages to quotes from Polybius to that effect. Clark has supported this rhetorically expressed cognizance by referring to various episodes early in the conflict, discussed briefly below. This formulation is too glib. There was no sudden flash of cognizance of the need for a powerful fleet. The war's course only indicates a piecemeal, though tenaciously stubborn, Roman struggle to cope with Carthage's ability to replenish her Sicilian entrenched garrisons due to the latter's command of the sea lanes leading back to Africa. Polybius was engaging in ex-post facto rationalization.

At first reckoning, the struggle in Sicily would essentially be a land battle to secure a substantive bridgehead on the island. Sicily at this time was divided among three powers. (1) Carthage held all of the western part of the island, including the important cities of Agrigentum in the south, Panormus in the north and Lilybaeum at the extreme promontory. (2) The south-eastern part of the island was under the control of Hiero II, the King of Syracuse, who ruled not only this city, but also some of the neighbouring towns. (3) The north-eastern corner of the island was in the possession of a body of Campanian mercenaries, who had originally been hired by the King of Syracuse to defend his authority against rival claimants; these invited guests, on returning homeward, were apparently unsatisfied with their war booty and thus had treacherously seized the city of Messana.

Casus Belli

Contrary to some modern commentaries, war between Carthage and Rome was not unavoidable. As can be gathered from the several naval treaties described previously, and the tacit alliance during the war with Pyrrhus, there had been general agreement about their respective spheres of influence, with Rome implicitly acknowledging Carthage's superior sea power and her commercial interests in Africa, Sardinia and western Sicily, Rome being permitted to conduct some trade with Greek colonies on Sicily. Clearly, during the period covered by the treaties,

Carthage did not see Rome as a threat or serious maritime competitor, with her trade, such as it was, more coastal than transoceanic.

Carthage had been contending for control of Sicily with the Greek city-states of the island, led by Agathocles, Tyrant of Syracuse from 315 BC until his death in 289. Among his troops was a contingent from Campania, at the base of the Italian boot, the Mamertines or the 'Sons of Mars'. In general, this band of unemployed mercenaries behaved as freebooters and occupied the strategic town of Messana in the north-eastern tip of Sicily. They were apparently not satisfied with their share of the loot from assisting the Syracusan leader. After Agathocles' death, a new leader, Hiero II, rose in Syracuse. Under his leadership, the Mamertines were defeated and forced out of Syracuse. The Mamertines eventually took control of Messana, facing the Straits of Messana and mainland Italy. Situated on the narrow strait that separates Sicily from Italy, Messana controlled commerce and communications between Sicily and the Italian peninsula. From there, the Mamertines raided the surrounding areas.

When Hiero attempted to dislodge the troublesome Mamertines from Messana in 265 BC, the beleaguered band enlisted the aid of a nearby Carthaginian fleet (the Carthaginians were the major power-brokers on the island at that time), whose swift intervention forced Hiero to withdraw; the Carthaginians installed a small garrison in the town, occupying the citadel. This situation was somewhat unsettling to the Romans; heretofore the Carthaginians had largely been active in the western half of the island, but now had a foothold on the point closest to Italy and in a position to interdict all Roman maritime activity in the narrow strait, trade which was becoming increasingly important to the Roman economy.

The Mamertines soon regretted the Carthaginian occupation, which became tyrannical, and for a second time appealed to Rome for protection, citing their status as fellow 'Italians'. Contrary to some modern accounts, Rome was initially hesitant to become entangled in a conflict outside of Italy or to come to the aid of the piratical Mamertines. Indeed, Rome had only a few years before executed a similar group of their own soldiers who had lawlessly occupied the Italian town of Rhegium. The Mamertines did not appear to have a just cause in Roman eyes. Yet Rome's fear of a Carthaginian stronghold so close to Italy – and greed for plunder in what they assumed would be a short war against Syracuse – outweighed their concerns. The Romans, under the command of the consul Appius Claudius Caudex, somewhat hesitantly invaded Sicily and marched to the Mamertines' aid.

The turmoil in Messana in 264 BC had thus provided the opportunity the Romans were looking for to check the worrisome expansion of Carthaginian power on their maritime approaches. The Romans sent in a small expeditionary force, sufficient to eventually compel the Phoenician garrison at Messana to return to Carthage and bring Hiero to their side.

Although the matter of honour – coming to the aid of an importunate neighbour – was the superficial *casus belli,* breaking the Carthaginian dominance of Sicily clearly became the ultimate motive. But this goal was not initially based upon any premeditated imperialistic programme on the part of Rome. As mentioned, the Senate was at first reluctant to provide the requested assistance. They did not wish to aid soldiers who had unjustly stolen a city from its rightful possessors. The decision to ultimately intervene appears to have been an opportunistic and improvised reaction to turmoil close to home. This mindset was to change as the struggle for Sicily dragged on and it became obvious that Carthage could resupply and reinforce its Sicilian bastions by sea at will, no matter what the Roman legions accomplished on land.

War in Sicily, Land Operations *vis a vis* Naval Warfare

When the Mamertines learned that the Romans were approaching, they persuaded the Carthaginian general to withdraw his forces from the city. The general, regretting this decision to abandon the city, took the fateful steps of allying with Hiero. The combined Carthaginian and Syracusan forces then besieged Messana. After attempts to negotiate a truce failed, Carthage and Rome began hostilities. Both sides were confident of a quick and decisive victory.

In 262 BC, Rome won many small victories in Sicily, giving it control over almost the entire island. It was a see-saw affair, various local rulers switching sides back and forth according to who they thought was in the ascendancy for the moment. But the Romans at length realized that they needed control of the sea for final victory, and Carthage was a formidable naval power. Rome's transport of troops to Sicily was achieved by being able to evade Carthaginian patrols in their landings on the eastern side of Sicily (maritime blockade was unknown in the days of the war galley), but the maintenance of supply corridors to the ferried legions was worrisome.

The Carthaginians' naval superiority did not initially seem to be much of an obstacle to achieving the Roman objective, and consequently the war began as a struggle on land for Sicily. However, a major problem for the Romans in their invasion of Sicily was the lack of a fleet to transport soldiers to Sicily and keep them supplied. At the start, Rome sent a small initial force under C. Claudius to Messana, and then moved his two consular legions using ships from Rhegium, Locri, Naples and other cities. He was fortunate in being able to evade the Carthaginian fleet by a ruse, under cover of darkness. Meanwhile, the office of *duovir navalis* (one of two officials in charge of the navy) had lapsed in Rome, which was unprepared for naval warfare, relying upon more naval-minded allies for help.

Clark ('The Influence of Sea-Power on the History of the Roman Republic') criticizes the Carthaginians as being ignorant and lethargic in their failure to stop the Roman crossing to Sicily at the outset. However, this smacks of facile present-mindedness in assuming that it was possible at that time to anticipate that the Romans would launch such a maritime venture, and then that the Carthaginians were positioned to blockade or interdict such an expedition. Mahan had observed, as will be discussed in his observations on the Second Punic War, that blockade and interdiction was a hit-or-miss affair at that point in naval development. He said it was relatively easy for the Romans to utilize stealth and deception on such a narrow crossing, especially under cover of darkness, when maritime excursions in the vicinity of coastal shallows were rarely attempted, let alone by one who had not evidenced any nautical enterprise up to that time. At any rate, the timid reaction of the Carthaginian commander when confronted by the Roman troops in Messana is indicative of the local Carthaginian reluctance to engage Rome in warfare at this point. This disinclination might explain the lack of Carthaginian naval interference with the initial Roman crossing, although surprise and stealth are the likely principal factors.

At first, Carthaginian naval domination of the narrow Messana Straits blocked the Roman crossing from Rhegium to Messana. But under cover of night, the Roman flotilla made the risky 3-mile crossing from Rhegium unimpeded and achieved a successful landing on Sicily, with the assistance of the *socii navales* on the mainland. Thiel lays the ability of Claudius to make the lodgment in part on Hanno's hesitation and the unwillingness of both sides to provoke a full-scale war at this point. Darkness and the careful utilization of favourable winds and currents assisted in concealing the move until it was too late. Carthaginian warships were too distant along the coast to intervene in time. The Carthaginian superiority at sea had been sidestepped for the moment, but this factor was to underpin Carthage's stubborn hold on key ports on the western side of the island.

Carthage, after crucifying the dilatory general who had lost the strategic initiative by permitting Rome's invasion, adopted the cautious strategy that they had honed in generations of intermittent fighting against the Sicilian Greeks. Their mercenary army, operating from fortified towns, would harass the allies of Rome and Syracuse, eventually sapping their will to continue the fight, while allowing Carthage to make expedient gains when and wherever an opportunity arose. It was a defensive strategy, designed to preserve a status quo that was quite satisfactory to the Carthaginians. But the Carthaginians would soon realize that the Romans were a decidedly more powerful and lethal foe than the loose confederations of Greek city-states that they had previously fought.

The Romans initially waged quite a successful campaign in Sicily without employing naval forces on a larger scale. Syracuse remained a loyal ally of Rome throughout the rest of the war, and its aid was invaluable in maintaining supplies to the Roman forces on the island. In 261 BC, however, Rome finally decided that there was the need for a substantial naval force. The reason for this change of strategy lay in a revision of the overall objective of the war; after three years of operations resulting in a firm foothold on the island, the Romans now set their eyes on capturing the whole of Sicily. The experience of the Sicilian land battles had shown, however, that the Carthaginians – due to their control of the sea – could, with impunity, both support their main harbours on the island and stage landing operations there in order to capture coastal cities behind Roman lines.

Furthermore, a long war facilitated the Carthaginians' favoured tactic of reducing areas held or captured by Rome by sieges, in which they could supply and reinforce their besieging forces by utilizing their command of the sea. The suggested riposte to this long-war strategy was for Rome to shorten the conflict by striking directly at Carthage's home base. In the ensuing months of 261, the war see-sawed. The Romans would intimidate the Sicilian cities with the power of their army, but that army could not be everywhere at once. The Carthaginian navy would then frighten many cities on the coast back into allegiance. Further, the Carthaginians were raiding Italian shores with impunity, burning and looting towns and sowing havoc.

In sum, the Romans became discouraged at how the Carthaginian fleet quickly recovered lost Sicilian coastal cities and ravaged the Italian coastline. Their dominance made it difficult to even reinforce Rome's Sicilian garrisons. We have noted that, contrary to some popular notions, the Romans had even at this time a small navy, about twenty vessels, plus perhaps another forty available from the Greek maritime cities. The ships, however, were only smaller triremes, that were no match for the larger and more experienced crews of the Carthaginian quinqueremes. Roman sailors had largely failed in the few naval encounters prior to the Punic Wars, and they had not been eager students. Nevertheless, Rome had no choice but to surrender or match the enemy's vessels.

In 261 BC, having failed to capture several coastal towns, and suffered Carthaginian naval raids on its home shores, the Romans decided to build a fleet. After several years of campaigning in Sicily, the Romans realized that they needed to control the sea themselves and, even more importantly, had to deny it to the enemy, otherwise the Carthaginian bases in western Sicily would probably be impossible to capture. In other words, the only way to control all of Sicily was to control all of the waters around it. It was Rome's allies with a naval tradition that had provided the navy used to transport the first Roman army to Sicily in 264; only in 261 did Rome decide to build its own fleet of 120 ships.

The large Roman fleet was therefore not built merely to support army operations or to act as some kind of flank guard in battles near the coast. It was built to fulfill a strategic function – to make effective operations by Roman armies possible in the first place by dominating the Straits of Messana and all the approaches to Sicily. This is exactly the substance of the rounded notion of 'sea power' promulgated by Julian Corbett.

Opening of the Naval Conflict: Land Warfare Afloat?

Tradition has it that in order to counter Carthage's naval superiority, Rome built a fleet of 120 ships, 100 of them quinqueremes supposedly modelled (reverse-engineered) on a stranded Punic vessel. Since they had no trained seamen or naval establishment, according to Polybius, the training in rowing and manoeuvring had to be conducted on a mock-up of the galley deck on dry land. But note my earlier statements about how Hans Delbruck questions (as does Michael Pitassi, more recently) these assertions as a specious Polybian literary device, meant to denigrate prior Roman naval competence in order to accentuate the 'miracle' of her rapid ascent to the status of Queen of the Mediterranean. Rome had the experience of her *socii navale* to turn to when it came to the construction of warships; if this would have only sufficed to build triremes rather than the larger quinqueremes, it may have been that some of the latter may have been available during the war with Pyrrhus when Carthage was a naval ally. Whatever the method, the Romans' speedy creation of a fleet to challenge Carthage in sixty days is impressive. While it is possible that the stranded Carthaginian quinquereme may have provided some guidance as to the constructional details – such as the method of mass-producing the keel, rib and plank components by lettering the various pieces – there was ample opportunity to replicate these vessels as they were also in the inventory of naval asoociates and allies.

Yet another controversy that is sometimes exploited to disparage Rome's nautical prowess is the adoption of the *corvus* early in the war. On the surface, this would appear to be a purely tactical matter, but it was a key factor underlying Roman strategy in the opening phase of the sea war, so merits some consideration here. Its use is glibly attributed to Rome's inexperience at naval warfare and is employed to underscore her landlubberly aim to thereby turn sea battles into land warfare, the latter being her forte. While this is true to an extent, I contend that it does not constitute a slapdash strategy, but a keen appreciation of limitations and strengths at sea. Again, it was an emergency measure, a temporary expedient utilized until Rome could get her 'sea legs'.

The *corvus* (translated as crow or raven, named for its beak-like configuration) was a boarding bridge mounted near the bow of Roman warships, probably 20–36ft long and 4ft wide, with a parapet on each side. This was attached to a pole on the fore section of the ship, and could be hoisted up at an angle by a system of pulleys. Underneath the far end was a heavy spike. The idea was that the ship with the *corvus* moved close to the enemy vessel, and then released the device from its supporting tackle. The spike would dig into the enemy vessel and pin it in place, while the Roman marines charged onto the opponents' ship. This allowed the Romans to take advantage of their superior infantry.

Both Thiel and Wallinga note that the ability to manoeuvre vessels so as to engage the *corvus* was emblematic of a high degree of seamanship. So the skill necessary to execute the complex manoeuvres incident to ramming was not the *sine qua non* of naval mastery. Note that, early on, Athens had to resort to boarding by marines before they developed the ram and the tactics to accompany it. Should Rome have been expected to have acquired the latter skill during the relatively low-key naval activities it had experienced thus far?

Also, the fact that the Romans relied upon their strong suit at sea while neutralizing the enemy's indicates proper application of a naval strategy – at least during the early phase of the war, before the Romans could evolve their seagoing skills. The reasons for the *corvus*' discontinuation after the opening naval battles – and the date of its last use – is a matter of contention, some saying that the device rendered the ships very unstable, accounting for Rome's heavy ship losses in storms, while others claim that the Carthaginians developed a counter-weapon and/or tactics that nullified the *corvus*. Both suggestions are asserted rather than proven.

The *corvus* was first used at the Battle of Mylae, in which the Carthaginian fleet was badly mauled. This was not the first encounter between the two navies. The preceding confrontation did not show any evidence of the Roman edge, as there was no opportunity to bring the *corvus* into play. Though a minor incident, relatively speaking, it warrants some mention here.

In 260 BC, as soon as some of the newly built Roman ships were ready for service, they put to sea under the command of consul Gnaeus Cornelius Scipio and headed south for the Straits of Messana. Roman inexperience showed during this foray, however, when a seventeen-vessel squadron, an advance party sent to assess the possibilities of using Messana as a reprovisioning depot, was ambushed. Polybius has it that Scipio had been apprised that since the main Carthaginian naval strength was concentrated at their major base at Panormus, the citizens of Lipara, a small island off the coast of Sicily, had taken the opportunity to cast off the Carthaginian yoke and sent word to the Romans that they would be welcome there. Steinby (*Rome versus Carthage*) believes that this mission was not merely a rash impulse of Scipio's, as Lipara could have provided Rome with an important naval station from which to reduce Carthaginian influence.

Parties in Lipara still loyal to Carthage were able to send intelligence of this movement to the Carthaginian admiral, who sent part of his fleet (twenty ships) to Lipara at night to cloak his movement. Alternately, this whole episode may have been a ruse by Carthage with the intention of luring the Roman ships into a trap. In any event, the Roman naval advance party was cornered in the harbour of Lipara. On finding themselves hemmed in at daybreak, the Romans beached their ships and fled inland. The consul surrendered and his ships were taken as prizes. As this war would go, it was a relatively small-scale affair; the loss still left Rome with 103 ships of its newly built war fleet. However, the consul was taken prisoner.

After the defeat and capture of Scipio at Lipara, his co-consul Caius Duilius took command of the Roman fleet's main body, which had awaited news of the scouting party. In a second skirmish, the main Roman fleet repulsed a Carthaginian force that accidentally crossed its path while it was rounding an Italian cape – the sources don't specify which one – enroute to Sicily: the Carthaginian ships apparently were a reconnaissance in force, dispatched to look for signs of the approaching Roman fleet. They stumbled upon the Roman vanguard as it rounded the cape. The Carthaginians, after losing an unspecified number of ships (probably twenty), were able to break off and outrun the Roman vessels, which were relatively ponderous and slow. But it was still clear that Carthage had the better fleet. This perhaps qualifies as the first victory of Roman sea power, but it was nonetheless fortuitous and the Carthaginians were able to salvage most of their vessels.

Word reached Duilius that the Punic fleet under Hamilcar was raiding the area of Mylae, on the northern coast of Sicily. He immediately led the balance of the Roman fleet out to face them. This raiding was likely done with the intention of drawing the Roman fleet out to battle with them, as the Carthaginians were confident that they had the edge and this was a chance to trounce the large fleet that their spies and scouts reported as having been made ready to face them.

Polybius states that the Carthaginians had 130 ships, but does not give an exact figure for the Romans. The loss of seventeen ships at the Lipari Islands from a starting total of 120 suggests that Rome had 103 remaining. However, it is possible that this number was larger, likely 143, thanks to captured ships and the assistance of Roman allies at the southern extremity of the Italian boot. The Carthaginians anticipated an easy victory because of their superior experience at sea; they advanced rashly in a disordered fashion, with no semblance of control, against the waiting Roman fleet.

Polybius notes that when the Carthaginians observed the *corvi* trussed up high at the Roman vessels' prows, they were puzzled, not knowing what to expect. Florus goes so far as to say that the Carthaginian seamen ridiculed the awkward and useless-appearing devices. This bit of embroidery may simply reflect the fact that the Carthaginians, without an inkling of the Roman 'secret weapon', figured the apparatus to be a rather clumsy oddity that could only further hamper the bulky Roman vessels' ability to manoeuvre in order to evade the deft movements of the swift Punic ships.

The consensus is that the *corvus*, a stupefying tactical surprise to the Carthaginian admiral, was very successful and helped the Romans immobilize, board and seize the first thirty Carthaginian ships that got close enough. This included the Carthaginian flagship, and their admiral was forced to flee. In order to avoid being grappled by the *corvus*-bearing vessels, the Carthaginians were compelled to utilize their superior speed to navigate around them and approach the Romans from behind or from the side. The Roman vessels were able to react by quickly pivoting so as to deploy the bow-mounted *corvi*, and grapple most oncoming ships. Thiel presupposes a second line of Roman vessels, kept in reserve for exactly this contingency, which seems logical enough. Once an additional twenty of the Carthaginian ships had been secured, immobilized, boarded by marines and lost to the Romans, Hamilcar retreated with his surviving ships, leaving Duilius with a clear victory.

Instead of following the remaining Carthaginians at sea, Duilius sailed to Sicily to retrieve control of the troops. There he saved the city of Segesta, which had been under siege from the Carthaginian infantry commander Hamilcar. Modern historians have wondered at Duilius' decision not to immediately follow up with another naval attack, but Hamilcar's remaining force of eighty ships was probably still too strong for Rome to overcome.

The Roman victory was substantial on a tactical level. Some fifty Carthaginian ships were either captured or sunk, and the balance of power at sea began to swing towards the Romans. Duilius was able to celebrate the first naval triumph in Rome, and some say he began the tradition of displaying the prows of captured ships in the forum, though others credit the victory over Antium as the start of this practice.

Jon Wintjes, in his study of command and control in Roman naval battles, ('Command at Sea – The Roman Perspective', *Mars & Clio* No.22, Summer 2008), has examined a number of Roman sea battles and suggests that '[Mylae] was the result of operational planning on a strategic level that … succeeded insofar as the battle actually took place'. Operational planning by the Romans is likewise inferred by the way in which the Roman ships successfully manoeuvred so they could always turn their prow-mounted *corvi* so as to grapple and hold, while avoiding being holed by the Carthaginian rams. He believes that the evidence shows that this was a coordinated fleet action rather than a hodgepodge of single ship-to-ship melees. Wintjes holds that it was indicative that the Roman commanders had issued a series of 'general fighting instructions' prior to the battle, and that in 260 BC the Romans had 'made the strategic decision to seek out the Carthaginian fleet in order to destroy it' and thereby gain control over the seas around Sicily, breaking the ground stalemate there.

This battle has been traditionally viewed as a watershed, marking the beginning of Roman success upon the sea. However, the innovation of the *corvus* proved to be no more than a temporary expedient to offset the acknowledged Carthaginian superiority in seamanship and naval tactics at the war's commencement. How transitory this was is not clear from the ancient sources, and modern authorities differ as to both the date and the reason for its abandonment. I will tackle this issue later.

Lazenby (*First Punic War*) observes that the Roman success at Mylae did not pay off in terms of domination of Sicily. He argues that the Carthaginian navy was still too strong, consisting of not only the eighty vessels it was able to salvage from the battle, but likely enhanced with as many as thirty additional ships from naval allies on Sicily. The later Roman raids on Sardinia and Corsica were, in Lazenby's view, not part of the strategy that ultimately led to the invasion of Africa a few years later. He feels, contra Wintjes (above), that as yet the Roman fleet was conducting a defensive strategy and Rome did not believe they could defeat the Carthaginian control of Sicily by use of their fleet.

Thiel notes that even after Duilius' victory at Mylae in 260 BC, it was more than three years (257/256) before the 'second naval plan' (ferrying legions to the Carthaginian homeland) was taken in hand. According to Thiel, the Roman peasants (and perhaps the Senate as well) put the plain question 'why new ships after a victory?', and they had to be gradually acclimated to and convinced of the necessity for the African expedition which required this new fleet. Another reason attested by Thiel was perhaps jealousy: they begrudged each other and Duilius a success. Whoever would be in charge of a new fleet fitted out for an illustrious expedition would win many laurels, and the other senators left behind could not brook this fame and glory going to a rival leading family.

Rome Gets Her Sea Legs

Clark and Grant have pointed out the cyclical pattern that, following each of the three Roman mass shipwrecks due to storms, Rome had tried to fall back upon the prowess of her legions to prosecute the war on land, but when they failed to come to grips with the Carthaginian centre of gravity were compelled to rebuild their fleet. Considering what a costly and labour-intensive task this was, her determination to persevere is a testament to Rome's belated recognition of the necessity of maritime mastery. This doggedly determined mindset was principally inferred by Polybius from Roman actions.

In 259 BC, Lucius Cornelius Scipio (there would be a confusing number of Scipios leading land campaigns in this war, much as the Carthaginians had multiple Hasdrubals, Hannibals and Hannos) invaded Corsica and quickly captured the town of Alalia. Attempts to repeat this success in Sardinia failed – the complete subjugation of Corsica would take another century – but the ultimate result was the loss of Carthaginian control of both islands. The following year saw a victory at sea by C. Sulpicius off Sulci in Sardinia. This battle, though rating hardly a footnote in Polybius, merits some attention here either as a curious sideshow or a portent of things to come.

Thiel *(Roman Sea-Power Before the Second Punic War)* doubts that the Sardinian venture reflects some broader strategy leading towards the Roman invasion of Africa, but suggests that at this point it was likely a ruse. The Roman commander, Gaius Sulpicius Paterculus, Thiel notes, likely feinted a move against Africa to draw the Carthaginian flotilla out of the harbour, and then, hiding his ships behind a mist, ambushed the Carthaginian ships, inflicting some casualties. However, Lazenby suggests that the assaults on Corsica and Sardinia may have been reactive rather than proactive, undertaken simply to eliminate Carthaginian bases from which the Punic fleet was making sorties against Sicily and the Italian mainland. Grainger (*Hellenistic and Roman Naval Warfare 336BC – 31BC*), on the other hand, suspects that the Romans may have been attempting to take Sulci as a more convenient naval base than distant Ostia and Messana from which to wrest control of western Sicily from Carthage. Lazenby (*First Punic War*) thinks it nonetheless reflects a defensive naval strategy, since it was merely an effort to stop Carthaginian raids against the Italian coast which were launched from the two islands. In any event, it signals increased sophistication and confidence among Roman seamen.

On land, in Sicily, Atilius Regulus attacked the city of Panormus and captured Mytistratus. The following year (three years after Duilius defeated the Punic fleet at Mylae), Regulus followed up his successes in Sicily with naval victories off Tyndaris and raids on the coast of Malta. The Tyndaris battle was interesting and bears further scrutiny.

The sources are contradictory as to the events preceding and accompanying this naval clash near Tyndaris in 257 BC. It seems that the Romans, in 258/257, had mounted a campaign against Lipara, the site of their earlier defeat off the Sicilian coast, and this victory was followed up by an attack on Malta. Gaius Atilius Regulus' fleet was anchored off Tyndaris when he observed the Carthaginian fleet sailing past, without it being arranged in a tactical formation. He gave orders for the main body of his ships to follow the leading ships. He then took an advance guard of ten ships and sailed towards the Carthaginians. The Carthaginians noticed that the advance guard had managed to outdistance the main body of the Roman fleet and that other Romans were still boarding their vessels. Taking the initiative, the Carthaginians turned and engaged the Roman squadron and sank nine Roman ships. Meanwhile, the rest of the Roman fleet arrived and formed a line. The Romans then engaged the Carthaginians, sinking eight and capturing ten of their ships. The remainder of the Carthaginian ships retreated to the Aeolian Islands. The subsequent attack against Malta, according to Lazenby (*First Punic War*), may signify a phased advance on the Carthaginian base in Africa. However, Dexter Hoyos, while admitting this may be the case, considers that the venture was a little counterproductive, as Malta is not best positioned for an attack on Carthage, and it alerted the Carthaginians that the Romans were indeed ranging far out to sea and to prepare a defence of home shores accordingly.

The Roman naval successes in this phase signalled a naval arms race between the two contenders, the Senate commissioning more ships, prompting the Carthaginians to do the same. When the two fleets met again in 256 BC, Rome manned 330 ships against perhaps as many as 350 Carthaginian vessels. The biggest naval battle of the war came in 256 BC as the initial phase of the Roman invasion of Africa. The two fleets met at the Battle of Ecnomus, probably the largest naval battle in history, at least in terms of the numbers of men involved, and once again Rome was victorious. In 256, the Roman fleet continued its successes, under L. Manlius Vulso and Atilius Regulus, in naval action off the coast of Sicily. Despite their victories, stalemate reigned in western Sicily and Rome felt the only way to achieve victory was to invade North Africa itself. In preparing to sail, the two fleets met at Ecnomus off southern Sicily.

Agathocles, a king of Syracuse, had already pointed the way to defeating the Carthaginians in the so-called Battle of White Tunis; with sixty triremes, Agathocles managed to escape a Carthaginian blockade of Syracuse in August 310 BC. His fleet narrowly avoided a naval battle with a pursuing Carthaginian fleet as they landed legions at Latomiae, near the modern Cape Bon, the headland of Tunisia. This relatively recent example of a bold overseas expedition, albeit ultimately unsuccessful, was to resonate with Rome.

How bold a move this was for the fledgling Roman sea power can be gauged by the fact that the initial invasion of Sicily eight years earlier entailed merely traversing a narrow strait 2-5 miles wide – and this with the essential aid of the naval associates, helped somewhat by Carthaginian laxity. It marked the first, albeit cautious, venture of Rome beyond Italian shores. In contrast, the African invasion entailed a bold crossing of some 85-100 miles of open ocean, endangered by a fully alerted, vigilant Carthaginian naval armada.

Ecnomus was a relatively complex battle, entailing the Romans proceeding with approximately 330 warships from Italy via Messana to the Ecnomus promontory on the south coast of Sicily, which was to be the jumping-off point for the invasion of Africa. Thiel, Christa Steinby and J.F. Lazenby have described the battle in some detail. It is not necessary to delve into the tactical complexities of this hard-fought battle to understand its strategic implications. Dr Steinby notes that the Roman flotilla skirted the southern coast of Sicily because the Carthaginians still had a number of ports on the north coast from which they could launch a strike at the fleet. She suggests that the Romans decided to hug the south coast of Sicily as far as practicable so as to reduce the distance of the open-sea crossing. The Roman ships had apparently picked up their horse transport, which had embarked the 40,000 troops and several thousand horses, at the staging area near the cape of Ecnomus as they were towing them when the Carthaginian fleet came out to meet them.

Both Steinby and Lazenby remark on the apparent increase in tactical skill shown by the Roman consuls. There is some difference of opinion as to whether the Romans had intended to draw the Carthaginian fleet out to do battle, but given that the former were encumbered by having to tow the unwieldy horse transports behind a wedge formation of soldier-laden warships, this is unlikely.

What probably happened is that the Carthaginian spy network in the Greek cities of Sicily informed the Punic commanders of the gathering of the vast Roman fleet at Messana and its progress along the southern coast. This gave enough warning for the Carthaginians to assemble their own fleet of roughly the same number of vessels, albeit all swift quinqueremes, and then proceed eastward along the southern coast to meet the oncoming Roman armada. The Roman warships had already landed to embark the horse transports at the staging area in southern Sicily. It was likely the Carthaginians planned to allow this to take place unmolested, as it was felt that the presence of the cumbersome animal transports would render the Roman fleet more vulnerable to the swiftly manoeuvring Punic ships.

Upon assessing the Romans' formation, Hanno and Hamilcar, the two Carthaginian commanders, adjusted their battle plan to try to isolate the Roman escorts from the horse transports and take the second tier in the flank and rear, while avoiding the ship beaks with the *corvi* of the outermost wings. Apart from one echelon that was trapped against the shore and almost forced to beach, the Roman fleet adjusted so as to bring their *corvi* to bear against the Punic ships as the latter attempted to ram them. Punic losses amounted to more than ninety vessels, while the Romans suffered just twenty-four ships sunk.

The victory at Ecnomus facilitated the invasion of Africa. Landing at Aspis in Africa, Regulus was at first successful in a series of battles on the Tunisian peninsula. Already discouraged by the steep cost of the war thus far, consul Vulso returned to Italy with part of the army to ease the financial burden, leaving Regulus with between 15,000-20,000 men. In the spring of 255 BC, the campaign was resumed and Regulus was on the verge of victory. But when the Carthaginians sued for peace, harsh terms demanded by Rome ensured a resumption of fighting. Carthaginian citizen levies having proved ineffective, Carthage looked to mercenaries to expel the invaders, in this case the legendary Spartans under Xanthippus. This expedient proved effective. The Spartans, along with Carthaginian elephants – a surprise weapon to rival the Roman use of the *corvus* at sea – met the Romans with equal force at the Battle of Bagradas and utterly destroyed the army of Regulus. Of the 20,000 or so Romans, only 2,000-3,000 escaped to Aspis; the rest, along with Regulus, were killed or captured.

News of the Roman defeat at the land battle of Tunis led to the rapid formation of a large fleet, possibly as high as 350-strong (though Thiel suggests a lower number, perhaps only 250, with the addition of the squadron waiting at Clupaea), under M. Aemilius Paullus and Fulvius Nobilior, which sailed across to Africa to rescue the survivors. Carthage managed to put together a fleet of 200 ships to face at least 210 in the Roman fleet, but after a series of defeats at sea their morale may have been poor, and the skill of the rowers perhaps lagging owing to the depletion of their numbers at Ecnomus.

En-route from Sicily to Africa, the Romans were driven from their course by a storm and reached the island of Cossyra (modern Pantelleria) some 62 miles south-west of Sicily and 37 miles east of Cape Hermaeum – a perfect way-station on the route to Africa, had the Romans been deliberately seeking one. They were able to plunder the islands for such water and victuals as they could find and then proceed to seek out the Punic fleet at Cape Hermaeum, which location their sources had divulged to them by this time. Thus they approached the cape in battle formation.

The Carthaginians, alerted to the oncoming Roman flotilla, were already predisposed to protect their rear echelons (*Zonaris* 1.1), and the sudden arrival of Roman reinforcements in the form of the contingent of forty ships from Clupaea caused them to post themselves close to land with their backs to the beach to avoid envelopment. However, they soon discerned that this arrangement posed the worse danger of being driven ashore by the oncoming threat of grappling by the Roman *corvi*, and they thus retired to escape being grappled. Thiel believes that this is the only explanation for the high ratio of undamaged ships that fell into the hands of the Romans with their crews: 114 Punic ships were captured and added to the Roman fleet, and possibly just sixteen destroyed. Tarn compares this battle to its converse in the Roman defeat at Drepana six years later (see below).

With control of the African coast secured, they were able to withdraw all the remaining troops at Aspis. Polybius, our main source for the First Punic War, is reticent about this engagement, a terseness which the reported lopsided victory does not warrant. Perhaps he judged that the ensuing shipwreck by storm eclipsed the victory by combat. Thiel, as usual, manages to craft educated speculation from sparse data, and I follow him here. Again, the tactical details of the battle are not important to my theme, but rather reflect how the incident affected Rome's evolving cognizance of naval strategy.

Neptune's Wrath: Storm Wrecks, Reversals and Recovery

On their return to Sicily, the consuls rashly decided to attempt to intimidate the Carthaginians and their remaining allies on Sicily, and attempted to sail along the south-west coast in a gratuitous show of force. A storm promptly blew up while this fleet was off Carmarina, and perhaps as many as three-quarters of the 264 Roman ships and their crews were lost, with approximately 100,000 rowers, marines and the rescued legionaries doomed when the ships were dashed against the rocks in coastal waters. The Romans, despite the incredible loss to available manpower, showed their resilience, and would eventually rebuild the fleet and retrain crews. However, for the meantime, she abdicated the naval initiative and concentrated on trying to consolidate progress on land in Sicily. This would, however, require a substantial naval component when attempting to break the firm Carthaginian hold on their powerful base at Lilybaeum.

In an impressive sign of the strength and stubbornness of Rome, another fleet of 220 ships was constructed the next year, which played a part in the capture of the fortress town of Panormus (254 BC), after which Rome pressed on with its naval operations. A raid along the African coast was interrupted by yet another improvident failure to gear up to meet an oncoming storm in 253 BC, which resulted in the loss of 150 ships of a Roman fleet at Cape Palinurus. This second costly shipwreck by storm found the Senate and the Roman allies alike nearly bankrupt and short of manpower. This crisis was thus followed by a period of quiet on the part of the Roman fleets, causing the Senate – at least in the short term – to concentrate on land warfare. By 252 BC, this switch to reliance on the legions brought about more success in Sicily with the capture of Lipara and Thermae, the defeat of a Carthaginian relief effort at Panormus and the onset of a lengthy siege of Lilybaeum. By 250 BC, the Romans regained confidence and decided to return to the sea.

Thiel correctly speaks of 'the relative imperturbability of public opinion in Rome' (p.242), as proven by the building of a new fleet in the winter of 255/54 BC after the further storm-related disasters of 255. The same cool-headedness might have permitted the building of new ships after Duilius' success at Mylae if the senators had agreed upon the strategy.

Rebuffing Carthaginian efforts to come to terms for a settlement, Rome rebuilt its fleet once more to protect its siege of Lilybaeum from the arrival of a large Carthaginian fleet, under Adherbal, lying near Drepanum. It was a sign of the strain that Rome was under that the blockading fleet of 253 BC was financed by private individuals rather than the state. A fleet of 123 ships under Publius Claudius Pulcher was sent to engage the Carthaginian resupply/relief force in an attempted surprise attack. Pulcher, relatively inexperienced at sea, was badly beaten, losing ninety of his ships against less than ten by Carthage, which initially had about 100 vessels.

Thiel notes that the Roman line-ahead formation anticipated that the Carthaginian admiral would be surprised while at anchor in the harbour, and Pulcher made another fatal error in having his command ship stationed at the rear to spur laggards, thereby losing the ability to direct the action of his vessels or gain an appreciation of what was transpiring. His line-ahead formation was not one that was advancing to engage the enemy, but planned merely to blockade in harbour a quiescent and sleeping enemy fleet. Thus when Adherbal quickly manoeuvred to escape to the open sea, where he could move to slice up the Roman line formation, Pulcher's reaction was dilatory. Pulcher escaped with only thirty ships of his original force. Incidentally, regarding the abolition of the *corvus*, Wallinga places this change *after* Drepanum rather than backing Thiel, who puts it *before* that action.

As if Poseidon was angry with Rome for her impudent encroachment on his domain, she suffered yet another in her run of weather-related shipwrecks when a fleet under L. Junius Pullus, including some of the few surviving ships from Drepanum, was destroyed in a storm near Camarina.

In the same year, the Romans sent a fleet (numbering possibly as many as 800 ships) around the southern tip of Sicily to supply their troops in the west of the island. This fleet was also destroyed in a storm on the south coast, near Camarina, and Rome broke off the war at sea completely. Punic raiders now harassed the entire Italian coast. The Punic fleet was able to bring reinforcements to Sicily undisturbed, and Hamilcar Barca there gave the Romans stiff resistance, especially in the struggles for Panormus and Lilybaeum. Finally, rich Roman merchants, citizens and shipowners built and crewed a fleet of 200 warships at their own cost. When it was learned in Carthage that the new Roman fleet had set out for Sicily, the Carthaginian fleet was also dispatched to support Hamilcar Barca.

With three Roman fleets decimated within a few years, the prospects for resuming a naval war looked bleak. The battle in Sicily was at a standstill, with a relatively quiet period of two years until 247 BC and the entry to Sicily of Hamilcar Barca (father of Hannibal, the scourge of Italy during the Second Punic War), who drove back all Roman attacks over a period of four years. While unable to expand Carthaginian territory in Sicily or bring the fight to the Italian mainland, he seemingly ended Rome's ability to dominate the war on the ground. As the cause seemed near to being lost, or her gains untenable, Rome's traditional stubborn tenacity took hold again. With a loss of one-sixth of their population and the liquidation of a vast treasury, they still persisted in the attempt to conquer Sicily. Wealthy citizens again advanced their own money to build a new fleet of 200 ships.

In 241 BC, one of the consuls for 252, Caius Lutatius Catullus, led the reconstituted 200-strong Roman fleet to Sicily with the apparent aim of forcing a naval battle. He met the Carthaginian fleet in a decisive victory at the Aegates Islands, off the western extremity of Sicily. The 170 Carthaginian ships were laden with grain and supplies for Hamilcar's army, holed up on Mount Eryx, and the fleet had thus lost its manoeuvrability. Further, the Roman ships, built without mounting the *corvus*, were thereby lighter and more manoeuvrable than the Carthaginian vessels, even if the latter had not been heavily laden.

In the resulting battle, over half of the Carthaginian fleet was lost. It was recorded that fifty of the Carthaginian galleys were sunk outright and seventy captured. The remaining vessels were only saved by a fortuitous change in wind direction, allowing them to escape back to Africa. The Romans took nearly 100,000 prisoners, and Hamilcar, with no way to be resupplied and after twenty-three years of war, was forced to sue for peace.

Following the Battle of Mylae, with both sides balanced, the war between Rome and Carthage had continued for twenty years until the war-weary Phoenicians gave up in 241 BC. According to Lazenby (*First Punic War*), 'To Rome, wars ended when the Republic dictated its terms to a defeated enemy; to Carthage, wars ended with a negotiated settlement.' At the end of the First Punic War, Rome won a new province, Sicily, and began to look further into the sea lanes, through which to project power and protect trade. This marked the commencement of Romans as empire builders, a task for which powerful fleets were haltingly acknowledged as essential. Carthage, on the other hand, had to compensate Rome for its heavy losses. Although the tribute was steep, it did not keep Carthage from continuing as a world-class trading power – and a rival to Rome. With both sea powers exhausted from the twenty-year conflict, it would seem that a protracted *modus vivendi* would logically follow. However, the peace would turn out to be no more than a twenty-year truce.

Implied Lessons of the First Punic War

Should she choose to heed them, Rome had been afforded important lessons regarding the employment of naval power in wartime; however, the warnings concerning its misapplication presented by the several Roman naval setbacks appear to have been overlooked. Briefly, the Roman mistakes may be summed up as follows. First, the popular assembly which accepted the alliance with Messana seems to have failed to realize that the Carthaginians were bound to try to eject them from Sicily. To fight Carthage, Rome would need a navy; she had none of her own, and even in the treaty with Hiero demanded no naval assistance from his fleet. The assistance furnished by the Greek cities of Italy's southern shores might have been sufficient to cross the narrow channel separating Sicily from the Italian coast, but would not suffice to fight the kind of protracted conflict Rome had courted, wherein lines of supply and reinforcement had to traverse contested waters.

Secondly, Rome made her struggle in Sicily much harder because she alienated all the Greek settlements on the island – erstwhile allies with naval experience and assets – by her ungenerous treaty with Hiero and the massacre of non–combatants at Agrigentum. Thirdly, she was very slow to realize that the only way to get the Carthaginians out of Sicily was to strike at Africa.

One conspicuous lapse in Roman strategy, pointed out by Thiel (*Roman Sea Power before the Second Punic War*), was that in 253 BC they should have started the systematic blockade of Lilybaeum, instead of the African raid, which was followed by the loss of the fleet in a storm. The one fatal Carthaginian blunder, he believed, was to let slip the opportunity of offensive action in Sicily in 248 BC. Late in the war, it was shown that breaking the Carthaginian sea line of communication and supply to her western Sicilian bastions would have sufficed to end the war on Roman terms. Thiel sees beneath the decision to fritter away time and ships upon a futile effort to intimidate and demoralize the Carthaginians by raids near the home base a split in senatorial factions in 253: one favouring a full-scale repeat of the invasion of 256-255, and the other a concerted sea-land blockade of Lilybaeum. The fact that Hasdrubal was able to strongly reinforce the garrison of Lilybaeum *after* the raids near Carthage demonstrates the failure of the African strategy. Of course the Romans could not have predicted the weather-inflicted disasters en route back to Italy, but they were well aware of the constant threat of storms on long sea passages. The decimation of the fleet left them open to the disaster at Drepanum, where numerical disadvantage was exacerbated by incompetent naval command.

Rome continued to change the command and appoint inexperienced men, though few were quite so incompetent as Regulus in the expedition of 256/255. His failure was on land, but it had implications for Rome's naval ambitions to strike at the Carthaginian heartland. When faced by the elephants and Spartan phalanx of Xanthippus, Regulus massed his legionaries, thus making them easy prey to the Carthaginians' human and animal battering ram. The invasion of Africa turned out to be a major failure for Rome, but its undertaking proved its entrance into the field of major players in the ancient world. That this lesson had been absorbed is evidenced by the fact that a more sophisticated plan for an African expedition was set in motion at the Second Punic War's outset, though postponed by the need to meet Hannibal's unexpected trans-Alpine overland invasion of Italy.

Most significantly for the naval lessons, Rome had shown that she could neither anticipate or deal with impending tempests at sea and take appropriate precautions. Romans certainly had not mastered the seamanship required to navigate around or, where unavoidable, through stormy seas. While the Carthaginians wisely took their vessels to sheltered waters or out of the path of oncoming storms where possible, Rome seemed incapable or unwilling to take these precautionary measures, resulting in ship losses from stormy seas that eclipsed those in battle. The renewed Roman fleets were to win a series of great naval victories, but suffer a shocking level of losses to storms and wreckage.

The more experienced Carthaginian seamen did not hesitate to abandon an exposed position and seek shelter when storms were approaching, something the Roman novices were slow to learn. It was only the sheer determination of Rome's magistrates and populace that allowed her to keep relying on her ships to defeat Carthage. There were only two prolonged pauses in this effort. In 253 and 249 BC, Rome had suffered considerable losses and the people could not at once be approached for fresh sacrifices. A breathing space of two and five years respectively was needed. However, when, after returning to land campaigns to try to squeeze the Carthaginian armies from their strongholds in the western third of Sicily, they realized that naval replenishment was the key to the resilience of Carthage's besieged garrisons, for a third time they built up a powerful war fleet.

The higher individual performance of Carthage's ships was probably due to the superior quality of their crews, at least until the last few years of the war. The bulk of the ships on both sides were quinqueremes, or 'fives', probably with three banks of oars. The main Roman tactic of naval warfare in the early phase of the conflict was the boarding attack deploying the *corvus*, with marines crossing over to fight on the target galley, in part explaining why the Romans did so well. These ships had a very large crew, in the Roman case some 300 men plus marines, resulting in the very large numbers of men present at some of the naval battles of the war.

The development and redevelopment of the Roman navy during the First Punic War reveals a number of qualities that were key to the Roman domination in the next few centuries. The Romans were able to make a strategic assessment that naval power would be important in prevailing over Carthage. They were imaginative and organized in their approach to building a fleet, showing much enterprise and determination, as well as the ability to draw on Roman resources and those of their allies. While their inexperience and over-confidence contributed to a number of naval disasters, ultimately they were able to learn from their mistakes and adapt their approach in order to defeat Carthage in the final battle off the Aegates Islands. The development of the navy clearly reveals the adaptability and resolve of the Romans, and their immense capacity to draw people and resources together to achieve their goals.

Whether Rome had in fact digested her experiences in this first venture beyond her shores can only be inferred from the preparation and operation of fleets in her subsequent expeditions to defend, expand and consolidate her overseas conquests.

The Interval Between the First and Second Punic Wars (241-218 Bc)

In the long interwar period, 241-218 BC, Carthage apparently made little effort to reverse the consequences at sea of the first conflict. The Carthaginian navy entered the Hannibalic War as a force already defeated, with little stomach for a decisive naval encounter. It is ironic that while Hannibal is credited with a long-range plan for war with Rome, the Roman fleet was far better prepared for this war than the navy of Carthage. Fleets were very expensive to maintain, so only a skeleton force was normally manned in peacetime. The Romans, as usual, were favoured by fortune. In 219 BC, the year before Hannibal crossed the Alps, Rome's consuls conducted a maritime campaign against the Illyrian pirates. So Rome had a fleet of 200 quinqueremes, fully manned and equipped, when the Second Punic War began. Some twenty additional ships were added to the fleet. Carthage, on the other hand, was able to man and deploy only eighty-seven quinqueremes in 218, although she had quite a few more ships in dry dock. Carthage had the money to hire crews for her many dry-docked ships, but perhaps lacked the leadership and will to raise the naval stakes.

In 238 BC, when Sardinian mercenaries rebelled against Carthage and solicited Roman help, Rome declared war again and Carthage was soon forced to yield Sardinia and Corsica. This was a morally dubious position, a point that even the normally pro-Roman Polybius admits. The islands were clearly allotted to Carthage by the treaty of 241 at the end of the First Punic War, but they were seized by erstwhile Carthaginian mercenaries in protest of loot/payment arrears from their service in that conflict. They in turn were expelled by a widespread rebellion by the native populations. The mercenaries had, in 239, appealed to Rome for help against the Carthaginians, but Rome was at the time preoccupied with the dangerous uprising of the Gallic tribes north of the Po River. The Roman pretext for seizure was thin – that the islands were in a state of anarchy, therefore did not technically 'belong' to Carthage and were available for appropriation. The eagerness to take advantage of this opportunity shows that the Roman senators were thinking in a 'sea power' geopolitical mode. They were, in effect, constructing a 'barrier reef' between Italy and North Africa. It showed how Rome had learned from the First Punic War to think strategically about its maritime interests. The very efficiently mounted expedition against Sardinia across 150 miles of open sea was another marker of increasingly sophisticated naval capabilities.

In her alteration of the terms of the original treaty, Rome also availed herself of all the smaller islands between Sicily and Carthage, which, though miniscule in comparison to Sardinia and Corsica, were nonetheless conceivable way-stations en route to Africa. Roman control of them would also deny Carthage such stop-overs should she determine to launch an assault from Africa to Sicily, and thence to Italy.

In 229-228 BC, Rome suppressed the Illyrian pirates in the Adriatic (covered in the next chapter), and brought the whole of that coastline under her control. In 237-227, the Carthaginian Hasdrubal conquered Spain as far north as the Ebro. Rome was at the time greatly troubled by the aggressive manner in which Hasdrubal was making progress in building an imperial outpost in Spain, but the Gallic threat in the north prompted the Senate to authorize a rather soft arrangement with Carthage.

In 226 BC, the Ebro Treaty between Rome and Carthage was signed, pledging the latter to forgo further conquests north of that river. When, however, Carthage attacked and captured Saguntum (an ally of Rome *south* of the Ebro), Rome declared war yet again. The rationale for this is a bit fuzzy. Even though Saguntum was technically in the territory in which Carthage was allowed to expand, Saguntum had been a 'friend' of Rome before that, and appealed to her for help against Hannibal. Rome hesitated, because before she could deal with Carthage, she had to put down the revolt of the Celts in northern Italy, an event that figured in Carthaginian commander Hannibal's calculations for the coming Punic war, and deal with resurgent piracy in the Adriatic involving the Illyrian sea robbers, after whom several campaigns were named.

These events, along with a consideration of the naval characteristics of the Second Punic War, will be discussed in more detail in the following chapter. In the event, when Saguntum at last fell to Hannibal, Rome demanded the evacuation of the city and that Hannibal be handed over to them. In hindsight it is easy to see that the ambiguous cause of Saguntum was merely the pretext for Rome to step in and stifle Carthage's apparent effort to build a war chest to finance a rematch and establish a forward base for that effort.

Chapter Four

Combatting the Eastern Mediterranean pirate Threat (Illyrian Wars) and the Naval Features of the Second Punic War

The loss of naval supremacy in the First Punic War not only deprived the Carthaginians of their predominance in the Western Mediterranean, but exposed their overseas empire to disintegration under renewed attacks by Rome. Even the Greek historian Polybius, a reluctant admirer of Rome, considered the subsequent Roman actions against Carthage aggressive and unjustified. A gross breach of the treaty was perpetrated when a Roman force was sent to occupy Sardinia, whose insurgent garrison had offered to surrender the island in 238 BC. The Romans replied to the objections of Carthage with a declaration of war, and only withheld their attack due to Carthage's compliant cession of Sardinia and Corsica and the payment of a further indemnity. One of the Roman rationalizations for this aggressive action was that the Carthaginians were using Sardinia as a base from which to harass Roman merchant shipping. This is a specious argument. It is more likely that Rome recalled how the two islands were used by Carthage as advance bases for resupplying her besieged towns in Sicily and in staging raids on the Italian coast in the First Punic War. Combined with the frenzied Carthaginian empire-building in Spain noted at the end of the previous chapter, this betokened trouble.

Contra Chester Starr, Rome's domination of the sea lanes doubtless loomed large in Hannibal Barca's calculated range of options for the inevitable rematch with Rome. However, it was likely of some consequence to his renowned decision to invade Italy via the tortuous land route that the Celtic peoples of southern Gaul and north-western Italy chafed under Roman rule – their recent rebellion was still smouldering – and could be useful allies as well as providing a forward base on land. Further, Carthage could tap into the rich resources of north-eastern Spain while preparing its expedition. But this was making the best of a bad situation, given that there could be no seaborne troop landings (other than possible pinprick hit-and-run raids) in either Sicily or the Italian peninsula so long as Rome held the balance of sea power along the Rome-Carthage axis.

After the First Punic War, Roman authority was extended in the north of Italy from the Apennines and the Rubicon to the foot of the Alps. Alarmed at the advance of the Romans, who were pushing northward their great military road, the Flaminian Way, Gallic tribes on both sides of the Alps gathered for an assault upon Rome.

From around 228 BC forward, the Celtic tribes in Cisalpine Gaul (the vicinity from modern Milan north-west to the French Alps) rebelled and launched attacks on Rome. By 224-220, Rome had succeeded in pacifying Cisalpine Gaul through its customary methodical severity. However, the Celtic peoples in that region remained restive, resenting the harsh repressive measures, and Hannibal was encouraged by the prospect of a tacit alliance with them when he invaded the Roman heartland several years later.

The suppression of the Celtic rebellion in the north of the Italian peninsula hardly need detain us further. But the anti-pirate campaign has been regarded as a naval event, or series of events, sometimes under the separate heading of the Illyrian Wars. Although the main thrust of this chapter concerns the Second Punic War, the interregnum bracketing the close of the first war and the opening of the second encompasses an interesting and relevant prelude.

It is clear that by 219 BC, Rome had established a protectorate in southern Illyria and northern Epiros as a counterbalance to both Macedonian and Illyrian ambitions, the kings of Illyria being still to some extent dependents of the former. It is likely enough that a similar arrangement was attempted after the first pacification, the greater part of Illyria being handed over to Demetrius, but with a possible rival to him remaining in the old royal house, which was not entirely divested. Being as these conflicts had a specifically naval component, they are worth examining in greater detail.

At the close of the First Punic War in 241 BC, Rome had at its disposal a considerable navy left over from that epic conflict. That navy was employed in smaller conflicts in the following years, but not until Pompey's anti-piracy campaign of 67 BC was it again employed in such large and sustained actions. We have seen how, in 238, the Romans annexed Sardinia and Corsica (Thiel, *A History of Roman Sea-Power Before the Second Punic War*, p.343), the occupation and pacification of which would have required a fleet, if in no other capacity than to transport soldiers to the islands. Thiel points out that it served as a 'fleet in being' (p.350), a strong presence which discouraged resistance, comparable to America's Great White Fleet of the early twentieth century. Around the same time, the Senate ordered a campaign against the pirates of Liguria, an area in the north-west of Italy. This was undertaken, so far as can be determined, mostly on land, but also showed concern for naval interests since the Ligurians presented a challenge at sea as well.

The First Illyrian War

A more substantial operation was undertaken by the Romans against the Illyrians (present day Croatia), beginning in 230 BC. Between 233-231, the Illyrian King Agron had gathered stronger land and naval forces than any prior king of that country. The Greek historian Polybius gives the number of the fleet as 100, and refers to the ships as *lemboi* (Greek), or *lembi* in Latin. These native ships of the piratical Illyrians had wider beams than typical warships of the day and lacked rams. They were well suited to coastal raids and 'cutting out' (ambush) operations against merchant vessels entering a land-flanked maritime chokepoint. They were fast, and their wider beams rendered them more stable than narrow triremes. They would suddenly emerge from hidden coves and inlets to attack and plunder lumbering merchant vessels as the cargo ships plied coastal waters, avoiding open sea for fear of storms.

Polybius relates that, after hearing of his success against the Aeolians, Agron celebrated so hard that he caught a cold and died. He was succeeded by his wife, Queen Teuta, who sanctioned extensive privateer activity and authorized her commanders to use their substantial forces to attack, besiege, pillage or plunder as they pleased. Epirus was pillaged in this way. The Illyrian pirates stepped up their attacks on Italian merchants, and repeated protests by the latter brought the matter to the attention of the Roman Senate. In the wake of the First Punic War, Roman maritime commerce was beginning to thrive and the Roman vessels were known by the pirate chieftains to bear particularly rich cargoes to plunder.

The senators dispatched two envoys, Gaius and Lucius Coruncanius, to Teuta. Receiving the Romans haughtily, the queen guaranteed only that the official forces of Illyria would make no attacks; she artfully declared that she could not be held responsible for the actions of pirates. Coruncanius responded angrily, asserting that these so-called pirates were obviously hers to command, and for this Teuta had him killed on his return voyage. This outrage angered the Roman people and senators, who consented to the raising of an expedition in 229 BC.

Thiel (in his *Studies on the History of Roman Sea-Power in Republican Times*) presents the case that the Senate had not ignored the piratical practices of the Illyrians for so long because of indifference, but rather because they were hamstrung without the approval of the *comitia centuriata*. This assembly, responsible for discussing and confirming military matters, was firmly in the hands of the plebeians, or lower-class citizens, who were wary of military operations outside Italy – in modern parlance, 'foreign entanglements'. Consequently, the Senate had to wait until the increased attacks created a situation severe enough to draw the attention of the plebs. The above-noted murder of the Roman envoy Coruncanius, apparently on Queen Teuta's orders, shifted the popular opinion in favour of war.

Thiel further points out that this was an opportune time for the Romans to go to war, as the Macedonians, Illyria's chief allies, were occupied with important matters elsewhere.

In 229 BC, the consul Gnaeus Fulvius set off for Illyria with 200 quinqueremes, while his counterpart Aulus Postumius brought a large contingent of soldiers across from Brundisium. Fulvius first set out for Corcyra, with hopes of relieving the siege by Illyrian forces there. He was too late, but the commander of the Illyrian garrison on Corcyra, Demetrius of Pharos, turned the island over to the consul. It was then placed under Roman protection.

Fulvius and the fleet joined Postumius and the army at Apollonia, and the Romans proceeded north, up the coast of Illyria, causing the Illyrians to abandon the sieges of Epidamnus and Issa, Rome then placing both of those cities under its protection. On the way, the fleet captured twenty *lembi* carrying off food in order to save it from capture, also subduing several coastal settlements. Teuta withdrew to her fortress at Rhizon for the winter, while the Romans left forty ships under Postumius at Epidamnus. Notably, the ships afloat and armies ashore operated in alignment: the legions subdued the inland tribes while the fleet proceeded up the coast to take possession of the harbours and coastal cities. This was a worthwhile experience in combined operations.

The following spring, in 228 BC, the queen sued for peace, the terms of which included her relinquishing portions of her kingdom, an amount of tribute to Rome and a prohibition against sailing south of Lissus with more than two unarmed vessels. Rome retained control of 120 miles of Illyrian coast, from Lissos to Epirus, and set up Demetrius of Pharos as ruler of a client kingdom north of Teuta's (Thiel, p.354). Thiel explains that the former act was not so much to chastise Illyria as to provide a barrier between Macedon and the sea. Roman policy was decidedly anti-Macedon during this time, and the latter country would ally with Hannibal during the Second Punic War, as elaborated below. Meanwhile, Rome had, at least for the time being, cleared the Adriatic of the pirate threat, securing naval stations that could be used to assure an entrée to the East.

Second Illyrian War

After the First Illyrian War, the Romans had to contend with the aforementioned major invasion of the Gauls from the north-west, which they successfully drove off. They were then faced with the appointment of Hannibal as Carthaginian commander in Spain and his subsequent attack on Saguntum.

Encouraged by these perceived weaknesses in Roman power, the Illyrian Demetrius of Pharos raised a fleet of ninety *lembi* and sailed south of Lissos, in violation of the treaty Rome had coerced from Teuta. He made several unsuccessful attacks on Pylos and then, taking fifty of his ships, began pillaging the Cyclades, a hemisphere of islets off the Greek mainland. The Romans responded quickly, hoping to put out the Illyrian brush-fire before Hannibal could bring the Carthaginian torch to bear, and sent Lucius Aemilius across the Adriatic in 219 BC.

The fleet quickly captured Dimale, previously regarded as impregnable, and moved toward Pharos, where Demetrius had encamped. Aemilius detached twenty of his ships to make a show in Pharos harbour, while the rest of the fleet secretly landed its troops behind the town. Demetrius sent his garrison out to meet the perceived threat of the twenty ships, and at that time the concealed Romans attacked his rear. The battle was decided in Rome's favour, and Demetrius barely escaped on a *lembus* to his benefactor Philip of Macedon. The Romans returned to Italy to face Hannibal, leaving unscathed Demetrius' ally Scerdilaidas and thus hastily concluding the Second Illyrian War.

The Second Punic War

After defeat in the First Punic War, Hamilcar Barca had sought to rebuild Carthaginian strength by acquiring a territory in Spain where Carthage might gain new wealth and manpower with which to redress grievances against haughty Rome.

Invested with an unrestricted foreign command, Hamilcar spent the rest of his life founding a Spanish empire (237-228 BC). His work was continued by his son-in-law Hasdrubal and his son Hannibal, who was placed at the head of the army in 221.

As we have seen, these conquests aroused the suspicions of Rome, which in a treaty with Hasdrubal confined the Carthaginians to the south of the Ebro River. At some point Rome also entered into relations with Saguntum (Sagunto), a town on the east coast of Spain, south of the Ebro. To the Carthaginians it seemed that once again Rome was expanding its interests into their asserted sphere of hegemony. In 219 BC, Hannibal had laid siege to Saguntum and carried the town in spite of stubborn defence. The Romans, who were placed in the position of guarantor of Saguntum's safety, responded with an ultimatum demanding that the Carthaginians evacuate the town and surrender Hannibal to them, or go to war. The Carthaginian council supported Hannibal and opted for war.

Mahan wrote:

'In fact, Roman sea power obliged Hannibal to undertake a perilous march through Gaul thereby wasting half his veterans, and enabled the elder Scipio to intercept Hannibal's communications, and to return to wage a war on land. Meanwhile, legions passed to and fro by water between Italy and Spain unmolested, unwearied, while Roman sea power sealed off the enemy's approaches by salt water, obliging them to come by land. Thus divided, the two Carthaginian armies were separated, and one was destroyed by the combined actions of the Roman generals.'

The Second Punic War eclipsed the First Punic War in the magnitude of the forces involved and the geographic scope of the conflict. The first war had been primarily a naval war for the island of Sicily, with only brief land-force penetrations into Africa and Sardinia. The second war was a massive struggle for dominion of the Western Mediterranean waged from the Pillars of Heracles to the Bosporus, from the Alps to the edge of the Sahara. It seems strange then that the recorded naval battles of the first war dwarf those of the Hannibalic War.

There are three main reasons for this anomaly. First, the size of the naval battles in the first war was likely exaggerated by the methodology employed by Polybius. Second, the fleets in the second war were dispersed in numerous theatres, unlike the earlier war. Finally, the Punic navy was broken in the first war and never regained its former fighting spirit and skill, though its army, especially under Hannibal, was much improved.

Casus Belli and Preparations

We have seen that after the end of the First Punic War in 241 BC, Carthage chose to concentrate at first on controlling Spain rather than going directly for the Italian jugular near the seat of power. Being as she had been deprived of forward naval bases on Sardinia and Corsica in the war's immediate aftermath, and there were no longer any reliable allies on Sicily, this was the best she could manage. One factor among several in determining the Carthaginian strategy in the Second Punic War, albeit a large one, is said to be the decline of Carthaginian sea power and the concurrent rise of Roman naval mastery at the end of the First Punic War. This conclusion is not due to anything explicitly stated – Roman literature, such as it is, rarely discusses maritime matters, certainly not in a triumphal manner – but rather is inferred from the course of the conflict.

In 219 BC, when Hannibal captured Saguntum after an eight-month siege, Carthage refused Roman demands for Hannibal's extradition and the relinquishment of the city, and both sides prepared for war.

It is curious that while Hannibal is believed to have devised a long-range plan for war with Rome, the Carthaginian fleet was largely absent from the planning. The Roman fleet was far better prepared for this war than the navy of Carthage, the former having more than 200 quinqueremes, fully manned and equipped, when the war began. Carthage, on the other hand, was able to man and deploy only eighty-seven quinqueremes in 218 BC, although she had a number of other ships in dry dock.

Roman Sea Power as Impediment for Hannibal

Being as the renowned American naval strategist Alfred Thayer Mahan's earliest thoughts about sea power were inspired by reading about the Second Punic War, it is worth examining his analysis of that war in more detail. Professor Starr advances a peculiar argument against Roman sea power as a deterrent to Hannibal. I alluded to this peculiar though useful little book (*The Influence of Sea Power on Ancient History*) in my preface and introduction.

The publisher implies that Starr's title should read *The* Limitations *of Sea Power in Ancient History*. Certainly Starr's own review of the Second Punic War belies this caveat. Starr concisely recapitulates the sequence of events as given in Mahan. His only quibble is that 'contrary to the views of Mommsen and Mahan … he [Hannibal] had to march by land not *simply* [emphasis added] because the Romans controlled the sea but by reason of his large forces of cavalry and elephants that could not easily have been transported by sea'. I shall return to this misconception later.

As Starr asserts, there certainly were considerations other than the Roman naval threat prescribing using the Spanish operational base to stage a march along a lengthy, twisting land route traversing extremely rough terrain: Carthage wanted to gain direct power over Spain's mineral resources and needed to mount an army of its inhabitants against the Roman legions.

In 218 BC, Hannibal set up a strong Carthaginian base at Saguntum, from where he planned to march across the Pyrenees and the Alps in winter to surprise the Roman army. Along the way, Hannibal recruited reinforcements from the warlike Celtic tribes who rejected Rome's recently established dominion. To maintain his hold in Spain, Hannibal left about 20,000 men under the control of his brother Hasdrubal.

Presumptive Carthaginian Plan of Action

Rome and Carthage enjoyed different military advantages than they had during the last war. Hannibal now fielded the best-trained and equipped army in the ancient world, while the Romans enjoyed complete naval superiority, which they could use to invade Carthaginian territory at will. Rome expected to exploit this advantage to wage a quick, offensive war that would compel Carthage to sue for peace on Rome's terms. Hannibal, however, had a plan to restore Carthage's supremacy in the Western Mediterranean. First, he would neutralize Rome's advantage at sea through a daring invasion of Italy across the Alps. Hannibal correctly saw that the presence of a foreign army in Italy would compel the Romans to abandon their planned assault on Carthage.

Once across the Alps, Hannibal planned to recruit soldiers from the recently conquered regions of northern and southern Italy, especially among the agitated Gauls, and convince other kingdoms in the East to join forces against Rome. At the head of this combined force, Hannibal would cut at the roots of Roman military power by disrupting the intricate web of alliances that bound the cities and peoples of Italy to Rome. It is important to note that Hannibal's goal at the start of the war was not to destroy the city or exterminate the Romans, despite the claims made by later Roman authors. Hannibal assumed that a few decisive victories in Italy would compel Rome to negotiate a new peace treaty on terms favourable to Carthage. At the least, he thought he could win a restoration of Carthaginian holdings in Sicily and Sardinia, and recognition of the new empire in Hispania. Roman resolve, however, would again surprise the Carthaginians.

Presumptive Roman Plan of Action Thwarted by Hannibal's Boldness

At the start of the war, the Roman strategy assumed that one army would pin Hannibal down in Hispania, freeing another to invade the Carthaginian homeland in Africa. But Hannibal, with typical daring, seized the initiative and marched towards Italy with a large army. He evaded the first Roman army sent against him and arrived at the Alps in late 218 BC with 38,000 infantry troops, 8,000 cavalrymen and thirty-seven war elephants. The brutal march over the mountains in the early winter cost Hannibal nearly a third of his army and most of his irreplaceable elephants. But his gamble worked: he was able to lead an intact army into Italy. Hannibal then won a cavalry engagement at Ticinus and forced the Romans to withdraw south of the Padus River. Facing an enemy army in Italy, the Romans recalled the forces that were being marshalled for the planned invasion of Africa. Hannibal had succeeded in forestalling the attack on Carthage: his audacity had gained him the chance to win the war in Italy.

The details and possible route of Hannibal's long march and subsequent rampage in Italy are too well known to bear repeating. In sum, there were some good reasons, other than Roman control of the sea lanes, for Hannibal to establish a base of operations in Spain where he could both recruit and exploit the natural resources to equip and feed his invasion force. But it is also clear that the perils of transiting short-sea crossings or coastal cruising in Roman-dominated waters loomed large.

Mahan, in his *The Influence of Sea Power upon History*, aptly delineates the position as follows:

'The military situation which finally resulted in the battle of the Metaurus and the triumph of Rome may be summed up as follows: To overthrow Rome it was necessary to attack her in Italy at the heart of her power, and shatter the strongly linked confederacy of which she was the head. This was the objective. To reach it, the Carthaginians needed a solid base of operations and a secure line of communications. The former was established in Spain by the genius of the great Barca family; the latter was never achieved. There were two lines possible – the one direct by sea, the other circuitous through Gaul. The first was blocked by the Roman sea power, the second imperilled and finally intercepted through occupation of northern Spain by the Roman army. This occupation was made possible through control of the sea, which the Carthaginians never endangered. With respect to Hannibal and his base, therefore, Rome occupied two central positions, Rome itself and northern Spain, joined by an easy interior line of communications, the sea; by which mutual support was continually given.'

Sketch of the Course of the War

Let us briefly examine the war from the maritime perspective. After the death of Hasdrubal in 221 BC, Hannibal assumed command in Spain. Weighing the risks of an arduous overland trek through the Alps versus Rome's ability to interdict troop-laden ships, he crossed both the Pyrenees and Alps and carried the war into Italy, winning a succession of victories: Ticinus and Trebbia (218), Lake Trasimenus (217) and Cannae (216). After these defeats, the Roman army avoided battle with Hannibal; their fleet, meanwhile, controlled the sea. In 217, there was an action at the mouth of the Ebro wherein a Roman fleet under Gnaeus Cornelius Scipio decisively beat the Punic squadron in Spain. There followed a series of see-saw land battles in Spain, Sicily and Greece, but command of the sea permitted Rome to redeploy her forces rapidly. In 215, successfully wooing the Greeks in southern Italy away from Rome, Hannibal concluded an alliance with Philip V of Madedon; but since the Roman fleet controlled the Adriatic, the Macedonians were blocked from intervening in Italy. These events are covered below under the rubric of the Macedonian Wars.

In 212 BC, the Roman consul Marcellus captured Carthage's ally Syracuse with his fleet and army, despite the ingenious defence by Archimedes (who died in the fighting). Meanwhile, on land, Hannibal captured Terentum (Taranto) and won a battle at Capua (211). In 207, Hasdrubal crossed the Alps with reinforcements, but lost a battle on the Metaurus River (near Sena Gallica) and was killed. In 206, P. Cornelius Scipio (to become known as Scipio Africanus) completed the conquest of Carthaginian Spain, while Hannibal's youngest brother, Mago, managed to land at Genoa with the remnants of the Spanish army. Here he attempted vainly to lead the Ligurians and Gauls against Rome once more. This evacuation of Carthaginian forces from Spain comprised the only large-scale Carthaginian sea operation during the Second Punic War.

In 204 BC, consul P. Cornelius Scipio, thanks to Roman mastery at sea, landed in Africa and won a battle at Tunis (203). Hannibal was thus compelled to evacuate southern Italy in an improvised transport fleet. In 202, P. Cornelius Scipio defeated Hannibal at Zama, and Carthage was finally forced to conclude peace. She lost Spain to Rome, and Numidia became independent. Carthage was obliged to pay reparations, hand over all but ten of her warships and could not declare war without Roman permission.

As Mahan pointed out in his *The Influence of Sea Power upon History*, Hannibal rejected taking the maritime hop directly across the Straits of Messana to Italy because of logistical difficulties resulting from the unfavourable position of Carthaginian sea power at the time. It was this state of affairs that provided Mahan with his germinal insight on the significance of sea power in more recent times. Nowhere in his brief (about six pages) passages on the Second Punic War does he suggest that the concept of blockade and sea control exercised by the British Navy from 1660-1793 is applicable to the war with Hannibal.

The rationale, per Starr, that Hannibal's heavy troops and their mounts could not be conveyed by sea is without foundation. Specially adapted Roman cargo ships (*corbitae*) could and regularly did convey horses as well as their riders and equipment for decades before the Second Punic War. While transits of several weeks were out of the question simply due to the problems of feeding and maintaining horses at sea, the short trip across to Sicily did not preclude the ferrying of cavalry. Scipio Africanus did this in the opposite direction near the war's end, culminating in the Battle of Zama.

The Phoenecians/Carthaginians were experienced in shipping bulky cargoes, including livestock. As for the elephants, it should not have been beyond the capacity of the ingenious Hannibal and his intrepid admiral Bomilcar to transport the beasts as deck cargo on a one-week's sea crossing. The rate of attrition for the animals would certainly not have exceeded that encountered in the long overland march through the Alps. The land route option was obviously heavily influenced by Rome's demonstrated capacity to overpower enemy ships.

Mahan never maintained that 'control of the sea' in antiquity consisted of an impenetrable, seamless blockade of all enemy maritime movements. In fact, he acknowledged that although the Romans in general 'controlled the sea', they 'permitted' Carthaginian admiral Bomilcar, in the fourth year of the war, following the stunning Carthaginian victory at Cannae, to land 4,000 men and *a body of elephants* (so much for Chester Starr's doubt that it could be done) in southern Italy. Nor did Roman command of the sea prevent Bomilcar in the seventh year of the war from evading the Roman fleet at Syracuse and reappearing at Tarentum, then in Hannibal's possession. Likewise, Roman naval mastery did not prevent Hannibal from sending dispatch vessels to Carthage, or from finally withdrawing the remnants of his army from Italy to Africa. These evasions and minor Carthaginian naval exploits create the impression that more help could have been given: that is, there should have been steady attempts to provide support by sea from the Carthaginian base in the likelihood that some ships were bound to get through unscathed.

Thus, Mahan asserts, we have to examine 'ascertained facts' to determine the kind and degree of 'influence'. It was the renowned historian of ancient Rome, Theodor Mommsen, who originally said (as cited here by Mahan) that at the beginning of the war Rome controlled the seas: in the Second Punic War there was no 'naval battle of significance'. Mahan finds that this situation, along with other 'well-ascertained facts', demonstrates naval superiority analogous to later, better-documented epochs such as the Royal Navy between 1802 and 1815.

Even though this control lasted throughout the war, it didn't preclude large or small maritime raids (as noted), but it did obstruct the sustained and secure communications which Hannibal needed. On the other hand, it was also plain that for the first ten years of the war, the Roman fleet wasn't strong enough for continuous operations on the sea between Sicily and Carthage, nor even to the south of a line drawn from Tarragona in Spain to Lilybaeum (now Marsala) at the western end of Sicily. Roman control extended from there around the north side of Sicily through the straits of Messana down to Syracuse, and from there to Brindisi in the Adriatic. During the early phase of Hannibal's campaign, he used whatever ships were available to maintain communications between Spain and Africa, which the Romans seemed incapable of impeding while keeping a watch on the coasts of Italy and Sicily to prevent direct reinforcement of Hannibal from Africa.

Roman sea power was consequently key to throwing Macedonia totally out of the war, thwarting Philip V's threat of aid, but it couldn't prevent Carthage from assisting its useful harassing diversion in Sicily. However, it did preclude Carthage from sending troops to Hannibal in Italy at a time of dire need. This is the type of 'sea denial' exercised by the Roman admirals during Hannibal's war. It certainly didn't match the 'razor sharp' capabilities of modern warships – whatever Starr meant by the phrase – but it was sufficient to deprive an invading army of sustenance during a crucial part of the war.

Johannes Thiel's take on the issue of implied Roman naval superiority adopts a slightly different tack from that of Mahan. In his survey of the Second Punic War, Thiel (*Studies on the History of Roman Sea Power in Republican Times*) had a distinct reassessment to offer, and one which made it at any rate questionable whether the common assumption is really justified, that the Roman naval superiority of about two-to-one gave them a position at sea which was unassailable. As Professor Thiel's mid-twentieth-century commentary is still persuasive, I will summarize it here.

Maritime Strategy of the Second Punic War According to J.H. Thiel

The Roman navy very early in the war was dispersed in squadrons permanently based in Spain, Sicily and Calabria (and after 214 BC in Greek waters), and though there was always a central reserve of ships not normally manned, the dispersal of the squadrons was wide enough to have enabled the Carthaginians to bring a superior force into action against any one of them without much risk, except in Greek waters, of the optimistic enterprise degenerating into a battle against odds. The movements of Bomilcar and Mago, the reinforcements sent to Hannibal and his evacuation of Italy by sea all suggest that the Carthaginian squadrons had considerable freedom of action, and that a more enterprising naval strategy might have paid them good dividends. Mahan had intimated such in his resumé of the Roman naval effort.

Thiel in fact believes (pp.82ff., and especially p.98f.) that Bomilcar had the opportunity of winning the war for Carthage by sea in 212 BC, when his decisive superiority in Sicilian waters (150 or 185 ships against 130) ought to have enabled him to force Marcellus into the role of Nicias in the Sicilian Expedition during the Peloponnesian War – expertly elucidated by Mahan in his 1915 book, *Naval Strategy Compared and Contrasted with the Principles and Practice of Military Operations on Land: Lectures delivered at the U.S. Naval War College, Newport, R.I., between the years 1887 and 1911.*

Thiel accepts the Livian (= Polybian) account of this year *in toto*, despite the doubts which it raises as to the movements of Bomilcar. It seems possible that it is not only these movements, but also the fleet-numbers of Bomilcar, that ought to be suspect: it was by no means impossible for Polybius himself to be misled by his sources (see e.g., Pol. VIII, i, cited by Thiel, p.87, n.156, and fleet-numbers in the First Punic War).

Thiel himself explains the inactivity of 212 BC by 'Bomilcar's faintheartedness', and the inactivity of the years after 211 (when the Carthaginians still should have had 130 ships intact) to a breakdown of morale and lack of manpower. All this is possible, but perhaps only just possible. I would prefer to distrust the Livian

(Polybian) figures which give Bomilcar 185 (or 150) ships in 212, ships which, as Thiel admits, seem to 'vanish as it were in smoke' in 210 and subsequent years. In the same way, I find it difficult to accept the tradition that Scipio invaded Africa unopposed with a fleet of only forty warships, while Carthage could still dispose of about 1,000: one of these two figures must surely be wrong. It seems likely that lack of manpower must have been the most important factor which limited the size of both navies.

Although Thiel is certainly correct in his interpretation of the evidence relating to Roman naval personnel, which was not in general (except for some of the marines) the same personnel that served in the legions or the allied military contingents, it seems possible that the general rule may have been broken in the long crisis occasioned by Hannibal. It is perhaps no accident that the maximum naval effort (280 ships at sea in 208 BC) comes at a time when the maximum effort on land (twenty-five legions in 212) has already been weak.

The traditional boarding tactics of the Roman navy made heavy demands on troops, and the First Punic War provided precedents for selecting picked troops from the legions (or *socii* of equivalent military value) for important naval occasions (Pol. I, 26, 5; 63, 1); but it would not be surprising if, in this war of no decisive battles at sea, the quality (and perhaps the quantity) of the marines was allowed to decline when the legions were needed so urgently in Italy and elsewhere. After 208 BC, there is a pronounced decline in the whole Roman effort at sea, attributable (as Thiel points out) to the war-weariness of the Roman and Italian peoples. Nevertheless, the minimum effort of this war was greater than the maximum of the wars that succeeded it. No new warships were built after 208.

Chester Starr Refuted?

What of Starr's stipulation about the limited sea-keeping capabilities of the 'racing-shell styled' ancient war galleys? He uses this assertion to minimize the relevancy of naval forces to this war. An apt riposte to this argument is provided by Boris Rankov's fascinating essay in *The Second Punic War: A Reappraisal*. Rankov recounts that by way of contrast to the First Punic War, the second war saw no decisive encounter at sea, which was precisely Mahan's point. Rankov points out that the reason for this is geographical. In order for large fleets to operate, they need to control harbours. As a result of the First Punic War, the Carthaginians did not have access to landing spots in Sicily, and thus could not support Hannibal by sea. The galleys' short sea legs – of which Chester Starr has reminded us in his alleged counter-Mahanian tract – did not matter when naval forces were moving along the shoreline and while legions marching along the coast parallel to the fleets could effect control of the harbours required for provisioning the ships and resting and refreshing the crews. At any rate, the geography of the Mediterranean basin was compatible with such coast-wise exercise of sea control.

This is a rational way to look at the actual meaning of 'sea power' in the context of ancient fleets, specifically that of Rome. It has implications for other periods of ancient history, where control of the sea (and landing places) proved less than decisive in the absence of an enemy who was prepared to contest the point. It was only when Rome could free up resources to take advantage of its command of the sea, that sea power mattered. As Chester Starr's narrative acknowledges, superior Roman sea power, in conjunction with operations on land, made a big difference in the Second Punic War, even if it wasn't as conspicuous an instrument that it proved to be in the first conflict with Carthage. Next, I will consider other episodes affecting the Roman Republic's command of the seas, those dealing with the transition from the Republic to the early imperial period. There was still plenty of scope for the exercise of Roman naval superiority in the immediate aftermath of the Second Punic War.

The strategies of the two contenders in the Second Punic War can be summarized as follows. Rome successfully attacked the Carthaginian centre of gravity, while the Carthaginians pursued a more peripheral strategy aimed at the allies of Rome. Carthaginian strategy focussed almost solely on its military (i.e., land) strategy, committed to war with Rome by a general unable to muster the strategic resources to win. Carthage never effectively employed its naval forces in concert with its land forces.

Hannibal's successes point out the importance of training and experience in senior leaders. However, the strategic assumptions of a campaign plan must be valid for that plan to succeed. Hannibal's campaign was based on the invalid assumption that Rome's allies would defect following defeat of Roman armies in the field. It was noted that the inability of Hannibal to receive resupply and reinforcement by sea played into the hands of Fabius' delaying strategy. So long as he could keep Hannibal at bay without affording him a knockout blow, the greater the chances of Hannibal's army being starved out and depleted.

Finally, successful campaigns consist of operations linked in space and time. Rome succeeded in linking its widely separated operations in Italy, Sicily, Greece, Iberia, and eventually North Africa. The Roman ability to inflict punishing blows on Carthaginian maritime troop and resupply movements weighed heavily on Carthaginian strategic calculations.

Roman strategy evolved as events dictated changes to initial plans. The ends of Roman strategy were to limit the resurgent power of Carthage, fuelled by Carthaginian conquests in Iberia, and to maintain Rome's pre-eminent military status in the Western Mediterranean. The ways of Rome's strategy were sea-launched land attacks against both the North African homeland of Carthage and the financial centre of the Carthaginian empire, Iberia. Initially, the two Roman consuls leading armies were to invade Iberia and North Africa, respectively. Scipio the Elder sailed for Iberia, while Sempronius, the other consul, was to launch an invasion of North Africa from Sicily. The Senate directed the military: the pre-eminent Roman navy and the legions of the Roman army.

Central to Roman strategy was the critical advantage of Roman sea supremacy. Their ability to control the sea lines of communication of the Central and Western Mediterranean enabled them to move and resupply large forces at will. The Romans maintained this advantage throughout the war, and were able to respond quickly to problems arising in distant areas.

This stands in marked contrast with Carthaginian naval efforts. Carthage possessed a potent naval force, but never successfully deployed it against the Romans. Roman strategy first changed when Scipio the Elder, en route by sea to Iberia, learned of Hannibal's movement towards the Alps while resupplying his invasion force at Massilia. Scipio failed in his attempt to intercept Hannibal west of the Alps, but did make the critical operational decision to send his army on to Iberia. Scipio returned to Italy to confront Hannibal with forces left to control the Gauls in northern Italy. Sempronius cancelled the North African invasion and also moved his consular army to northern Italy.

Roman military strategy changed again after repeated tactical defeats. The Romans concluded they could not beat Hannibal on land on the tactical battlefield of his choosing, and the war in Italy became one of survival for the Romans. There they adopted the policy of Fabius Maximus (renowned in military textbooks as the Fabian Strategy) to rely on their walled cities and road network to shadow Hannibal's army in Italy, limit his ability to forage for supplies and prevent his reinforcement. Fabian military strategy acknowledged that Roman defeats would weaken the hold of Rome on its allies, but depended on Hannibal's inability to get supplies and reinforcements from Spain or Carthage wearing him down faster than the defection of Roman allies at home would cripple Fabius' jab-and-feint approach. Rome focussed on removing Iberia as a source of wealth and manpower for Carthage. The success of Romans in Iberia convinced the Carthaginian oligarchy, despite Roman losses at Cannae, to divert reinforcements planned for Hannibal to Iberia. Rome reinforced successful efforts in Iberia and Sicily, and thwarted Carthaginian attempts to regain Sardinia. Rome's success in Iberia was based on her control of the sea lanes.

I have tried to look at the Second Punic War at the strategic level and attempted to answer the question of why Hannibal, one of the great captains of military history, failed so completely. I have abstained from examining Hannibal's tactical and operational prowess on land, except where those events provide an insight into strategic factors bearing on the naval situation. A description of the rival strategies was followed by an analysis of why one succeeded and the other failed. I have tried to provide lessons a modern strategist can extract from the failures and successes of both Carthage and Rome during the second war.

The Roman navy had maintained its overall superiority throughout the conflict. Rome was never really challenged, and the lacklustre Carthaginian navy never won a single victory in this war (other than the unusual battle at Castra Cornelia). In five recorded naval actions, Carthage suffered a total loss of seventy-seven ships captured and eight sunk. Rome's total recorded loss was one ship damaged. Of course, Rome wrote the history books, which may have glossed over many losses, including the presumptive naval manpower shortage referred to above. Nevertheless, it was a remarkably one-sided result. This disappointing performance by the once-great Carthaginian navy contributed decisively to their eventual loss of the Second Punic War.

Implicit Lessons of the Second Punic War

All major battles of the Second Punic War were fought on land, but sea power played a pervasive role. The Romans effectively leveraged their land and naval forces into a coherent grand strategy. Rome used its fleet to transport its land forces to several different theatres and maintain them once deployed. The Roman alliance with Masinissa, king of Numidia, in North Africa, combined with possession of Corsica and Sardinia, allowed the Romans to control the northern half of the Western Mediterranean. Carthage was never able to penetrate the Adriatic and assist Philip V, and therefore the alliance of Carthage and Macedon never reached its full potential.

Carthage, on the other hand, was a major regional power engaged in a war far from her shores, and conceded control of the seas to her enemy. This prevented strategic surprise by large movements of troops; resupply, reinforcement and evacuation were also difficult. The Romans could easily disrupt Carthaginian trade, and the North African shore was open to Roman raids. There is evidence that Carthage had the means to effect a naval strategy. Five hundred Carthaginian warships were burned as part of the peace settlement ending the Second Punic War. Carthage successfully moved a large army to Sicily, and also moved large forces to Sardinia and repeatedly to Iberia. A Carthaginian fleet spent two years in Greek waters without significantly assisting their most potent ally, Philip, before withdrawing. Late in the war, they still had the ability to move Mago's small army as far as Genoa in northern Italy. The Carthaginian allies of Syracuse and Tarentum also had significant naval assets. Carthage had the resources and certainly a strong naval tradition, but had lost the will to use its navy. During the Roman siege of Syracuse, the Carthaginian admiral Bomiclar had superior numbers of warships, and yet he retreated at the appearance of a smaller Roman fleet. Scipio seized a substantial Carthaginian fleet still moored to its docks when he took New Carthage in Iberia. The existing records do not adequately explain why Carthage failed to employ its naval assets.

Sea power played a critical role in defeating Hannibal. It conditioned his strategy of invading Italy. He was forced to take the long, costly overland trek, rather than a maritime voyage. The overland move from Iberia through the Alps cost Hannibal tens of thousands of veteran soldiers. Roman sea power consistently prevented adequate reinforcements from reaching Hannibal. Hannibal was only able to evacuate Italy during an armistice period with Scipio, who was already in Africa. Roman success underlines the importance of a 'fleet in being'.

Here it might be instructive to turn from the contest in the Western Mediterranean between Rome and Carthage, to the Eastern Mediterranean, where Rome would encounter enemies – as well as allies – as adept at wielding the naval weapon as Carthage had once been. Already during the closing years of the Second Punic War, maritime adversaries had been fomenting trouble for Rome's sea-minded associates near the Mediterranean's eastern rim. The arena of hostilities was considerably farther from the Roman heartland than was the fight with Carthage. Here, I will pass quickly over the general course of the wars and the Byzantine political intrigues to highlight the naval aspects.

Having suggested how the Romans apprehended the value of naval 'presence' and command in the absence of a clear-cut requisite for sea battles in the Second Punic War, I will next discuss how this lesson-learning continued during the so-called Macedonian Wars that evolved from the former conflict.

Chapter Five

Expanding Horizons: Consolidating Sea Control Through the Eastern Mediterranean

The Macedonian Wars

First Macedonian War

During the hostilities with Carthage in the Second Punic War, the Romans quickly reacted to the Macedonian threat. As mentioned above, Hannibal sought to divert Roman sea power to the east by having Philip V stir up things in Macedonia and its maritime neighbours. Roman praetor Laevinius moved a force across the Adriatic, defeated Philip and forced him to burn his fleet and withdraw. Philip waited in vain for support from the Carthaginian fleet, while the Romans used diplomacy to conclude an alliance with the Aetolian League. These Greek states were quickly joined by the additional Greek city-states of Elis, Messina, Sparta, Pergamum, Thrace and Illyria in the struggle against Macedonia. Rome not only prevented help from reaching Hannibal, but the war in Greece was shifted onto Greek shoulders. This was clearly an economy of force theatre for the Romans, who through skilful diplomacy persuaded the Greeks to fight the Macedonians and prevented significant Carthaginian support to Philip by dominating the Adriatic lines of communication.

The Carthaginians were accordingly never able to fully leverage their Macedonian allies. Macedonia could not reinforce Hannibal in Italy due to Roman domination of the Adriatic Sea, either directly or by means of the naval forces of the Aetolian League. Carthage had the means in the number of ships and certainly the tradition to challenge Rome at sea, but never did. This reluctance is implicit acknowledgment of the ability of Rome to skilfully provide for naval potency in new theatres of war far from the homeland. Much of the following information on the First Macedonian War was adapted from the timeline on the online blog, HistoryOfWar.org (http://www.historyofwar.org/articles/wars_first_macedonian.html).

This so-called First Macedonian War was actually little more than a sideshow of the Second Punic War, discussed above. It was induced by Philip V of Macedon's tacit alliance with and material assistance to Rome's nemesis, Hannibal, who later retired there after finally being checked in his rampage on Italian soil. We have seen how, in 230-228 BC, the Romans had intervened to prevent the Illyrians from gaining too much power on the coast (First Illyrian War), and in 219 had returned, this time to prevent their former ally Demetrius of Pharos from upsetting the balance of power (Second Illyrian War). In the aftermath of his defeat, Demetrius had fled to Philip's court, where he soon became one of his chief advisers. During the First Macedonian War (214–205), the Romans had aided the Greeks in rebelling against their Macedonian rulers on the imperial principle of keeping their enemies – actual and potential – divided and fighting one another. This was Britain's method of keeping continental enemies at bay during the eighteenth and nineteenth centuries. As we have seen, at the conclusion of the Illyrian Wars, Rome was left in possession of (or alliance with – one and the same thing in Roman strategic thinking) several Greek colonies near the Dalmatian Coast. So far as can be deduced, at this time Rome didn't harbour any territorial ambitions in Macedonia.

Phase One: Rome alone versus Philip

In the summer of 215 BC, an embassy from Philip, lead by the Athenian Xenophanes, reached Hannibal's camp to negotiate a treaty with the Carthaginian commander, who seemed on the verge of dealing Rome a crushing defeat after the massacre at Cannae the previous year. The vague terms likely reflected Hannibal's confidence in a quick victory. Philip and Hannibal were to act as allies against Rome, although neither was required to send any direct help to the other. Once victory was achieved, peace terms to be dictated to the Romans stipulated that they would agree never to attack Philip, to abandon all of their 'possessions' on the Illyrian mainland (at this stage this referred to their official friends and allies) and were to return the households of Demetrius of Pharos, captured by the Romans during the Second Illyrian War.

The Romans discovered the terms of the treaty when a ship bearing a draft copy and the Carthaginian delegation was captured off the coast of Calabria. In response to this disclosure, Rome reinforced the twenty-five warships anchored in a staging area on Italy's south-east coast with an additional thirty vessels under the command of M. Valerius Laevinus, who was delegated to ascertain whether the treaty was genuine or not. If so, he was then to cross to Macedonia and bottle up Philip so as to thwart his plan.

In the spring of 214 BC, Philip made a second attempt to capture Apollonia from the sea. His fleet apparently consisted of 120 light *lembi*. This fleet reached the bay of Aulon, capturing the port of Oricum. Philip then began a siege of Apollonia, but as in 216 the Romans were quick to respond. Laevinus quickly recaptured Oricum, and then threw reinforcements into Apollonia. The Romans and Apollonians then launched a successful attack on Philip's camp. Philip was forced to burn his boats and retreat across the Pindus Mountains into Macedonia. Here, once again, we find evidence of ships and armies working in close cooperation.

In the autumn of 214 BC, Philip's attempt to take Messene ended in failure. In revenge, Philip pillaged the territory of Messene, resulting in the city's factions uniting against Philip and leaving the Greek (Achaean) League, moving closer to the Aetolians. The Achaean League was further weakened in the following year by the death of its leader, Aratus.

In 213 BC, Philip made an overland attack on Illyria. This was far more successful than either of his naval expeditions had been. Failing to take Apollonia and Dyrrhachium, he was able to subdue the Atintanes and Parthini tribes and capture Dimallum and the fortress of Lissus, driving a wedge between the Romans at Oricum and their ally Scerdilaidas. He also gained a foothold on the Adriatic coast, which could have served the Carthaginian fleet well in an attack on Italian shipping had they opted to exploit it.

Phase Two: Rome and Aetolia vs Philip

By 212 BC, the deteriorating situation on the Illyrian coast spurred the Romans to look for a Greek ally. Further, Hannibal had captured Tarentum, while a large Carthaginian fleet was engaged in an attempt to break the siege of Syracuse. Part of this fleet could easily have been sent around the Italian coast to Philip's new coastal possessions, posing a risk that Philip might transport the Macedonian army to Italy.

The only effective ally in Philip's neighbourhood available to the Romans was the Aetolian League, which was based on the northern side of the Corinthian Gulf. By 212 BC, the leading figures in the league were both hostile to Philip. It seemed a propitious time to renew the war. Achaea was weak and leaderless, while Philip's intervention in Messene had turned the rest of the Peloponnese against him. Further east, Attalus of Pergamum, a long-standing friend of the Aetolian League, had been tied down in Asia Minor by the Achaean revolt, but that had now been put down, freeing him to agree to come to the aid of the league.

Either late in 212 or during 211 BC, Laevinus visited Aetolia with his fleet, the first time that a Roman war fleet had entered Greek harbours. He met with the federal assembly of Aetolia and agreed a treaty of alliance. The Romans agreed to provide twenty-five quinqueremes, while the Aetolians provided the majority of the soldiers. Elis, Messene, Sparta, Attalus, Pleuratus and Scerdilaidas were all free to join the alliance if they so wished. The two parties also agreed not to make a separate peace.

The new alliance initially targeted Acarnania, an ally of Philip's located on the coast west of the Aetolian heartland. In the autumn of 212 BC, Philip captured territory along the northern borders of Macedonia. Encouraged by his preoccupation in the north, the Aetolians invaded Acarnania. The fiercely determined Acarnanians held off the Aetolians until Philip was able to return from the north.

The Romans, employing their naval assets, were more successful. Laevinus used his fleet to capture Oeniadae and Nasus from the Acarnanians, and all of Zacynthus – apart from the acropolis – from Philip. All three cities were then handed to the Aetolians.

Next, in 211 BC, Laevinus' ships captured Anticyra in conjunction with the Aetolian general Scopas. The Romans handed over the town to the Aetolians, who shortly lost it to Philip. Late in the summer of 211, Laevinus was replaced by the proconsul P. Sulpicius Galba, who would command the Roman fleet for most of the rest of the war.

In 210 BC, Philip took the initiative in an effort to expel the Aetolians from Phthiotic Achaea (Thessaly). If successful, this would give him access to central Greece. The principal effort focussed on the siege of the coastal city of Echinus. The Aetolian general Dorimachus and Sulpicius, in cooperation with the Roman fleet, attempted unsuccessfully to break the siege, and the city fell to Philip.

The sole Roman success of this first expedition into the Aegean was the capture of the island of Aegina. The island was then handed over to the Aetolians. Lacking a fleet, the Aetolians sold the island to Attalus of Pergamum for 30 talents. This brought Attalus' fleet into the war. In response, Philip made an alliance with Prusias of Bithynia, who promised to bring his own fleet into the Aegean.

This same year, Sparta joined the war, this time on the side of Rome and the Aetolians. The entry of Sparta into the war greatly complicated Philip's tasks, for his allies in Achaea were now under attack from three sides. In 209 and 208 BC, Philip would be forced to come to their aid.

In 209 BC, the Aetolians' defeats on land at least temporarily convinced them to seek peace. An armistice was agreed and peace negotiations began, but they broke down when both Sulpicius and Attalus arrived with reinforcements. Philip resumed his campaign in Achaea, inflicting a defeat on the Romans at Sicyon. Philip's further efforts failed, whereafter he was forced to return to Macedonia to deal with a Dardanian invasion.

The campaign of 208 BC began inauspiciously for Philip. Sulpicius, Attalus and their fleets were operating in the Aegean, the Aetolians had fortified Thermopylae in an attempt to confine Philip to the north, and it was rumoured that the Illyrians and Maedi were planning to invade Macedonia. As it turned out, that year demonstrated the limitations of Roman strength in Greece at this time. They were reliant on the Aetolians in any campaign on land. While they exercised command of the sea, they lacked the troops to exploit this advantage – evidence of the validity of Corbett's sea-land interdependency conception.

The combined fleet unsuccessfully assaulted Lemnos, Peparethus and Chalcis. On land, Philip was able to force his way through the pass of Thermopylae, and came very close to capturing Attalus at Opus in Locris. This marked the end of Attalus' involvement in the war in Greece; Prusias of Bithynia finally entered the war on Philip's side, invading Pergamum, and Attalus was forced to return home to defend his kingdom. The loss of this associate ultimately represented a serious weakening of Sulpicius' alliance, although he was able to achieve some further success in the short term.

With Attalus out of the war, Sulpicius retired to Aegina with the Roman fleet, leaving Philip free to campaign in Locris, where he captured Thronium, and in Phocis, where he captured Tithronium and Drymaea. He was then forced back into the Peloponnese to repel a Spartan attack on the Achaeans.

Phase Three: Philip vs Aetolia

The final stage of the war saw the Romans withdraw from the Aegean. Clearly they had no hegemonic ambitions in this region at that point. Although Sulpicius sacked Dyme, the most westerly of the Achaean cities, thereafter the Romans concentrated on patrolling the Illyrian coast. From their point of view, the war had achieved its aim, keeping Philip away from the Illyrian coast at a time when the danger from Hannibal was at its most extreme. In addition, 208-207 BC saw Hasdrubal's invasion of Italy in an effort to link with Hannibal, and it is possible that Sulpicius' legion was withdrawn to help deal with this threat. It was also clear after ten years that Carthage was not going to help Philip.

This left the Aetolians in a vulnerable position, made worse by an unexpected revival of Achaean strength which enabled the latter to defeat the Spartan phalanx.

With no distraction in the south, Philip was able to concentrate on finishing off the Aetolians. He was able to drive them from Thessaly and recapture Zacynthos (in the Ionian Islands). He then invaded Aetolia from the north, sacking the Aetolian federal sanctuary at Thermum.

The defeats of 207 BC and the lack of Roman support convinced the Aetolians that it was time to make peace. In the autumn of 206, and in violation of their alliance with Rome, the Aetolian League made peace with Philip. Most of the areas lost to Philip during the fighting remained lost, including most of Phocia. The Aetolians also earned the hostility of Rome.

The Romans made one more attempt to renew the war, sending the proconsul P. Sempronius Tuditanus to Illyria at the head of a force of 10,000 infantry and

1,000 cavalry. This army was too small to face Philip alone, and was clearly meant to encourage the Aetolians to resume the war, but without success.

Both sides now had little reason to continue the war. Philip realized by now that Carthage was going to lose its war with Rome – in 205 BC, Scipio Africanus was preparing for his invasion of Africa the following year. If Philip was willing to make peace on good terms, then Rome had no need to continue to fight. When the magistrates of the Epirote confederacy offered to organize peace negotiations, the Romans agreed.

Rome eventually signed a peace treaty in 205 BC, but only so that they could concentrate on defeating Hannibal. Distracted as they were by the fight with Carthage closer to home, the war had been conducted in a desultory manner. There was only minor skirmishing by the force that Rome dispatched across the Adriatic, and that merely to occupy some slight slivers of coastline sufficient to hinder the piracy against Roman mercantile traffic provoked by Macedon, which Rome had hoped would have ended with the pacification of Illyria.

The peace treaty (Treaty of Phoenice) was accordingly rather inconclusive, merely postponing the final reckoning with Philip. Its terms were, on balance, favourable to Philip as it left him with his conquests in Illyria intact. However, it served notice that Rome's sphere of influence was about to take a quantum leap across thus-far unsettled waters. At worst, Rome had failed to check Philip's conquests in Greece, though it had made his advances more costly and compelled him to settle for less than he desired. The upside was that Rome was able to dispatch naval units to eastern waters in spite of having to guard the seas off the Italian and Spanish coasts against Carthaginian vessels attempting to reinforce Hannibal. It deterred Philip from coming to the aid of Hannibal and served notice on Carthage and any other would-be naval opponents that Rome's navy had a long reach.

Second Macedonian War

Significantly, after the conclusion to what was, in effect, the expansion of the Second Punic War into the Eastern Mediterranean, Macedonia was down but not out, and its truculent resilience led to the Second Macedonian War, spanning from 200-196 BC. It is known as the Second notwithstanding that the First, as indicated above, was not really a war *per se*, but a sideshow incidental to the Second Punic War.

Philip V of Macedonia and Antiochus III of Syria combined to share Ptolemaic possessions in the Aegean and Judaea/Palestine. Philip began harrying Pergamum, Rhodes and other Greek city-states of the Aegean. Philip's successes in Asia Minor caused the lesser states in this area to fear for their independence, and Rhodes, Pergamum and Byzantium together declared war on Philip.

So far as Rome was concerned, Philip still had to be suppressed, because what he had done several years earlier was emblematic of a deep-seated pattern of exploiting Rome's preoccupation in wars with other enemies to form alliances against her. Thus the Second Macedonian War began in 200 BC.

Rome proclaimed that she wanted the liberation of all Hellene *poleis* from Macedonian rule. This sort of strategy – posing as liberators from tyranny – had been used many times before by the Hellenistic empires, but it still worked. Many central and southern Hellenes sided with Rome. In 197 BC, Philip was defeated at the land Battle of Cynoscephalae and forced to become an ally of Rome. The next year, at the Isthmian Games, the Roman general Flaminius dramatically declared the independence of all Hellene states. In 194, all Roman troops were pulled back from the Balkans, after everything had been arranged.

Being as the war was decided by a land battle, Cynoscephalae, in 197, and there were no grand sea battles to record, one has to ask what role the fleets played in the victorious conclusion of the war. As it happens, it was a significant one. This great land battle was facilitated by less conspicuous, though no less important, movements on the seas.

In 201 BC, the Roman Senate, even though the country was exhausted by the previous wars, determined to take an active part in eastern affairs. Rome watched warily as a Macedonian fleet captured Samos and destroyed the Egyptian fleet there, thus checking Ptolemaic naval activity in the Aegean. Accordingly, it sent M. Valerius Laevinus with thirty-eight ships to the Aegean. In that same year, there occurred the Battle of Chios, wherein the allied fleets of Rhodes and Pergamum defeated the Macedonian fleet, Philip losing twenty-seven large and sixty-five small ships. At the request of the allies, Rome entered the war against Macedonia.

The ancient sources testify that the fleet was active during this conflict. After the first step of dispatching Laevinus with thirty-eight ships to the East in 200 BC, during the first campaign Claudius Cento was sent to Athens with twenty vessels. This squadron succeeded in checking the inroads of pirates, and later surprised and sacked Chalcis in Euboea. Owing to its small size, however, this fleet was unable to capitalize on these achievements. This same force, however, was able to thwart Philip's attack on Athens. In 199 BC, King Attalus of Pergamum received instructions to unite his ships with the Roman fleet at Aegina. The combined fleets proceeded to Oreus and captured the place, enabling attacks on the Macedonian coast.

During 198-195 BC, several expeditions in search of plunder were set in motion against Philip's ally Nabis, the Spartan tyrant. Successful seaborne raids were launched against Andros, Icus, Cassandrea (which naval sortie was repulsed) and Acanthus. Eretria was captured and Cenchreae blockaded. In 197 BC, Lucius Flaminius brought the fleet to Leucas, bringing about its surrender.

While none of these foregoing actions rise to the level of a decisive fleet engagement, a closer examination shows that ships played a significant role in bringing the war to a successful conclusion. This was a demonstration of Corbett's dictum that while fleets alone rarely decide a war's outcome, they facilitate the land campaigns that do so. For example, the provisioning of the army from secure forward bases in Greece was an important component in the Roman victory.

When Flaminius entered Epirus, foreseeing a shortage of provisions, for example, he ordered that the transports come to the Ambracian Gulf. It was the consul's policy to spare the country (i.e., not ravage the natives' farms and storage facilities), and thus the army was in need. Not until the ships arrived and provisions were brought up from the sea was the consul able to move inland. Again, when engaged in the siege of Atrax, the Romans found it impossible to subsist in winter so far from the sea and were obliged to retire to Anticyra. These are but two specific references which support the inference that the army was frequently dependent on the fleet for supplies.

Thiel, in *Studies...* (pp.247-49), contains an interesting discussion of why Rome, in the final operations of the war in 197-196 BC, had mounted fleet operations from the western flank of Greece while the army debarked on the eastern side of the Greek peninsula, whereas combining the two efforts might have secured tangible benefits. His explanation is quite lucid. This question has also been deliberated by Clark in his 1915 dissertation. The following is a summary and reflection on their arguments.

In light of the difficulty of provisioning the army when distant from the sea, it seems odd that the fleet was not used to transport the troops to the eastern coast of Greece, where a direct attack could have been delivered at the heart of Philip's power and at no distance from the coast. It may have been that the Romans were afraid of transporting a large body of troops in waters that were at that time little-known to them, and that to make the short voyage across the Adriatic and to deliver the main attack from the west seemed the safer, if the more drawn-out, method of campaign. Perhaps the Senate was not quite alive to the advantages which were theirs by virtue of supremacy at sea. Yet at the same time, the Romans did follow a definite policy by which the army pushed its attack inland from the west while the fleet served as a check on Philip's movements in the east.

That the policy was a deliberate one with reference to both fleet and army, it is not difficult to see. The Senate, at the outset, recognizing the importance of a strong fleet, set about its naval preparations, despite the fact that debts incurred in the Hannibalic war remained to be paid. Livy makes it plain that Corcyra was retained as the regular base for fleet operations and as a wintering station for the ships. So as not to leave the eastern waters wholly unpatrolled, ships were also wintered at Piraeus. Also noteworthy is the Romans' eagerness to utilize Attalus of Pergamum and the Rhodians as naval allies, thereby alleviating their initial disadvantage in numbers of vessels available in the theatre and their unfamiliarity with navigational hazards in eastern waters.

Some late-nineteenth-century commentators, notably the German scholar William Ihne (*History of Rome*, Vol.3, p.78), held that the naval war contributed little to the Roman victory. He asserted that even though some successful blows were struck at hostile ports, the Roman ships were unable to engage the Macedonian fleet as it never ventured out of the port of Demetrius, nor did the Roman fleet attack Macedonia itself. Written just a few years before Mahan's first *Influence of Sea Power* volume was translated into German, it could not apply his sea-power dicta as a corrective. The American admiral, had he considered the Second Macedonian War, would have noted the fact that the Roman fleet was able to keep the Macedonian ships bottled up in Demetrius was an indicator of the dissuasive influence of command of the sea. Considering its victory over the Rhodians at Chios prior to Rome's entry into the conflict, it is apparent that Philip's fleet was a worthy opponent and could have put the Roman flotilla at a disadvantage.

Had Macedonian ships been permitted to patrol freely along the eastern coast, they likely would have rounded the Peloponnesus and attacked the Roman forces on the western shores. This would have likely resulted in a reversal of the actual situation: not Philip, but the Romans would have been caught between the two forces, their provisions intercepted and their communications cut. But, in the event, the naval force under Heraclius was unable to sortie from Demetrius, fearing being caught by the Roman ships, while the arrival of the Roman fleet at Oreus exposed the shores of the Macedonian homeland to Roman sea power, should the Romans opt to strike. Thus, the Roman fleet was effective at a distance, so to speak, leaving the Macedonian fleet paralyzed due to the uncertainty about where and when the Romans might strike and thereby depriving Philip of a potentially powerful auxiliary arm.

On the strategic level, it was unfortunate that after its successful initial attack, the Roman fleet was unable to hold Chalcis. This situation pointed up the importance of controlling the Strait of Euripus, for if the Roman naval strength had been sufficiently large to both retain Chalcis and protect Athens, then both Chalcis and the Euripus Strait could have been seized from Philip. This would have given the Romans an important advantage at the beginning of the war. Much as Thermopylae Pass was a potential land chokepoint for armies entering Greek territory, as proven in the Greco-Persian War, so control of the Euripus Strait could block entry by sea.

Roman naval presence along the eastern coast not only kept a check against Philip's fleet, but hampered the movements of his army, as demonstrated by the cases of Athens and Eleusis. The arrival of Cento and his fleet provided security for Athens, while later the approach of the Roman ships from Piraeus saved Eleusis from being attacked by Philip.

Finally, the presence of the Roman fleet was a strong influence in both winning over new allies and holding on to those already committed to aid Rome. For example, the Aetolian confederation was convinced to join the Roman cause by the arrival of the Roman ships at Oreus, raising the prospect of investing Macedonia from the sea. Further, just at the point when the allies were beginning to despair, the Achaens were largely influenced to join up with Rome thanks to the latter's command of the sea. This foresight is emblematic of what today is known as coalition warfare. The British Empire, and later the Commonwealth, wisely chose allies who might provide military assistance at times when Britain was insufficient in land-power strength in vital theatres. Similarly, Rome tapped the naval prowess of maritime allies to supplement its meagre naval resources in the East.

After his defeat at Cynoscephalae in Thessaly (197 BC), as a measure of the growing importance of naval forces in Roman strategic thought, Philip was forced to negotiate peace and hand over his fleet to Rome, retaining only six ships. But this did not put an end to the Macedonian threat. After Phillip's defeat at the hands of Rome, the Seleucid emperor King Antiochus III absorbed his conquests in Asia Minor, and began to extend his rule to Thessaly and Greece. This event precipitated a new round of conflict, which is known as the Syrian, Seleucid or Asiatic Wars.

The Syrian War (aka The Asiatic War)

Causes and Prelude To War

The end of the Macedonian Wars really settled nothing and gave rise to the conflict with Antiochus III, who opportunely tried to regain ancestral territories in Asia Minor and Thrace. The Second Macedonian War (200-196 BC) had ended Macedon's role as a major player and preserved Rhodian independence. Rhodes would continue to play an important balancing role as a naval power and erstwhile ally of navally neglectful Rome for another century or so, after which its maritime strength waned.

The Seleucid King Antiochus III of Syria was Rome's next opportunistic adversary to roil Adriatic waters. As early as the autumn of 201 BC, envoys from some important Greek states arrived in Rome to report that Philip V of Macedon, stirring up trouble once again, had joined forces with Antiochus III, with the intention of destroying the domain of the child-king Ptolemy V, ruler of Ptolemaic Egypt. If true, this would result in a concentration of tremendous power or, even worse, the supremacy of one of these two bellicose monarchs to form a new geopolitical threat in the East following shortly from the narrow victory over another existential threat, Hannibal.

Eckstein in *Rome Enters the Greek East*, chapter 8, 'Hegemonic War II: Rome and Antiochus the Great, 200-188 BC', believes it likely that the Greek envoys warned the senators that Antiochus' formidable navy of 100 quinqueremes could soon be merged with Philip V's own large and newly built fleet of fifty quinqueremes, and pointed out that in the summer of 201 BC the latter's fleet had proven itself highly effective off the coast of Asia Minor. However, they failed to observe that Philip's naval losses in this battle (the Battle of Chios) left his fleet greatly weakened. At the same time these concerned envoys were making their case in Italy, fierce fighting was raging between Philip on one side and Pergamum and Rhodes on the other. Regardless of any other danger spots in the south-eastern Aegean Sea, it was this burgeoning naval menace that should command Rome's urgent attention.

By this time, the Roman Senate was keenly aware that sea power had been instrumental in preventing Philip from attacking Illyria, and possibly even forestalled his assault on Italy under Hannibal's guidance. Rome's control of the seas to the east was once more endangered. The Senate strengthened its naval forces on its eastern periphery to mount a watch over the threat from that direction.

As the envoys had not verified that an imminent attack from Syria was being prepared, A. Atilius Serranus was dispatched to Greece, Marcus Baebius Tamphilus took some legions to Tarentum and Brundisium, and a fleet of twenty ships was ordered to protect the Sicilian coast. The importance of the fleet at this juncture is indicated by the fact that the person in charge, L. Salinator, was invested with 'the imperium' and immediately proceeded to Sicily. Additional instructions were dispatched to Baebius, who then crossed with his forces into Apollonia on the Corinthian Gulf.

Overview of the War

Some Hellenes, especially those of the Aetolian League (the alliance of Hellenic nations that had aided Rome against Philip), felt that Rome hadn't done enough for them to repay their loyalty. They captured the stronghold of Demetrias and invited Antiochus to liberate Hellas. Antiochus, who had recently campaigned in Anatolia and Thrace and thus fomented tension between Rome and his empire, accepted the invitation and sent a small expeditionary force into Hellas in 192 BC. The Romans defeated it at Thermopylae and thus expelled him from Europe. They then marched into Asia and defeated Antiochus at Magnesia in 190. A final treaty was signed in 188 at Apamea, stating that Antiochus had to retreat behind the Taurus Mountains, pay a large tribute and give up his war elephants and navy to Rome. His Asian possessions were divided between Rhodes and Pergamum. The Romans had also crushed the Celtic Galatians in Asia, a potential threat to Pergamum, and destroyed the Aetolian League for being disloyal.

This war is significant because it ruined the last chance for any Hellenistic nation to become powerful again. Rome was omnipotent now and could do whatever she wished, as she would show during the following decades. This war is of interest here, more so than the Macedonian Wars, because of its considerable naval component. Fleet operations were even more conspicuous than in the Macedonian Wars.

Course of the War

Ever eager for opportunities to retaliate against his arch-foe, Hannibal was present at Antiochus' court and proposed a plan of campaign to the king. As in the Second Punic War, he was determined to take the war to Italy and deal Rome a knockout blow. To accomplish this, he requested that Antiochus provide him with 100 warships, plus infantry and horse, with which he would sail to Carthage and convince his compatriots to back his plan. After initially agreeing, the king subsequently rejected this approach. He apparently assumed that all Greece would welcome him with open arms, and thus he would require no assistance from the Carthaginians. So he sailed to Demetrius with a token force, thereby precipitating the conflict.

Philip of Macedon was greatly riled by the treatment which he received from the Romans after the peace with Antiochus; the subsequent course of events was not sufficient to appease his wrath. His neighbours in Greece and Thrace, mostly communities that had once trembled at the Macedonian name, now similarly trembled at the Roman's. They now diligently sought, as was to be expected, to retaliate on the fallen great power for all the injuries which they had received at the hands of Macedon since the time of Philip II. Rome no longer had any troops in Greece, yet it was clear that the regional powers of Greece had been allotted their territories with a view towards Roman aims.

To the Aetolian League, who felt betrayed, Rome's high-handedness seemed intolerable. It appeared to the Aetolians that Greece was being treated as though she had been conquered. This sense of grievance played into the hands of the Syrian monarch.

At length, the Aetolian League appealed to Antiochus III to come to their aid. Antiochus had concluded his successful war against Egypt and even achieved an alliance with King Ptolemy V Epiphanes. He had also made peace with Rhodes. Antiochus' standing was unrivalled among the rulers of the successor states of Alexander's old empire. Now this great king was called upon to liberate Greece from what the league perceived as Roman oppression. Moreover, a ready, powerful ally already awaited him, with the promise that others would follow if only he led his forces into Greece. The diplomatic jockeying and motives are complex, but were generally as follows.

At the councils of the various confederacies, the Hellenes had arduously pleaded their case against Macedon. They similarly appealed to the Roman Senate for aid. The Romans had allowed Philip to retain what he had taken from the Aetolians; but in Thessaly the confederacy of the Magnetes alone had formally joined the Aetolians, while those towns which Philip had wrested from the Aetolians in two of the other Thessalian confederacies – the 'Thessalian', in its narrower sense, and the Perrhaebian – were reclaimed by the latter on the grounds that Philip had only liberated these towns, and not actually conquered them. The Athamanes conceived that they might request their freedom; and Eumenes demanded the maritime cities which Antiochus had possessed in Thrace proper, especially Aenus and Maronea, although in the peace with Antiochus the Thracian Chersonese alone had been expressly promised to him.

As a measure of the importance of sea power in this conflict, one has only to consider the activities of Rome to ready itself when, based on both rumour and spy reports, it anticipated that Antiochus was preparing to bring the war to Sicily. Baebius Tamphilus was ordered to build thirty new ships and repair any others that might be made fit for service. Additionally, two praetors were to provide 100 quinqueremes. The fleet was originally intended to sail against Nabis of Sparta, but was held back pending the report of the ambassadors from Antiochus. When it was learned that, contrary to earlier reports, Syria was not preparing for an immediate attack in Italian waters, Atilius was sent to Greece, Baebius was ordered to Tarentum and Brundisium with the legions, and twenty warships were sent to protect Sicily.

Rome was again ill-prepared for another war in Greece, not least because she had wars in Liguria (a Celtic uprising) and Spain to contend with. War commenced on a small scale in 192 BC. What few troops Rome deployed soon found themselves cut off in Boeotia. In 191, Rome therefore sent a force of 20,000 infantry, accompanied by cavalry and elephants, under the command of consul M. Acilius Glabrio. Glabrio marched on Thessaly and Antiochus at once retreated to the Pass of Thermophylae, where King Leonidas of Sparta had held back Xerxes' vast horde in 480 BC. We need not dwell on the details of this land battle, which Rome won.

To counter the sizeable Seleucid navy, the Romans enlisted the aid of the Rhodians and mastered the enemy in the Battle of Myonnesus; Antiochus was defeated on land and in the ensuing peace of 189 BC he gave up all but twelve of his warships. By then every naval power in the Mediterranean, apart from Rome itself, had vanished; the once formidable naval might of Egypt was a broken reed and what was left of the Seleucid naval forces was likewise weakened. Rome had won its mastery of the Eastern Mediterranean primarily by land battles, but wherever and whenever naval forces were useful, they had been provided out of

Roman resources of funds and men. The Macedonian and Syrian Wars should have driven this lesson home more forcefully than ever: but Rome drew the wrong conclusion from them.

Review Of The Naval Aspects Of The Syrian/Asiatic War

Having determined that he would not require Hannibal's services (and the distraction from his own plans to serve as saviour of the Greeks), Antiochus sailed westward with his fleet and landed at Demetrius with a surprisingly meagre force, thereby commencing hostilities. Having augmented the fleet to a total of 130 quinqueremes – originally devised to confront Nablis of Sparta – Rome held this force back until the ambassadors to Antiochus returned with intelligence on the nature of the threat.

While Rome's vessels were poised to take any action necessary to resolve the eastern crisis, they presented Philip of Macedon with an ultimatum that unless he made peace with 'the Greeks', Rome would declare war on him. At the same time, an embassy had been sent to Antiochus to warn him against invading Egypt proper. Although temporarily heeding the Roman 'advice', Antiochus refraining from attacking Egypt, he did seize all Ptolemaic holdings in Lebanon and Judaea. However, upon hearing that Ptolemy V had died in 196 BC, he once again prepared to conquer the Nile region. Being as Rome had withdrawn its forces to Italy in the settlement of 196, her threats may have lacked some credibility.

For his part, Philip rejected the Roman ultimatum and the two states resumed warring against each other. Rome immediately went on the offensive, landing a large expeditionary force in Greece at the same time as a large Roman war fleet, augmented with Pergamene and Rhodian squadrons, swept the Aegean of Philip's ships and severely weakened Macedon's Greek allies. This fleet, numbering approximately 100 quinqueremes, fifty-five of which were Roman, outnumbered Philip's naval forces two-to-one and deterred him from confronting them at sea. It is said that the leader of the Achaean League, just prior to switching sides from Macedon to the coalition in 198 BC, said, 'The Romans have the sea in their power.'

To sum up, the Romans had withdrawn from the Balkan Peninsula, but the resulting power vacuum quickly attracted Antiochus and, as a result of opportunistic intrigues, the Romans then easily polished off (in 192-188 BC) the last Mediterranean power that might even vaguely threaten their homeland. They ultimately depended on the assistance of the very capable and experienced Rhodian navy. That navy, reflecting the dominance of Roman sources, has been unfairly treated as a mere adjunct to the Roman fleets; but in reality it was, at the time, *the* major naval force in the Eastern Mediterranean. In essence, the Roman conquest was completed largely thanks to the unappreciated maritime expertise of their Rhodian ally. Having provided Rome with valuable naval help – to put it mildly – in her first foray into Asia, the Rhodians were rewarded with territory and enhanced status.

Jorit Wintjes (in 'Command at Sea – The Roman Perspective', University of Würzburg, *Mars & Clio* No.22, Summer 2008, pp.2-15) makes some interesting points concerning the navies in this war. The Syrian War saw several large-scale engagements; in this context, the Battle of Myonessus of 190 BC is of particular interest. At that time the war had already gone badly for Antiochus, who, having had his attempts at getting a firm foothold in Europe frustrated, now faced a Roman invasion into Asia Minor. In 190, his fleet, which was based at Ephesus, was the only major asset left to him that was theoretically capable of preventing such a Roman incursion. In a move perhaps comparable to that of the Carthaginians at Mylae in 260, he attacked a small coastal town to the north of Ephesus which was known to have good relations to Rome, hoping that this would draw out the main Roman fleet which was based at Samos, where it had effectively blockaded the Antiochene fleet.

The Romans did indeed react in the way Antiochus had hoped, moving first towards Teos in order to gather supplies. There the Seleucid commander Polyxenidas had hoped to trap the Roman fleet inside the harbour of Geraesticum, a bay completely surrounded by rocky promontories that did not allow more than two ships coming out of it at the same time. Fortunately for the Romans, the commander of their allied Rhodian squadron had pointed out the dangers of Geraesticum and recommended another harbour instead. Deprived of the opportunity to destroy the Roman fleet, Polyxenidas then offered battle on the next day off the cape of Myonessus. Polyxenidas could field a force of around ninety heavy ships, whereas the Romans and Rhodians had only eighty ships between them – around sixty heavy Roman ships, the rest being Rhodian ones of lighter construction. Many of the latter, however, were armed with fire pots, making them dangerous opponents. Having a shorter line, the allied force faced the grave danger of being outflanked by Polyxenidas, and apparently it was exactly that which he had in mind. Instead of leading his line from a central position with the van of his fleet, he stayed on the left flank as the opposing forces closed on each other. On seeing this development, Eudamas, the commander of the Rhodian squadron – which seems to have been either near the Roman left flank or to the rear – reacted by moving his ships swiftly to the Roman right, thus preventing Polyxenidas from hitting the Roman ships in the flank. The Rhodian manoeuvre is a testimony to the tactical skills of Eudamas and shows once again that it must have been possible to get at least a general idea about enemy dispositions during the initial phases of a battle. Of course, communications were of paramount importance here.

Eudamas not only must have conveyed his planned reaction to his own captains, but also to the Roman commander – who might have had an uneasy moment or two at the sight of his allies suddenly leaving their original positions in the face of an enemy superior in numbers. After heavy fighting, the Seleucid fleet gave way first in the centre. Polyxenidas, now himself threatened in the flank by the victorious Romans, fled the scene, while the Antiochene right was the last to break off the engagement. It was the manoeuvre of Eudamas that really decided the outcome of the battle, denying Polyxenidas the advantage of his numerical superiority and throwing the Antiochene left into disarray. As a result, the fleet of Antiochus lost a considerable number of ships, while the allied forces lost only three. With the defeat at Myonessus, the strategic initiative finally went over to the Romans, who invaded Asia Minor and eventually brought Antiochus to battle near Magnesia at the end of the year.

There were various naval lessons to be learned from this war. Several blunders by Antiochus on the naval side stand out. (1) His navy, despite its good commander, Polyxenidas the exiled Rhodian, was not on par with the combined Rhodian, Pergamene and Roman fleets. Although he most likely deemed his navy to be superior, Antiochus needed to build more ships and train the crews for several months before engaging in operations. Without control of the seas, Antiochus did not stand much chance in this war. (2) After his naval defeat, Antiochus made an inexplicable mistake. He abandoned Lysimachia in Thrace, which could have held the Romans for months, and simultaneously left the shores of the Hellespont, allowing the Romans to land their ships easily on the opposite side. For her part, Rome had leaned heavily on sea-minded allies to defeat the Seleucids and, from her subsequent naval demobilization, learned the wrong lesson from this; i.e., she need not bear the expense of rebuilding, crewing, provisioning and repairing a fleet while she enjoyed the respect and cooperation of such maritime allies. Events were to show that she lacked the British skill of some eighteen centuries hence in managing alliances and power blocs with friends who could provide the bulk of the land forces while Britain furnished the naval support. In Rome's case, the land–sea equation was reversed, but the principles were the same.

In spite of the confusion which prevailed in Crete, and the rapacious character of its inhabitants, it seems that Rhodes was able, for the most part, to keep the seas clear of predators during the interval between the Second and Third Macedonian Wars. However, the outbreak of piracy which accompanied the Syrian War showed that in abnormal times, the Rhodian maritime patrols were insufficient. But with the rapid decline that followed the withdrawal of Roman favour after the Third Macedonian War, it became obvious that the Rhodians were no longer equal to the task.

Other Minor Wars of the Second Century BC

After some years of peace, the Adriatic again fell into a disturbed state. In 181 BC, the inhabitants of Brundisium and Tarentum were complaining of piratical descents on their coasts. When the piracies of the Ligurians necessitated the maintenance of a special squadron to patrol the Tuscan Sea, a similar force was commissioned to protect the southern part of Italy as far as Barium. In the complaints received by the Romans from Apulia there was special mention of the Istrian raiders, and the praetor, Duronius, was empowered to act against them. In his report, he stated that all the pirate vessels operating in the Adriatic came from the kingdom of Genthius, the new king of Illyria, but apart from a demand for the release of Roman citizens detained at Corcyra, no action was taken at the time against Genthius himself. The general effect of Roman naval activity in this period was that of deterrence, as Roman ships acted as a brake on wider piratical attacks on allies in the Adriatic.

Third Macedonian War

Although this conflict had little in the way of discrete naval actions, such as we have seen to a limited extent in the First and, more extensively, the Second Macedonian Wars, and the Syrian/Asiatic War, sea power nonetheless had a role to play in a more nuanced way. Rome, and its naval associates and allies, sent warships to confront Perseus, son of Philip V, but in the end there was not much for them to do. The background to this war involves complicated diplomatic jockeying and covert fifth-column type missions, which need not detain us here.

Thiel devotes some fifteen pages to the Roman navy in this war, but, as there were no significant naval actions to report, mainly speculates on lost opportunities in the failure of the navy to cooperate with the legions by landing marines at key strategic points, which might have turned some of the disastrous early land battles into victories. Notably, had the fleet effected a troop insertion at Pydna in 171 or 170 BC, this would likely have severed Macedonian communications and starved Perseus' army.

Instead, the praetors kept the ships busy looting Boeotia and punishing the inhabitants for their support of Perseus, who had also stirred up the ever-troublesome Illyrians to rebel against Roman rule. The fleet's relative idleness (though, arguably, they had kept the Macedonian warships at bay) compounded the poor performance of the Roman army commanders.

Early in the war, Rhodes had offered to provide their excellent ships – some forty of them – to augment the dilapidated Roman fleet, but this was inexplicably refused. However, contributions of other naval allies in the east were accepted, though, as it turned out, these were were unnecessary since Rome did not exploit her naval edge to secure any advantage. Notably, the naval contributions of the allies consisted of smaller, faster warships, *lemboi*, in contrast to the large Roman quinqueremes, which cannot have escaped the attention of the Roman commanders.

Near the end of the conflict, the fleet made a contribution by anchoring off Heracleum and disembarking 5,000 legionaries, and remained to supply and feed this force, which forced Perseus' army towards Pydna, where the Roman legions moving from the east were successful. The fleet pursued Perseus to Samos, where he fled, and captured him.

In essence, there was poor or non-existent cooperation between the Roman fleet and the legions. Thiel believes that had this been achieved during the first few years of the war, it might have avoided Roman setbacks. Further, the depredations of the Roman fleet commanders alienated segments of the Greek populations which otherwise might have assisted the Roman war effort.

Third Punic War

The *coup de grace* delivered to Carthage in 146 BC was almost a foregone conclusion, and holds little of naval interest, although of course it was Rome's supremacy at sea that enabled it to mount a combined land and sea siege of the Carthaginian home base unmolested.

By the time the Second Punic War had ended, Carthage was a mere shadow of its former power. Notwithstanding the exhaustion of the treasury, Hannibal proved to be as good a governor as he was a general, and Carthage soon recovered. However, Masinissa, governor of Numidia and a strong ally of the Romans, was able to pick at Carthage until, painfully aggravated, Carthage attacked Numidia in 150 BC, breaking the treaty that ended the Second Punic War. Rome had done little to stop Masinissa. Whenever Carthage complained to Rome about his actions, Rome sent a tribunal to them, and then decided in Masinissa's favour. Basically, Carthage was pushed into fighting again, a not very honourable course of action for Roman diplomacy.

Rome declared war on Carthage in 149 BC, and an army landed in Africa after a long, unchallenged blockade by both sea and land, as further evidence of Rome's naval mastery. Carthage could not handle the onslaught of Roman might. The Roman terms were bitterly opposed by Carthage, as they called for the physical destruction of the city. This was in no small part due to the constant calls of Cato the Elder, who ended each speech he made in the Senate with 'Carthago delenda est!' ('Carthage must be destroyed'). Carthage managed to withstand the Roman siege for three years before yielding.

In 146 BC, Scipio Aemilianus (S. Africanus Minor) stormed and sacked Carthage, and Hannibal, not wanting to give the Romans the pleasure of seeing him as a prisoner in Scipio's procession, committed suicide. The Roman army then turned up stones, ploughed the land over and salted it. By salting it, rendering the fields sterile, they guaranteed that no new Carthage could rise up from the ruins of the old. The territory was incorporated into the Roman province of Africa. Again, this episode contains little of naval import, apart from a Carthaginian attack on the Roman fleet with fire-ships which damaged several vessels, the war being largely a demonstration of complete Roman sea control. However, it would soon be seen that this sense of maritime supremacy was an illusion – Carthage's sea power was a nullity by this time in any event. The real challenge for Rome's freedom of navigation would come from the increasingly lethal piracy menace.

A second war with Crete (the first was a concommittant of the Second Macedonian War discussed above) that broke out about 155/154 BC taxed Rome's resources to the utmost, and during its course we learn that a Cretan fleet ravaged the island of Siphnos. The formerly reliable aid from the Rhodian fleet was missing: Roman jealousy over the control of trade had weakened Rhodes, the one sea power in the Aegean that was capable of dealing with the pirates, and nothing was put in its place. While Rhodes could still furnish valuable naval help, it would from here on require any prospective ally to furnish its own sizeable naval component in order to avail itself of Rhodian assistance. In another quarter of the Eastern Mediterranean, a similar policy was promoting one of the most dangerous outbreaks of piracy that ever threatened the ancient world.

Chapter Six

Rome's Further Schooling in Sea Power: The Mithridatic Wars, Fighting the Cilician Pirate Menace and the Civil War at Sea

Lapse of the Fleet and the Regrowth of Rampant Piracy

After the Punic Wars, the Romans maintained a significant navy for the first half of the second century BC, but afterward, specifically after the fatal razing of Carthage in 146 BC, they saw no reason for the continued maintenance of a large fleet. In any event, the sixty years between the destruction of Carthage and the onset of the Mithridatic Wars saw no significant naval activity, as the wars in the interim primarily occurred on land. The Roman navy relied almost exclusively on the allied Greek cities of southern Italy; the ships and crews were called upon as needed from these allied squadrons, and this seemed sufficient. Then, as now, naval forces were the most costly weapons systems extant. There was no need to squander scarce funds to own a navy when they could simply rent or borrow one from reliable naval associates as the need might arise.

Thereafter, the Romans carried out a comprehensive naval disarmament and let their own naval establishment rot away. This cavalier neglect of sea power produced retribution in one of the worst waves of piracy in classical times. Pirates could not base themselves on shores that the Romans directly occupied, but there were other lairs, partly in Crete but more handily in the rocky, crenelated and thereby well-protected harbours of western Cilicia (in south-eastern Asia Minor), known as 'Rough Cilicia'.

Rhodes, The Essential Naval Ally

Much has been made about the declining naval power of Rhodes, which was intermittently a naval ally of Rome and was for a time especially helpful in the fight against piracy. As discussed in the preceding chapter, her help was quite valuable to Rome in its war against Antiochus.

The Rhodian foreign policy – the avoidance of entangling alliances and the concern for the power balance among the great states – had long been the brilliant key to the survival of Rhodes. In this sense, Rhodes anticipated the policies of

Great Britain some 1700 years later. In the aftermath of its alliance with Rome, it certainly lost some of its influence on the sea, but not to such a drastic extent as to render it incapable of policing for pirates. However, the great pirate crisis of the Late Republic was alarming to say the least, and certainly called for more than policing. Henry A. Ormerod described it (quoted in Philip de Souza's *Piracy in the Ancient World*, pp.227–28), writing, 'Four hundred cities are said to have been sacked … so great was the impunity of the pirate, who, without fear of molestation, caroused on every shore and carried his raids inland, until all the coastal districts were uncultivated, and the Romans themselves were deprived of the use of the Appian Way.'

Eastern Power Struggles and Chaos: A Platform for Piracy

Two factors contributed to the rise of piracy. To start with, the powerful Seleucid Empire, which had controlled the seas and been beaten by Rome, started to disintegrate after circa 150 BC, when a usurper named Alexander Balas became king. Paradoxically, Rome's success in diminishing Seleucid naval power left a vacuum at sea in which the pirates could flourish. The noted reduction in the naval capacity of Rhodes, which had successfully kept the piracy under control, exacerbated this situation. There was also the fact that the Roman elite had to buy slaves to work on the large plantations (*latifundia*) in Italy, and the pirates supplied a ready trade in cheap slaves. So the patrician bloc in the Senate had a built-in disincentive to act until and unless piracy threatened their very livelihood.

Although Rome sent a naval force, commanded by a praetor named Marcus Antonius, as early as 104 BC, it was reluctant to take comprehensive measures, largely due to the aforementioned fact that the gentry needed the pirates to feed its demand for slaves. Their opposition lasted until these raids on coast-dwellers grew to epidemic proportions.

The formal passage of the *lex de Cilicia Macedoniaque provinciis* shows that Rome did not ignore the problem of Cilician piracy after Antonius' expedition of 104–103 BC: Cilicia was again designated as a *provincia* for 99 BC (in all likelihood), and the terms of the enactment contained language about eliciting cooperation from the Eastern kings. However, this was an unrealistic goal, more of a desperate wish in view of Rome's scarcity of naval resources; under the conditions prevailing, it was hardly practicable.

The end of the Scordiscan-Thracian wars and return to a defensive posture in Macedonia and Thrace, mandated in the law, might have roughly balanced accounts and precluded the commitment of substantial new resources to the East. But these measures also had their limitations.

The concentration of Roman attention on Cilician piracy specifically is not difficult to explain. Among the pirates' chief activities was, as noted above, the enslavement of seafarers and coastal dwellers to supply the burgeoning slave market at Delos. Even more troubling, from their lairs in Cilicia, along the coast of Asia Minor, and on Crete, pirates disrupted supplies to Rome, and by the 70s and 60s BC, even stopped the flow of grain from Africa. Rome was finally driven to conduct a formal war against them. As will be discussed further below, the proconsul Servilius and Marcus Antonius the elder campaigned for years with varying success, until finally the pirates became downright impudent. But before that all-out war with the pirates, there had been a series of conflicts with a challenger from Asia Minor who is said to have worked hand-in-hand with various pirate colonies.

The Rise and Sway of Mithridates VI

Pontus was located on the north-eastern rim of what is now modern-day Turkey, fronting on the southern shore of the Black Sea, while another piratical threat emanated from the opposite side of the Turkish promontory, on the northern shore of the Mediterranean, in the kingdom of Cilicia. The Cilician threat was more or less constant and half-measures had been taken at various times, while the other menace, from Pontus, was exacerbated with the advent of Mithridates VI.

When Mithridates VI inherited Pontus around 120 BC, this new monarch's regional aspirations set off a series of wars spanning thirty years, which were to become known as the three Mithridatic Wars. The politics and diplomacy of these conflicts – both in Asia Minor and at Rome – are rather complex, and mainly superfluous for a survey of naval strategy. They include the clash between Roman commanders in Anatolia and Sulla's difficulties in the homeland. Of more interest here, Mithridates' ambitions to become regional hegemon more or less enlisted the aid of various pirate clans which infested the waters surrounding the Turkish peninsula. Thus Rome's entanglement with this power struggle had naval implications. The pirates would prove to be one of the most intractable problems spawned by Mithridates' emergence as a territorial challenger in the East.

Some commentators have dismissed the branding of Mithridates' maritime allies as 'pirates' as a Roman rhetorical device to discredit their opponents. Nevertheless, there is no doubt that the loose confederation of freebooters lining the sinuous south-eastern coast of Anatolia saw advantage in securing the sponsorship of Mithridates against the Romans. After all, the Romans seemed determined to eliminate them rather than employ or appease them, as was customary with the regional powers abutting their lairs.

In 129 BC, Rome had annexed the Kingdom of Pergamum, in south-western Asia Minor. Rome turned Pergamum into the province of Asia. The south-east region of the Asian province was later reassigned to the province of Cilicia. In 104, in order to suppress piracy along the southern coast of Asia Minor, Rome acquired portions of Cilicia. The new entity was dubbed, prosaically enough, the province of Cilicia. It was intended to present a permanent challenge to the pirates based in Cilicia Tracheia, a rugged mountain district formed by the spurs of the Taurus range, which frequently terminate in rocky headlands with small sheltered harbours. In classical times, these afforded a string of havens for pirates ranged along this coast, affording them ideal hideouts from which to launch maritime ambushes on merchant ships which usually hugged the coastlines.

The titular province of Cilicia was more of an ad hoc command post than a permanent base. The Senate assigned a middle-ranking city magistrate of Rome, praetor Marcus Antonius, to conduct the war against the Cilicians. He aspired to achieve the rank of consul, and a resounding military success in his assigned province would grant him a celebratory triumph and be a big boost for his candidacy.

Given the depleted condition of Rome's naval assets, Antonius' task force appears to have been largely made up of contingents supplied by Rome's Greek allies, especially the Rhodians. In any event, the vexation of these maritime allies was most likely the chief catalyst for the campaign. With this naval assemblage, Antonius attacked cities on the southern coast of Turkey which were identified as pirate bases. We do not have a detailed account of his campaign, so much is speculation. De Souza believes that the coastal pirate enclaves may have been attacked overland, with some assistance from warships offshore. Apparently it was at least temporarily successful, since Antonius earned his triumph and was elected to the consulship in 99 BC.

However, despite warranting a triumph, Antonius' victories of 104–103 BC did not remove the threat; they merely alleviated it for the time being. One important consequence of the campaign, however, was the creation of a permanent command in the waters surrounding Cilicia. At first it consisted merely of the environs of the city of Pergamum, originally established by the Attalid rulers and gradually expanded.

Notwithstanding their acquiring a forward base in the new Cilician province, and Antonius' vaunted 'victory', shortly after 100 BC the Cilician pirate problem had again become rampant. Ideally, there would be some kind of confederation with the Seleucid rival kings of Syria, Egypt, Cyrenaica and Cyprus against the pirates; but in no way were these quarrelsome monarchs going to fight on the same side. In addition, there needed to be some vigorous campaign mounted against the coastal strongholds to the east of Pamphylia. Neither happened. The dispatch of a second praetor for Cilicia did not really address the problem, as his scope of action was constricted in the easternmost areas, in deference to the prerogatives of the friendly rulers in that sector – who, as we have noted, did little. This quadrant was exactly where the pirate threat was most acute.

Thus, despite the seriousness of the pirate menace, nothing was done navally to deal comprehensively with the problem before the onset of the Mithridatic Wars absorbed all of Rome's available resources in the area. While Rome's riposte to the Cilician pirate threat was deferred, the Mithridatic conflicts would bring home the way in which piracy could become not merely a nuisance but an existential threat.

In order to meet Rome's episodic challenges to their lucrative predations, the pirates sought a new associate, which they found in the person of the avaricious Mithridates around 90 BC. This loose, informal alliance was similar to that between the Barbary corsairs and the Sultan of Turkey in the 1500s.

The Expanding Mithridatic Threat

Mithridates split the kingdom of Paphlagonia with King Nicomedes IV Epiphanes of Bithynia. Next, between 104 and 103 BC, he conquered Colchis (modern Georgia), parts of Armenia and looked south to Cappadocia and Galatia. This caught the attention of Rome. Initially, Rome had not paid much attention to, nor cared about, Mithridates' conquests on the northern Black Sea, for it was much too concerned with its campaigns in North Africa and defending against Germanic tribes to its north. While Rome was thus preoccupied, Mithridates managed to enlist regional actors in his bid to wean away the kingdoms of Asia Minor who were under Roman 'protection' by pointing out that Rome taxed and bullied them, stifling their economic potential, whereas an alliance with him would prove beneficial. Skilfully managed alliances fell into place. Greek cities in the area appealed to Mithridates for help against their enemies. Scythian nomads aligned themselves with Mithridates, as did, most portentously, the pirates of the Eastern Mediterranean. His empire grew, arousing the fear and ire of Rome. Luckily for him, Mithridates had as allies some of the most competent Greek mercenaries.

The disputed area of Cappadocia lay inland to the south of the two disputants: Pontus, a wealthy, mountainous kingdom in the north-east of modern Turkey, on the Black Sea, and Bithynia, a kingdom to the west of Pontus, also fronting the Black Sea coast. Mithridates, leader of Pontus promised to comply with the proposed terms of the agreement, but because of subsequent events in Rome and the death of his Bithynian opponent, he was not compelled to keep his word. Rome couldn't worry too much about this region at this time, though, because of its noted problems closer to home.

A Roman envoy named Manius Aquillius had been sent to Asia in 90 BC to settle the Cappadocia/Bithynia problem, which, after several military setbacks, he did, but he also created new ones by urging the rightful king of Bithynia to attack areas long controlled by Pontus. Accordingly, Mithridates VI invaded Bithynia in 88, forcing Nicomedes IV to flee to Rome. In the process, he massacred tens of thousands of Italians residing and doing business in the Greek cities of Anatolia. The victims were Roman and Italian merchants, slave traders and tax collectors, the deeply detested settlers in Rome's new province of Asia. In response to these butcheries, the ousting of Nicomedes and Mithridates' growing power, the Senate declared war against Pontus and, in 88, sent the consul Sulla east to govern as *propraetor* and defeat the aggressive Pontic ruler. While in the area, he forged an agreement which temporarily shelved the quarrel between the two rulers.

It was at this point that Sulla secured for himself the command in Asia Minor which was tasked to put an end to Mithridates' mischief-making once and for all. The course of this long conflict is rather tangled; I will here gloss over the political plots and details of the land battles to trace the naval dimension. The sources are inconsistent as to the chronology and the division of the long conflict into three distinct wars is convenient but difficult to determine. In the following analysis, I have tried to sort out the sequence of events; however, my focus is not upon the see-saw battles but with the role of sea power in the overall struggle.

Conflict with Mithridates, with 'The Pirates', or both?

One issue confronting us here is whether the naval wars against Mithridates were, in effect, anti-piracy campaigns. In other words, who *were* these 'pirates' said to be allied with Mithridates and to what extent did he coordinate his operations with their raids?

Begin with the fact that Mithridates was a long-standing enemy of the Romans and eager to tap any local forces that could hamper their military and economic endeavours. At times, during his series of wars fought against the Roman Republic from 89-63 BC, he controlled most of Anatolia and parts of mainland Greece. He exploited a variety of mercenaries and military allies, and was often accused by the Romans of recruiting Cilician and Cretan pirates to his cause and promoting piracy. This 'coalition' appears to have operated in much the same way as that of the earlier arrangement of Diodotus Tryphon, who, in his rebellion against Seleucid rule in the 140s BC, encouraged and was assisted by the coincident operations of Cilician pirate squadrons, but never supervised these moves.

It is natural that the Romans would exploit the fear of piracy engendered among citizens of the Greek cities of Anatolia by presenting Mithridates as an ally of the pirates. H.A. Ormerod, in *Piracy in the Ancient World* (pp.209 ff and 219 ff), has

Mithridates working in complete unison with the pirate bands, which is surely an exaggeration. On the other hand, there is little doubt that the freebooting raids and ambushes conducted by various pirate chiefs were a boon to Mithridates in his war against Rome.

As these pirate groups were independent operators, it is difficult to say much other than that while Mithridates was probably encouraged by the troubles they caused for Roman shipping, he did not orchestrate their predations. So, while it is likely that Mithridates and various pirate groups of the first century BC cooperated, one can no more speak of an alliance than one can say that the informal seventeenth and eighteenth-century Caribbean pirate confederation known as the 'brethren of the coast' were actually collaborators with the British, even though they were at times helpful in furthering Britain's campaigns against Spanish forces there.

FIRST MITHRIDATIC WAR

The first of the three conflicts between Rome and the ruler of Pontus was for the most part decided on land. However, taking Corbett's sense of the term, sea power played an offstage role, allowing Rome to utilize her relative freedom of the seas to send troop contingents to the Anatolian peninsula and resupply them. Conversely, Corbett (and perhaps Mahan too) would have noted how a relative lack of sea control in the first war hampered Sulla's ability to follow up his land victories to deal a decisive blow to Mithridates' armies – and to prevent their escape and regrouping – when they were on the ropes. That said, there were no naval engagements of any consequence in the initial round. Some modern commentators have incorrectly retrofitted the important sea battle of Tenedos to the first war, whereas it occurred in the third. In fact, all sea combat of any consequence took place in what modern analysts call the second and third conflicts between Rome and Pontus. This confusion no doubt arises because the ancient sources treat the struggle as one long war, whereas it is the modern observers who have created the convenient, if arbitrary, three-war division.

From the outset, Mithridates had his own fleet. Ancient sources (chiefly Appian) mention a fleet of 300 larger decked warships and 100 biremes with two banks of oars. These figures are probably too high, but they suggest that the Romans and their allies were badly outnumbered at the start of the war, even without considering such assistance that the pirate fleets might offer Mithridates. Mithridates had created this fleet in the years before the dust-up with Rome when conducting operations along the Black Sea coast in order to repel barbarian attacks on the Greek cities there. In any event, this navy was sufficient to take control of the Aegean and facilitated his initial conquests in Greece.

Interestingly, Mithridates perceived early on the Rhodians, the only significant naval power in the Aegean, as an impediment to his conquests, and accordingly sent his fleet against that island. Both the inclement weather and the superior Rhodian navy forced Mithridates to redirect his attention elsewhere. Rhodes would continue to play a large part in the naval balance of power in the region for some time to come.

Mithridates' successes on the Asian mainland encouraged the Athenians, partly inspired by the tyrant Aristion, to break with Rome and invite Mithridates to operate in Greece. Mithridates responded in the late summer or autumn of 88 BC by sending a fleet and army under the command of Archelaus to Athens. On the way across the Aegean, Archelaus captured the Cyclades islands and the sacred treasury at Delos, giving the treasure captured there to Aristion to bolster his support at Athens. Apparently, the Greeks of the Cyclades did not welcome their new Pontic overlords. Archelaus landed at Piraeus, and encouraged by the presence of his army, large parts of southern Greece, which had been chafing at Roman rule, rose against the Romans.

While it is true that there had been a Roman naval squadron stationed at Byzantium guarding the entrance to the Euxine (Black) Sea, a defeat on land compelled this force to withdraw, leaving Mithridates in command of the straits.

Sulla's initial goal was the immediate conquest of Mithridates' strongholds in Greece. Athens and its main port, the Piraeus, were the obvious targets and Sulla ordered a direct assault. Since the port was defended by Mithridates' able commander, Archelaus, the Roman plan nearly came to disaster. Sulla had landed in the Greek city of Epirus. Gauging which way the wind was blowing, Greeks in the area switched alliances from Mithridates to Rome. Sulla next went to the area near Athens known as Boeotia, where he defeated two of Mithridates' generals. He then invaded Athens, but his lack of a fleet made delivering a knockout blow difficult. The walled port was in an excellent defensive position, with access to reinforcement by sea. Sulla was forced to withdraw in order to secure local funding and prepare proper siege equipment. The entire campaign year of 87 BC was spent besieging both Athens and Piraeus, with little success. By the winter, Sulla abandoned his plan regarding the Piraeus, while keeping the siege of Athens intact. Inasmuch as the lack of naval assets was obviously the major impediment to Rome, one may wonder at this Roman oversight.

Rome's naval strength had been depleted since the end of the Illyrian campaign. The Republic eschewed the expensive and manpower-intensive upkeep entailed in maintaining a standing navy, especially in light of the destruction of Carthage, which event seemed to them to eliminate any serious naval threat. This ignores, of course, the persistent pirate danger, which Rome had left to more naval-minded allies such as Rhodes to control. After all, Rhodes, with its mercantile interests, had at least as great an interest as Rome in ensuring freedom of navigation in Eastern Mediterranean waters.

Accordingly, at the beginning of the war, after most of Greece fell into Pontic hands, Sulla was obliged to raise a fleet from Rome's allies around the Eastern Mediterranean. In 87-86 BC, in an effort to cobble together an allied naval force, his emissary Lucullus sailed from Ostia with only six ships, and despite traversing pirate-infested waters, managed to reach Crete and Cyrene (Libya) where some – though not many – ships were added. However, pirates destroyed most of this little squadron en route from Cyrene to Alexandria. Once again, it is not clear whether these pirates attacked Lucullus' expedition at the behest of Mithridates, or were merely engaging in their accustomed predatory practice. In Alexandria, the Egyptians were welcoming, but failed to offer Lucullus any practical assistance, other than seeing to it that his onward voyage to Cyprus was unmolested.

Lucullus' luck improved when he landed at Cyprus and moved on to petition officials in Phoenicia (Lebanon) and Pamphylia (on the southern Turkish coast, between Lycia and Cilicia) for ships and crews; by the spring of 85 BC, after almost a year-long quest, Lucullus finally had a fleet said to number almost 100 ships. Combined with that of allied naval power Rhodes, who ultimately agreed to provide assistance, this naval force posed a major threat to Mithridates' freedom of the seas. While not engaging in any sea battles *per se*, the arrival of this flotilla sailing along the Ionian coast was nonetheless instrumental in encouraging restive Greek inhabitants to drive the recently conquering Pontic land armies out of the Greek Cyclades islands of Cos, Cnidos, Colophon and Chios. Today's naval pundits would label this show of force 'gunboat diplomacy'.

Meanwhile Sulla had succeeded in cutting off Athens from its harbour and defeated the city. Many were slaughtered, but the city was delivered. He then defeated the Greek-Pontic army at Chaeronea in March 86 BC, causing serious loss to Mithridates' forces. After Sulla defeated Mithridates in Boeotia at Orchomenus the following year, the Pontic king left Europe.

Following the death of Marius while in office, the Roman replacement or suffect consul of 86 BC was Valerius Flaccus. He led an army to Asia to replace the forces of Sulla, who did not want to be relieved and did not know Flaccus was coming. After arriving in Thessaly, Flaccus chose to head to the Hellespont, preferring to confront Mithridates than Sulla. By this time, Sulla had a fleet and could cross the Hellespont (the strait between Greece and Asia Minor joining the Aegean Sea and Propontis), but he wanted to return to Rome to deal with Cinna.

In 86 BC, after Sulla's victory in Orchomenos, he initially spent some time re-establishing Roman authority. His legate soon arrived with the fleet he was sent to gather, and Sulla was ready to recapture lost Greek islands before crossing into Asia Minor. The second Roman army under the command of Flaccus meanwhile moved through Macedonia and into Asia Minor. After the capture of Philippi, remaining Mithridatic forces crossed the Hellspont away from the Romans. The Romans, under Flaccus' subordinate C. Flavius Fimbria, were encouraged to loot and create general havoc as they went, creating problems between Flaccus and Fimbria. Flaccus was a fairly strict disciplinarian, and the behaviour of his lieutenant led to discord between the two.

At some point as this army crossed the Hellespont while giving chase to Mithridates' forces, Fimbria seems to have started a rebellion against Flaccus. While seemingly minor enough to not cause immediate repercussions in the field, Fimbria was relieved of his duty and ordered back to Rome. The return trip included a stop at the port city of Byzantium, however, and here Fimbria threw down the gauntlet by taking command of the garrison, rather than continuing home. Flaccus, hearing of this, marched his army to Byzantium to put a stop to this manifest insurrection, but walked right into his own undoing. The army preferred Fimbria (not surprisingly, considering his leniency in regard to the legionaries' plundering prerogatives) and a general revolt ensued. Flaccus attempted to flee, but was captured shortly after and the rightful consular commander was executed. With Flaccus out of the way, Fimbria took complete command.

The following year (85 BC), Fimbria took the fight to Mithridates while Sulla continued to operate on the Greek islands of the Aegean. Fimbria quickly won a decisive victory over remaining Mithridatic forces and moved on the capital of Pergamum. With all vestige of hope crumbling for Mithridates, he fled Pergamum to the coastal city of Pitane. Fimbria was in hot pursuit, laying siege to the town, but, lacking naval assets, he could not prevent Mithridates' escape by sea. Fimbria called upon Sulla's legate, Lucullus, to bring his fleet around to hem Mithridates in, but it seems that Sulla had other plans.

Sulla apparently had been in private negotiation with Mithridates to end the war. He wanted to develop lenient terms so as to get the ordeal over as quickly as possible. The more quickly it was dealt with, the faster he would be able to settle simmering political problems back in Rome. With this in mind, Lucullus and his navy refused to help Fimbria, allowing Mithridates to flee to Lesbos.

Later, at Dardanus, Sulla and Mithridates met personally to negotiate terms. With Fimbria re-establishing Roman hegemony over the cities of Asia Minor, Mithridates' position was completely untenable. Yet Sulla, with his eyes on Rome, offered uncharacteristically mild terms. According to the treaty they agreed to, Mithridates kept Pontus, but Sulla forced him to give up the section of Paphlagonia he had earlier promised to withdraw from, give up prisoners and deserters, and give Sulla what he had needed so badly, warships and lots of money. Sulla then stationed Fimbria's men in an Asian garrison, restored the vassals and organization of the Roman province of Asia and collected what became crippling fines.

Mithridates was compelled to give up all his conquests (which Sulla and Fimbria had already managed to take back by force), provide a fleet of seventy ships to Sulla – along with supplies – and pay a tribute of 2,000–3,000 gold talents. In exchange, Mithridates was able to keep his original kingdom and territory, and regain his title of 'friend of the Roman people'.

According to Michael Pitassi (*The Navies of Rome*), the naval units used to escort Flaccus in 84 BC were taken into Lucullus' command, together with the most suitable of the surrendered Pontic ships, and Lucullus was thus able to dismiss his initial ad hoc fleet, pieced together from the contributions of volatile naval allies. Orders were given that a number of the warships be laid up in reserve in various coastal cities around the Aegean, so as to provide a naval force which could be quickly mobilized if and when needed. This is a similar provision to that made some sixty-five years earlier, in 148 BC, and seems to have had a similar negligible effect on subsequent events. Nevertheless, it probably represented a part of a larger overall plan of Sulla's for the long-term defence of Anatolia, which he never returned to complete.

Second Mithridatic War

At the end of the First Mithridatic War, the command of the Roman army in Asia Minor was given to Licinius Murena, a Sulla protagonist and legate. Murena was left in charge of Fimbria's legions. Nominally colleagues, the two men had rather different views of the future of relations between Rome and Pontus. Distracted by domestic challenges to his power, Sulla wanted to maintain the peace with Mithridates, but Murena is said to have been looking for a chance to resume the war, hoping to win himself a triumph. A pretext for war was not long in coming. In some modern studies, this occurrence is mingled with the events of the Second Mithridatic War, and perhaps by rights belongs under this heading.

When Mithridates began making preparations to fight local peoples chafing under his control, Murena read the movements as a threat to his forces, and so marched into Cappadocia, where he faced Mithridates' forces in Comana, a country Mithridates ruled. Meanwhile, Murena arbitrarily determined that Mithridates was re-arming, and consequently Murena invaded Pontus. Among the preparations which Murena construed as being directed against Rome and her allies were the assembly of a fleet, which, according to Appian, was intended for use against the Bosporan tribes and not to confront Roman sea power. These tribes were in fact later subjugated by Mithridates. Murena also organized naval forces, requiring the cities of Asia to furnish ships as part of their tribute to Rome. The king wrote to Sulla for help, since he avowed that Murena was violating the treaty terms they had agreed to. Ignoring the directives of consuls sent by Sulla for him to desist, Murena plundered this and other territories owned by Mithridates, which action, he asserted, did not violate any treaty as there was no written treaty.

In 82 BC, Murena launched a second raid into Pontus, and this time, believing that the Romans had actually declared war, Mithridates reacted. An army under Gordius, a Cappadocian aristocrat who was one of Mithridates' nobles, carried out a raid into Roman territory, and then faced up to Murena. Due to the Civil War going on in Rome at this time, Sulla was unable – some say unwilling – to provide support for Murena's army, and the latter was defeated. At that point, there was no alternative but to make peace on terms somewhat unfavourable to Rome, which merely delayed resolution of the issue as it essentially restored Mithridates' status quo. His regional ambitions to contest Roman influence in the Eastern Mediterranean were thus only temporarily checked by the two settlements.

Apart from naval reinforcement, positioning and posturing, there was little of direct naval interest in this second conflict with Mithridates and his confederates.

Third Mithridatic War

Inception And Overview

A new war erupted in 75 or 74 BC occasioned by the deceased king of Bythnia bequeathing his kingdom to Roman rule, which entity was considered by Mithridates to be under his suzerainty – producing a clear *casus belli* on his part. Accordingly, Mithridates invaded Bithynia and sent his forces around Asia. Rome dispatched Lucius Licinius Lucullus to Asia. Marcus Aurelias Cotta, Lucullus' consular colleague, was sent to Bithynia with a fleet. Lucullus was designated to handle the land issues and safeguard the the provinces of Asia and Cilicia. He had to discipline the men left by Sulla at the garrison in Asia. While so engaged, Mithridates' Pontic fleet beat Cotta's naval forces at Chalcedon. Roman ships sought refuge inside the harbour, but to no avail: the Pontic fleet made their way into the port, where they destroyed or captured the Roman fleet. Mithridates then went on to put the Roman-controlled town of Czyicus under siege. Lucullus was able to help Cotta cut off Mithridates, who withdrew, but in his retreat he lost a large part of his army at the Battle of Cyzicus. In 73, the Roman fleet cleansed the Aegean of Mithridatic ships. Lucullus invaded Pontus and defeated Mithridates in battle at Cabira.

Crassus had been left as general in Italy, where he soon had to deal with the uprising of the slaves led by Spartacus, starting in 73 BC. Mithridates fled to Armenia to get help from his ally Tigranes. Meanwhile, Lucullus captured most of Pontus by the middle of 70. He moderated the taxing burden of a bankrupt Asia at the expense of equestrian bankers back home.

Mithridates was still a threat, so Lucullus told Tigranes to give up Mithridates. Tigranes refused, so Lucullus attacked territories Tigranes had recently annexed (in 69 BC). Tigranes met Lucullus in battle and was defeated. Syria had been in Tigranes' hands; now it was in Roman ones, but the Roman troops were unhappy with Lucullus' leadership. When Lucullus advanced into Armenia, his men, incited by Clodius Pulcher, refused to fight, so Lucullus had to withdraw to Mesopotamia, where he captured Nisibis and made it his winter headquarters. Tigranes recovered many of his losses and Mithridates defeated the Romans in Pontus.

Meanwhile, piracy was plaguing Rome. At first its base had been in Cilicia, and then in Crete. Finally, Pompey was given powers to dispense with the pirate menace, which he did, and was then given control of all of Asia Minor by means of the Manilian Law.

In the spring of 66 BC, Pompey invaded Pontus and defeated Mithridates' last army at Nicopolis. Tigranes would no longer help, but submitted to Pompey and Rome. Pompey's (unearned) victory was complete when Mithridates was killed in his hideout in the Crimea.

Outline of Operations

The final, Third Mithridatic War (75-65 BC) was the longest and bloodiest of the three. As in the first war, Mithridates was the aggressor. Rome responded by sending two generals, Lucius Licinius Lucullus and Marcus Aurelias Cotta, to Anatolia (Asia Minor). Lucullus attacked by land and Cotta commanded a Roman fleet numbering sixty-four vessels, mostly gathered from Rome's allies in the area. Mithridates outmanoeuvred Lucullus and attacked Cotta. Without the support of Lucullus, Cotta was outmatched. Appian puts Mithridates' forces at about 150,000 (though that may be exaggerated). Regardless, he outnumbered Cotta and captured or destroyed over sixty Roman ships.

Cotta was forced to retreat and wait for assistance from Lucullus. Mithridates may have become overconfident because he moved his army onto the island of Acrtonnesus, on which was the city of Cyzicus. He needed the city to resupply his army. But the move was ill-advised, as when Lucullus arrived, he simply blockaded the island and trapped Mithridates. As winter approached and Mithridates' situation became desperate, Lucullus attacked. Mithridates' army was routed, but he was able to escape by ship in the heat of battle. Part of his army also managed to escape, and he had reserves back in Pontus. Lucullus then launched a campaign in 69 BC against Armenia, where Mithridates had fled.

Armenia was ruled by Tigranes (the Great), who was Mithridates' son-in-law and ally. This brought Rome into contact with both Armenia and its neighbour, the

Parthian Empire, for the first time. Lucullus defeated Tigranes, but Mithridates escaped and returned to Pontus. Lucullus allowed himself to become sidetracked, perhaps because of personal ambition. Rather than pursue Mithridates, he turned east and tried to conquer all of Armenia. This undermined his troops' morale and the campaign ultimately failed. The Romans turned to their greatest general of the time to bail them out: Pompey the Great. He arrived in Asia Minor in 67 BC and had to start by suppressing rampant piracy. The Third Mithridatic War began its final phase the following year when Pompey won the Battle of Nicopolis. Mithridates fled north and was eventually killed by the Celts.

Roman Attitudes Towards and Actions Against Piracy

Although the Roman elite benefitted from the pirates' activities in the availability of cut-rate slaves, they sometimes sent out soldiers to punish them. These attempts to restore order were usually half-hearted. In 74 BC, the son of the aforementioned Marcus Antonius, also called Marcus Antonius, received special powers to fight against the pirates of Crete. After he had expelled them from the Western Mediterranean, he invaded their base in the winter of 72/71. However, he was defeated, died soon after, and no one really cared about pursuing the war. (His son is known to us today as Mark Antony, the successor of Julius Caesar, who was defeated by Octavian at the great naval Battle of Actium in 31 BC.)

After 100 BC there was plenty of Roman military activity in the Eastern Mediterranean, but there is little evidence that it was directed against pirates. From 78-74, Publius Servilius Vatia, one of the consuls of 79, campaigned strenuously in the province of Cilicia. Servilius is credited with defeating pirates but, while it is clear that he captured some coastal cities which were used as bases for piracy, his main priorities were to enhance his own prestige and assert Roman control over a strategically important area. The same was true of other Roman aristocrats who campaigned in the region in the 80s and 70s BC.

Cretan pirates were blamed for many incidents of piracy. Another commander, Quintus Caecilius Metellus, was sent in 69 BC with orders to bring the whole island under Roman control. The official reasons for his expedition were the suppression of piracy and the punishment of the Cretans for helping Mithridates, but the Senate had actually been on the verge of clearing the Cretans of these charges and declaring them allies of the Roman people. It was only at the last moment that an ambitious politician, Lentulus Spinther, intervened and forced the Senate to declare war. The conquest of Crete should not, therefore, be seen simply as a further measure to suppress piracy. An extended campaign of this kind offered numerous opportunities to obtain booty and, for the victorious general, prestige and influence in Rome. The Romans had recently annexed the wealthy kingdom of Cyrenaica, and an expedition against Crete had already been attempted in 72 by the son of Marcus Antonius the Orator. It is reasonable to surmise that many Romans saw Crete as a profitable addition to their growing empire.

Historical sources provide evidence of continuing attacks and spectacular cases of kidnap and ransom by pirates in the 70s and 60s BC. The story of one famous victim illustrates the extent to which most Roman provincial governors were indifferent to the problem. In late 75 or early 74, an aspiring Roman aristocrat called Gaius Julius Caesar was sailing to Rhodes, where he was to study rhetoric, when he was captured by pirates who held him for about forty days until he was ransomed. Having been released, he collected together a small fleet in Miletos, went after the pirates and captured them. He took them to the Roman governor of the province of Asia, Juncus, to demand that he deal with them, but got no satisfaction. Juncus appears to have been more interested in obtaining the pirates' loot than in punishing them, so Caesar had to organize the executions himself.

A similar lack of enthusiasm for dealing with pirates was displayed by Gaius Verres, the Roman governor of Sicily between 73-71 BC. Verres was put on trial for extortion when he returned to Rome. He had made himself so wealthy during his period as a governor – through corruption, extortion and even murder – that he expected to have little difficulty in bribing the jury to acquit him, but he had to give in to a vigorous prosecution mounted by Cicero. A recurrent theme of Cicero's case against Verres was his neglect of his duty to protect the province from pirates.

Pompey Smashes the Pirates: Foretoken of the Imperial Fleets

In the years following the Third Mithridatic War, the Roman Republic faced an alarming number of pirates. The impact these pirates had on shipping became severe enough to eventually result in almost unprecedented powers being voted to Pompey in 67 BC. His brilliant and successful campaign in the Mediterranean wiped out the pirate forces that had impeded Rome's precious grain supply and had been a thorn in her side since at least 102. Until Pompey's success, however, the pirates had almost free rein in the regions around Cilicia. Several other commanders had been thrown at them with special powers from the Senate, but with little success. For thirty-five years, the western seas were crawling with pirates.

Rome was driven to conduct a formal war against the sea robbers. During the previous half century, proconsul Servilius and Marcus Antonius the elder had campaigned for years with varying success, until finally the pirates became downright impudent. In 67 BC, in Ostia, Rome's harbour, the pirates attacked a squadron being prepared for service against them. This audacious raid was emblematic of Rome's naval decline. The situation called for extraordinary measures. In 67, Pompey was given absolute command of Mediterranean waters and land within 50 miles of the coast, with great powers to finance his campaign. The Senate balked, but Cicero convinced them to acquiesce in this emergency measure.

Pompey was then given exceptionally sweeping executive powers, and placed in command of 500 ships and an army of 120,000 men. In a brilliant three-month campaign, he secured the Western Mediterranean, and then he defeated the pirates in their eastern lairs during the following three months: we are told that 10,000 pirates were killed and 20,000 captured. Pompey had defeated the pirates in just six months instead of the three years of his writ. However, delegating special powers to Pompey proved to be the first step towards dictatorship. In 60 BC, he formed the First Triumvirate with Caesar and Crassus. In 56 in Quiberon Bay (Gaul), Caesar's fleet of galleys defeated the great sailing ships of the Gallic Venetes, assisted by a deficiency of wind, which becalmed his opponents.

The perhaps fortuitous consequence of Pompey's comprehensive campaign was territorial expansion. In 65 BC, Armenia became a province, followed in 63 by Syria. Consequently, Rome controlled Asia Minor, with Armenia as a buffer state between it and the Parthians. As the Roman Republic unravelled in the period of civil war, competing Roman forces once again built up their naval might. Sextus Pompeius – son of Pompey – in his conflict with Octavian, amassed a fleet powerful enough to threaten the vital supply of grain from Sicily to Rome. Octavian, with the help of Marcus Agrippa, built a fleet at Forum Iulii and defeated Sextus in the Battle of Naulochus in 36, finally putting an end to all Pompeian resistance. Octavian's power was further cemented against the combined fleets of Mark Antony and Cleopatra at the Battle of Actium in 31. This last naval battle of the Roman Republic definitively established Rome, with Octavian in sole command, as the supreme naval power in the Mediterranean. After this, he formalized several key naval harbours for the Mediterranean and the now fully professional navy had its main duties consist of protecting against piracy, escorting troops and patrolling the river frontiers of Europe.

The rapidity and thoroughness with which the reduction of the pirates had been achieved created a great impression among Pompey's contemporaries. There are also indications that he endeavoured to render his work permanently effective by arranging for the establishment of a standing fleet to patrol the seas. Before his departure from the East, he had given instructions that the maritime states should continue to supply their contingents of ships, and after he returned to Rome, it was at his suggestion that arrangements were made to patrol Italian waters. Unfortunately, however, he still preserved the old system of dependence on foreign states for the provision and maintenance of warships, the inadequacy and dangers of which are illustrated by the sequel.

Julius Caesar – Pioneer of Joint Land-Sea Warfare?

Although it was a sideshow to his Gallic campaign, an excursus on Julius Caesar's two temporary invasions of Britannia in 55 and 54 BC is apropos here as it was a precursor to the larger-scale and more permanent cross-channel Claudian campaign of nearly a century later. It was the type of 'operation in the littorals' – to borrow a contemporary phrase – that would, along with fluvial operations, characterize the bulk of naval activity for the next few centuries until the decline of the Western Empire, when 'barbarians' who had mastered naval expeditionary warfare arrived by sea.

The reasons for these excursions across treacherous waters have been well presented in Caesar's own account of the campaign in Gaul. He could clearly see that Britain posed a backdoor threat to his latest and greatest conquest (ancient France), whose subjugation Caesar had now enforced after eight years' hard campaigning. During those years, the Celts of Britain had aided their Gallic kinsmen against Caesar, who judged that until Britain was his, the northern coast of Gaul would always be vulnerable to surprise attack. He thus decided on an amphibious campaign against Britain.

Caesar's First Invasion of Britain, 55 BC

The first expedition provides an illustration of a reconnaissance in force with lessons learned regarding actual tactical/strategic requirements, particularly as to an assault zone/troop landing. This and the follow-on invasion of the next year are rare examples in antiquity of a landing force having to fight its way ashore.

In the summer of 55 BC, Caesar assembled his ships for the invasion. The armada of mercantile vessels were to transport infantry, cavalry and the heavy war machines of the day, consisting of catapults and rams. With two legions, the VII and X (10,000 foot soldiers and 500 cavalry), the invasion was launched in August. After a reconnaissance-in-force to ascertain the topography of the landing site, he embarked a small fleet of war galleys and eighty transports from the Gaulish ports of Boulogne and Ambleteuse, embarking the cavalry contingent from the latter port.

This force landed near Dubra (Dover) after rowing along the coast searching for a suitable beach. Due to their high freeboard and relatively deep draft, the mercantile ships lacked the requisite manoeuvrability for the tight arena of an opposed beach assault, nor did they have effective means of disembarking troops in such a landing operation. Due to these limitations, the transports could not get close to the beach, resulting in many troops being drowned as they attempted to reach the shore, weighted down with their armour and weapons. Those who survived were attacked by the Britons as they staggered in the surf. The Romans were further hampered by their inability to coalesce into their usual combat formation, resulting in monumental disarray. As more ships moved up to discharge more troops, the confusion only increased, as they were unable to disembark in any order. The Britons, clad only in light animal skins, were able to dart around the immobilized Romans with ease and strike them at will. The disembarkation was fiercely contested, with savage hand-to-hand fighting in the surf. It was supported by 'heavy artillery' (catapults and ballistae) mounted on ships held just at the water's edge, but these had difficulty in directing fire upon an enemy so extensively intermingled with friendly forces.

The only saving grace in this initial operation was the skilful deployment of Caesar's shallower-draft war galleys that carried the intended 'shock troops', along with the smaller more mobile missile-launchers. These vessels were able to get in close enough to the shore to rake the flanks of the attacking Britons and drive them back. This enabled the badly impeded heavy troops to finally get ashore and establish a beachhead after incurring many casualties.

Due to the failure of the cavalry to arrive in good time, the landing force was unable to push further inland. When the eighteen cavalry-carrying vessels arrived four days later, a storm forced half of them to return immediately to Gaul. The other half sought sheltered coves along the British coast, but another storm sent them back to the continent as well. Accordingly, after negotiating a truce, thanks to his inability to move inland with supporting cavalry, Caesar stayed only three weeks. With the weather deteriorating, and running short of supplies, he managed to repair enough of his damaged ships to return to Gaul for the winter.

Caesar's Second Invasion of Britain, 54 BC

During the winter of 55-54 BC, Caesar built a fleet of 800 specially designed vessels suited to amphibious warfare, configured with shallower drafts and broader beams, specifically to move and land troops and war engines close inshore and with the stability to withstand a surging surf. They also had low freeboards to facilitate easy disembarkation of men and equipment.

On 6 July 54 BC, Caesar's second amphibious force arrived off the coast of Britain. This time, rather than bunch all his military units together, he landed simultaneously on several well-reconnoitred beaches, meeting little resistance. The new assault vessels worked splendidly, their shallow draft permitting them to proceed close enough to the shore to permit an easy landing of men and equipment, with the infantry landing in a disciplined, protected formation and thereby quickly establishing a beachhead. He then offloaded his cavalry and war machines prior to attempting to move inland. At this point, Caesar abandoned the oversight of the landing zones and moved inland in command of his advancing forces, completing a successful invasion.

For the second expedition, Caesar undertook a more forceful probe and a major intelligence-gathering mission, Mediterranean anchoring techniques proving unsuitable for tough climate and sea conditions. Caesar himself supervised the design of suitable transport vessels and the proper deployment of the fleet, the fire support in particular worked out by him in person.

The natives were demoralized by the size of the vast fleet and its warship support, and melted into the countryside leaving the construction of beachheads and supply depots unopposed. The Romans then withdrew in good order, but British seas were now under total Roman control. Note that absolutely no native British seaborne interdiction occurred at any point in this campaign; all the potential maritime threats emanated from northern Gaul.

Julius Caesar's quasi-invasion comprised but a full-scale dress rehearsal for the Claudian assault by the then termed *Classis Germanica* (the *Classis Britannica* was formed in the wake of that later, more purposeful invasion of AD 43), the 'dry run' greatly benefiting commanders and logistic supply units. The Claudian expedition was essentially a three-pronged battle group assault (from one initial beachhead) on the southern coast of Britain, the future Emperor Vespasian commanding the II Augusta legion with the toughest job, the reduction of the enemy fronting the south-western beachhead. It now transpires that the most recent attested archaeological record shows us that the XX legion kept close to the shore for logistical and interdiction backup from the boats along the whole length of its campaign trail to subjugate this area. We will return for a more detailed look at the large-scale landing operations under Claudius in a later chapter.

The following section covering the Civil Wars will demonstrate the restoration of the centrality of control of shipping and maritime supply as a key element in Roman war-making.

Civil Wars of the First Century BC

In the Civil War, Pompey and his senators had fled to Greece, but Julius Caesar was temporarily prevented from following him as Pompey still held the navy under his control. The inability of galleys to catch sailing ships in a good wind was likely a key factor. Caesar ordered ships to be built in every Italian port; Pompey prepared his forces to confront this fleet.

The record of the previous three centuries demonstrated that in order to fight effectively at sea, the Romans had to change their traditional thinking. Yet for centuries, during the Punic Wars, the Macedonian Wars and endless adventures against piracy in the Mediterranean, Rome had been content not to have her own *bona fide* standing navy. Instead, she relied on using – renting – small squadrons of vessels from her maritime allies, such as the Greek city-states on the Italian mainland and on Sicily. It was a policy that had worked, but one that had more than once almost proved disastrous, such as when Sextus attempted to cut off all supply routes in 40 BC, almost succeeding in blockading Rome into submission.

Octavian thus chose to build a fleet from scratch, recalling Rome's emergency programme for her first fleets of the Punic Wars, and he chose his very able deputy, Agrippa, a naval technician, to build and command it. Four-hundred ships were built from the wooded areas near Naples and trained on Lake Lucrino, a few miles north of Naples. (The violent seismic activity in the sixteenth century that formed the hill of Montenuovo right next to the lake also emptied most of its water.) Agrippa joined Lake Lucrino to the adjacent Lake Averno and the Gulf of Cuma by canals in order to form a single large naval base, *portus Iulius*. (A chariot tunnel from Averno to Cuma was built at the same time and has partially survived the ravages of time.)

The Roman vessels were somewhat smaller than those of Mark Antony. The Roman fleet that trained at Lucrino and Averno was made up of small, fast triremes (sailing ships with three banks of oarsmen) as well as 'fives' and 'sevens' (here, the number refers to the number of rowers on each oar). The Romans specialized in speeding into close quarters and boarding by grapnel to let their superb infantry swarm onto enemy vessels. Antony's fleet, on the other hand, was the last great one in history built along lines pioneered by the Greeks. Some of the ships were monsters, virtual sea-going cities with boarding towers, artillery and large infantry forces on board. They were propelled through the water by sail and as many as ten rowers on a single oar.

Joining up with Pompey, Bibulus was placed in charge of Pompey's fleet in the Adriatic to ensure that Caesar and his troops could not cross from Brundisium in Italy to Eprisus. Letting his guard down because winter was approaching, and assuming that Caesar would not cross any time soon, Bibulus was caught by surprise when, on the evening of 6 November 49 BC, Caesar and his fleet successfully crossed the Adriatic, landing at Palaeste. Although Bibulus was stationed near Corcyra, some 50 miles south of Palaeste, he had not sent out scouts and his ships were not ready to be put to sea to intercept Caesar's transports. When he finally heard of Caesar's crossing, he ordered his rowers to return to their ships, and sailed northward, hoping to capture the ships carrying Caesar's reinforcements from Brundisium. Again too slow, he managed to get there for their return journey to Italy, capturing and burning thirty of Caesar's transports. He then manoeuvred to prevent any further ships crossing to reinforce Caesar, but only succeeded in capturing one transport, which had been chartered by private individuals and had refused to obey Bibulus' orders. Enraged, he ordered the killing of the entire crew of the transport.

Bibulus then proceeded to blockade all the harbours along the coast, hoping to prevent any further crossings from Italy and leaving Caesar stranded in Epirus. Unfortunately, he found that he could not resupply his ships without abandoning the blockade, so he attempted to bluff Caesar's legates at Oricum into getting Caesar to agree to a temporary truce in order that he could resupply. However, when Bibulus refused to guarantee the safety of Caesar's envoys to discuss a peaceful settlement with Pompey, Caesar realized it was a bluff and pulled out of negotiations. Determined to continue with the blockade, Bibulus pushed himself too hard; he fell ill in early 48 BC and died near Corcyra before the end of winter.

When some ships were ready, Caesar evaded the blockade of Brundisium and crossed the Adriatic in the winter of 48 BC. Bibulus caught some vessels on the return and sank them, but eventually Antony went to Italy. As Cicero wrote to a friend, 'Pompey holds with Themistocles that those who are masters of the sea will be victors in the end.'

Although Pompey used his naval power to provide his own army and deny food to Caesar, the battlefield of Pharsalus in September 48 BC saw a complete Caesarian victory. On land, Caesar was a tactical genius who inspired the blind loyalty of his troops; but on the sea, he was barely competent. In invading Britain during his Gallic campaign, Caesar had failed to realize that there were tides in the Atlantic and so had his ships stranded on the coast. Such success as he eventually achieved was gruelling and costly due to his disregarding the available lessons concerning navigating tempestuous seas.

The problem of maintaining a fleet in the Western Mediterranean, moreover, was now easier, for the Civil Wars had scattered seafarers all over the coasts. Yet Octavian's first squadrons were destroyed in storms and defeat in battle. Unable to cope with Sextus, he recalled his main military aide, Agrippa, from Gaul to build new warships in 37 BC. New ships were built far more heavily than those of Sextus.

Pompeius Magnus' venture against the pirates and the last episode in the struggle between Octavian and Antony mark a turning point in Rome's attitude towards the sea. Soon Antony, bewitched according to Virgil by the Oriental siren Cleopatra, was drawn into war with Octavian. Perhaps we will never know whether Antony's alliance was guided more by realpolitik than amorous attraction, but in any event he could incorporate the Egyptian queen's warships with his own fleet. The fact that the struggle was settled by a naval battle reflects the importance sea power had attained, but the final result was clearly foreshadowed by the physical and psychological skirmishing before the battle proper. Thus commenced the Battle of Actium. It was not until the conclusion of the war with Sextus that Octavian – soon to be hailed as Augustus, Princeps – was able to turn his attention to the eastern shores of the Adriatic, where piracy still flourished on the coasts, and disturbances among the barbarian tribes of the interior demanded vigorous action.

The Battle of Actium in 31 BC: The Last Great Naval Battle of Antiquity?

As quite a bit of ink has been spilled regarding this culminating battle of the Republic, I will just note a few salient points here, which portended the shape of the naval establishment for centuries hence.

The political machinations which ended the Second Triumvirate and precipitated the last phase of the Civil War – the conflict between Antony and Cleopatra on one side, and Octavian and his associates on the other are convoluted and superfluous to this treatment. Since the assassination on 15 March 44 BC of the last dictator, Gaius Julius Caesar, by a conspiracy of senators who feared that Caesar's popularity might bury Republican government forever, Rome had been plunged into turmoil. It is sufficient here to note that Antony had proposed Caesarion, the son of Julius Caesar and Cleopatra, as the rightful heir to Caesar, undermining the legitimacy of Octavian's claims. This declaration subverted the rule-sharing arrangement of the Second Triumvirate; Octavian's declaration of war against Cleopatra was a de facto proclamation against Antony and precipitated the Civil War.

Antony, with 500 ships and 70,000 infantry, made his camp at Actium, which lies on the southern side of a strait leading from the Ionian Sea into the Ambracian Gulf, located on the west coast of Greece. He utilized towers on land and a row of ships in the water to guard the entrance to the gulf. Octavian, with 400 ships and 80,000 infantry, arrived from the north and, by occupying Patrae and Corinth, also managed to cut Antony's southward communications with Egypt via the Peloponnese. Desertions by some of his allies and a lack of provisions soon forced Antony to take action. Either hoping to win at sea because he was outmanoeuvred on land, or else simply trying to break the blockade, Antony followed Cleopatra's advice to employ the fleet.

On 2 September 31 BC, Antony moved out to meet Octavian. Antony's fleet consisted primarily of massive quinqueremes with bronze plates protecting the hull, while Octavian's fleet was made up mainly of smaller Liburnian vessels. The quinqueremes had the advantage of height from which to attack, and the plates which protected them from ramming. But the Liburnian ships were much more manoeuvrable. At the time, the primary nature of Roman naval battles was to manoeuvre into position to ram the opponent and thus sink their ship. Since the quinqueremes could not manoeuvre quick enough to ram the faster Liburnian ships, and the Liburnians could not do much damage even if they did ram the plated quinqueremes, the contest progressed more as a land battle than a standard sea one.

Antony drew up his ships outside the bay, facing west, with Cleopatra's squadron behind. The ensuing naval battle was hotly contested, with each side's squadrons trying to get around the other. Antony's fleet rowed out in two wings, where Octavian's ships were gathered at the entrance to the gulf. Antony tried to outflank Octavian's right, but the sudden move threw his own centre into confusion. When Octavian's centre took advantage of the confusion, the fighting became heavy.

All day long the strange battle progressed with the land tactics of arrows and spears being fired back and forth, without much chance of tangible gain. Late in the afternoon, Cleopatra and her squadron of sixty ships suddenly raised their sails and fled, racing away from the centre of the battle to the open ocean. Antony then broke off and managed to follow her with a few ships. While there have been various reasons advanced for his inexplicable action, what is certain is that a quarter of Antony's fleet left without warning in the middle of the battle, leaving the remainder of his fleet to their doom. The residue of his fleet became disheartened and surrendered to Octavian, with Antony's land forces surrendering a week later.

The naval lessons of this battle were not a good guide for the ensuing battles of the Empire, as the enemies of Rome would henceforth be the 'barbarians', with varying degrees of naval skill and in theatres where great warfleets were superfluous. It soon became plain that the ponderous 'fives' and 'sixes' inherited from the late Hellenic navies were rendered obsolete. Naval operations in conjunction with the legions along rivers and in coastal estuaries became more typical.

Recap: Naval Involvement at the End of the Republic

Accompanying the civil strife in the middle of the first century BC, there had been a long series of wars with the tribes of the Illyrian coast, which lasted almost continuously from the outbreak of the Civil War to the Battle of Actium. The campaigns organized by Julius Caesar, and later by Octavian, were alike intended to form the prelude to a wider scheme of conquest, which had for its object the rectification and extension of the whole of the northern frontier of the Empire. To this extent, they constituted the foundation of a Roman grand strategy, however rudimentary.

Octavian himself was unable to give his personal attention to the task until after the defeat of Sextus, and his initial conquests on the Illyrian coast and in the Alps were again interrupted by the war with Antony. It is clear, however, that the pacification of the Illyrian coast had been achieved by the time of the Battle of Actium, and although the region was again disturbed during the Pannonian and Dalmatian revolt (covered in a later chapter), the principal obstacles to peace had been removed by the disarmament of the tribes of the interior and the gradual spread of civilization from the trading stations on the coast.

We have no further mention of piracy on the coast. No doubt the police measures undertaken by Archelaus and his successors were sufficient to suppress petty marauders, and behind them lay the strength of the now fully organized Mediterranean fleets.

The wars against Mithridates and rapid campaign against the pirates had shown the importance of naval power, forgotten since the Punic Wars. F.E. Adcock noted that, 'in their most difficult campaigns, Pompey's victories were based on naval power and Caesar trusted the sea; in serious situations, the last word was left to the sea.' He is referring to operations around Dyrrachium (Durazzo), where the powerful fleet of Pompey was defeated by Caesarean forces. Here we have a further proof that the exercise of command of the sea was regarded by the Roman generals as a pledge of victory. During the Civil War, fleets became more and more powerful. Sextus Pompey, using maritime cities of Asia, managed to gather a force of about 300 vessels at the beginning of 48 BC; this was the son of Pompey the Great, who, possessing the mastery of the Western Mediterranean, directed the supply of grain to Rome and made raids on Italian shores to plunder and weaken his opponents' rule between 42-40.

In 38 BC, the future Augustus and Agrippa, his military and technical adviser, built a fleet of 400 ships that triumphed over those of Sextus, from Mylae fought in 37, to Nauloque in 36 and finally at Actium in 31. The naval force became the nucleus of the future imperial fleet. It is possible to discern in this activity an outline of naval thinking wherein Octavian, the future Augustus, was the political and strategic guide, while Agrippa was his collaborative technician; Agrippa was the inventor of harpax, a kind of grapple launched by catapult, and was honoured by the new Caesar, who gave him a naval crown, never hitherto granted to anyone (Livy, CXXIX).

Initially, the primary Roman fleet was oddly based at Forum Iulii, where part of the fleet was built. This site had been chosen, some time prior to 37 BC, in what is now the Provence region of the French Mediterranean coast. Forum Iulii was sited in the Ligurian Gulf, at what is now the French province of Frejus, where Octavian had gathered the galleys captured after the Battle of Actium. It served the purpose of watching over the maritime approaches to the province of Gaul. But as the imperial writ expanded, it was deemed advisable to station the two main fleets in Italy. A military port was established closer to Rome at Portus Julius in the Gulf of Puteoli (Pozzuoli), and a training centre in Lake Averno, which occupies a crater, a site perfectly sheltered from all winds.

The only significant naval occurrences, aside from Caesar's crossing to Britannia, for the remainder of the Republic had come during the Civil Wars that would end the current system of situational construction – as needed – and reliance upon the good will of maritime allies. The Battle of Actium, between Octavian's Legate Marcus Vipsanius Agrippa and the combined forces of Mark Antony and Cleopatra, was the last major naval battle in the Mediterranean until the Middle Ages. Victory for Octavian ensured the collapse of the Republic and his confirmation as Augustus of the Roman Empire. With a fleet already raised for use against other Romans, Augustus virtually wiped piracy off the face of the Mediterranean, but this time the fleet was more reasonably maintained to protect Rome's trade.

Rome no longer had a 'worthy opponent' in the Mediterranean, being the sole naval power. The imperial fleet – with its main centres in Ravenna and Misenum – prevented the emergence of a maritime enemy and had largely only police duties, at least initially. The Parthians, Rome's only remaining genuine rivals, were a land power without access to the Mediterranean. Until the battle to clarify the question of power between Constantine and Licinius against the Dardanelles, there was therefore more than 300 years with no more great naval battles. Rather than signifying the irrelevance of sea power, however, this fact demonstrated its centrality to maintenance of Roman sway. In any event, there was plenty of trouble on the various frontiers to keep the various fleets, sub-fleets, squadrons and ad hoc naval detachments busy.

Sextus Pompey's experience in subduing the piracy menace and the last episode in the struggle between Octavian and Antony mark a turning point in Rome's attitude toward the sea. The victor finally understood the absolute necessity of keeping very tight control over both the shores and sea lanes in order to guarantee freedom of economic relations among the various areas of the Roman world, and above all to guarantee that food would arrive regularly in Rome, thereby ensuring that the population would stay calm. This meant that Rome could no longer count on the small fleets from the maritime cities with allied status, nor on fleets constructed only in time of need. Since the great Eastern fleets were gone because of Rome's victory, Rome recognized for the first time in her history the need to build powerful, well-organized, permanent fleets with safe, strategically located ports as bases. This task, begun by Octavian/Augustus, was continued by his successors and extended into the western waters and also into the big coastal rivers.

It was with the organization of the standing fleets maintained by the emperors at Misenum and Ravenna, with auxiliary squadrons in Egypt, Syria and Cyrenaica, that for the first time in history the whole of the Mediterranean was adequately patrolled, and the inhabitants of its coast obtained respite from marauders. With the reduction of the piratical communities, improved methods of government in the provinces and the provision of an organized maritime police, piracy almost disappeared from the Mediterranean during the first two centuries AD.

I will next consider the organization of Roman imperial sea power and how it was tailored to meet the needs of the Empire's maritime commerce and freedom of the seas. This was a dynamic evolutionary process that occurred over the five centuries of Roman power, as various contingencies arose and waned. The source material for the exact location, size and composition of the fleets at any one time is lacking. Naval archaeology, in a few instances, can help fill in some blanks, but this data is far from complete or conclusive. Thus there is no neat 'table of organization and equipment', as is often applied to modern conflicts. At the end of this next chapter, I shall also note the maritime commerce – a vital unperpinning of sea power – to include cargoes, ports, routes and navigational considerations.

Chapter Seven

A Naval Establishment to Serve the *Pax Romana*: The Fleets and their Respective Theatres of Responsibility

It is important to note that Rome had no concept of a navy as a singular entity. Instead, its sea force was comprised of several fleets: two major imperial fleets positioned at Misenum and Ravenna in Italy, and several smaller provincial fleets scattered throughout the Mediterranean, Black Sea and North Sea, and their related estuarial and riverine systems. In essence, each fleet acted independently of the rest, having its own commander and its own sphere of duties, which could vary greatly depending on its location and circumstances. In a sense, following the formation and siting of these task-oriented squadrons provides an overview of the evolving maritime strategy of the Principate.

Bases: Background and Rationale for Siting the Fleets

The permanent establishment of harbours as dedicated fleet bases had to await the advent of the Roman imperial phase. As the Greek city-states were small self-contained entities, there was no idea of different naval bases since their warships, as with their merchant vessels, were stationed in the main port of their limited territory. When alliances were formed, whether in peace or war, the warships of the strongest member would host the combined fleet. These fleets were usually assembled for particular crises. The exception to this rule during this period was the Ptolemies in Greece, who maintained a fleet with its dedicated excellent home base, and the Carthaginians, with their great base ideally situated in a protecting bay which nonetheless commanded all ship traffic to the east and west which had to thread the bottleneck between Sicily and Cape Bon in Africa.

Once Augustus authorized the standing fleets, Rome augmented existing ports with installations to handle warships or expanded military outposts to accommodate ships, as well as creating entirely new facilities. There was no general plan for this expansion. The creation of the individual fleets and attached squadrons of varying composition generally followed the exigencies of an ongoing campaign or was determined by the strategic needs of a future campaign. Defence against assaults by barbarian tribes often required building of makeshift fleets with various landing stations, and these might later be strengthened to accommodate other expeditiions.

Without exception, each fleet possessed a main base, in which a *praefectus classis* (fleet prefect) performed his service. During the construction period, a fleet had a *praepositus classis* (high staff officer; this today is likely equal to the admirals frequently stationed at navy yards).

As there were frequent changes in jurisdiction, a list can never be exact. However, it has been shown that ports that were associated with only one fleet could also include facilities for other fleets, either because they were once managed by one fleet or because they were also strategically located for another.

Along the rivers, practically every settlement with a military contingent comprised a quasi-base because the supply function was mainly dependent on ships. In this case, one must not think of large-scale harbours with shipyards, supply depots, warehouses, etc. They were probably paired with only nominally larger river settlements. In late antiquity, as the overland routes were increasingly uncertain, even individual fortified posts (upgraded to castles) received a mini-fleet docking facility.

Although the Romans took to sea in the First Punic War in 264 BC, they never possessed a standing navy before the establishment of the Principate by Augustus in 27. Gnaius Pompeius Magnus (Pompey the Great) was the first to come up with the idea of a standing navy, after having completed his mission of ridding the Mediterranean of piracy. Recall that the Cilician pirates had gained such momentum at this time that they halted Roman trade in the East, sank a consular fleet at Ostia and kidnapped Roman praetors and travellers from Italy, including a young Julius Caesar who was then ransomed for 50 talents.

The notion of Roman ownership of the Mediterranean was prevalent as early as 67 BC, when by defeating the pirates Pompey 'had restored the rule of the sea to the Roman people'. In the years of the Civil Wars, several conflicts revolved around sea power: battles between Caesar and Pompey Magnus, Octavian and Sextus Pompey, and finally Octavian and Mark Antony.

However, it was with the battle with Sextus Pompey that Octavian truly learned to value fleets, leading him to maintain them permanently: first at the Forum Iulii in southern Gaul, then at Misenum and Ravenna. Sextus was given, by the Senate, command of the remaining ships from Caesar and Pompey's war in order to offset the power of the Second Triumvirate. Victims of proscriptions, war survivors and brigands soon flocked to him, turning to piracy to terrorize Italy and loosen Octavian's control of the mob by starvation.

Pompey's numbers further increased in 43 BC following the Battle of Philippi, when allies of the conspirators joined forces with him, bringing more ships. Octavian, however, had turned his gaze to the northern Adriatic and the Illyrian pirates. He established a fleet at Ravenna in 39. Such encounters with pirates served to convince Octavian that a standing fleet would not only be beneficial, but crucial for maintaining the people satisfied with his policy. This object lesson in sea power sowed the seeds of the imperial fleets.

When Augustus set out to reorganize the defences of the newly established Empire, he primarily looked to rationalize and streamline the setup of the legions. However, the key role of the navy in deciding the outcome of the recently concluded struggle for the crown seems to have loomed large in his consciousness. After winning the Civil War, post-Julius Caesar, Octavian wanted to assure the Roman aristocracy and masses of the return of normality, meaning peace and republican procedure in rule. He began with gestures in this direction. Octavian disbanded the majority of the mobilized war-era legions, annulled illegal orders and declared an amnesty for most Civil War antagonists, with the exception of Mark Antony's chief lieutenants at Actium.

With his increased powers under the two 'settlements' of 27 and 23 BC that determined the authority of the new Principate, Augustus undertook to reorganize the civil and military administration. Under this new more upwardly mobile scheme, the best *equites* procurators could rise high, either to govern key provinces such as Egypt or Judaea, to the prestigious palace guard known as the Praetorian Guard or, more germane to my purpose, to the prefecture (command) of the fleet or to safeguard the vital corn (i.e., cereal grain) supply.

The legions were reorganized to match the 'containment' mission of the newly minted Roman Empire, which sought to rationalize and consolidate its frontiers. But it was Augustus' transformation of the naval component of imperial defence that most strikingly broke with tradition. No longer would there be a draw-down of the navy, to be hastily rebuilt to face any new crisis. No longer would the *Princeps* have to bribe (with money, special privileges or power-sharing) fickle maritime allies to perform essential naval tasks. For the first time, Rome established permanent fleet stations at strategic locations, designed to handle the domestic and foreign responsibilities of a world power.

It should be borne in mind that during the entire history of Rome up until the accession of Augustus, the war fleets, largely built ad hoc as the various crises demanded, or 'borrowed' from maritime provinces and allies, had no dedicated bases. To make a modern analogy, the chief American naval bases at Norfolk in the east and San Diego and Pearl Harbor in the west served in varying degrees the needs of a home-based main fleet, with specialized and ancillary stations such as the submarine base in New London, Connecticut, and the naval air station in Pensacola, Florida. These were the functional equivalents of the Misene and Ravennate Italian home fleets established under Augustus. The diverse and fluctuating provincial 'fleets' of the Empire had transitory operational bases similar to the Mulberry harbours set up in Normandy in the wake of the Allied invasion in 1944 and those improvised facilities built by US Navy Seabees in the recaptured island chains of the Pacific in the latter days of the Second World War – the 'forward bases' promoted by Mahan in his later writings, such as at Guam, Wake Island, Majuro in the Marshall Islands and those at Kwajalein and Eniwetok.

Augustus' lasting legacy, then, with regard to the shaping of Roman imperial sea power was the stationing of permanent fleets in Italian waters. The antecedent for this measure was his sending part of Mark Antony's fleet to Forum Iulii (Frejus in southern Gaul, on the Côte d'Azur of modern France) following the Battle of Actium. He subsequently raised this port to the status of a colony. This base may also have formed the foundation of a military – land-based – auxiliary unit. Thus, the fleet from Forum Iulii, which seems to have absorbed part of Antony's fleet after it had fallen to the victor, was tasked with keeping watch over the coasts along the arc between Gaul and Italy (the *sinus ligusticus*, the Ligurian Gulf, the present Gulf of Genoa) and of the indentation between Marseille and Spain, the *sinus gallicus* (the Gulf of Gaul, or the Gulf of Lions), and to prevent the recurrence of piracy in an area where natural conditions favoured it.

This fleet also patrolled the military/strategic and mercantile sea routes between the Italian and Iberian peninsulas. Its base was a newly built town with a good, semi-artificial port created by using a lagoon adapted for the purpose, and a protected canal linking it to the sea. But we do not know much about the Frejus fleet because it disappeared rather quickly and seems not to have survived the civil wars that brought victory to Vespasian in AD 70.

Soon, however, it became clear that Italy could be much better defended from the motherland itself. Finally, probably advised by Agrippa, Augustus decided on two harbours, one on the west and one on the east coast of Italy: Misenum on the northern headland of the Bay of Naples and Ravenna on the Adriatic. In recognition of their function to defend the Empire's political and economic centre, the fleets based upon these harbours were designated as the praetorian fleets.

It has been shown that the construction of a permanent fleet, already planned by Pompey in 62 BC, was begun immediately after the Battle of Actium. At that time, Augustus had over 750 ships at his disposal, including the remnants of Antony's fleet. As demonstrated at Actium, the heavy ships – primarily quinqueremes – of this fleet were considered too sluggish and difficult to manoeuvre; they were burnt or otherwise destroyed. The remainder were added to Augustus' new fleet.

A possible precedent for Augustus to create these Italian-based fleets occurred when Pompeius Magnus, after he defeated the pirate menace early in the first century BC – and having been assigned all available ships to operate against them – proposed that the emperor thereafter base a fleet offshore of Italy to act as a permanent deterrent against the recurring scourge of piracy. One

Lucius Staius Murcus, who had been governor of Syria in 44 BC, was awarded command of this fleet the following year. Murcus had earlier been posted to blockade the fleet of Cleopatra as she came to the aid of Mark Antony against Octavian. Domitius Ahenobarbus was sent to assist him in this, and the two formed a highly successful partnership, which resulted in dominance over the seas between Greece and Italy. Murcus was later joined by Sextus Pompeius, who appears to have followed him to a similar command. Taken together, this information betokens the remnants of an official fleet-in-being stationed off Italy in the late Republican period. However, the size of the fleets stationed at Misenum and Ravenna has not been determined with any confidence.

There were varying functions for these home-based fleets. Ranking near the top, witness the aforementioned precursors (or remnants thereof), was the deterrent effect upon piracy: Augustus was quoted as boasting to having made 'shipping safe'. The grain trade from Alexandria (and increasingly North Africa) was the likely beneficiary of this protective umbrella. A minor, albeit steady, employment for the Italian fleets were setting up the awnings that shaded spectators in the amphitheatre and assisting in staging naval battle re-enactments as entertainments in the Coliseum in the first century AD. Their sail-handling expertise qualified them for this unrelated task.

Stationing the fleets adjacent to the seat of power inevitably entailed some political use of the home-based crews, but this was not as prevalent with the sea service as was the case with the traditional land force Praetorian Guard. At times, covert operations were undertaken by the Rome-based sailors. One striking example is when Nero contrived to murder his mother-in-law, Agrippina the Younger, in AD 62, and another during the counteraction to the Pisonian Conspiracy in AD 65.

Being so close to the seat of power, it was also inevitable that the Praetorian fleets were often utilized by the competing factions during the civil wars afflicting the Empire. It will be noticed that the crews and shore-based personnel were often employed as a kind of strategic reserve for the land army, since the sailor/soldier divide was not as sharp then as is common with modern navies, and the seamen were readily adaptable to fighting on land and in fact were practically interchangeable with the legions.

The delineation of the various fleets and their operating bases does not lend itself to straight chronological exposition; the literary and epigraphical evidence is disjointed, even for the two principal Italian or Praetorian fleets. When we get to the provincial fleets, one can often only make an informed guess as to beginning and end dates. Nomenclature varies as the fleets conjoined with legions and river forts wax and wane according to the state of affairs on the frontiers. The terminology of the several flotillas differs from source to source, and the time frames are garbled. Underwater archaeology helps to fill in some *lacunae*, but not much.

Here I will only set out the positioning of these various fleets, with a brief outline of their likely provenance and roles so far as is known. More detail will come out in the chronological survey of naval endeavours in the following chapters. But it will be seen that in the existing record, fleets, squadrons and naval detachments come and go, at times seemingly defunct, then reconstituting themselves or being subsumed by other entities, only to 'go silent' once more for no apparent reason. How much this reflects actuality – e.g., bases and ships falling into enemy hands, absorption into other fleets or absence of notable activity, etc. – rather than the unreliability of sources may merely be inferred from the record of operations.

Regarding the latter, it is well to bear in mind that addressing maritime matters was scarcely a concern of the chroniclers, who were mostly interested in either glorifying or vilifying the ruling classes, in accordance with the prevailing political currents. And it was the legions that held their attention, maritime affairs only being of interest in connection with the doings of the land forces.

The Home or Praetorian Fleets

Augustus saw, as with the army itself, the need for a permanent arrangement for maintaining the peace, but the most strategic and economical situations which would inform the siting of the main bases had yet to be evolved. Forum Iulii controlled the north-western Mediterranean, but soon further bases were needed to protect Italy itself and the corn supply to Rome and the Adriatic. An obvious choice was Misenum on the Bay of Naples, and considerable harbour works and buildings were started by Augustus, the port thereafter remaining the most important naval base throughout Imperial times. Augustus also constructed a new naval harbour at Ravenna at the head of the Adriatic, helping to deal with any potential trouble to the East, especially from Dalmatia and Illyria, should it arise.

The positioning of these home fleets to guard Rome's maritime spheres of influence recalls the British siting of its home fleets in the nineteenth and twentieth centuries to safeguard the various maritime approaches and the near seas (North Sea, Channel approaches, Atlantic, Baltic, etc.).

There is no evidence of naval convoys in the modern sense for the grain fleets, much less so for the large luxury freighters from the Eastern trade. The maintenance of the sea lines of communication was prophylactic – warships did not shepherd the cargo vessels, such as with the Allied convoy system for protection against the U-boat menace in the First and Second World Wars. This was highly impractical in any event, given the ship technology of the day and the constricted orbit of warships. But the patrolling vessels were vigilant for any piratical activity that might threaten seaborne commerce along the established itineraries. Being as the bases of these marauders were located in what today would be called 'failed states', it was a matter of scouring their coastal enclaves and destroying as many of their ships (and related infrastructure) as possible.

The Misenum and Ravenna fleets were not engaged in exploration *per se*; this function seems to have fallen upon those provincial or purpose-built invasion fleets on the Empire's fringes, and for the purpose of military reconnoitring, not scientific curiosity. Nor, until the second half of the second century AD, were the Praetorian fleets employed for the large-scale transport of men and supplies. In effect, they are best regarded as comprising part of the military forces immediately available to the emperor. Much as with the lesser urban forces in Rome, an important role was to serve as an adjunct to the Praetorian Guard, to be used against perceived enemies of the state when operating by sea was the most appropriate avenue of attack.

As the name betokens, the *classis Misenensis* was stationed at Misenum, in the northern end of the Bay of Naples, though small *vexillationes* (detachments) were based at every major coastal city and settlement in Italy. Marines and sailors from this fleet also likely provided a garrison for Corsica and Sardinia. Some hundreds of Misenum marines were always garrisoned in Rome, serving alongside the Praetorian Guard. The Misenum fleet supported Vespasian in the Civil War of 69 AD, and he spent the rest of his reign enlarging it. By the end of the first century AD, it consisted of fifty vessels and had a strength of 10,000 marines. The Misenum fleet maintained its reputation as Rome's largest and most prestigious naval force at least as late as the Severan period (193-235 AD), when it won the honorary titles of '*Pia*' (loyal) and '*Vindex*' (victorious).

The Ravenna fleet was created in 25 BC, and was based predominately at Ravenna, on the north-western, Adriatic-facing quadrant of the peninsula, with occasional outlying ancillary posts. At least in the first century AD, small units of Ravenna marines were garrisoned in Rome and Dalmatia; it is likely that Dalmatia/Illyria was a major recruiting ground for this and other fleets. It is believed that the Ravenna fleet was almost exactly half the size of the Misenum fleet, though it was also enlarged during the reign of Vespasian. This fleet appears to have been active in the West somewhat later than the Misenum fleet, which was last mentioned at the turn of the fifth century. It was directed largely to the Eastern waters, particularly to combat Illyrian piracy.

From the modern point of view, one might think first of the protection of trade, which reached its ancient height in the Early Empire. But then Chester Starr says, regarding grain shipments from Alexandria in Egypt:

'It is, however, unlikely that the navy had any real responsibility in patrolling this vital route; sailing ships came directly from Alexandria, but galleys could not keep to the sea for more than about 100 miles before they needed to touch shore for food and water. The general peace of the Mediterranean, moreover, prevented any serious interference with seaborne trade.'

Starr is correct about the relatively short action radius of galleys propelled solely by oar power, but the galleys did have masts and sails, which were stowed or placed ashore when clearing for action. There was nothing to prevent the galleys from utilizing sail power for longer open-sea transits.

The real utility of the Mediterranean fleets in general military assistance was in swift dispatch of letters and orders. Michael Redde goes on to say that 'at least once' in the Early Empire the essential military role of Mediterranean fleets became more visible. In the Year of Four Emperors civil wars following Nero's death, Vespasian, erstwhile governor of Syria, was victor both by reason of his own ability and the cooperation of the Balkan generals; but a minor, yet important, factor was the support of the Italian squadrons and his control of the food supplies provided to Rome from Egypt.

Praetorian Fleets: Roles

The fleet at Misenum was primarily military. The town itself, on the Bay of Naples, was a veteran colony where sailors settled their families. Seeing that Nero and Vespasian raised two legions from it in 68-69 AD, the fleet itself ought to have numbered approximately 10,000 sailors, rowers and marines. With this much manpower, the fleet was divided into several outposts throughout the Western Mediterranean. The Ostia detachment, for instance, was responsible for transporting senators to their provinces, shipping grain from Ostia to Rome and conveying news back and forth from the provinces to the city. The skill of the sailors was also used within Rome, where they camped with the Praetorians, formed a part of the *vigils* and managed the awnings in the Coliseum. A Corsican detachment guarded timber shipments from the island to Italian shipyards, and policed Gaul and Spain. Another detachment was placed in Sardinia, where rebellions occasionally flared. Ships of the Messene fleet also had several ports of call in the Eastern Mediterranean, including the Piraeus and Seleucia.

Meanwhile, the Ravenna fleet was strictly military, policing Dalmatian and Liburnae pirates. It was Italy's first line of defence in case of attack from the north. A heavy naval presence in Italy was necessary for the security and rapid evacuation of the emperor in case of emergency, since Italian infantry presence was weak. In the meantime, the provincial fleets were established where the Italian fleets could not reach in good time. The Mediterranean fleets in Alexandria and Syria were used as police forces and guards of trade. The Syrian fleet was the launching point of every emperor's Parthian expedition. An additional fleet in the Nile was responsible for fiscal action along the river and suppressing revolts.

We will examine these episodes in more depth in the concluding eight chapters delineating key naval operations and functions from the time of Augustus to the fall of the Empire.

The Provincial Fleets

Overview

It is true that large fleets continued to operate away from the adjacent coasts of Italy under Augustus; however, these were not permanent establishments as of that period, but rather what we might call 'invasion fleets' – specially commissioned for a specific threat. Eventually, over the next couple of centuries, smaller fleets were stationed permanently in the provinces, most often attached to legionary forts or outposts. It is not often clear when operations attributed to the 'provincial' fleets were actually conducted by ad hoc invasion fleets due to the accelerated depletion of the outlying standing naval units as the barbarian incursions became more frequent and eroded the staging areas normally assigned to the provincial flotillas. This muddled accounting will be seen in the discussions of the various naval operations in chapters eight to ten. I will endeavour to try to untangle this disorder in my narration of the campaigns.

Fleets stationed along the northern frontier on the Rhine, Danube, Black Sea and in Britain were mostly militaristic. The first three had the dual role of dividing the two banks against crossing intruders, and uniting them in communication between legions along and across the rivers. They had the duties of guarding and promoting trade along the river, transporting both supplies and men. The Pontic fleet was responsible for quelling occasional Caucasian invaders and providing communication of the legions placed along the Caucasian coasts, transporting troops across the Hellespont and collecting tariffs from the Black Sea. Furthermore, a fleet located at the mouth of the Danube, the *classis Moesica*, was left to defend the Dacian frontier from invasion without legionary support in AD 68-69, allowing some barbarian tribes to invade. This fleet is repeatedly featured in Trajan's Column and serves as the main evidence for the importance of the fleet in an expansion mission as conductor of supplies, reinforcements and news. The *classis Germanica*, being on the most heavily guarded frontier, had several achievements after its establishment by Drusus the Elder in 12 BC. Germanicus, on his mission to the Elbe, decided to sail his force to central Germany and make reconnoitring missions along the coast. The massive 1,000-ship fleet was manned by landlubbing soldiers, and the results were disastrous as the entire fleet was scattered around the coast, some ships reaching Britain. Its strategic placing also allowed it to encourage trade between Gaul, Germany and Britain, thus developing a steady economy along the northern frontiers.

Finally, and perhaps most obviously, a Roman fleet played a crucial part in the maintenance of the province of Britannia. It had been first established by Claudius, who enlisted Mediterranean sailors for the conquest of the isles. It had several posts around the island, making excursions, as Tacitus writes in his *Agricola*, to Scotland, Ireland and Wales. The fleet established by Claudius must have declined, since Agricola did not always have a fleet disposable for his conquests. Tacitus writes the amusing tale of the conquest of the island of Anglesey off Wales, which had to be achieved without ships. Agricola's cunning plan was to send a number of auxiliaries skilled in swimming with weapons and horses. Thus he completely blindsided the natives, who were expecting a naval battle. Once his fleet was established, however, Agricola made great use of it, sending ships ahead of his infantry along the coast to inspire terror in the enemy, weaken their defences and employ divide-and-conquer tactics. The greatest impact of the British fleet was in the revolt of the governor Carausius, who proclaimed himself *imperator* in AD 286. He strengthened the *classis Britannica*, protecting his realm successfully. Carausius was the first usurper to have based his power entirely in a fleet, minting coins with ships and maritime imagery.

The Northern Fleets

It will be seen that, at least for the first several centuries of the Empire, the fleets operating in the north and north-west sectors were the busiest. The term '*classis Germanica*' is mentioned for the first time by Tacitus in AD 69. However, both the availability of warships for Domitius Corbulo's naval operation against the Chauci in AD 47 and the extensive preparations for the invasion of Britain in AD 43 indicate that both the German and British fleets go back to the Principate of Claudius.

The headquarters of the German fleet was located on a branch of the Rhine, 3km (about 1¼ miles) south of Cologne (Colonia Agrippensis), although the site may have been utilized earlier by the land forces. Some of the rowers were Batavian, although the *nautae* (sailors) in the fleet were probably professional sailors from elsewhere.

The main base of the *classis Britannica* was at Boulogne (Gesoriacum, later Bononia) in Gallia Belgica. In the second century AD, the fleet had a second HQ in Britain at Dover (Dubris). Agricola fully utilized the British fleet during his campaigns in the north under Domitian. With Agricola in the lead boat, the seaborne component advanced northwards in combination with the land forces. This fleet is said to have inspired terror in the Britons. In one incident, a newly recruited auxiliary cohort from 'east of the Rhine' mutinied and seized three liburnians for the return to Germany. Each of these vessels embarked up to 150 troops, who ordered the *gubernatores* (navigating officers) on them to serve as their helmsmen. Following his final victory at Mons Graupius, Agricola used this fleet for exploration, ordering the *praefectus classis* to circumnavigate Britain, most likely bearing a landing force of marines. Indications are that the British fleet was already of a considerable size by the date of this voyage.

The Mauretanian Fleet (*Classis Mauretanica*) originated in the middle of the first century AD when Mauretania was made a Roman province. It had its beginnings as a detachment of the Alexandrian Fleet, but gradually developed its own identity. Very little is known about this fleet. Apparently it patrolled along the North African coast to the Strait of Gibraltar.

The Danube

During the Illyrian campaigns of Octavian/Augustus prior to the Battle of Actium, the future emperor deployed an invasion fleet on the Danube. Later, in AD 50, the fleet that provided refuge to Suebian chieftain Vannius is presumed to be the *classis Pannonica*. Professor D.B. Saddington (in '*Classes*, the Evolution of the Roman Imperial Fleets', in *A Companion to the Roman Army* by Paul Erdkamp (ed.), Blackwell Publishing Ltd, 2011) deduces from a fragmentary diploma found near Zagreb that the fleet may have already been in existence in AD 45. The main base of this fleet was most likely at Tarunum (Zemun) at the mouth of the Sava River, near the Danube.

The *classis Moesica* patrolled the lower Danube, where Saddington deduces that it was already in existence from AD 56 under Nero. He finds evidence for two ship types utilized by this fleet: the *ratis*, an oar-propelled raft which was also a type of flat skiff which could be mounted on pontoons for river crossings; and the *pristia*, a type of lembus, a flat vessel used for both reconnaissance and troop transport. Lembi were used for the latter purpose by Julian when he crossed the Danube in AD 361.

Fleets in the East

When Nero turned the kingdom of Pontus into a province, he confiscated its royal fleet and used it to patrol the Black Sea as the *classis Pontica*, comprising forty ships principally based at Trapezus (Trabzon). Agrippa had used its facilities in 14 BC during his expedition to the kingdom of Bosporus (the straits of Kerch).

The *classis Syriaca* is first attested to in circa AD 93. Its main base was at Seleucia Pieria (Kaboussie), where in AD 75, an artificial tunnel and a canal to divert a river which was silting up the harbour were built at the port. Detachments of the Misene fleet were also stationed at Seleucia. Some documents attest to the presence of triremes there in AD 166.

The Egyptian Fleet

The *classis Alexandrina* has been authenticated as early as the reign of Gaius Caligula, and its rowers are mentioned under Nero. During the Jewish Revolt of AD 66-73, it employed transports to convey troops up the Nile. There are further references to a prefect of this fleet during the Jewish Revolt of AD 115-117 under Trajan. The Alexandrian fleet was raised in the early first century AD – probably by Augustus. It was based in Alexandria, with detachments serving across the coastline of Egypt. Its precise function is unknown, since the Nile was guarded and patrolled by a local Egyptian militia rather than Roman forces. Mention is made of vessels belonging to this fleet patrolling the Nile later, in the second and third centuries. The Alexandrian fleet is believed to have contributed marines to land campaigns during the wars with the Sassanid Persians in the mid-late third century, but it falls out of history in this period.

There are vague references to a *classis Nova Libyca* (the New African fleet), to which Marcus Antonius had appointed a trierarch to deal with pressing problems in safeguarding the corn supply. As was the case with all of the naval contingents, fleet personnel might be used in non-naval tasks, such as road-building, working in the stone quarries and building field fortifications, tunnels, canals, etc.

Legionary Naval Squadrons

The uncertainty in attributing specific fleets to operations can be illustrated by the following, which shows that certain squadrons were not under the command of the regional fleet organization but rather were attached to the legions.

In a series of Roman provinces, a river formed the border of the Empire. In Europe, this was the case for the provinces on the Rhine and the Danube. We know of three provincial fleets here, the *classis Germanica*, *classis Pannonica* and *classis Moesica*. Although one could conclude from their names that their areas of operations stretched over both provinces bearing their corresponding name, this was not the case. Thus, so-called military diplomas clearly show for the *classis Pannonica* and *classis Moesica* that they belonged to the army of Pannonia inferior and Moesia inferior respectively.

As for Germania inferior, one can see the same from the distribution of inscriptions and tiles, which are limited to Lower Germany. The sole exception is the Brohl Valley, which lay in Upper Germany, but the stone quarries there were exclusively used by the army of Lower Germany. That the *classis Germanica* belonged to the army of Lower Germany was recently confirmed by a military diploma dating to Trajan. It was found in the Netherlands and names, beside the auxiliary troops of the Lower German army, the fleet as well. For the protection of the Empire's borders, there was certainly a chain of forts along the corresponding rivers in all three provinces, but an effective control of the border was only possible with ships undertaking daily patrols, as the author Ammianus Marcellinus still describes for the fourth century. But Lower Germany, Lower Pannonia and Lower Moesia were not the only provinces with a riverine border with the non-Roman world. Since the fleets did not operate beyond their provinces, however, one must ask who was in charge of surveillance here.

There are other indications of legionary fleet detachments in the *Notitia Dignitatum*. A special feature of the province Moesia inferior provides a first indication for this. Although the province had its own fleet, the *classis Moesica*, there have been found in the legionary fortress of Novae tile-stamps bearing the name of the locally stationed *Legio I Italica* in a frame shaped like a ship. Moreover, this is not any ordinary ship, but a warship displaying the typical concave prow and a sternpost decoration, such as seen on liburnae on Trajan's Column. This extremely seldom seen way of stamping tiles gives every reason to believe that the *Legio I Italica* was equipped with its own squadron of warships. The tiles clearly belong to the second century. This means, however, that in Moesia inferior, alongside the fleet itself the naval squadron of a legion was also stationed. The reason for this lies in the area of operations of the *classis Moesica*. Its inscriptions and tiles are to be found only on the western and northern coasts of the Black Sea and in the Danube delta. They are absent further upriver. One can assume, therefore, that the *classis Moesica* possessed mainly seaworthy ships with a deep draft, which were unsuitable for use on the rivers. As a result, the *Legio I Italica* took charge of surveillance on this section of the Moesian border using more suitable ships.

Summary and Conclusion: The Fleets as Military Tools

The new imperial navy of Rome was in fact organized according to a general design that has the clear imprint of strategic foresight and Agrippa's naval expertise. Miseno was chosen as the principal permanent naval base, as it was optimally located for coastal defence of the Tyrrhenian Sea while being close enough to Rome to be readily available at the emperor's command. The naval base of the second imperial home fleet was based on the west coast of Italy at Ravenna, a well-sited locale from which to maintain naval control of the northern Adriatic and also optimal for maintaining a connection with the Balkan hinterland through the navigable tributaries of the Danube (Drava and Sava). Both of these fleets, which were styled 'praetorian' (at the emperor's direct service), thus covered the entire Mediterranean.

Among the other permanent imperial fleets, some were established directly under the rule of Augustus (Foro Julius fleet, Augusta Alexandrian fleet, Germanic fleet). Others were initially set up in the same period but were not formally established until later by some of the immediately succeeding emperors, such as the Syrian fleet, established by Vespasian; Pannonian and Moesican fleets, instituted by Domitian; and Arabica fleet, established by Trajan. Further fleets were formed only later, such as the British fleet, initially, in embryonic form, instituted by Gaius Caligula; the Pontic fleet, instituted by Nero; Nova Libyan fleet, set up by Commodus; and Mesopotamian fleet, inaugurated by Trajan. The bulk of these fleets (nine of thirteen) therefore go back to Augustus and Agrippa, a testament to the organizational genius of the latter, as this type of organization is similar to those adopted today by the largest navies in the world.

Readers unfamiliar with the role of ships in maintaining the Roman Empire may well ask, 'Why create such a comprehensive array of fleets if there were no longer any challengers at sea?' As will be shown in the concluding chapters of this book, the absence of other major maritime powers did not mean that the situation at sea was secure. The Empire still required a visible and credible permanent naval presence to inhibit the flourishing of any threat to the smooth performance of maritime activities, most of which remained of vital necessity to the Roman metropolis and the other outlying cities of the Empire.

It will be seen that the main function of the fleets of Imperial Rome was to ensure there was no interference with Rome's maritime lifeblood across the sea and river conduits. The Roman fleets, therefore, made regular patrols to ensure necessary control and surveillance of these waterways. They had to maintain the appropriate level of training and a smooth functioning of the requisite logistics. These were the silent, unsung, though vital operations of the fleets, which served as a crucial underpinning of the *Pax Romana*, albeit rarely exciting the notice or interest of the authors of surviving scraps of literary evidence.

From the time of Augustus onwards, therefore, the Roman military fleets maintained full dominion of the sea – the entire Mediterranean, as well as all other seas washing the shores of the Empire's provinces and allies. For the first and only time in history, the waters of the known world were subject to the law of a single state. This control, however, did not mean that Rome retained the exclusive privilege of exploiting the sea's resources and maritime navigation for strictly selfish purposes. Under common legal usage in the early Empire, the sea fell into the category of '*res communes omnium*', i.e. the joint property of mankind: it was thus necessary to guarantee freedom of navigation for all, as well as free exploitation of marine resources: harvesting salt, fishing, creation of coastal ponds for fish farming and exploration to locate sources for the products used in luxury items, such as corals, pearls, the murex for purple dye and the shells for cameos.

Rome likewise found it in her best interests to encourage all economic activities associated with the sea, beginning with commercial shipping as needed for the city's requirements, as well as to unite and communicate with all the shores of the wide sea around which stretched the Empire. Accordingly, in addition to employing their war vessels to ensure the safety of their commercial sea routes and freedom of navigation, Rome adopted a series of measures to boost and encourage the merchant marine: improving and augmenting the shipyards, multiplying and enlarging ports and creating a network of lighthouses, all this without imposing customs duties, and, on the contrary, putting into force tax relief measures for shipowners.

The port system of the Eternal City was greatly enlarged: the city of Rome's river port was gradually expanded downstream, reaching the Emporium area, where huge warehouses were erected, while the adjoining landfill embedded with amphorae landed by vessels began to grow increasingly, eventually forming the present-day Mount Testaccio.

Drawing on their technical and organizational skills, the Romans ensured thereby an extraordinary development of sea lanes of communications, facilitating all links by which to secure supplies necessary for Rome's sustenance and growth, in addition to the more intensive and beneficial cultural and political interchange between all the shores of the Empire. It has been estimated that the merchant fleet operating during the Roman Empire period reached a size never seen previously, and was likely to remain unsurpassed until the nineteenth century, when the great modern era of shipping companies flourished.

This situation enhanced trade and travel by sea, extending the trade routes to the most remote shores in search of more lucrative commerce, and pushing naval exploration beyond the limits of the known world. While the ports in India became commonly frequented by Roman cargo ships, there were likewise regular contacts with several ports of the South China Sea and of Serica (modern China). Serica was one of the easternmost countries of Asia known to the Ancient Greek and Roman geographers. The term is generally taken as referring to northern China during its Zhou, Qin and Han dynasties, as it was reached via the overland Silk Road, in contrast to the Sinae, who were reached via the maritime routes. Military fleets also had occasion to make voyages of exploration, such as those conducted at the time of Augustus in the North Sea, up to the Baltic Sea and down to the Red Sea, and that of the fleet of Agricola, who circumnavigated Britain, leading to the sighting of the mystical Arctic legend island of Ultima Thule (probably the Faeroe Isles).

Enjoying a sustained peaceful state of affairs which the ancient world had never before known, all the peoples of the Empire were able to take advantage of freedom of navigation and the increase in vessel traffic. The shipping-lane network became denser, more regular and more efficient, allowing all conveyance of people and necessary supplies, and determining a general elevation of the economic conditions, prosperity and well-being of all the realm's populations. All along the coast, maritime activities flourished: fishing, seaside villas and even recreational boating. Finally, as a historically much more significant result, the mutual exchange of knowledge and values that constituted the real breeding ground of Roman civilization was privileged, among all the shores of the Empire, which then spread and took root to the point that it remains the basis of our Western civilization.

Chapter Eight

Trade and its Protection: Ports, Cargoes, Seafaring Factors and Trade Routes

Trade was vital to Ancient Rome. The Empire cost a vast sum of money to run, and trade brought in much of that money. The population of the city of Rome was one million at its peak in the first century AD, and such a vast number of people required all manner of things brought back via trade, certainly exotic spices, baubles, textiles, oils and wines for the patricians, but most crucially grain to feed the burgeoning populace. While mercenary commerce was considered to be beneath the dignity of the equestrian class, it was nonetheless a very necessary evil in oiling the wheels of empire. Then there were Italian, and later provincial, exports to all parts of the Empire as well as trading entities not under Roman rule.

The Roman Empire was criss-crossed with trade routes. There were sea routes that covered the Mediterranean and Black seas, and numerous land routes using the roads built by the Romans. Trade and moving the Roman army around were the two principal reasons for building roads. As Mahan and Corbett would agree, this was also the case with the various naval and merchant fleets. Before examining the mercantile traffic, I will take a look at the ports and harbours serving both the military and commercial requirements of the Empire. The siting of these *entrepôts* was as much driven by mercantile considerations as naval strategic imperatives.

The Ship Havens and Their Facilities

We should distinguish between port and harbour, since the two terms are often confused. A port is a man-made coastal or riverine facility where boats and ships can load and unload. It may consist of quays, wharves, jetties, piers and slipways with cranes or ramps. A port may have magazine buildings or warehouses for storage of goods and a transport system, in modern times typically railway, road transport or pipeline transport facilities for relaying goods inland. In short, a port is used mainly for marine trading and a harbour is used as a parking space or a storage space for ships and does not customarily maintain the infrastructure incidental to mercantile trade that the harbour contains.

While many of the Empire's shipping terminals were newly built, there were also some that had been radically modified to suit new duties.

The small port was a simple marina consisting of a well-protected cove and an adjacent beach, near which a ship could drop anchor. It was adequate both as a fishing port and trading port. Moving trade goods by land was hampered due to excessive cost and relatively small quantities of merchandise that could be moved. Thus, small ports would benefit from coastal shipping by functioning as distribution centres for areas difficult to access by land routes.

The big harbours were always at least partly man-made. They were either adaptations of favourable natural sites or were entirely built up. They had either one or several basins and were located either directly on the coast or at the mouth of a river – using the latter term in a broad sense to include streams capable of floating shallow-draft 'shuttle' craft trans-shipping goods to and from the deeper-draft seagoing vessels. For example, the harbour of Alexandria was pretty much left the same as it had been in Hellenistic times; thus we do not have to consider it as being newly fashioned with the Empire.

During the period of the Republic, Rome never had a port commensurate with her size and importance. Ostia, at the mouth of the Tiber, was founded in the fourth or third century BC, but not as a harbour *per se*, rather as a maritime defence post to fend off an enemy approaching by sea and prevent him from coming up the river. Early in Rome's history, small merchant vessels did come all the way to Rome, where at the foot of the Aventine – one of the seven hills of Rome – an *emporion* (trading port) surrounded by grain silos and porticos evolved. But as the city of Rome grew, this combination river and sea port proved inadequate.

During the Second Punic War, Rome started work on the Greek port in the Bay of Naples, then named Dicaearchia (or Puteoli), as her chief trading port. Julius, then Augustus, Caesar found this situation inadequate and wanted to rectify it by augmenting the man-made port at Ostia, but this did not actually transpire until the reign of Claudius. Ostia was formally opened by Nero and was soon doubled in size by the time of Trajan. Thus the harbour to become known as Portus (Latin word simply denoting 'port') was developed alongside Ostia, maintaining close relations with both Ostia and Rome.

Claudius had constructed a circular basin, with the entry channel divided into two branches by moles (piers or jetties). This basin was not very well protected from storms coming across the open sea; in AD 62, 200 ships anchored there were destroyed by heavy seas. This condition provoked Trajan to construct a hexagonal basin almost half a mile in diameter, built further back on the landward side and connected to Claudius' port, which thereafter served it as an outer harbour. It was also connected to the Tiber, upon which small craft could transport goods all the way to Rome.

All around the basins there were numerous warehouses, porticoes and shipyards. There were also many warehouses in the Ostia complex. These new installations finally provided Rome with a harbour commensurate with her needs. Because of the importance of this complex, it was placed under the authority of a *praefectus annonae*. As Portus/Ostia grew in importance, the old harbour of Puteoli in the Bay of Naples lost most of its trade.

Following the decline of Puteoli, Ostia became the most important port as it was the nearest major port to Rome itself. (The naval base for the *classis Misenensius* was at Naples some 120 miles to the south). Ostia was situated at the mouth of the River Tiber and was only 15 miles from Rome. Many ships travelled between Ostia and the North African city of Carthage (an important trade *entrepôt* after the destruction of the Phoenician base there in the second century BC), a journey that took between three and five days. Ships also arrived at Ostia from Spain and France. All their goods could be quickly moved to Rome itself, taken in barges to the city up the River Tiber after slaves had transferred the products from the merchant ships. Ironically, Ostia was to play a major part in the downfall of Rome when Alaric the Goth captured Ostia in AD 409, knowing that this would starve Rome of much-needed food.

The Romans did what they could to make sea journeys safe – lighthouses were built, as were safe harbours and docks. The Roman navy also tried its best, and largely succeeded, in making the Mediterranean safe from pirates, a task driven by trade requisites as concomitants of naval strategy.

The Romans made trade as easy as possible. There was only one currency used and there were no complicating customs dues. Trade was also encouraged by many years of peace within the Empire. Trade was vital to the success of the Empire. When the Empire collapsed, trade throughout the lands that had once made up the Roman Empire also collapsed. The Mediterranean became a dangerous place for merchants, as there were no powers remaining who could control the activities of pirates who marauded as far north as the English Channel.

What was Acquired from Where?

The Romans imported a whole variety of materials: beef, corn, glassware, iron, lead, leather, marble, olive oil, perfumes, purple dye, silk, silver, spices, timber, tin and wine. The main trading partners for these commodities were in Spain, France, the Middle East and North Africa.

Britain exported lead, woollen products and tin. In return, it imported wine, olive oil, pottery and papyrus from Rome. British traders relied on the Romans to provide security within the Empire. When this collapsed and Europe was seemingly overrun by 'barbarians', no one could guarantee traders that their produce would get through. Also, without the power of Rome, who would be willing to buy what was produced in Britain and other parts of Europe?

This vast flow of goods to Rome from far-flung corners of the Empire was only one of, if the most notable, aspects of the commerce of the imperial age. Soon all of Rome's provinces were trading among one another as well as with the capital. Casson (*The Ancient Mariners*) provides the following survey of trading partners and sources, indicating the value of sea trade to the Empire's well-being:

'Exports:

'Italy *exported* pottery, metalware and, up to the end of the 1st century AD, quantities of wine – after that time, the provinces (formerly Rome's best customers for exported wine) began not only to produce wine for themselves but to export it to their former supplier;

'Spain was exporting 'garum', a syrupy sauce used to flavour food made from a fermented fish extract, to France and dried fish to Greece;

'Asia Minor sent coloured marble for Roman building projects in North Africa;

'Athens sent statuary to adorn the homes of the rich throughout the west; and

'Egypt shipped papyrus all around the Mediterranean.

'Imports:

'From Africa and Arabia, Rome and its associated entities received frankincense and myrrh;

'from Africa and India, ivory;

'from India, pepper and other spices, certain drugs, cottons; and from China, silks.'

By AD 117, during Emperor Hadrian's reign, Rome was a city of more than one million people. Its empire stretched from the Upper Nile to the Sea of Azov, from the Caspian Sea to northern England, and from Morocco to Germany. During this period it cost more to cart a large quantity of grain just 75 miles on land than to ship it from one end of the Empire to the other by sea. Trade by sea flourished during what is referred to as the *Pax Romana* (Roman peace).

A graphic recital of the seaborne lifeblood of the Empire is recounted in the following passage by Lionel Casson in *Ships and Seamanship In The Ancient World*:

'The Roman man in the street ate bread baked with wheat grown in North Africa or Egypt, and fish that had been caught and dried near Gibraltar. He cooked with North African oil in pots and pans of copper mined in

Spain, ate off dishes fired in French kilns, drank wine from Spain or France, and if he spilled any of his dinner on his toga, had it cleaned with fuller's earth from the Aegean islands. The Roman of wealth dressed in garments of wool from Miletus or linen from Egypt; his wife wore silks from China, adorned herself with diamonds and pearls from India, and made up with cosmetics from South Arabia. He seasoned his food with Indian pepper and sweetened it with Athenian honey, had it served in dishes of Spanish silver on tables of African citrus wood, and washed it down with Sicilian wine poured from decanters of Syrian glass. He lived in a house whose walls were covered with coloured marble veneer quarried in Asia Minor; his furniture was of Indian ebony or teak inlaid with African ivory, and his rooms were filled with statues imported from Greece. Staples and luxuries, from as near as France and as far as China, poured into the capital, enough of the one to feed a million people, and of the other to satisfy the extravagances of the political, social and economic rulers of the western world.'

Sea Routes

There were two principal governing factors determining the orientation of the commercial navigation: (1) supply and demand governed the points at which sailing originated and ended; (2) there were also maritime factors, principally wind patterns, but to some extent currents and navigational hazard zones. The way in which maritime routes all converged on Rome (actually first on Puteoli, then on Portus and finally on Rome) was a function of the political and economic centrality of Rome.

Maritime archaeology and ancient manuscripts from classical antiquity show evidence of vast Roman commercial fleets. The most substantial remains from this commerce are the infrastructure remains of harbours, moles, warehouses and lighthouses at ports such as Civatecchia, Ostia, Portus, Leptis Magna and Caesarea Maritima. At Rome itself, the thousands of amphorae forming Monte Testaccio testifies to the scale of this commerce. As with most Roman technology, Roman seagoing commercial ships had no significant advances over Greek ships of the previous centuries, though the lead sheeting of hulls for protection seems to have been more common. The Romans used round-hulled sailing ships. Continuous Mediterranean 'police' protection over several centuries was one of the main factors of success of Roman commerce, given that Roman roads were designed more for feet or hooves than for wheels, and could not support the economical transport of goods over long distances. The Roman ships used would have been easy prey for pirates had it not been for the fleets of Liburnian galleys and triremes of the Roman navy.

Bulky low-valued commodities, like grain and construction materials, were traded only by sea routes, since the cost of sea transportation was sixty times lower than land. Staple goods and commodities like cereals for making bread and papyrus scrolls for book production were imported to Italy from Ptolemaic Egypt in a continuous fashion.

In Augustus' day, over 100 ships sailed each day from Myos Hormos or Berenice, the major ports on the north-western Egyptian shore of the Red Sea. This was six times the number under the last of the Ptolemies. To guard against pirate attack, these vessels embarked troops of archers and were probably escorted by warships of the Roman navy patrolling the Red Sea. The term 'escorted' is used very loosely here and does not comport with the close convoy escort adopted in the twentieth century's two world wars. As was typical at that time, the Roman warships likely pre-emptively patrolled to attack the pirate bases, or did so retroactively after merchant vessels had been attacked or threatened. This seemingly lethargic notion of protection of trade is reflective of the limited ability of the ships of the era to sail against the wind and to keep up with merchant vessels, whose primary means of propulsion was sail rather than oars.

The trade over the Indian Ocean blossomed in the first and second century AD. The sailors made use of the monsoon to cross the ocean from the ports of Berenice, Leulos Limen and Myos Hormos on the Red Sea coast of Roman Egypt, to the ports of Muziris and Nelkynda on the Malabar coast. The main trading partners in southern India were the Tamil dynasties of the Pandyas, Cholas and Cheras. Many Roman artifacts have been found in India; for example, at the archaeological site of Arikamedu near present-day Pondicherry. Meticulous descriptions of the ports and items of trade around the Indian Ocean can be found in the *Periplus of the Erythraean Sea*.

What follows is a brief run-down of the routes favoured by merchant vessels, subject to the vagaries of tide, winds, currents and season.

The most famous route is the one associated with Alexandria's 'wheat fleet' (although from the time of Nero, most of Rome's grain supply came from North Africa – present-day Libya and Tunisia). The difficulties encountered with this route all centred around the onset of the summer winds, known as 'the Etesians'.

Prior to the commencement of these winds, the most probable route for the shipping was a 'middle course', going by way of the southern coast of Crete. Then, once the summer winds arrived, there were two likely possibilities: (1) along the African coast, utilizing the alternating land and sea breezes, which could be felt up to about 13 miles from the coast; and (2) a route going north as far as the area around Rhodes, and from there, with some difficulty, to the western regions. The routes coming from the east and from Asia Minor joined up with this route.

Heading westward, the three major routes were as follows:

(1) the African routes, which, starting from the area north of the province of Africa (the area around Carthage) went up to the eastern coast of Sardinia and along its shores, after which the ships sailed before the wind into the Italian ports; (2) the route from Spain (and variants thereof); and (3) the routes from Gaul.

The route from Spain started either from the south, from Cadiz on the Atlantic coast, from the centre or from the north – from Malaga, Carthago Nova (Cartagena), Terraco (Tarragona) or from other ports in the area (Dertosa, Emporiae).

From the south, the route most frequently taken after going through the Strait of Gibraltar was one passing to the south of Sardinia and linking up with the African route. From central and northern points, the ships took a median course that led them through the Straits of Bonifacio between Corsica and Sardinia, which explains why a whole ships' graveyard has been found there.

With regard to the routes from Gaul, the first of them left from Narbonne and was similar to the Spanish route from the north, that is, it was a route on the open seas towards the Straits of Bonifacio. The second, leaving from Arles or Marseilles, went to Corsica, then on to the Italian coast via the island of Elba.

Thanks to her control of these sea lanes, Rome could pride herself on being the marketplace of the entire *oikoumene* (known world). These routes made it possible for Rome to re-export goods and also contributed to the renown and prosperity of her ports. We know that these trade operations were still in effect at the beginning of the fourth century because, in the maritime sections of Diocletian's *Edict on Maximum Prices*, the rates for transporting goods from Rome to a number of different places are given.

Routes Outside the Mediterranean

With the development of the western regions of the Roman world, routes in the Atlantic, the English Channel and the North Sea took on great importance. They were connected to the Mediterranean routes, either by the Strait of Gibraltar, by the isthmuses of Gaul (the valleys of the Garonne, the Loire and the Seine) or by the Rhone-Rhine axis. This creates a most insoluble problem for understanding how products from the Mediterranean reached Gaul. When we find, for example, an Italian wine amphora in the middle of the Loire country, there is no way of knowing whether it got there via the Atlantic and the lower Loire, or via the Rhone and the upper Loire after a short portage.

In any case, the size of the ports on the Atlantic is evidence that ocean-going shipping between the Iberian peninsula and the big estuaries of Gaul and the British Isles was of some magnitude. R. Dion's studies from the 1950s on the transshipment of goods across France in this period have shown how difficult it was for ancient seamen to go from the Atlantic Ocean into the English Channel. In view of the fact that rounding Brittany is depicted as an all-out expedition, perhaps we should think that there were actually two navigational areas almost totally separate from each other. There is nothing to prove it, but nothing to disprove it either.

At the other end of the ancient world, direct trade relations developed during Roman times between the Empire and the lands in the East and the Far East without the agency of the Arab world. The desire to eliminate interference from Arab middlemen and pirates (at times indistinguishable) provoked the earliest recorded sea-land campaign under Augustus (discussed below). This trade was censured by Pliny the Elder, a querulous and traditionalist thinker, who says that it was simply a matter of importing luxury items, and this trade upset the Empire's trade balance and was thus the cause of the Empire's economic decline.

A brief note on the configuration and capabilities of the trading vessels themselves is in order here. Illustrations and conventional specifications of the vessels are shown in illustration number two, while illustration number one depicts a typical cargo vessel of circa the second century AD. Much of the following is derived from Casson's *The Ancient Mariners* and his *Ships and Seafaring*, as well as Rouge's *Ships and Fleets of the Ancient Mediterranean*.

Merchant Ships

The smallest merchant vessel considered suitable for open seas was 70-80 tons burden. By the fifth century BC, carriers of 100-150 tons were in common use and vessels of 350-500 tons were not rare. The larger ships were said to carry as many as 600 passengers on long voyages, but this seems a stretch. While standards of habitability have changed drastically over the millennia, such a large mass of human cargo in a vessel of perhaps 400 tons for more than a couple of days' passage would seem to invite illness, not to mention great discomfort. *Syracusia*, the largest merchant ship of the ancient world, was launched about 240 BC. Archimedes, the Greek mathematician and engineer, supervised construction of the three-masted, three-decked grain carrier of about 1,800 tons burden.

The dimensions of *Syracusia* are not known, but those of a Roman grain-carrier of a couple of centuries later were 180ft long with a beam of 45ft. The depth from deck to bottom of the hold was 43½ft. Classical scholars and nautical experts have determined that the Roman vessel's cargo capacity was 1,100-3,500 tons, depending on the length of its keel, which is not known. Wooden hulls often leaked and on smaller vessels bailing was manual, using buckets. On larger ships, sophisticated devices such as an Archimedean screw operated by a treadmill performed the arduous task. Ballast was usually stone or sand.

By the fifth century BC, a dramatic advance in rigging introduced the foremast. A second mast, with a slight forward rake, was set midway between the mainmast (amidships) and the prow. The second mast also carried a square sail, smaller than the mainsail, usually used to aid steering rather than as a driving force.

Thucydides wrote that a merchant ship required eight days to sail around Sicily. Literary works such as his have allowed scholars to calculate a sailing speed of about 4–6 knots for the period, as well as later eras. There was a distinct contrast other than armament between merchant ships and warships. Merchant ships had strong, wide hulls to hold cargo, while warship hulls were light and narrow for speed and manoeuvrability. Unlike warship galleys, merchant galleys were often tub–like in shape and had to rely almost exclusively on sail, being rowed only when absolutely necessary. Their oars were almost useless and Aristotle likened the sight of a merchant ship under oars to a large insect with small, weak wings, trying to fly.

Chapter Nine

Testing the Waters:
Naval Operations Under Augustus

Haaving described the various ports, maritime trade routes and cargo vessels, I will next discuss the foreign policy, or grand strategy if you will, that prescribed and was more or less supported by the mercantile and combat fleets. Before considering the operations under Augustus, I will briefly outline the grand strategical situation confronting the newly minted Empire. I have telescoped several centuries into a few paragraphs in this prefatory survey in order to provide a context for the following critical review of the employment of fleets to advance or protect the Empire's policy requisites.

The shrinking resources of the Empire had to be devoted rather to desperate efforts at maintaining military strength, and this was concentrated in the legions. During the third century AD, every type of political and natural calamity, including a great plague, weakened the imperial structure. Pretenders to the throne rose freely, and few real emperors had reigns of any length. In the East, the Sassanian dynasty, which had replaced the ineffectual Parthians, was a far more serious threat, and at times advanced as far as Asia Minor. There were challenges at both the eastern and western extremities, but that in the East posed the most serious threat.

Roman Foreign Policy/National Security Overview 1: The West, South-West and North-West

At its greatest extent, the Roman Empire included all the lands bordering on the Mediterranean Sea, and reached far into Northern Europe and the Near East. The northern limit was in Britain, where, after an unsuccessful Antonine attempt to annex southern Scotland, the frontier was eventually established on Hadrian's Wall, which stretched from the Tyne to the Solway. The whole of the Iberian Peninsula was occupied, and divided into the provinces of Tarraconensis, Baetica and Lusitania. Gaul extended as far as the Rhine, and comprised Gallia Narbonensis (Provence and the south), Gallia Aquitania (south of the Loire), Gallia Lugdunensis (between the Loire and Seine) and Gallia Belgica (northern France, reaching to Germania Inferior on the banks of the Rhine).

Along the southern bank of the Danube lay the provinces of Rhaetia, Noricum and Pannonia. Virtually the whole of the coastal strip of northern Africa was part of the Empire, divided into the provinces of Africa, Mauretania, Numidia, Cyrenaica and Aegyptus (Egypt).

The earlier chapters have testified how, after conquering nearly all of the Italian peninsula in the third century BC, the Roman Republic gained control over long stretches of coastline strategically located in the centre of the Mediterranean Sea. This geopolitically advantageous position boosted the wealth of Rome, and provided a push to build up a powerful navy, as they frequently came into conflict with the Carthaginians, who had dominated the northern coasts of Africa along the southern shores of the Mediterranean. The Roman navy eventually challenged Carthage for dominance of the Mediterranean, leading to the Punic Wars. Rome would achieve victory, rewarding it with hegemony across the all-important sea, enabling it to control all trade. This was also an insurmountable military advantage, allowing Rome to position troops anywhere along the coast to quickly reach far-flung battlefields.

The maritime hegemony achieved as a result of the first two Punic Wars extended from Sicily westwards and permitted unfettered access by Roman merchantmen to the lucrative trade with her colonies in Spain and southern Gaul, and with the North African markets. There would be no serious challenges to Roman freedom of navigation, nor threats from the sea flanks in the Western Mediterranean, until late in the Western Empire's reign.

Nearly all Celt peoples in modern Spain, France, Germany and England were subjected and completely assimilated into the Roman Republic, and later into the Roman Empire. However, aside from losing some territories, the Germanic peoples largely resisted the Roman advance, despite a concerted effort by the Romans to take them under their control.

The primary reason for the inability of Rome to successfully conquer the Germanic 'nation' was the decentralized nature of the Germanic peoples. Unlike the more organized Celt tribes, which clustered into small villages and settlements, the Germanic peoples were a collection of very numerous, loosely affiliated tribes. It was thus not possible to assert control over a large group of people by simply conquering a few strategic settlements. The inability to pacify the Germanic tribes to the north would prove to be a major cause of the collapse of Rome later in history, as mass Germanic raids and migrations along the long, northern border of Rome would severely weaken the Empire.

In order to subdue the resilient, restive Germanic tribes, Rome would utilize the river networks extending up through the Gallic heartland, eventually debouching on the wild North Sea coast and extending her reach across the English Channel to Britannia. Legionary forts and staging areas were sited along the various watercourse systems linking the Italian homeland ultimately to the Scheldt estuary in what is now Holland.

It is ironic that the most serious threats to the Roman Empire began not with the restive western Germanic tribes of the Roman frontier but the eastern Germanic tribes, particularly the Goths. The Roman Empire during the early third century had a series of weak emperors and a strong challenge from the Parthian Empire of Persia. The resources of the Empire were debilitated, and the Goths challenged the Romans for control of the area at the mouth of the Danube River at the Black Sea. The Goths controlled the area north of the Black Sea and the Romans had conquered a territory north of the Danube, which they called Dacia (present-day Romania).

The attacks of the Goths began in 247 AD, and in 251 they lured the Roman army under the command of the Emperor Decius into a swampy region and defeated it at Abrittus. Decius was killed in the battle. Emboldened by this victory, the Goths built boats and ships and raided the cities of the Black Sea and Eastern Mediterranean. The Romans under Claudius I were finally able to defeat the Goths decisively in 269 and brought peace to the region. The Emperor Claudius was thereafter known as Claudius Gothicus, but his rule did not last long and he was succeeded by the Emperor Aurelian.

Aurelian recognized the realities of the military situation in Dacia, and in 270 AD withdrew Roman troops from the region, leaving it to the Goths. The Danube once again became the northern frontier of the Roman Empire in Eastern Europe. In 324, the Emperor Constantine concluded a treaty with the Visigoths that made them confederates of the Empire, which meant that in return for annual subsidy they agreed to help defend the Empire. Nominally, Dacia was again counted as part of the Empire, but controlled and defended by the Visigoths.

The Ostrogoths were located to the east of the Visigoths in the region beyond the Dniester River. There were significant differences between the Ostrogoths and Visigoths; the Ostrogoths generally represented a more archaic form of Gothic society. At the apogee of the Western Empire's power, and the commencement of its decline, it was the maritime folk, the Ostrogoths, Vandals and Franks, who challenged the dwindling strength of Roman sea power (see John Haywood's *Dark Age Naval Power: A re-assessment of Frankish and Anglo-Saxon seafaring activity* for an excellent survey of the capabilities of these invaders over land and sea).

Roman Foreign Policy/National Security Overview 2: The East

Roman rule over the Semitic provinces of the Middle East extended across some seven centuries. In 64/63 BC, Pompey the Great entered the area and, refusing to restore the former Seleucid Hellenistic dynasty – which had declined into warring factions – organized what was left of their kingdom as the Roman province of

Syria. At the other extreme, the annihilation of the field army of the Emperor Heraclius at the Battle of the Yarmuk in AD 636 ended forever Roman rule over the lands south of the Taurus Mountains.

The military requirements of the region varied greatly with the changing political and economic background. There were, however, at all times two main considerations determining the size of garrisons and their distribution: the need to secure and police the population, particularly those of the great urban centres and in the mountainous areas and desert fringes, and the need to protect from external threat the sources of wealth – the cities and their rural populations, and various important natural resources. A limiting factor to the routine implementation of a policy was the need to place major units where they could be sustained with food and supplies. Ancient agricultural surpluses were low, and troops had to be located where either they would not be competing with some existing major population centre or food could be brought in. In practice, the dispositions made for either of these could overlap with those required for the other.

Internal Security in the East

Most of the great cities were within 80km of the coast, some of the largest being in the north. The concentration of so many people in a single centre such as Antioch raised the danger of disturbance amongst what was a racially mixed and, on occasion, volatile population. In the south, Jerusalem was not only a large city but also the political and religious centre of a numerous people. The Jews became increasingly alienated from Rome in the Early Principate. Sporadic insurrections were followed by bloody rebellions in the time of Nero and Hadrian. There may have been an uprising of some sort as late as the reign of Septimius Severus (AD 193-211), and the Caesar Gallus (351-354) certainly had to put down a rebellion in Galilee. Clearly, however, the wholesale slaughter and dispersal of the Jewish population of Syria Palaestina in the first and second centuries ended the major revolts. By the late third century, the two legions that had been based there since the early second century had both gone.

The External Threat: Parthia

External threats came from two directions: on the one hand, the Parthians and their Persian successors; and on the other, the Arab nomads of the Syrian desert. When a Roman army first arrived on the Upper Euphrates in eastern Anatolia, probably in 96 BC, much of the great sweep of land from Mesopotamia across Iran to Afghanistan was subject, directly or through subordinate kings, to the Parthian Arsacid dynasty. Until conquered by Alexander the Great, this region had been the heartland of the Achaemenid Empire (550–350) of Cyrus, Darius and Xerxes. Alexander's successors, the Seleucid kings, had ruled over it from their twin capitals of Antioch on the Orontes and Seleucia on the Lower Tigris. However, in the generation before the arrival of Rome on the Euphrates, Iran and even the eastern capital at Seleucia had gradually been lost to the Parthians. For the next six centuries, first the Arsacid dynasty of Parthia, then their neo-Persian Sasanian successors, were to represent the single most potent threat to Rome on her eastern frontier, the only power comparable to herself in size or might she faced on any of her frontiers.

Not that the threat was unremitting. Far from it. Although early amicable contacts between representatives of the two empires soon deteriorated, wars were in fact uncommon before the third century. The reasonable Parthian expectation that the boundary between the two empires might be the Euphrates was soon to be dashed by Pompey, whose forces crossed the river in the mid-60s BC and drove deep into Armenia and the Caucasus. Indeed, they even crossed the Upper Tigris and one Pompeian general returned to Syria across the breadth of northern Mesopotamia.

A major reversal came a decade later when the Triumvir, M. Licinius Crassus, for reasons of personal ambition, provoked a war with Parthia and invaded Mesopotamia. His disastrous defeat and death at the Battle of Carrhae in 53 BC opened Syria to the first Parthian invasion. Raids took place in 52, and in 51 came a major invasion. Though Cassius, the de facto governor of Syria after Crassus' death, inflicted a defeat, a Parthian army wintered in northern Syria and the province remained in turmoil. Internal dissension within the Parthian royal family, however, ended the invasion and the Parthian threat faded for a few years.

Pompey negotiated with Parthia for support in 49 BC at the outset of his civil war against Caesar. It was not until 45, however, that a Parthian force appeared in Syria and was able to raise the Caesarian army's siege of a Pompeian army inside Apamaea. In 44, some of this force was found with Cassius, who sent them home to seek more extensive support for him in the new round of civil wars. Once again their support was too late; the decisive battle was fought at Philippi a few months later. However, in 40, soon after the victor of that battle, Mark Antony, had passed through Syria to Egypt, a major Parthian invasion of Syria took place. Alienated by widespread Roman corruption and extortion, many cities opened their gates to the Parthian prince, Pacorus, and all but Tyre fell into his hands. The occupation was short-lived. Antony's general, P. Ventidius Bassus, soon drove them out in a succession of victories – the second resulting in the death of Pacorus – in 38 and 39. It was to be two centuries before a Parthian army again appeared in Syria.

The wars, however, were not over. Antony's attempted revenge for Roman defeats and loss of prestige nearly ended in disaster when he led an army through Armenia into Media in 36 BC. Yet that was to be the last direct clash of Roman and Parthian asmies for nearly a century.

There had been important lessons for both sides. By the end of the 30s BC, each had tasted victory as well as defeat. Rome was to remain the more aggressive, but there was now an undoubted wariness of the military ability of a state which had seized much of the former Achaemenid and Seleucid empires, and inflicted signal defeats on major Roman armies.

It was now clear that although Roman expeditions could take many months to prepare, Parthia's lack of a standing professional army revealed a great weakness, already evidenced by her slowness in responding to the appeals of Pompey and Cassius. However, if the feudal nature of her organization made her slow to gather strength for aggressive warfare, the reaction time for countering a Roman invasion of her territory was rather faster. More important for Syria was that the scene of likely and actual warfare moved northwards. The mountains of Armenia not only offered Roman armies some protection against the formidable Parthian cavalry, but geographically the region became a bone of contention until Rome gained a more lasting advantage in the second century AD. At that point the war zone moved south to Mesopotamia. However, the Roman planners did not enjoy our hindsight. Even if Roman expeditions until the time of Trajan were in practice to be across the Cappadocian rather than the Syrian frontier, the Parthian threat to Roman territory was long perceived to be towards Syria. The Syrian Euphrates was literally and figuratively the direct point of contact between the two empires.

The Emperor Augustus threatened war with armies on both the Cappadocian and Syrian frontiers, but ultimately achieved his ends – the recovery of the lost eagles of Roman legions and a dominant role in Armenia – by diplomatic means. Disputes arose over Armenia, but it was not to be until the reign of Nero (AD 54-68) that a great war broke out in that region. Even then, and only on one occasion, and in Armenia not Syria, did Roman and Parthian forces clash. Not that Syria did not seem threatened. The historian Tacitus explicitly tells us how in 62 the governor of Syria, C. Domitius Corbulo, fortified the Euphrates bend in the face of a possible Parthian attempt to break into his province. None of his forts has yet been identified.

So much for the big picture. I will now critique the several documented instances of the Empire's deployment of ships to support these responsibilities.

Protecting the Trade Links With The East: A Flawed 'Joint Operation'

Among the earliest recorded naval operations in the newly minted Empire are, fittingly enough, those associated with the security of the commercial links to the lucrative spice/luxury trade with India – the East. From the time, circa 30 BC, when Egypt became a Roman province, Roman merchants increasingly turned to establishing a steady sea trade with India, which led to strong competition with the dominant trading partners in this Indian commerce, the Arabs. Augustus sought to improve the situation for Roman merchants by conducting a military operation.

Chester Starr observes, in his book on the various imperial fleets, that the resulting Red Sea operation offers an extraordinarily clear example of a political/military action being based on commercial motives. This is in line with Mahan's observations about freedom of commerce being one of the principal motivations for the exercise of sea power. Originally, there had been no idea of subjugating such an unruly and militarily dangerous stretch of seacoast, because the trade links had heretofore been manageable by use of carefully nurtured middlemen. But when these agents decided to cut themselves in for a hefty piece of the action, their Roman 'senior partners' decided to rein them in.

In 25 BC, Augustus sent Aelius Gallus, praefect of the new colony of Egypt, to conquer the Sabaeans (whose name is derived from 'Sheba') in south-western Arabia (Yemen), who were the middlemen in the Indian trade. The Sabaeans, like the other Yemenite kingdoms of the same period, were involved in the profitable spice trade, especially frankincense and myrrh. Although the proximate precipitating cause is ill-defined, it seems that the Sabaeans were becoming prickly and demanding associates in this trade, comprising a shaky link in the coveted Indian goods trade chain. The Arab jobbers thus turned from being partners to competitors, or at the very least extortionate dealers. Rome had not yet mastered the direct maritime passages to India, and thus was still dependent on reasonable terms from their Arab middlemen.

As one recent analyst of the campaign has observed (Philip Mayerson, 'Aelius Gallus at Cleopatris (Suez) and on the Red Sea', *Greek, Roman and Byzantine Studies*, 36(1), 1995, pp.17-24), it has received considerable scholarly attention in order to ascertain:

> ' the political and economic reasons behind it, the identification of Arabian sites mentioned in the sources, Gallus' misadventures caused by the duplicity of his Nabataean guide Syllaeus or by his own miscalculations, and his inglorious retreat to Egypt. Arabia has been the focal point of interest, understandably so since little was known of Rome's relationship with this exotic region at the end of, or prior to, the first century BC.'

This expedition can only have had commercial motives, because Rome was not previously involved in the region as a matter of military or political interest, nor did Augustus have any general programme for the acquisition of all of Arabia. This campaign is worth examining in more detail, as it manifested the combined obstructive effect of uncharted tidal waters and unsuitable ships upon military operations in a littoral zone. This was a lesson painfully learned by Julius Caesar in his amphibious campaign against the Veneti, discussed previously. It, along with taking precautions in threatening weather, was a steep learning curve for Roman seafaring. In modern naval parlance, these expeditions comprised 'conjunct operations' or 'joint operations'.

The Romans at this time controlled at least the northern half of the Red Sea, but a Roman fleet was never permanently stationed there. Modern criticism that this failure to station a permanent naval force there is a sign of negligence is unwarranted, as up to this point, diplomatic and fiscal negotiation seems to have secured any necessary trade concessions. Furthermore, naval operations in the Red Sea were made difficult by the lack of good harbours, the unsuitability of Mediterranean craft to the region and the fact that suppression of ancient piracy always entailed occupation of the coasts which served as pirate bases. The conquest of the barren Arabian and Ethiopian coasts was a costly task, perhaps impossible in itself and perhaps not directly remunerative; operations in the Indian Ocean itself were impracticable. Patrolling of this area was perhaps undertaken by the Axumite kings, who were chiefly interested in protecting their own traders of Adulis (modern-day Eritrea). In any case, the rudimentary economic thinking of the Roman Empire quickly perceived a dangerous lack of balance in the Indian trade which required at least a limited imperial response.

In 25 BC, Gallus built a fleet of eighty warships and 130 transports. The noted lack of a permanent fleet dealing with this area required such a crash building programme. The naval personnel to man them were drawn from the fleet at Alexandria. This armada sailed to transport Gallus' army of 10,000, which included 1,000 Nabataeans and 500 Jews sent by King Herod of Judaea, across to the eastern shore of the Red Sea. Allied contingents joined him at Leuke Kome – the southernmost town of Nabatea (close to the modern Al Wajh, a town on the north-west Red Sea coast of Saudi Arabia). This village was part of the Nabataean territory at the time of the expedition. After Leuke Kome, Gallus marched to the south, through Nabataean-controlled lands. This use of allies – or more precisely client-states – as naval allies in this campaign has been seen as a common thread throughout the Late Republic and Empire. In fact, the port of Caesarea Maratima in Judaea, built with Roman engineering expertise, would not only serve Herod's maritime needs, but would function as a Roman forward naval base in times of emergency and a depot for Roman merchant vessels trading with the East.

Strabo describes the nature of the region and the campaign with these words:

> 'Gallus moved his army from Leuke Kome [*sic*] and marched through regions where water had to be carried or supplied by ship. Gallus wanted to subdue the region to protect the trade from the piracy coming from

this area. His plan was to occupy all the cities found in this dangerous tract, but he did not find any city until he reached Najran [around 23 BC]. Gallus occupied Najran, then Asca [within Yemeni territory]. Going south, he occupied a city called Athrula, then advanced toward Marsiaba [probably Ma'rib, the capital of Saba]. He assaulted and besieged the city for six days, but desisted for want of water. He lost only seven soldiers in war against the Arabians of Najran and in the battles south of it. Most of the losses in his army came from lack of water and supplies and disease.'

Further, Strabo (16.4.23.780) criticized Gallus for wasting resources and men building a fleet while the Arabs did not have one, and most importantly for the time he wasted in so doing. His remit was to invade Arabia across the Red Sea. An intriguing papyrus fragment (P. Oxy. 2820) seems to imply that he (if not an earlier governor) had incorporated ships from Cleopatra's navy into the fleet.

The 160-mile Red Sea crossing took him two weeks because of the hazards posed by reefs, dangerous tides, etc.; the slowness was most likely due to cautiousness in command and navigation rather than any inherent limitations of materiel capacity. He thereafter abandoned plans to sail down the Arabian coast and decided to advance overland, with his sea flank covered by the navy and troops being supplied by ships along the way. The ensuing march through the desert to Yemen decimated the army – thirst was the main culprit – and it failed to reach the south-eastern shores of the Arabian peninsula, thereby forsaking control of the southern Arabian coast.

Whatever the ineptness of this operation, it cowed the Sabaeans of southern Arabia (known as the Biblical Sheba, or roughly modern Yemen) – who had been the balking middlemen for the Romans in the Indian trade – into recognizing the 'friendship of Rome'. Although it might be said that Gallus returned in failure, at least the demonstration manifested Roman interest in the Red Sea and the Indian trade thrived prodigiously without further military efforts.

Despite the expedition's inability to subdue the piratical tribes at the base of the Arabian peninsula, the trade routes eastwards to India were not seriously threatened. This is due to the fact that the Romans still controlled the northern shore of the Red Sea and did not require a Red Sea fleet, because the economic interests of the rulers along this route – as they realized – were the best guarantor of unhindered Roman trade. Again, the Sabaeans of modern Yemen were impressed enough by the Roman effort along the Red Sea coast to become reliable trading partners. It had at least manifested Rome's determination to persevere in pursuing 'free trade' with the Indian markets.

The inference remains that the construction of this fleet constituted an extravagant time-wasting, labour-intensive digression, inasmuch as the Sabaeans did not possess a fleet requiring such action. The putative Arabian navy that would potentially disrupt Roman mercantile traffic was said to be either an invention by Gallus' duplicitous Nabataean guide, Syllaeus, or an error due to his own overestimation of his Arabian foes' naval assets.

Philip Mayerson has expressed the problems in both executing and memorializing this poorly planned operation ('Aelius Gallus at Cleopatris (Suez) and on the Red Sea', *Greek, Roman and Byzantine Studies*, 36 (1), 1995, pp.17-24):

> 'It is evident that Gallus could not have built and equipped over 200 ships in a period of four or even six months. It is further evident that he undertook the expedition without seeking information regarding alternative routes, both by land and sea, and the nature of the terrain in Arabia. Bungling and naive he may have been, but the likelihood is that he lacked military experience in the field (as his brief resumé in RE seems to indicate). As for Strabo's account of events at Cleopatris and on the Red Sea, there is a deeper subtext to it than use of Syllaeus' duplicity as the cause of a friend's misfortune; but lacking confirmation in other sources, it has to be considered as a questionable part of an ill-conceived and poorly executed military operation.'

This operation comports with Mahan's dictum that the strategic object of sea power was not offensive in nature but fundamentally defensive, to safeguard access to the sea and the free working of the global trading system. In this case it was to break the stranglehold of duplicitous, quasi-piratical Arab middlemen on the trans-shipments of increasingly important goods from India to Rome. It may have also demonstrated the unpreparedness of the Roman fleets to master unfamiliar and treacherous shores. It certainly, in this case, appears to have corroborated Thiel's ascription of 'landlubberly' qualities to the average Roman. Having neither instinct nor affinity for seafaring, they continued to tackle the naval side of martial expeditions amateurishly, and therefore stumbled when crossing the shore's edge.

Early Troubles in Germania and Along the North Sea Coast

The other major naval activity under Augustus occurred at the opposite end of the Empire, in Germania. These operations are worth examining in some detail, as they show Rome's naval forces in what was to become a familiar role: what the British sea-power theorists called conjunct operations. The series of campaigns thereby evoke modern analogues, such as the British Mesopotamian campaign in the First World War, where ground forces advanced in conjunction with and supported by riverine warships and supply vessels. Julius Caesar's landings in Britannia and the recently completed Red Sea campaign of Gallus, just described, were earlier examples of such naval support of land operations. In Caesar's case, the planning errors were overcome by sheer determination and improvisation, whereas the Red Sea operation had failed on a tactical level, but more or less succeeded on the diplomatic front.

The best literary sources are to be found in Dio Cassius, Velleius Paterculus and Tacitus, who describe four expeditions of Roman fleets along the North Sea coast. This occurred in connection with the Roman attempt to conquer Germania up to the River Elbe. Perhaps too much has been made of this campaign comprising a joint operation, glibly evoking the modern-day amphibious task force, but there are similarities on a broad strategical level.

The Roman fleet on the Rhine was the product of Augustan expansion which had placed the Balkan boundary on the Danube. In the Rhenish sector, Augustus apparently aimed at advancing the frontier to the Elbe in central Germany, and operations to this end were begun as soon as Tiberius had conquered Illyricum (the Balkans). His general on the Rhine, Drusus the Elder, is designated here as the creator of the German fleet, for according to the Roman historian Lucius Annaeus Florus (latter half of the first century AD, in his *Epitome de T. Livio Bellorum omnium annorum DCC Libri duo*), Bonn and 'Caesoriacum' (Mainz) were the bases for a fleet. Bonn may well have been a temporary port, but there is no doubt that Drusus actually did form a Rhenish fleet, later to be designated as the *classis Germanica*. He even excavated a canal, the *fossae Drusianae*, between the Rhine and the *Isacus Flevus* (Zuyder Zee) to open a shorter passage for the Rhine fleet to the North Sea.

During Octavian's role as a triumvirate responsible for the western provinces, his legate Marcus Vipsanius Agrippa led a considerable campaign from 39-38 BC against the Suebi (also old enemies of Caesar). The low point seems to have been a Germanic Sugambri invasion into Belgica (17-16 BC) which resulted in the loss, and ultimate disgrace, of one legionary standard.

In response, Augustus sent his stepson Drusus, while Tiberius was busy in Pannonia, to oversee a reorganization of the Germania provinces (Superior and Interior), which were essentially military frontiers roughly encompassing the Rhine valley

The Romans, under the leadership of Drusus, risked the first attempt; the second expedition followed in 5 BC under Tiberius. Germanicus undertook the two final voyages in AD 15 and 16 (described in Chapter 10), both ending in catastrophes, when huge waves coursing along an incoming tide destroyed the ships.

Drusus' campaign of 12 BC reflected a plan of enormous scope, entailing well-defined political and military objectives, integrated combined operations and substantial logistical support – primarily ship-borne. Although ending in a tactical stalemate, the campaign was successful from Augustus' perspective: Rome once again demonstrated its ability to strike into the heart of a belligerent's homeland. As a warning and deterrent, the campaign succeeded in preventing Germanic aggression for the next ten years. Subsequent campaigns even achieved regional stability for decades.

The valley of the Lippe opposite Vetera and the valley of the Main River (in modern-day Bavaria) across from Moguntiacum furnished the only easy routes of approach to the area of operations; the Roman base in the German wars accordingly shifted between these two points. Drusus built forts on the Lippe, and succeeding commanders attempted to provide adequate roads in the broken, wooded territory of western Germany. Nonetheless, the German fleet remained useful, and literary evidence gives us a fine picture of the experiments in its employment during the war on the Rhine from 12 BC to AD 16. Along with supply ships, it presumably penetrated to the head of navigation on the Lippe and Main rivers; naval control of the Rhine must also have facilitated the plan of attack. The Romans, that is to say, often used several independent parallel or converging columns, a risky method except against barbarians, and dangerous even then if lateral contact was not maintained at least in the rear.

From advanced positions secured by Drusus the Elder in northern Holland, the fleet was able to reconnoitre the German coast and explore the estuary and lower reaches of the River Visurgis (Weser) and then of the Alibis (Elbe) itself. The *classis Germanica* thus extended its operations along the lower Rhine and Ems and into the German Bight in support of the new advance. The formerly primarily river-based fleet was strengthened by the addition of seagoing ships for this extended role, so as to release the channel squadron to its former duties. Lack of experience in these unfamiliar waters led to some of the ships becoming stranded on a falling tide on one occasion, presumably to be recovered later. The Chaucians and Frisians had little with which to oppose the superior numbers and tactics of Roman vessels when they penetrated the mouths of the Weser and Ems. The resident tribes capitulated. The Romans did not consider the Germanic vessels (primitive dugout canoes) to be a direct threat to their communications, and thus did not bother to deploy their naval units to patrol the North Sea coasts.

The reason for all four operations was always the same: it was necessary to bring a part of the army of occupation by ship as close as possible to the theatre of war. Along with the soldiers, equipment and provisions were also loaded on the ships newly constructed for this purpose. Tacitus (Annals 2, 6) describes the ships employed in the German campaign. They had wide hulls, but narrow sterns and bows. The keel was flat, so that the ships did not run aground, even at low tide. All could be sailed and rowed. Some possessed a cover to protect the cargo from wind and weather. A series of these characteristics survived up to the fourth century, as demonstrated by the five Roman military ship remnants from Mainz. Their design showed that Drusus had accurately gauged the navigational conditions along the German rivers and estuaries that had to be traversed in this campaign.

As an early and quite sophisticated case study in what we now call 'combined operations', 'joint warfare' or 'littoral/riverine warfare', these early operations along and near the Scheldte estuary warrant further scrutiny. As this campaign is a harbinger of how Roman sea power will be employed on inland waterways and along sea coasts, I will examine it in more detail. The following analysis will highlight aspects and details pertinent to modern sea power concepts.

From the Rhine-Donau border to the shorter Elbe, part of the fleet was engaged in the task of securing the sea flank, supplying the legions and effecting landing operations. They were attempting to accomplish Agrippa's plan of extending the border to the Elbe. Agrippa had been the governor stationed there since 38 BC, and in 19, during his landing operations on the Rhine, he had designed the strategic concept which guided future pacification of this sector. Germania is bordered by the sea on the north-west, hence it was important for the Roman navies and the legionary supply units to be able to utilize the rivers coinciding with their primary supply lines unhindered: the Amaziah (Ems), Visurgis (Weser) and Albis (Elbe).

In 12 BC, Drusus' fleet sailed down the Rhine, then through his newly dug canal to the sea, accepting the submission of the Frisians, who most likely had earlier received some diplomatic assurances of amity and thus accepted status as a 'friend of Rome' peacefully. By coasting east to the lands of the Chauci, he became the first Roman general to venture on the North Sea. The previous travails of Caesar's beachheads in Britain had not yet fully acquainted the Romans with the vagaries of the ocean, and Drusus' ships were stranded by an ebbing tide on one occasion. Local naval opposition was slight; after one battle against the Bructeri on the Ems in 12 or 11 BC, the Romans met no challenge to their control of German waters.

Having secured the compliance of the Frisians, Drusus had next to deal with the Chauci. In order to accomplish this task, he is said to have built 1,000 ships (likely an exaggeration) and dredged a canal – the Canal *Fossa Drusiana* – from the Rhine to the Zuiderzee, linking the Rivers Waal, Ems and Rhine to the North Sea via the lakes of Holland. He led this augmented Rhine fleet past the Zuiderzee into the North Sea. Note that, although I use the modern-day designation 'the Zuiderzee', that inlet in its present configuration was not developed yet. It was much smaller than its later forms and its connection to the main sea was much narrower; it may have been a complex of lakes, marshes and channels, rather than a single lake ; thus there was still a land barrier to the North Sea which had to be breached.

As the Frisians and the Chauci had only light naval units, Drusus brought his superior naval strength to bear in the Weser estuary, where he was also able to land legions. Inasmuch as the Romans advanced seaward into the German Bight from the rivers, riverine craft had to be augmented with seagoing vessels. While Drusus' specially built fleet was the primary force employed, the roots of what was to become known as the *classis Germanica* were laid during a campaign to the south-east. In 15 BC, a separate Bodensee (Lake Constance) fleet had been established. In achieving domination of this area, the largest sea-battle ever to occur on the Bodensee took place – the Celts from Bregenz (in western Austria, along the eastern shores of Lake Constance) against the Romans. As Lake Constance feeds into the Rhine, there is a reasonable inference that at least a component of this fleet was also employed for Rhine operations. Later, Drusus and Tiberius most likely utilized this naval force extensively in executing the Roman plan of extending the boundaries of Roman power as far as the Elbe.

Having secured the seaward flank, the invasion of Germania could proceed. The landward drive could be supported by using as lines of the supply the Rivers Lippe and Main, which flow into the Rhine from the east. Naval support also enabled the legions to make simultaneous parallel drives into enemy territory whilst retaining secure lines of supply. The border was pushed forward to the Visurgia (Weser) by the following year (10 BC) and established on the lower Elbe by 9 BC, in which year Drusus died following an accident. Tiberius took overall command and continued the work of pacification and consolidation of the intended new province of Germania.

By AD 4, Tiberius had the fleet operating along the Elbe and north German coast. He campaigned again in AD 5 by land and sea, and further exploration was undertaken by the fleet northward up the Norwegian coast. Pliny describes how Roman naval squadrons passed the eastern regions over Cape Skagen (the north tip of Denmark), which is called the Kimberncap (Cimbri Cape) as the Cimbri resided in North Jutland. After they rounded this cape to the north-east coast of Denmark, they encountered a sea which is depicted by the ancient Roman author Vellelius as previously only having been described in hear-say – this was the North Sea. Intelligence about a Roman fleet in this area may explain why the German coastal tribes did not join up with the Cherusci to take advantage of the Roman defeat in the Teutoberg Forest in AD 9.

Drusus the Elder acquired an even larger fleet for his expedition in Germany east of the Rhine. It was also used for exploration (and intimidation): as Augustus said, '*classis mea*' ('my fleet') sailed as far north as the land of the Cimbrians (that is, Jutland, Res Gestae 26.4). After Drusus' death, Tiberius continued his combined land and naval incursions, as did Germanicus, who built a fleet of 1,000 ships in AD 16 (Tacitus, Ann. 2.6): it is not certain whether the otherwise unknown Anteius, who was placed in charge of the fleet, was accorded the title of '*praefectus classis*'. Harbours used during these German wars have been recorded by archaeologists, most notably one at Haltern on the Lippe, where there is a block of eight wooden ship sheds suitable for boats the size of liburnians.

Such fleets were not standing fleets stationed in the areas concerned on a permanent basis, but were specifically constructed for a particular war. As such, they may be labelled 'invasion fleets', or in today's parlance 'naval task forces'. Drusus' later campaigns in particular bear further examination as they exemplified the use of ships in conjunction with land armies.

The above described campaigns of Drusus in 11-9 BC were waged from Vetera (Moguntiacum, modern-day Mainz). Moguntiacum had been the site of legionary and auxiliary forts since 16 BC, when Augustus' son-in-law Drusus started the first expedition into Germania on the other side of the Rhine. The naval mishap (stranding by ebb tide) possibly discouraged prosecution of the war on the seacoasts. Strategically, such naval expeditions were subsidiary operations, as a successful conquest of the Cherusci, Chatti and other 'cross-Rhine' tribes could be mounted only on the basis of a methodical advance by land from the middle and upper Rhine.

By coasting east to the lands of the Chauci, Drusus became the first Roman general to venture on the North Sea. The previous difficulties of Caesar's landings in Britain had not yet fully familiarized the Romans with ocean sailing, leading to Drusus' ebbing tide stranding. *Classis Germanica* extended its operations from the lower Rhine and Ems into the German Bight in support of this new advance. By AD 4, Tiberius had the fleet operating along the Elbe and north German coast. He campaigned again in the following year by land and sea, and further exploration was undertaken by the fleet northward up the Norwegian coast, as described earlier.

Although Julius Caesar had encountered the strange vessels of the Britons and north-eastern Gauls some forty years earlier, the craft of the Teutons were different, ill-suited to operations offshore and in the English Channel. The Germanic tribes along the North Sea and Baltic Sea at that time possessed only riverine vessels without a keel or sails, which were propelled by paddles. They rarely exceeded a length of 12 metres (40ft), though some have been found in North Schleswig 16 metres (54ft) long and 2 metres (7ft) broad. These double-ended canoes were the boats with which the Frisians attacked in 12 BC. Romans entering the Ems at Borkum (Burcana) were met with numbers of these craft, but the Frisians were repulsed and thereafter the Frisians between the Ems and the Zuiderzee acknowledged Roman supremacy.

The Romans did not regard these canoe-like Germanic vessels as a direct threat, and therefore judged that the Germans on the North Sea posed no naval danger to them. The thrust of Tiberius to the Elbe in AD 5 was facilitated by a combined naval and land operation. The fleet sailed up the River Elbe to the district of Lauenberg, where they were joined by the army. This same year, Roman units pushed far to the north to confront the Cimbri, but the exact route and terminus of this expedition are unclear. However, Tacitus describes them as arriving at the *Herculis columnae* (Columns of Hercules) in the north, which is now believed to be the island of Heligoland.

Campaigns in South-Eastern Germania and in the Balkans

The next move was to be the conquest and annexation of Bohemia, and with it the headwaters of the Elbe. Domitius Ahenobarbus advanced northwards from the Noricum along the River Saale to join the upper Elbe. In AD 6, while he was in the final stages of securing Bohemia, revolts broke out in Pannonia and Illyria. A hasty peace had to be made with the Macromanni of Bohemia, and Tiberius and his forces diverted to deal with it.

Caecina Severus, commander of the Moesian legions, relieved Sirminium in Lower Pannonia (today's Serbia) from the siege conducted by the rebels. Tiberius kept a firm hold on Siscia (Sisak in modern Croatia), and in AD 7, reinforcements from the eastern armies opened the Save River (Sava in the Balkans). With the Save in his hands, Tiberius moved with confidence and by AD 9 had stopped the Pannonian revolt.

Apart from the ill-defined operations across the Danube in Dacia, which necessitated naval support based on Siscia (Sisak in modern Croatia), the middle Danube saw no further action until this Pannonian revolt of AD 6 recalled Tiberius from his campaign against Maroboduus, king of the Marcomanni, in southern Germany. Tiberius then crossed the Danube as part of a campaign against the Marcomnni at Carnuntelm (Petronel, Austria). The task of the the Danube fleet consisted of securing the crossing of and supplying the army. Further activity was stopped for the moment, due first to the revolt, and then to the infamous Varian disaster in the Teutoberg Forest in AD 9, but in the following campaigns of Germanicus, from 14–16, yet other prospects for naval action were patterned on the first campaign of Drusus the Elder.

Although the cliché maintains that Rome 'ruled' the seas surrounding the peninsula of Italy, from AD 6 on, this did and could not connote absolute mastery. There were increased threats from Sardinian and Dalmatian pirates, requiring a constant and increased naval presence along the coast for the protection of trade. The Sardinian pirates were probably petty buccaneers of no great concern. However, the Adriatic (Dalmatian) coasts were vexed by marauders, and the danger in this sector was somewhat more serious, but naval forces could not deal with this maritime threat when the whole hinterland was aflame in the Pannonian revolt.

Chapter Ten

Pacifying The Empire's North-Western Frontier

Further Operations in Germania

The next Roman naval action of note occurs in the same corner of the Roman world that had earlier engaged Drusus the Elder – Germania. It was a direct consequence of the military disaster of Varus in the Teutoberg Forest in AD 9, and also appears to have been precipitated by a revolt by the discontented Germanic legions. The context of the revolt is a bit puzzling, as is the relationship to the Varus disaster. However, so far as can be determined, the gist of the accepted narrative is as follows.

Following a hiatus due to the aforementioned Pannonian revolt and the Varus calamity of AD 9, in 15-16, Tiberius' adopted son Germanicus commenced a campaign against the Bructeri located on the upper Ems. The Rhine fleet transported four legions from lower Germany through the Drusus canal and the Zuiderzee, and landed 40 cohorts at the present-day Rhine-Ems confluence, i.e., along the Rhine up to the Ems, on the Frisian coast in an effort to unite the country and solidify Roman rule. Among other things, they tried to locate the site of Varus' battle. The Roman army had to withdraw two, and later four, legions with heavy losses. In the second campaign of 15, Germanicus packed the four legions of lower Germany onto the troopships and sailed through the Zuiderzee to the Ems, where he met the foot troops and cavalry of upper Germany, and united with them.

Due to the approach of the equinoctial storms by the time of his return, Germanicus had to lighten his ships by embarking only two of the four legions, but the two that had to march along the shore were so badly buffeted by tides and storms that he finally packed them aboard ships along with the other two.

In the spring of AD 16, Germanicus assembled a fleet of over 1,000 ships that had been built by his shipwrights over the previous winter. If accurate, this would be Rome's largest shipbuilding project since the Punic Wars. Having been so aggravated by the congested and difficult trek by the land columns, he hit upon the bold plan of shipping his entire army along the North Sea coast, and from there to the middle of Germania for a spring campaign. Taking a clue from the craft of the indigenous Germanic folk, the ships built were designed with flat bottoms and beamy mid-sections, others with double sets of rudders. These were mission-specific troop and horse transports, all galleys. This fleet was constructed at the island of Bavatorum (Beveland) formed by the two principal estuaries of the Rhine (islands of Beveland and Walcheren). Four legions were brought in via the canal system and the North Sea coast. This force alone needed 200 ships to transport it and its supplies to the lower Rhine ports; in addition to the specially built craft, there were probably a number of civilian ships included.

In all, Germanicus embarked eight legions, along with auxiliaries and supplies, and entered the Drusus canal (after first invoking the spirit of his father to assist the son in effecting a very similar exploit to that of Drusus the Elder along the North German coast and its river estuaries in 12 BC, described earlier). This fleet carried the legions a distance up the Ems in the area of persent-day Jemgum in the north-west of Saxony, near the North Sea coast border between Germany and Holland.

The vessels were most likely dragged ashore at this place (on the western shore), and put under guard while the army marched upstream, crossing the Ems on bridges, for what appears to have been a very lackadaisical campaign. After several victorious battles with the Bructeri in midsummer AD 16, they besieged the Bructeri and Cherusci, and the Romans embarked again towards the Rhine frontier from the Ems estuary through the 'seaway' to the Rhine. During an autumn storm, almost the entire fleet, along with the troops, became victims to the tempest. Germanicus himself managed to escape in a trireme to Chauci territory.

Then in AD 28, the fleet lost control of the Teutonic coast to the Rhine estuary thanks to an uprising of the Frisians. That same year, the Rhine fleet was used to transport an army to combat an uprising in this area (said to have been instigated by the dictatorial demands of a Roman officer). The garrison of the besieged fortress of Flevum (possibly on the island of Vlieland) was relieved with the assistance of the fleet, but the aged Tiberius seemed content to let this region go rather than mount yet another comprehensive combined operation. Having satisfied Roman honour and bloodied the noses of those who had aided Arminius, Rome decided that there was no need to stretch its power across the Rhine.

Operations in Britain

Prelude

During the century or so from Julius Caesar's expeditions (covered in some detail previously) to the death of Tiberius, the tribes of south-east Britain had the status of client kingdoms ruled by kings educated at Rome, with close ties of friendship and possibly intermarriage between each other. With the notable exception of the inhabitants of Kent, these tribes were by and large enjoying increasing prosperity from the developing trade with the Empire and were becoming increasingly part of the Roman world. Their interest and that of Rome was in maintaining a stable status quo.

Such stability does not seem to have been compromised, notwithstanding Julius Caesar's warning, by the subjection of the Trinovantes by the Catuvellauni sometime during this period, a step now more advantageous for the Catuvellauni because it gave them control of Colchester, the British hub of the developing Essex-Rhine trade network. Significantly, the import of corn from Britain became vital to victualling the Rhine garrisons. Thus at the death of Tiberius in AD 37, the most powerful tribe in the south-east would have been the Catuvellauni, who had shifted their capital to the former Trinovantian centre of Colchester.

South of the Thames, the Atrebates and Durotriges also prospered from trade with the Empire, while the Kent of Caesar's four kings was at this time still an impoverished backwater; its people still had not coalesced as a tribe (later they become the Cantiaci). In AD 37 and the years immediately following, stability was threatened on both the Roman and British sides. The death of Tiberius brought the highly unstable Gaius Caligula – who within four years would be assassinated by the commanders of his Praetorian Guard – to the throne, to be succeeded by his uncle Claudius (who was unprepared for this unexpected honour). The conquest of Britain had been seriously mooted by Caligula during his four-year reign (AD 37-41). He had begun extensive naval preparations, including construction of transports and galleys (tiremes), and building lighthouses at Gesoriacum (Boulogne-sur-Mer), along with extensive harbour improvements designed to make this a naval base.

When the soldiers of Gaius' army balked at making a cross-channel attack, and Gaius dropped his plans for conquest, a fleet on the English Channel became superfluous. In order to make the return voyage, he first attempted to sail the triremes he had built to protect the transports during the aborted crossing, but then sent them overland to Rome. The reluctance of the naval commanders to sail these vessels across the Bay of Biscay and around Spain into the Mediterranean indicates both the sailors' lack of confidence and the unsuitability of Mediterranean craft to navigate the open ocean. Both of these considerations were to restrict the activities of the later British squadron in the area.

After Cunobelinus, the king of the Catuvellauni, had occupied south-eastern Britain concurrent with the reign of Caligula, from AD 37-41, Claudius began the major invasion of Britain. A. Plautius Sylvanus landed with his fleet four legions in Kent to commence their march to the north. Up until the completion of the conquest of Britain in 85, the fleet maintained its prominent role on the island nation, supporting the amphibious operations of the army.

The earlier fiasco under Caligula was not totally in vain. The harbour of Gesoriacum remained as an important naval base, and most likely some of Gaius' fleet was laid up there available for future contingencies.

Claudian Invasion of Britain, AD 43

Upon his accession after the assassination of his mad nephew, Gaius Caligula, Claudius was considered to urgently need a military triumph to consolidate his new position. On the British side, some time after the death of Tiberius, Cunobelinus banished his son Adminius, who fled to Gaul, where he surrendered to Gaius. The death of Cunobelinus was followed by the succession of two more of his sons, Togodummius and Caratacus, who began a programme of aggression and enlargement. This was followed by the arrival of another wave of asylum-seekers in Rome, including former king Verica of the Atrebates. This triggered an outbreak of disturbances among the Britons. As Suetonius said, 'Britons were in an uproar over failure to return some refugees.' Some have speculated that this 'uproar' involved raids on the coast of Gaul or riots threatening Roman merchants in Britain. Whatever events were implied, relationships between Rome and Britain had reached a crisis point. This situation would be quite serious for the Romans if it threatened the exports of corn, which would have been of strategic importance, particularly to the legions on the Rhine.

Caligula had, as we have seen, already put in hand preparations for the invasion of Britain, developing naval facilities at Boulogne including the building of its lighthouse. But with his unstable temperament, he was not the man to carry it through. It fell to his uncle to meet the crisis when it was much further advanced.

In light of the above, the overall strategic objective of the military operations of AD 43 would have been to secure the uninterrupted continuation of the staple exports from Britain to Gaul, thence to the Rhineland. The Roman high command, in the person of the Emperor, had determined that this would be achieved by the invasion and occupation of Britain.

The successful prosecution of that overall objective could only be achieved by the defeat and submission of Togodumnus and Caratacus and their Catuvellauni, and the seizure of the strategically important hub of Colchester and its hinterland. To be committed to the invasion, the senior ranks of the army would have needed a better rationale than the restoration of some petty British king or the promotion of Claudius' military reputation. Better cause is to be found in the increasingly unstable relationships between Britain and the Empire. These troubles date from the death of Tiberius and the accession of the mad emperor Caligula, reaching a crisis point with the death of Cunobelinus, the uncertainty over his succession and the consequent likelihood of a campaign of aggrandizement initiated by his sons, Caratacus and Togodumnus. Ultimately, this instability threatened the supply of strategically important commodities, notably to the Rhine legions.

Caligula's failure to resolve the British problem forced Claudius to undertake his more successful attack. His generals undoubtedly built additional warships and transports, and skilled sailors from the Mediterranean were drafted to man the *classis Britannica*. The task that faced the Roman naval planners was to provide for the safe passage across the Channel of four legions, together with auxiliary units, including cavalry, numbering perhaps some 35,000–40,000 men, and to follow this up with the safe passage of Claudius himself and his war elephants. The limited capability of the available ships, particularly of the transports built in the Romano-Celtic tradition, must have meant that the passage could be contemplated only in good weather, with light and favourable winds.

The first Channel crossing, under the command of consul Aulus Plautius, was set to take place early in the campaign year, but consternation among the troops caused considerable problems. Roman infantry had long been known to have misgivings about naval crossings, but sailing to the mysterious island of Britain, where even the great Caesar had faced considerable problems, was another matter entirely. It was completely unknown territory to them, only described in legend. The situation was eventually resolved through the intervention of Claudius' freedman adviser Narcissus, but the affair was delayed for some time

In terms of naval practices, which were essential for the crossing of the English Channel, the Romans created an entirely new ship, the Mediterranean war galley, which was of much thicker wood and more stable on rough waters. Much as Julius Caesar had done a century earlier, the design of these galleys borrowed from local practice. The troop transports, which, as I have noted, were rarely mentioned in the annals, were also apparently modelled on native craft which were more suitable for the rough seas separating Gaul and Britannia. However, they tended to be clumsier and impossible to tack when facing adverse winds. This fact argues for the more direct westerly crossing to Richborough favoured in traditional accounts, as opposed to the longer, less direct passage to the Solent which some recent authorities have proposed.

In AD 43, the expedition left Gesoriacum and made three landings on the south-east coast of Kent, from which the campaign progressed triumphantly. The force seems to have landed near Rutupiae, or modern Richborough. Though some evidence exists of additional landing places, there is no question that Richborough developed into the main entry port in provincial Britain. The landing was rather uneventful compared to likely expectations. Navigators found a landing spot on Rutupiae Island, on the coast of Britain near the mouth of the Thames River, that was adjacent to an easily traversable channel leading to the British mainland. The landing was completely unopposed by British forces, something completely unexpected by the Romans. Several reasons likely contributed to this. First, diplomatic relations with local tribes from the time of Caesar likely reduced resistance in general, and secondly, the delay of the invasion made the British tribesmen, particularly the Belgic, tired of waiting, and they simply went home. Thus the Romans began marching into southern Britain after establishing a permanent beachhead camp near Richborough, and, as Dio tells us, finally encountering resistance from the two Belgic brothers, Togodumnus and Caratacus.

The Romans arrived at the Medway River, an area that Caratacus felt they could not cross without a bridge. However, the Romans were, unlike crossing the sea, very skilled at river crossing, and employed an effective strategy that took Caratacus by surprise. Plautius made two crossings of the river, one of which was intended to be the main attacking force and the other a distraction. Roman engineers found a ford that was traversable at low tide near modern-day Rochester, and crossed the main force at this location. Caratacus, realizing what the Romans were doing, attacked and nearly defeated the legions. However, after a day of fighting, reinforcements proved too powerful for the Belgic, and they retreated. Medway would come to be the decisive battle in Britain, rendering the Belgic kingdom helpless and open for Roman occupation, effectively ending organized resistance to Roman invasion prior to the formation of the province. After Medway, Plautius occupied the trade bridge on the Thames, the last defence between Rome and the Belgic capital.

It seems that the fleet most likely assisted in scouting and outflanking local resistance along the seashore; otherwise, it shuttled chiefly between the Gallic base and the bridgeheads in Britain. The Roman navy, which was ranked as quite inferior prior to the invasion of Britain, became a much more professional and respected branch of the Roman army due to its skill in resolving amphibious difficulties in this invasion.

The transport of men and materials from the continent to Britain remained the chief function of the British squadron. Its stations were, in consequence, concentrated on the English Channel, and Gesoriacum in Gallia Belgica remained its headquarters. Gesoriacum, the chief port in northern Gaul, was also the western terminus of the 'high road' to the Rhine (the medieval chemin de Brunehaut), which served as a major link between the German and British-based legions. The fleet, which furnished the necessary prolongation of the route across the Channel, occupied the port from the reign of Claudius into the fourth century.

Chapter Eleven

The Imperial Fleets on the Ascendant

Bosporous, *Circa* AD 43-46

In AD 38, Caligula had revived Agrippa's plan by giving the Bosporus to Polemo II of Pontus. Three years later, Claudius revoked this grant of the northern kingdom (which Polemo most likely had not put into effect anyhow) and gave Tiberius Julius Mithridates (also known as Mithridates 2) the whole Bosporan kingdom to rule. Claudius recognized and appointed him as the legitimate Bosporan king. Mithridates was apparently not content with this and tried to throw off Roman suzerainty, but the governor of Moesia, A. Didius Gallus, expelled him in 44 or 45 and installed Mithridates' younger half-brother, Kotys I. In the campaign against Mithridates' kingdom of Bosporous, Didius Gallus had conducted an expedition, presumably with the Moesian provincial units (*classis Moesica*) of the fleet, to the Crimea. The actual transport of men and supplies seems to been assigned to merchant vessels requisitioned from Byzantium and the other coastal cities. During this operation, Kotys was established as the new king. A few legionary cohorts under Julius Aquila and parts of this fleet were stationed in the Crimea for his protection. Mithridates, in an attempt to regain his throne, enticed leaders of local tribes into an alliance and was preparing to attack Julius Aquila, when in 46, the latter seized the initiative and launched an offensive against Mithridates' bases of operation.

The fleet units crossed the Bosporous Cimmerius (Strait of Kerch), entered the Maeotis (Sea of Azov) and reached as far as the mouth of the River Tanais (Don). The only losses of shipping were caused by grounding on the relatively unknown and unsuspected shoals in shallow waters. The use of the Moesian fleet on the northern coasts of the Black Sea began with Claudius, and the intimate connection of the Bosporan kingdom with the army of Moesia.

Frisians Again, Lower Danube, Balkans and Black Sea Regions

In AD 46 and 47, there was a brief subjugation of the Frisians once more, but they regained their power, which the assaults of the Rhine fleet were futile to turn back. At the beginning of Claudius' reign, the Chauci, who had been marauding on the coast, were defeated by P. Gabinius Secundus, the governor of Germania Inferior. In 47, Corbulo, the new governor of Germania Inferior strengthened the fleet again, defeated the restless Chauci and regained Frisian territory. Claudius, however, needed troops elsewhere and ordered the evacuation of the right bank of the Rhine.

The legate Corbulo, probably starting the work in AD 48, built a 27km (17-mile) long North Sea canal in today's southern Holland between the mouths of the Old Maas and the Old Rhine. Troop and supply transports were able, by traversing this waterway (called the *Fossa Corbulonis*), to avoid exposing themselves to a more lengthy passage on the open sea.

In AD 50, the Romans rescued part of the Germanic tribe of King Vannus, known as the Suebi, by helping him escape across the Danube with his cohorts by employing warships of the Pannonian provincial fleet to escort them to safe haven into Roman-controlled territory.

The Danube was patrolled by the *classis Pannonica*, which had moved forward from the Save (Sava) River (occupied previously by Tiberius while putting down the Pannonian revolt of AD 6-9) at some uncertain date.

We have noted above that in AD 45, there had been a naval expedition to the Bosporan kingdom. In 46, a temporary fleet was formed for the annexation of Thrace. With success in Thrace, coupled with certain naval operations in the northern Euxine (Black Sea) in the years immediately preceding, there commenced a more aggressive policy by which Claudius brought the Black Sea permanently within the Roman orbit. This temporary fleet formed for the conquest of Thrace may be what has been called the *classis Perinthea* under the equestrian procurator of Thrace. It incorporated elements of a previously little-known Thracian royal fleet. Apart from controlling the Propontis, it had an important role in ferrying troops and supplies between Europe and Asia. The uneventful tranquillity of the Black Sea following the reign of Trajan probably brought about this fleet's dissolution.

Neronian, Black Sea and Lower Danube Operations

In AD 46, several expeditions penetrated deeply into the region bordering the Black Sea and along the Don River, reaching as far as Chersonesus (Sevastopol) by 57. In 57, a Roman expeditionary force was transferred to Chersonesus under the command of Plautus Silvanus, most likely transported by the Moesian provincial fleet. A stricter control of the northern shores of the Black Sea accompanied Nero's annexation of Pontus Polemoniacus. The new era of dating which Tyras began in 56-57 indicates the submission of that independent Greek city on the Black Sea to the north of the Danube, and a famous inscription of Ti. Plautius Sylvanus

Aelianus, governor of Moesia, from about 58 throws a clear light on Rome's advance. Besides defeating the Sarmatians and settling 100,000 trans-Danubian natives in Roman territory, this energetic governor freed the independent city of Chersonesus from a Scythian siege and so pacified the Euxine (Black Sea) that he, the first of all the Moesian governors, could ship grain to Rome. Here again the intervention of Plautius in the Bosporus undoubtedly called upon the Moesian squadron.

Yet another example of the indifferent seamanship and weather sense of Roman rulers and commanders occurred in 64, when numerous units of the Misenium main fleet fell victim to a storm. Blame for this disaster rests firmly upon Nero. He commanded the fleet after a visit to Formia and ignored the warnings of the strengthening southerly storm, which had already damaged or sunk some vessels. While attempting to round Cape Miseno, the struggling ships were thrust against the Campanian coast, resulting in the loss of numerous triremes and smaller transports. Pitassi gives the date of this disaster as 62, and says the storm hit the Roman coast and the harbour of Portus, wrecking 200 ships there and also some of the Misene fleet ships, which were caught off Cumae.

The persistent problem of giving the capital city of Rome easy access to her shipping prompted Nero to seriously consider digging a canal to link the city with good natural harbours around Puteoli, some 160 miles away, most of the distance lying across the Pontine Marshes. The canal was to be sufficiently wide to accommodate the widest quinqueremes. This project died with the emperor. There was also a Corinthian canal project under Nero that was started, but the work likewise ended when Nero was assassinated.

Naval Operations in the Jewish Revolt, AD 66–73

In the first Jewish War (AD 66–70), Jewish pirates operated from the port of Joppa (present-day Jaffa/Tel Aviv). They disrupted grain shipments from Alexandria and threatened Roman seaborne supply and troop movements. During that period, there were only a few warships stationed in Syrian waters, insufficient to protect the Syrian and Phoenician coastal shipping, especially waterborne supply to the legions in the area. The Jews utilized a light shallow-draft coastal craft adapted from Egyptian models, which sufficed to interdict coast-wise traffic but were incapable of keeping course in stormy seas further offshore. Vespasian's legions attacked by land, forcing the pirates to flee by ship and hover a few miles out to sea, beyond the range of the legions' missile weapons. The weather finally came to the Romans' rescue. A storm decimated the Jewish raiding ships, smashing most of them against the rocks along the shore, and Joppa was then taken overland by one of the legions, which wiped out the town so it could no longer serve as a base for Jewish pirate operations.

In the course of the fighting, there was a battle on the Sea of Galilee near the town of Tarichae. The struggle between the light, swift, albeit unsteady improvised Jewish skiffs and the heavy Roman rafts ended in favour of the Romans. Josephus describes this close-in fighting vividly:

> 'Thus pursued, the Jews could neither escape to land, where all were in arms against them, nor sustain a naval battle on equal terms. For their skiffs were small and built for piracy and were no match for rafts, and the men on board were so few that they dare not to come to grips with the dense ranks of the Roman enemy. Some tried to break through, but the Romans could reach them with their lances, killing others by leaping upon the backs and passing their swords through their bodies; sometimes as the rafts closed in, the Jews were caught in the middle and captured along with their vessels. So these wretches died on every side in countless numbers and in every possible way … One could see the whole lake stained with blood and crammed with corpses, for not a man escaped.'

Viereck incorrectly states that Sextus Cornelius Dexter distinguished himself in this battle and was subsequently designated as prefect of the *classis Syriaca*. However, he actually received the honour only after his participation in the later Jewish Revolt of 131-134 under Hadrian (the Bar Kochba Revolt) described later. The importance of this naval victory is evidenced by Roman coins struck to celebrate it.

Civil War, AD 68-70

This next section, dealing with the upheavals in the succession for the Principate following Nero's assassination – known as 'the year of the four emperors' – will be dealt with at some length, as it provides an excellent illustration of the significance of sea power for the fledgling Roman Empire. Although it occurred more or less simultaneously with the Jewish insurrection in Judaea, it was conducted independently of that more circumscribed conflict.

During the civil conflict between forces loyal to Vitellius and Vespasian, the loyalty of the fleets was even more crucial. It clearly reveals that Vespasian knew and fully understood how important the fleets would be in helping him to obtain power. The cooperation between the Black Sea and Syrian fleets enabled Vespasian's forces, led by Antonius Primus, to move unhindered and with full logistical support into Italy and down to Rome. The fleet at Alexandria handed over control of grain supplies to Vespasian, who could thus exert powerful economic and political as well as military pressure on Vitellius. If Vitellius could not guarantee the provision of foodstuffs to the Roman populace, he would swiftly lose the confidence of the malnourished masses.

The defection from Vitellius of the Ravenna fleet (which created a furore in his army) and the sailors of that fleet's insistence on marching against him as a *legio classica*, taken together with the revolt of the Misenum fleet (commanded by Apollinaris) and its spontaneous march on Rome, which diverted Vitellian troops south from Rome to Terracina to deal with the problem, made it impossible for Vitellius to launch any surprise counter-attacks. To make matters worse, the capture of Valens, the top Vitellian commander, by a naval squadron acting on its own initiative destroyed any chance of reinforcements coming from Spain and Germany. Finally, the ex-sailors of *Legio I Adiutrix* (by now in Spain) declared for Vespasian, leading the way for the other legions in Spain to do the same, with *Legio Secunda Augusta* (Vespasian's old command) doing the same in Britain.

To quote C.G. Starr: '[Vespasian] chose to stress sea power as the most significant factor in his success. In the commemorative coinage of 71 and succeeding years, the only type which specifically refers to the civil war bears the legend *Victoria Navalis* – '(Lady) Victory of the Fleet'. The *I Adiutrix* continued as part of the permanent legionary forces in Spain while the sailors of the Ravenna fleet, who forced Antonius Primus to enroll them as legionaries after the second battle of Cremona, were formally organized by order of Vespasian in March AD70 into *Legio II Adiutrix Pia Fidelis* (Dutiful and Steadfast). The *II Adiutrix* went on to serve in Britain – at Lincoln in 71 and at Chester in 75.'

Vespasian honoured the provincial fleets as well. The Alexandria and possibly Syria squadrons received the title Augusta for their aid and the fleet in Germany was honoured for standing firm against a revolt by the German tribes during the civil war. The two Danube fleets – in Pannonia and Moesia – were awarded the title Flavia for withstanding the Dacian revolt. Finally there was further recognition of the role of the two home fleets at Ravenna and Misenum: the prefects in command were raised from the rank or status of sexagenarius to that of ducenarius – an income of 60,000 sestertia raised to 200,000.

Vespasian relied heavily on the grain embargo coupled with the steady advance of Mucianus' forces. According to Tacitus' discussion of Vespasian's strategy, now that Vespasian commanded both Egypt, with its control of the grain supply, and the revenues of the wealthiest provinces (Asia Minor and Syria), the army of Vitellius could be forced to its knees merely by a lack of pay and supplies.

Primus' invasion of Italy had been against Vespasian's orders. Antonius Primus had been commander of *Legio VII*, and became the commander of Vespasian's second army, complementing that of Mucianus which was advancing steadily through Asia Minor. His orders at this earliest phase were to halt his advance at Aquilea – east of Venice – to allow Mucianus to catch up and combine forces. But Antonius was lucky not to be soundly thrashed. Vespasian had wanted to avoid a premature, bloody and risky battle.

A further step in Vespasian's plan was the conquest of Africa, which he was planning to invade by seaborne land forces, when the news of Antonius' bloody triumph at Cremona arrived. It is difficult to say definitively if and when the Eastern fleets were assisting Vespasian as Tacitus is somewhat inconsistent in his references to them in his descriptions of Vespasian's battle strength.

This statesmanlike strategy for victory was swept aside by Antonius' precipitate actions, but even the more limited actual service performed for Vespasian by the navy was significant. Some insight into this can be found in the conflict of opinion during the council of war that Antonius held in Poetorio prior to the beginning of his campaign.

Antonius was arguing for a speedy advance of his forces, stressing that Vitellius, once in command of the Mediterranean – and especially the Adriatic – could get reinforcements from across the sea, enabling him to attack the Balkans if he wished. Yet others at the table disputed this, arguing that Vespasian held the sea, the navy and the provinces, thereby denying Vitellius access to any reinforcements. In a sense, both were correct. Antonius was thinking that Vitellius held Italy and the great Praetorian Italian fleets. On the other hand, the opponents of his thinking were stressing the frame of mind of these squadrons. The rank and file despised Vitellius (they had favoured Otho) and wore a thin cloak of loyalty to the upstart emperor. There is even some evidence that Vespasian had secretly sent emissaries to the two fleets, preparing for their revolt at a suitable opportunity.

The actual course of events leads one to believe that Vespasian counted on the assumption that Vitellius could not rely on the Italian fleets. Otherwise, Vespasian would not have been as confident of his ability to hold Egypt when all he had were the eastern fleets with which to oppose the powerful Italian squadrons. Plus, if Mucianus had seriously considered sailing to Italy, he must have been confident that the Italian fleets would not oppose his small Pontic fleet. Strongest proof of this attitude in the Italian fleets is the fact that as Antonius moved into Italy, the fleets changed sides rather quickly. For example, the Ravenna fleet deserted Vitellius once Antonius' advance past Aquileia guaranteed the safety of its secession from Vitellius' command.

Although the naval praefect Sextus Lucilius Bassus (who had the unique joint command of the Misene and Ravenna fleets) encouraged and advanced the revolt (without the express sanction of Vespasian), the treiarchs commanding the sailors had already elected their choice for praefect, Cornelius Fuscus, and the fact that he came up quickly from Primus' army suggests that there had been prior arrangements. This rapid transfer of allegiance was probably due to the fact that most of the sailors of the Ravenna fleet came from the Balkans, whose armies had already declared for Vespasian. Vitellius, who was dallying at Aricia on the west coast of Italy, south-west of Rome, and his general, Valens, who was moving north (with troops and concubines) to stop the advance of Antonius Primus, were both understandably alarmed at the news of the defection of the Ravenna fleet, since the entire Adriatic coast of Italy was now open to Primus. He used the fleet to safeguard his flanks as far as Ariminum (modern Rimini), some 25 miles south of Ravenna on the Italian east, or Adriatic coast. He had previously tried to guard his line of communications with the Balkans against an unexpected naval assault before the Ravenna squadron had defected to Vespasian. Now this was secure.

His supply situation became easier, and that of Vitellius' forces on the Po more difficult. Further, and more importantly, the loyalty of the Misene fleet was now suspect, although this very atmosphere of uncertainty ruled out any drastic action to keep its loyalty. He quickly appointed Claudius Apollinaris as praefect of the Misene fleet, and Vitellius attempted to both strengthen its loyalty and decrease its numbers by drawing a temporary legion (*legio classica*) from the sailors to assist his barricade of the Apennines.

When his position grew more desperate and the Misenian fleet did revolt (going over to Vespasian) along with much of Campania (a detachment at Forum Iulii also went over to Vespasian, capturing Valens, but fled after the second Battle of Bedriacum), Vitellius was forced to take rapid action. If this rebellious fleet maintained its position, Rome's food supply – and thereby Rome itself – would be lost.

Vitellius returned to Rome and sent Claudius Iulianus, who had been lax in his governance of the fleet, to pacify the sailors. When he deserted, Emperor Vitellius sent his brother Lucius to recover Campania and went so far as recapturing Tarracina, inflicting heavy losses upon the rebelling sailors. However, events were moving too swiftly on other fronts, and Vitellius fell. Promptly after the defeat of Vitellius, Vespasian dispatched large quantities of Egyptian grain to strengthen his popularity among the Roman populace.

After the civil war of AD 69, Vespasian chose to stress sea power as the most significant factor in his success in coins. The permanent military formation developed during the conflict as *legio classica I Adiutrix* was continued, and the Ravenna fleet sailors who had forced Antonius Primus to enroll them in a *legio classica* after the second Battle of Bedriacum were formally organized by Vespasian in 70 as the *legio II Adiutrix*. He also honoured members of the Pannonian fleet who had accompanied Antonius Primus to Italy. In summation, the honours which he heaped upon the fleets were greater and more extensive that those awarded to any other force. As a final gesture, Vespasian raised the praefects of the Praetorian fleets from the grade of *sexagenarius* to that of *ducenarius*, thereby making the heads of the Misene and Ravenna fleets two of the great equestrian praefects. In his treatment of the fleets, Vespasian might justly be called a second Augustus.

The fleets were also shown to have played an important role in a near-contemporaneous and somewhat related event that has become known as the Civilis Revolt, or alternately the Batavian Revolt.

Civilis' Revolt

During the later stages of the civil wars in AD 68-69, the legions, auxiliaries and fleet of 'the Germanies' were caught up in the intrigues of the Batavian known as Iulius Civilis. When Civilis raised the standard of Vespasian in the Batavian country (roughly modern Netherlands) as a pretext for revolt, Romans abandoned the forts along the lower Rhine, where vessels of the fleet had been harboured, and assembled the twenty-four ships of the *classis Germanica* in Batavia, making auxiliary units available at the eastern end of the *insula Batavorum* (island of the Batavi, modern-day Walcheren). The abandoned forts were likely Katwijk and Voorberg, possibly also Fectio. Note that Viereck says these twenty-four ships *defected* to Civilis. Since the Batavian rowers were native Batavians, as well as part of the auxiliaries, they were thus deemed to be unreliable – virtual fifth-columnists – allowing the the attack of Civilis to swiftly destroy this force.

With this defeat inflicted upon the Roman fleet and auxilia, Civilis' revolt had an auspicious start. The level of the Rhine River fell so low that it was almost impossible to mount naval patrols, and the forays of Germanic tribes could only be guarded against by instituting foot patrols on the river banks. Next, thanks to the creeping paralysis of the Roman administration, distracted as it was by the ongoing struggle for power in Rome, Civilis dominated the Rhine River past Novaesium. Because the Rhine was both a frontier and an avenue of military action, challenges beset the Romans on all sides. Allied Germans streamed across the river in large numbers to aid Civilis. Transport of Romans down the current became impossible, and supplying Lower Germany became a crucial, difficult problem. Shortly after the new year (AD 70), the principal loyal general was murdered and the entire Rhine yielded allegiance to two Gallic nationalists, Classicus and Tutor, who were engaged in a quixotic attempt to create an Empire of All Gaul.

In AD 70, a squadron of twenty-four ships of the Rhine fleet fell into the hands of the rebellious Germans led by Civilis through treachery. Civilis promptly turned these surrendered warships against the Romans. According to Chester Starr, it was this improvised fleet that harassed the Roman grain ships coming up the Gallic coast. In the spring of 70, the new government of Vespasian took firm steps to put down this upstart empire and to break Civilis' domination of the Rhinelands.

In order to counter this purloined flotilla, elements of the *classis Britannica* had to be brought across. Also in AD 70, this British squadron attempted to land on the western coast of the *insula Batavorum*.

A vigorous general, Cerialis, crossed the Alps with fresh troops and moved down the Rhine, forcing the collapse of the Gallic Empire. But Civilis remained defiant, and in the ensuing operations aimed at toppling him, the endemic failure (common at this time) of the Roman army to provide local security cost them severely.

The *classis Britannica* transported the *legio XIV Gemina* across from Britain to Gaul, but it was suddenly assailed by the Canninefates tribe (at that time active in the estuarine North Sea areas of the Rhine) as it was anchored near the Gallic coast, most of it being destroyed. The Rhine fleet was unable to intervene in the fighting. This absence, coupled with the Roman setback, encouraged the Germans to mount a successful attack against the berthing place of a squadron, where they were able to capture several ships, among them the trireme serving as the flagship of the commander, Q. Petillius Cerialis. Meanwhile, Cerialis himself, sailing down the Rhine from Novaesium with a squadron, was surprised as he lay camped on the shore, losing every one of his ships.

Notwithstanding this setback, the arrival of Cerialis at least, in the words of Tacitus, 'brought tactical skill and an aggressive spirit'. In the light of this impending onslaught, Civilis withdrew rapidly northward and crossed to the *insula Batavorum* before Cerialis could make contact. Tacitus suggests that the war would have ended then if the Rhine fleet had been available to cut off his retreat. In fact, Cerialis had ordered this fleet to join the army, but its rowers had been diverted to shore duties the previous autumn when the Rhine had been yielded to Civilis, and it took some time to reorganize the fleet.

At last, other ships appeared at Cerialis' camp on the Waal River, opposite the *insula Batavorum*. Civilis then launched his boats to invigorate his men and try to dishearten the Roman grain ships coasting up from Gaul. Finally, elements of the Rhine fleet arrived to engage the enemy, whereupon the two opposing squadrons met at the Maas river estuary. The Batavian ships far outnumbered the Roman contingent, but the Romans clearly possessed superior vessels and better-trained crews. There was a brief exchange of missiles as each file of ships passed one another, neither choosing to close with the enemy at boarding range, after which the two fleets separated. At the conclusion of this brief fire-fight, Civilis withdrew into the area at the northern end of the Rhine, affording the Romans the opportunity to land infantry units upon the *insula Batavorum* and devastate the place.

Although this, the only naval encounter of the Civilis revolt, is rather ludicrous – the two fleets merely passing each other and perfunctorily exchanging a few missiles – the event is nonetheless significant: Mediterranean naval techniques had quickly given the Romans mastery of northern waters, but the 'barbarians' acquired this technique and gradually eroded Roman naval superiority. They were thus, by the mid-first century, able to challenge the Romans at sea.

The readiness of the Batavians to challenge the Roman fleet in AD 69 presaged the more serious naval challenge posed by the free Germans in the next century. During the campaign, the reappearance of a Roman navy on the Rhine was important in itself. Cerialis' advance down the Rhine was likely prompted by the knowledge that his right flank, which rested on the Rhine, would be secure. The arrival of some portion of the fleet in the lower reaches of the stream indicated that the river above the Roman camp could be once again used as a line of supply. Neither side showed much trained discipline, but Civilis figured his heterogeneous flotilla to be weaker and withdrew from the *insula* to the country of the Frisians, shortly thereafter surrendering and ending the revolt.

Neither the *classis Britannica* nor the Rhine fleet had succeeded in scoring any decisive victories against the uprising. The fighting continued until AD 71. It was only the pressure of the Roman legions on land that forced the surrender of Civilis, after Cerialis inflicted defeats in land battles at Trier and Xanthene. Vespasian did not honour the Rhine fleet with the title 'Flavia', but did grant it the less significant 'Augusta'.

Campaign in Scotland

In AD 78, Britannic governor Gnaius Julius Agricola commenced his campaign against the Caledonians in northern Scotland, supported by his naval units. The following year, Mount Vesuvius erupted and the noted author of natural histories and praefect of the Misenian fleet, C. Plinius Secundus the Elder (Pliny), sailed the larger ships of the fleet to rescue residents in the area of Pompey and Stabiae, meeting his death in the effort.

Between AD 82-84, there were many incursions of British 'Brythonic' (Brythonic = variously, Britons, Celts or Normans) units on the east coast of Scotland to participate in the campaign against the Caledonians. In 84, Julius Agricola, during a flank protection operation in support of the legions, circumnavigated the Promontorium Caledonia, which today is known as the northern tip of Scotland, or Duncansby Head. Here he discovered the Orkney Islands: the Shetland Islands were also fully visible from the Orkneys. They may or may not be identical to the northern islands dubbed Thule by the Massilian explorer Pythias some three centuries earlier.

It seems that the flotilla had scouted ahead of Agticola's column moving northward along the east coast in AD 83 (as it had done in 82), and Tacitus reports that the Britons were stupefied at the sight of a fleet, 'constant of the sea, the open secret of his conquered had their last refuge closed' (author: my rough translation from the Latin). After his decisive land victory at Mons Graupius in 85, Agricola placed a detachment of soldiers on the fleet and sent it north with orders to circumnavigate Britain. It appears that the cruise was intended merely to officially determine that Britain was an island. It 'received the submission' of the Orkneys and spotted the Shetlands (likely the Romans' 'Ultima Thule'), after which it returned to the port of Trucculum, likely on the Firth of Forth, its starting place. Due to the rough seas surrounding them, these lands were not fully incorporated into the Roman sphere of influence. It seems incontestable that Roman warships had reached the northern end of Britain for the first and only time.

Saturnius' Revolt on the Rhine and the Dacian Expedition of AD 86

In AD 89, the *classis Germanica* defeated an incursion across the Rhine. This was a threatened assault by Chatti raiders in support of a usurpation attempt (speedily put down) across the frozen Rhine, aided by a sudden, early thaw. About 1 January 89, L. Antonius Saturnius, governor of Germania Superior, proclaimed himself Emperor, but within the month he was crushed by L. Appius Norbanus Maximus, governor of Germania Inferior, in the vicinity of Bonna. The Chatti, who had planned to cross the Rhine in support of Saturnius, were foiled by an opportune break-up of the ice. The fleet's part in this winter campaign can at best have been slight, but Domitian bestowed, along with every other unit in the army of Germania Inferior, the title *pia fidelis Domitia* in grateful memory of their swift assertion of loyalty.

The eventual overthrow of Domitian did not bring about any internecine warfare. For a time, Nerva's successor reign tottered, but the adoption of Trajan secured the new regime. There is mention of a 'Suez canal project' of Domitian in AD 92, and later Trajan's restoration of the canal from the Red Sea to the Nile – the *Augustamnica* – but not likely leading to any Red Sea dominance.

Domitian had reorganized the defence of the lower Danube in AD 85/86 by dividing Moesia into two provinces – Inferior and Superior – and adding two legions to the garrison. The *classis Flavia Moesica* was assigned to Moesia Inferior. Prior to the above reorganization, the Dacians had, in AD 85, struck across the lower reaches of the Danube inflicting serious losses on the *classis Moesica* and breaking the sea connection between the Danubian legions and the Bosporous.

The Moesian fleet took some part in the disastrous Dacian expedition of Cornelius Fuscus in 86, and in the more successful campaign of Tettius Julianus, whose victory at Tapae in Dacia permitted peace. The Dacian settlement effected by Domitian was not destined to be permanent. The first great action of Trajan's rule was a new solution to the Dacian problem through force. As part of his thorough preparations for this campaign, Trajan had strengthened the Moesian fleet, and also constructed a towpath to facilitate deployment of the Pannonian fleet on the lower Danube. He also apparently built a 2½-mile canal enabling the Moesian and Pannonian fleets to link and navigate over the entire course of the Danube. The subsequent series of campaigns from 101-106 brought about the complete conquest of Dacia. As this later series of campaigns has been meticulously documented in the commemorative column bearing Trajan's name, I will devote some space to these events. The Danubian frontier, much more than the Rhine, would remain a war zone well into the Byzantine era and beyond. Conflicts under Domitian and Trajan attempted to plug the dyke, plugged again in Hadrian's early years (117–120) and shored up yet again in Marcus Aurelius' Marcomannic wars (169–180) before the third century's deluge of invasions

Chapter Twelve

Resisiting Pressure on the Peripheries

Trajan's Dacian Wars

The wars of Trajan constitute a prime example of the transportation of troops by the navy. Trajan's column is the main source. The carvings highlight the importance of the fleet for the maintenance of the army and the incomparable route for this task furnished by the Danube. The main service of the warships was to so dominate the river that the clearly differentiable freighters could proceed unhindered in ferrying supplies to the legions, and the troopships likewise could keep moving. After the meticulous preparations detailed on the column, Trajan and his forces crossed into Dacia on their bridges of boats and the war began.

The first year's campaign was based on the locales of Vimacium and Tsierna. Late in the winter of AD 101-102, the Dacians, aided by the Roxalani, broke across the Danube below Drobeta, where Trajan most likely wintered and ravaged the countryside for provisions.

In the two Dacian wars of Trajan, in 101-102 and 105-106, the fighting legions were transported and sustained in crossing the Danube by troop transports and supply ships of the Pannonian fleet. At the opening of the Second Dacian War in 105, Trajan sailed hastily by night from Ancona to Dalmatia, accompanied by his Praetorians.

For his conquests in Parthia in AD 114-117, Trajan built a fleet of fifty warships on the Euphrates and Tigris rivers. Both land and naval forces cooperated to take the Parthian capital of Ctesiphon, which lay on the Tigris. By 116, Roman units reached the Persian Gulf.

In the first Dacian campaign of 101-102, the galleys of the Moesian flotilla, which most likely had been assembled at Drobeta for the winter, carried Trajan and his expeditionary force, with horses and supplies in transports, down the river as far as Novae. Having crushed the invaders, Trajan sailed upstream to open the second campaign. Two separate Roman columns plunged into the heart of Dacia, whereupon the frieze morphs the broad Danube into unnavigable mountain torrents. Yet the Danube continues to be shown in the background of the frieze, demonstrating that it was the lateral line of communication that made such a division of the troops possible – the Moesian fleet continued to patrol the length of the Danube throughout the wars.

After his final victory, Trajan reorganized the defence of the lower Danube along lines it retained well past the third century AD. The Danube remained the first line of protection, and was where most of the legions were stationed. Various posts, depots and naval stations were supplied by grain ships, which were guarded by details from the army.

As for the positioning and designation of the fleets, thanks to the inscription of C. Manlius Felix we can assume with great probability that there were two fleets in operation, the Pannonian and the German. In the inscription, Manlius Felix is described as '*Praefectus classium Pannonicae et Germanicae*' (Admiral of the Pannonian and German fleets), so one can safely assume that he commanded both simultaneously. The concentration of fleets stationed far apart was usual during campaigns in later times, too. The inscription of Valerius Maximianus mentions his special responsibility during the Marcommanic Wars of the Emperor Marcus Aurelius (AD 168-175). He had to secure the food supply for both the Pannonian armies. For this purpose he had under his command sections of the Misenum, Ravenna and British fleets. It is pertinent that the Pannonian fleet, i.e. the regular provincial fleet in the theatre of war, was not part of this assignment. Apparently, it was needed for other operations. These could have involved the transport of troops and equipment, as well as patrolling the Danube. After all, if the army alone was involved in the war without the fleet, the Danube – as the Empire's border – would have been defenceless against enemy attacks.

Trajan's Parthian Wars, Jewish Kitos and Bar Kochba Revolts

At the outset of the Parthian War, Trajan sailed with a large force via Athens to Seleucia. On this trip, which occurred in the winter of AD 113-114, the sailors of a quadrireme named 'Ops' performed some extraordinary service which earned the crew an immediate discharge with full privileges. Starr speculates that this comprised the transport of Trajan himself safely through a storm.

A considerable part of the Misene fleet remained in the East during Trajan's campaign in the suppression of the Jewish Revolts, which plagued Trajan's last years. When the Jews rose in Cyrenaica, Egypt and Syria in AD 115-117, Trajan singled out Q. Marcus Turbo, praefect of the Misene fleet – probably promoting him to a special command – and sent him against the Jews with both land and naval forces. This expedition quickly stamped out the revolt in Egypt, Cyrenaica and Cyprus. In this campaign, sailors may have served on land to strengthen Turbo's forces, as they regularly received military training.

With unrest in the Levant, Cyrene and Egypt to contend with, units of the *classis Misinensis* were sent to and stationed in the East to assist in restoring order, landing marines and sailors and escorting the Emperor, and generally reinforcing the local squadrons in keeping the coasts and sea lanes secure. In the Third Jewish War of 132-135, the Syrian naval fleet fended off attacks by

Jewish sea forces against key coastal ports and depots, securing the grain supply of the legions.

These eastern crises of the second century AD highlighted how, in a crisis, the Alexandrian fleet, like its Ptolemaic predecessor, might supplement the upper Nile River guard police force by sailing up the Nile both to transport troops and land marines. The first, and among the greatest, of such exigencies in the Empire was the above-noted general Jewish revolt of 115-117, which completely disrupted Roman control of the land and defied the full strength of the Egyptian army. On the re-establishment of peace, the two flotillas – the fiscal (i.e., tariff enforcement) and the military squadron – were united under a single praefect. Formerly, they had been constituted as the *potamophylacia*, an independent service – not part of the Alexandrian fleet – which exercised fiscal and police supervision over the waterways of Egypt, levying tolls and inspecting commerce.

In the second of the two mentioned Jewish rebellions in the second century, the Jewish War of AD 132-135 under Hadrian, the *Legio X Fretensis* was strengthened by sailors from the Misene fleet who had been utilized as soldiers ashore (most likely marines). The cohort *I Aelia classica* came from naval detachments of the *classis Britannica* put on shore to cope with a British rebellion under Hadrian. Also under Hadrian, just before the outbreak of the Bar Kochba revolt, the Emperor ordered a Roman naval squadron into the Red Sea on an expedition to sweep away pirates there, after which he could expand trade with the East.

The Parthian offensive of AD 162-166 into Armenia and Syria was largely a land war, but the *classis Syriaca*, operating between Alexandria and Seleucia Pieria (the latter being the port for Antioch in Asia Minor, modern Syria) patrolled the Cilician coast and was reinforced and built up to some 600 ships. Lucius Verus went east, attended by units of the *classis Misenensis*, which remained in the area, carrying out troop transport and dispatch duties. They may also have transported some of the numerous army vexillations required by the eastern crisis.

In AD 162, vessels of the Misene fleet carried the co-emperor Lucius Verus from Brundisium to Antioch to manage the Parthian War. These vessels likely carried news and orders between the East and West.

Marcomannic Wars

The onslaught of the Marcomanni and Quadi in AD 166 was likely to have overrun the Pannonian fleet at its anchorages, the fleet being decimated or captured. It was only with the commencement of the First Marcomannic War from 167-175 that the invaders were pushed back over the border once more. The advance of these rampaging tribes seems to have reached Aquilea in the Gulf of Trieste. Noricum (roughly modern Austria, in the west of Pannonia) and Pannonia were both overrun by the attackers. Marcus Aurelius spent from 170–175 fighting to drive the invaders out and restoring the border.

In both Marcomannic wars, the Pannonian fleet played a significant role. Its units operated from Carmuntum (Petronell, Austria) to Castra Regina (Regensburg), and also marched to the Naab River (tributary of the Danube in Bavaria, flowing into the Daunube at Regensburg) and River Tisza (mostly in Hungary), when the Romans utilized the base of Aquincum (Alt-Ofen=Old Oven) in Hungary.

In the Second Marcomannian War (AD 178–180), Marcus Aurelius started to push up past the Danube and into the territory of his enemies. The reconstituted Pannonian fleet, reinforced with newly built vessels to replace the losses suffered in the incursions by the Germanic tribes in 166, was again a major factor.

The Emperor Commodus negotiated a peace treaty which forbade ownership of ships by the Germanic tribes along the Danube border, and also forbade them from entering the Danubian islands, demarcating a 7–14km-wide buffer zone on the far side of the Danube in which was prohibited any Germanic settlement.

The Moesian and Pannonian fleets were constantly in action during these campaigns, providing support and transportation for the legions along the Danube and its tributaries, helping Marcus Aurelius to pursue the raiders into what is now the Czech Republic and across the plains of Hungary. In the winter of AD 170–171, Marcus Valerius Maximianus was sent with detachments of men from the Italian and British fleets to bring supplies down the Danube to Marcus' army, supported by cavalry from North Africa scouting the river banks against attacks on the boats. These men must have had to augment whatever boats they could commandeer locally with rafts and boats built for the occasion.

Further Operations Suppressing Frontier Disturbances, Late Second Century

Meanwhile, in AD 170 and 171, the Moor tribes south-west of Mauretania in North Africa began raiding the African and Hispanic coasts. The *classis Misinensis* had to send a major fleet to suppress this seaborne activity, operating far out into the Atlantic seaboard and reinforcing the local garrisons while the army dealt with the tribesmen on land. The Moors ravaged widely in the western Mediterranean. In order to hold the line against the rebelling Moors in Baetica (presently the Andalusian coast at the southern tip of Spain), who were harassing both the Spanish and African coasts, the province was temporarily switched from senatorial to imperial control and was joined to Hispania Tarraconensis. A special 5,000-strong task force under procurator Julius Julianus was sent against the rebels. As well as the Misene fleet playing a part agaist the Moors, there is a Ravennate tombstone in Spain that betokens some participation of the Ravenna fleet. The war was ended by 173, but the Moors seem to have erupted again in 177, providing more work for the troop transports of the Praetorians fleets.

The failure of Commodus to press his father's hard-won success against the Marcomanni to its conclusion required the strengthening of the river defences along the Danube with forts, whose positions faced detected secret passages utilized by the tribes – portages, fords, etc..

During the last decade of Marcus Aurelius' reign, the Mediterranean was more disturbed than it had been since the Civil Wars of the dying Republic. In AD 170, the Costoboci probably invaded Greece by sea; this is inferred by the fact that the *classis Pontica* was shifted from Trapezus, on the north-east coast of Asia Minor, to guard the Hellespont. The revolt of Avidius Cassius unsettled the East. Both Marcus Auerilius and Commodus visited Syria and returned from Athens to Brundisium by sea. There is naval coinage from this period commemorating their safe escape from danger during a storm suffered during this passage. The naval coinage under Commodus reflects both his activity in ensuring the safety of the vital grain fleets and his interest in 'Isis navigation' – most likely meaning sea travel by way of the vicinity of Egypt.

Meanwhile, there was further unrest in the British Isles. Against attacks across the sea against the North Sea and Channel coasts by the invading Saxons and Frisians, coastal forts were built from AD 187-196. One of these which is presently well-preserved is the Roman fort of Gariannonum, which, due to its location atop a cliff overlooking the Waveney valley, dominated the Waveney River estuary. Built for defence against Saxon raids, it is now the site of Burgh Castle in Norfolk.

In conducting his war against the Parthians, Septimus Severus was obliged to build many riverine warfare vessels on the Euphrates River. The connecting canal between the Euphrates and Tigris was reconstructed and thereafter utilized by the fleet. At the point where the two rivers' courses are closest, the Romans crossed to the Tigris, where they seized and looted Ctesiphon, the Parthian capital. During the combat operations, the ships supported the legions on both rivers, and also furnished a good deal of the supplies required. The fleet arrived once more in the Persian Gulf by AD 197.

Unrest on the Peripheries, Compounded by Internal Power Struggles

Summing up the the second two centuries of the Common Era, throughout the century of the Antonines (the seven emperors spanning from Nerva to Commodus, AD 96-192), the historic role of the navy had been that of an adjunct in frontier defence. During the following 100 years (192-292), this duty continued, for the pressure on the frontiers was unremitting; even more, the Mediterranean fleets now witnessed the plague of civil strife. Commodus was murdered on 31 December 192, and the reign of his successor, Pertinax, endured but a few months. Then Didius Iulianus at Rome and three contenders in the provinces all claimed the throne. Just as in 68-69, the tottering emperor in the capital resorted to the Italian (Praetorian) fleets to bolster his power. But the campaign took a different turn and this time the navy had a smaller scope for action.

The Ravenna fleet, notwithstanding Didius Iulianis' attempts to strengthen its loyalty, deserted to Septimus Severus as he entered Italy along the same route which Antonius Primus had followed 125 years earlier. Iulianus did summon the Misenium fleet sailors to Rome to help him, but these were unable to hinder Severus' rapid advance – Cassius Dio scoffs at the poor military training of the Misenian fleet sailors. After his victory over Iulianus, Septimus Severus was kinder to the Italian fleets than he was to the former Praetorian guards because he needed their support in his campaign against another challenger, Pescennius Niger. In July 193, Severus moved eastward to assist his generals who had blocked Pescennius' progress at the Hellespont. While Septimus moved by land, the Italian fleets transported part of his army to the Balkans at Dyrrachium and then proceeded to the Aegean. They most likely arrived at the Hellespont after Pescennius had fallen back into Asia Minor – where he was crushed – but they may have aided the crossing in turn of the Severan generals. Some part of the navy had possibly made a demonstration toward Egypt – this is inferred from the fact that this province came over to Severus before the final Battle of Issus concluded victory in the East.

Most of the navy remained in the East to aid in the siege of Byzantium, which had declared for Niger and held out after his suicide until the winter of AD 195-196. One official of the Misene fleet rendered such good service that Severus took the unprecedented step of promoting him to the Senate and advanced him steadily thereafter. In 197, Severus sailed east from Brundisium for his Parthian War, described above.

While Mesopotamia was once more annexed as a province of the Roman Empire after Severus' second war against the Parthians, he did not have it all his way. The strategic fortress city of Hatra was besieged twice without success, making it clear that not all of Mesopotamia was in Roman hands.

In Severus' final years (after AD 200), he campaigned along the northern coasts of Britain with the *classis Britannica* in support. Severus intended to settle the disquiet on the northern border once and for all by conquering the whole island. Leaving younger son Geta in charge of the province to the south, the Emperor and his elder son, Bassianus, campaigned into Caledonia in 209 and 210, imposing terms on the tribes as his campaigns pushed northward. During the campaign against the Caledonians in the north of Scotland, Severus' army was supported by the Britannic fleet, which protected the army on its sea flank, and transport ships both carried and supplied the legions. While no sea battles took place, the ships penetrated to the northern tip of the British isles.

The successors of Septimus Severus did not pursue a policy of open expansion, so the fleets were mainly employed in border security, combating piracy and transporting grain and troop supplies. These less spectacular exertions of sea power oiled the wheels of the Empire. At Severus' death in AD 211, the complex geographical and administrative frame of imperial sea power still enabled it to meet difficulties similar to those of 193 against Piscennius Niger's challenge. The siege of Byzantium indicated that the imperial fleets still controlled the Mediterranean. The greater upheavals to come, nonetheless, were to show that imperial appreciation of sea power had slowly diminished.

The shrinking resources of the Empire had to be devoted rather to desperate efforts at maintaining the military strength of the legions. During the third century, every type of political and natural calamity, including a great plague, weakened the imperial structure. Pretenders to the throne rose freely, and few real emperors had reigns of any length. In the East, the Sassanian dynasty, which had replaced the ineffectual Parthians, was a far more serious threat, and at times advanced as far as Asia Minor.

During the first half of the third century, the Italian squadrons continued to perform their usual functions in eastern campaigns. In AD 214, an accident sank Caracalla's galley while crossing the northern Aegean, but he was saved by an unnamed naval prefect. As late as Gordian III (238-244), the Emperor moved east by sea, at least part of the way, for the Persian Wars. Ships were thus still the main means of speedily and timely ferrying leaders to and from hotspots.

Chapter Thirteen

Seagoing 'Barbarians' at the Gates

On the northern frontier, the 'barbarians', now often partly civilized by long contact with Roman traders, grouped themselves in larger units and repeatedly broke the Roman defences. More gravely, from about AD 253-269, the Goths ravaged the eastern provinces, at first by land and then by sea.

In the period AD 250-270, a tribe known as the Carpi were an important component of a loose coalition of transdanubian (in Modavia, now eastern Romania) 'barbarian' tribes that also included Germanic and Sarmatian (Scythian) elements. These were responsible for a series of large and devastating invasions of the Balkan regions of the Empire which nearly caused its disintegration. The Carpi were joined in this devastation by the Borani, a Sarmatian or Gothic tribe of the Dnieper steppe.

Emperor Gallus Trebonianus had no time to respond to Persian king Sapor's devastation of the Syrian provinces; Sapor's invasion was not his only problem. During his reign, there operated for the first time Germanic tribes – these were actually probably Scythians – upon the sea, and they ravaged the coasts of Asia Minor to Ephesus and Pessinus. On the Danube, Scythian tribes were once again on the loose, notwithstanding the peace treaty signed in AD 251. The Bosporan kingdom in the Crimea had succumbed to the onslaught of the numerous tribes and the Romans had practically, by abandoning the peninsula's outposts, left it open to her enemies. The Scythian coalition took advantage of this situation by accumulating a flotilla of some 500 ships on the Euxine (Black Sea) through a combination of captured and newly assembled vessels, likely *liburnae* variants. In one foray, they managed to get these through the Propontis (Sea of Marmora) into the Aegean and, in combined land-sea assaults, attacked Macedonia, Athens, Cassanraeia (in Macedonia), Sparta and Corinth before being checked by both the legions and Roman fleets. Their attacks were defeated primarily on land, but naval forces of some type did meet and stop the naval threat in battles off Rhodes, Crete and Cyprus. Most probably, these latter were the *classis Moesica* in the western Black Sea, the *classis Pontica* operating from the south shore and the *classis Syriacae* in the Aegean.

Being as elements from all three fleets likely participated, the incursion was probably costly for the invaders, but they were not discouraged by their losses. By now the Goths had migrated to the northern shores of the Euxine and had a long tradition of navigating along large rivers of Russia and the Ukraine down from the Baltic. They developed even more seaworthy boats from these hardy riverine craft to navigate on the open seas. They became more adventurous as they gained seafaring experience, and ranged their raiding forays as far as the Anatolian and Balkan coast. The Bosporan kingdom was *de facto* dominated by the Goths by this time, rendering the Sea of Azov a Gothic lake. Effective Roman naval control of the north Euxine basin was lost.

Unidentified pirate raiders, most likely other Gothic elements, penetrated the Propontis to make plundering raids along the Anatolian and Greek coasts. They most likely only had relatively small (compared to the Roman ships) flat-bottomed craft, but sailed together in groups of several dozen ships manned by several hundred men. Individually, the Roman warships and crews were superior to the 'barbarian' flotillas, but the sheer numbers, frequency and area coverage of the so-called 'pirate' swarms made interception difficult. While, as I mentioned, the various Roman naval squadrons fought the intruders to a standstill in battles off Rhodes, Crete and Cyprus, those which were able to take their loot back home encouraged others to emulate their lucrative success.

In AD 254, 'barbarians' utilized Bosporan ships with captured crews to raid along the northern coast of Anatolia, but were beaten badly when the vessels and crews were caught ashore.

A massive attack by the Borani (along with the allied Carpi tribe) was finally stopped at Pityus (Pitsunda, in modern Georgia) and the marauding 'barbarians', who had carelessly sent their ships back, barely succeeded in preserving control of the northern shore of the Black Sea, where Roman control had been relinquished in AD 253, when the Goth-Scythian forces had crossed from Thrace to Ephesus. On their expedition they also took Pityus and Trapezus. Inflamed by the rich haul of loot, the Goths themselves had their merchants and slaves build them light boats, with which, in 256, they made a coastal raid along Moesia and Thrace to Byzantium. On this exploratory expedition, they pushed their devastation only as far as the coastal cities of Bythnia. For about another ten years (256-266) there seems to have been a hiatus when the Goths did not venture on the sea.

These series of attacks entail significant maritime components, and as such bear further scrutiny.

Utilizing their fleet of 500 motley vessels, they sailed through the Propontis and conquered Byzantium. The Greek cities of Athens, Corinth and Sparta were also looted. As the crews moved inland, they left their vessels inadequately guarded and the Romans exploited this laxness to destroy the 'barbarian' ships. The invaders then retreated northward, and the Roman army caught and defeated them at the Macedonian-Thracian frontier.

At the peninsula of Athos, jutting into the Aegean Sea south-eastward from Macedonia, the enemy fleet split. One portion sailed to Crete, Rhodes and Cyprus, while the other was en route to Thessaloniki and Athens Cassanraeia in Macedonia. Their attacks on these locations were not devastating, and the prefect of Egypt engaged these vessels with his *classis Alexandrina* and defeated them in a series of running naval battles off Crete, Rhodes and Cyprus.

In AD 267, it seems that the Goths ravaged Bythnia and Lydia, sacked Nicomedia and Ephesus among other cities and were finally met by the Palmyrene prince Odenathus, before whom they hastily retreated, having lost a naval battle.

In AD 268, there came an even greater penetration, when the migratory Germanic folk known as the Heruli, along with some Goths, set sail from the Danube in 500 light boats. This appears to have been a combined force of East and West Goths, Heruli, Peucini Bastarnae and Gepids (an East Germanic tribe closely related to the Goths). While some sources report a fleet of 2,000 ships and allegedly 300,000-320,000 men, these figures are certainly exaggerated. The invaders debouched from the Tyras River basin (now the Dnieper) and spread along the coasts of Asia Minor, Greece and Thrace.

The process of refortification in Asia Minor was only beginning at that time, and the militarization of the population was perhaps less advanced there than in other provinces. What resistance could be offered was offered by local police forces. More significantly, the fact of this raid revealed a glaring hole in Rome's maritime defences. There was a fleet on the Rhine that was charged with preventing raiders crossing the North Sea, and there appears to have been a fleet on the Danube, though how well organized it was after the disasters of AD 250-251 is a matter for conjecture; the ability of the 'Scythians' to sail past it may be the best indication.

Otherwise, the two main fleets of the Roman Empire were those of Misenum and Ravenna. Their primary duties had long been the protection of lines of communication from Italy to the provinces and, probably, the suppression of piracy. These great battle fleets of the Late Republic, in the absence of enemies, had long since degenerated, and there is no reason to think that there were any substantial forces available to patrol the coasts of the Aegean. It would appear that the 'Skythai' went home when they felt that they had acquired enough plunder.

The provincial fleets were in no condition to put up a defence, and the main Praetorian fleets at Ravenna and Misenum were not ready to be deployed. In any event, there were no naval units which could be brought to bear in the stricken sector. Byzantium had taken steps to improve the Roman defences in the area, and they fortified Thracian cities exposed to the Gothic attacks. Apparently, Emperor Gallienus had accomplished these tasks while on a personal tour of the regional defences *circa* AD 263.

A certain Venerianus appears to have organized a separate scratch naval force out of elements of fleets that had already suffered Goth attacks, and was able to defeat the invading fleet in the Propontis. His squadron seems to have been a new creation, conscripted most likely from Thracian coastal cities that had provided naval expertise, ships and manpower in the past. Venerianus' death in the battle, however, temporarily demoralized this scratch force, and the 'barbarians' took advantage of this hiatus to push their way into the Aegean. The citizen militia of Athens was able to repel the naval attackers. The imperial fleets, under the command of Cleodamus and Athenaeus, stopped the 'barbarians' by sea, while Gallienus killed a great number returning overland through Thrace. However, he was distracted by the revolt of Aureolus in Italy and had to break off his pursuit, leaving the job half-finished.

In the further course of events, the Pontic, Thracian and Syrian fleets were so weakened that they were unable to fight the massive raids by the Goths, Heruli and Peucini Bastarnae in AD 267. These Germanic (Gothic) coalition forces were then able to penetrate into the Aegean Sea.

The sources are a bit confusing, but it does appear that the invasions of AD 268 and 269 are two separate events, not a single invasion as some have tried to prove. If there were two distinct invasions, elements of each have become mixed-up in our sources. It is certain that fresh naval forces did pass through the Hellespont in 269, this time without Roman opposition. The 'barbarians' halted near Mount Athos to repair their ships, which had spun out of control in the rapid Hellespont current and collided. From there they made their way safely to Cassandria and Thessalonica, where the greater part of the ships disembarked their forces to besiege the two cities. These forces were wiped out by the new emperor, Claudius II, earning him his title of Gothicus. Those Goths who remained with the fleet found that, thanks to Gallienus' inspection tour of 263, all the cities of Thessaly and Greece had been fortified, so they went on to attack the islands of Rhodes, Crete and Cyprus but were defeated by a fleet under Tenagino Probus, governor of Egypt. They were afflicted by a plague and only a remnant returned home.

The Fleets that Fought the Gothic Invasions

These Roman naval forces which met the Goths are not readily identified with any previously existing forces. As noted, Venerianus' squadron was a scratch force recruited from Thracian local coastal units. In AD 268, the fleet did good service, but its failure to appear in 269 suggests that Venerianus' ships had returned to their native cities during the winter. The Egyptian prefect, Tenagio Probus, appears likely to have cobbled together his naval force prominent in the 269 hostilities from remnants of the Alexandrian and Syrian flotillas which may have survived. The direct cause of this revamped naval power in the East appears to haven been Gallienus' visit, but the project was short-lived. The invasion of Queen Zenobia of Palmyra swept it away, and no new units of a permanent nature appear in the Eastern Mediterranean for the rest of the third century.

During the upheavals in the Empire from Decius to Aurelian (AD 249-270), we have seen that the Romans employed temporary expedients on a kind of chaotic *ad hoc* basis. On land, the emperors, especially Galleinus (253-268), used hastily improvised military units, *de facto* forming a mobile field army composed of mainly cavalry. The naval forces of the Empire were apparently beset by the same disintegration of the formal organizational structures of the past, but the records are confused and murky for this chaotic period. The old naval units were superseded or underwent drastic changes. Temporary formations of a new type crop up. The task of combating piracy and 'barbarian' marauders over wide swathes of the Empire was turned over to local strongmen – for example, Valerius Statilius Castus was credited with providing security on sea and land in Pamphylia (the southern coast of modern-day Turkey). However, there was no formation of a new naval organization that was better adapted to dealing with the changed situation.

There are other reasons why the Italian Praetorian fleets did not give more assistance against the persistent raids and incursions of the Goths. The answer seems to be that they already had their hands full in the west attempting to maintain order. The governor of Egypt, Mussius Aemilianus, seems to have made trouble of some kind in AD 260-262, and this disturbance was perhaps put down by a naval expedition from Italy under the general Aurelius Theodotus. Around 260, Emperor Gallienus appointed M. Cornelius Octavianus, praefect of the Misene fleet, to deal with the native Bavares under their chieftain Faraxen. This was a revolt that spread across North Africa from Mauretania, through Numidia. Also, a band of Franks who had settled in Thrace seized vessels and made a marauding trip through the Mediterranean to the Strait of Gibraltar, and then returned to their homeland. This Frankish escapade occurred about 280. If true, it was an amazing journey for a supposedly non-seafaring folk.

On the northern frontier, the 'barbarians', now often partly civilized by long contact with Roman traders, grouped themselves in larger units and repeatedly broke the Roman defence. Again, we encounter the story of the marauding Franks. Everywhere piracy is once again a problem.

At the other end of the Roman Empire, the Britannic fleet fought Saxon pirates, starting in AD 275. With their agile boats, the Saxons raided wildly with surprise attacks from hidden coves and inlets against the Channel and East Coast of Britain. This struggle with the pirate fleets lasted until 287.

The Augustan naval set-up had disintegrated, but only on the northern frontiers did a solid substitute spring up to replace its fragments. Beset by wars and civil unrest, the emperors of this period tended to abandon the Mediterranean to pirates and 'barbarians'.

Troubles in the North-West: Gaul and Britain

On the Rhine frontier, the Germanic fleet had to be employed in AD 280. Several *naves lusioriae* (river warships) were burned during the fighting. A casual reference in the *Augustan Histories* indicated that Roman *lusioriae*, built perhaps by Aurelian or Probus, patrolled the Rhine in 280. Gallienus had partly rebuilt the Rhine defences; those ships that the Romans had burnt, but the restoration of the frontier by Maximian, the colleague of Diocletian, undoubtedly entailed the construction of other light vessels.

By AD 285, the Franks and Saxons had begun raids along the English Channel, which continued until they became settlers and rulers in the fifth century. However, in this period Diocletian quickly took steps to check this unrest in the west. His assistant in the area, Maximian, appointed an army officer, Marcus Aurelius Musaeus Carausius, to command the Britannic fleet at Gesoriacum. Born to a Gaulish tribe with a seafaring tradition, Carausius had come to the attention of Maximian through his bravery and skill as a pilot.

At first, Carausius seems to have pursued his duties with skill and zeal, yet ugly rumours soon began to percolate back to his imperial master. In AD 286, Carausius was combating an influx of Frisians, Franks and Saxons raiding along the English Channel, for which task many new naval vessels were built. In the course of a dispute over the spoils of war, tensions arose with the Emperor Maximian. Carausius was said to have betrayed the movements of merchant ships to the Saxon pirates and to let them raid with impunity. Then, when the pirates were returning home, he would swoop down on them, seize the booty, and keep it for himself.

Orders for the arrest of Carausius and his officers were issued, but he caught wind of them before they could be carried out and took the fleet to Britain after first destroying shipping all along the coast of Gaul to prevent pursuit. Bypassing the direct route through Dover, he effected a landing on Britain's north-west coast. Evading, or perhaps bribing, the garrisons along Hadrian's Wall, he marched on London. Quintus Bassanius, governor of Britain, hurriedly gathered together a force to meet him. When the two forces met, Carausius managed to bribe much of Bassanius' army to stay neutral, and the governor, as well as his senior staff, were slaughtered in the ensuing battle.

The victorious Carausius declared himself emperor and made London his administrative capital. For the first time in more than 200 years, Britain was independent of the Roman Empire. Most of Britain looked to him as a deliverer and he fulfilled the role as much as possible by providing competent government and sweeping the seas of pirates from the Channel to the mouth of the Rhine. His control extended as far north as Hadrian's Wall, and he even maintained a presence in Gaul at Boulogne and other parts of the Channel coast.

This was the only occasion in the entire history of the Roman Empire when a usurper rested his rule on sea power.

While Maximian was occupied elsewhere, he could do nothing against the powerful seaborne forces commanded by Carausius, including naval infantry (marines) and cavalry. In order to fight the insurrection (or secession), it was imperative for Maximian to construct a new fleet. The ships had to be built and placed on the great rivers in the interior of Gaul, as the coastal sites, most importantly the port of Gesoriacum (Boulogne), were firmly in Carausius' hands.

Another problem for Emperor Maximian was the crews. Experienced sailors were not available, and the commanders could only manage 'dry exercises' as Carausius dominated the high seas with his warships. When the Roman fleet entered the English Channel, it promptly encountered a storm and was sunk.

Although, under Carausius, the Romans had held the German tribes in check, the Franks nonetheless succeeded in AD 288 in taking the area occupied by the Batavians and the islands lying off the Rhine and Scheldt estuaries. The Frisians occupied the island of Walcheren, the homeland of the Canninefaten folk. The members of both of these tribes had been displaced since the first century BC and served as mercenaries in the Roman legions.

In the meantime, Carausius' usurpation had been neither forgotten nor forgiven, and the Empire made preparations to strike back. Thanks to Carausius' destruction of Channel shipping, this took a while to accomplish and the newly built Roman fleet did not sail for Britain until April 289. Owing to poor weather and inexperienced pilots, the Roman fleet was heavily defeated and Emperor Maximian was forced to come to terms with Carausius. The usurper was recognized as an independent imperial colleague, at least so far as Britain was concerned. Carausius received some part of Belgica, issued coins bearing galleys and other symbols of naval power, and successfully guarded his realm against sea raiders.

Meanwhile, the Germanic tribes, foremost the Franks and Saxons, took advantage of the internal problems of the Romans to mount their own expeditions along the coasts of Gaul and Britain. For the first time, they utilized Roman warship designs, but those were adapted to suit their requirements. One example of this type of ship has been discovered and is preserved in a museum as the Nydam ship.

In AD 293, both the Augusti chose two Caesars and assigned to one, Constantius Chlorus, the task of guarding Gaul and reconquering Britain. Constantius isolated Carausius by besieging the port of Gesoriacum (Boulogne), and invading

Batavia in the Rhine delta, securing his rear against Carausias' Frankish allies. At Gesoriacum, a mole was constructed outside the mouth of the harbour, damming it up and preventing reinforcements and supplies from reaching the beleaguered garrison. With all hope of relief gone, the city was eventually forced to surrender. If they had held out just a little while longer, things might have ended differently, for the first high tide after the fall of the city burst through the dam and reopened the harbour. The fall of Gesoriacum was a terrible blow to Carausius' prestige and one from which he never got the chance to recover.

Carausius' grip on power was lethally undermined. Allectus, whom he had put in charge of his treasury, assassinated him and assumed power himself. His reign would last only three years. After the capture of Gesoriacum in 293, Constantius spent three years in building a fleet, which sailed from the Seine estuary in the spring of 296 in two divisions.

An expeditionary force was embarked for Britain under the command of Asclepiodotus. Undetected by the usurper Allectus, due to foggy weather, the units could disembark unhindered along Southampton Water. One rebel squadron was posted to Insula Vectis (Isle of Wight) but failed to locate either of Constantius' forces and was not engaged. Asclepiodotus allowed his ships to be burned and marched immediately to Londinium (London). This behaviour shows that the rebel fleet, as previously, was superior. Allectus dispatched his ground troops and a few marines who were stationed in the southern ports to join the fighting. Somewhere in north Hampshire or Berkshire, Asclepiodotus' army fought the British forces and routed them. The usurper Allectus lost his life in the battle. Constantius sailed from Gesoriacum with the rest of his fleet and crossed the Thames estuary. This second invasion fleet was merely supposed to protect the first fleet to land troops on the Kent coast, but became separated in the fog, eventually landing near Londinium. This turned out to be a lucky break for there they met and annihilated some of the survivors of Allectus' army, including Frankish pirates who had made their way back to Londinium with the idea of looting the place before dispersing. This enabled Constantius to declare himself the victor and the deliverer of the city, commemorating his success by issuing a large medallion showing him on horseback with the personification of the city kneeling before him, and inscribed 'Restorer of Eternal Light'. Britain was once again a province of the Roman Empire and would remain so until the Legions withdrew forever in AD 410.

What of the *classis Britannica*, the first British navy? Whatever remained of it after the defeat of Allectus, whether it retained that name or not, was integrated back into the Roman forces. When the legions finally withdrew from British shores, they were transported by its descendants and the name vanished into history.

Chapter Fourteen

Naval Renaissance

Situation Circa AD 300

Evidence for the Italian squadrons does continue for a time, but more and more naval activity rested on temporary flotillas recruited for the occasion, as had been the practice in late Republican times. Naval forces (under Diocletian and Constantine) on the northern frontier were yet necessary, and continued as long as Rome could control the waterways. However, the carefully organized squadrons of the early Empire were supplanted by new, smaller flotillas, each based on a single port and patrolling a small area. While the Praetorian fleets had been greatly diminished in this period, there is some evidence that the Italian fleets may have at least been somewhat reorganized by Diocletian at the end of the third century. It was these reorganized squadrons that were presumably used by Maxentius, the tyrant of Rome, in AD 311 to restore his control of Africa, but they were unable to retain control of the Tyrrhenian Sea for him against Constantine's fleet in 312. Just as earlier with Vespasian, an invader of Italy found it essential to cut off the grain supply of Rome by blockading the west coast ports.

To sum up the situation at the end of the third century, the Roman navy had declined dramatically. Although Emperor Diocletian is held to have strengthened the navy and increased its manpower from 46,000 to 64,000 men, the old standing fleets had all but vanished, and in the civil wars that ended the Tetrarchy, the opposing sides had to mobilize the resources and commandeer the ships of the port cities of the Eastern Mediterranean.

Fleet Operations of Constantine

Constantine, son of Constantius who had brought Britain back under Roman control, proved to be a ruler who had recognized the strategic importance of sea power in all its aspects, and his single-minded fleet operational policy sustained this virtue. Since AD 306 the Emperor of the western parts of the Empire, based in Eboracum (York) – and later sole ruler (324-337) – realized, from his study of the situation, that the isolation of the British fleet, separated from the continent by a then formidably rough Channel, made it problematic to amass deployable naval units in a corner of the Empire. He analyzed with great clarity a situation created by the sequestering of Britain's warships and the resulting waste of the Britannic fleet.

With the legacy of his father's invasion of Britain still fresh in his mind, as well as Maxentius' more recent invasion of Africa, Constantine may have felt that he could draw from a reservoir of naval experience that his opponent, Licinius, would be hard-pressed to match. News that a fleet was building would give Licinius something to worry about: was Constantine's plan for a direct assault, or was it to land troops by sea somewhere in the rear of his army? Anything that would inject a degree of uncertainty into Licinius' deliberations would be useful – he had shown himself rather too competent when it came to a straight-up confrontation.

Thus, Licinius strengthened the Rhine frontier, not only with military fortifications, but also by reorganizing the Germanic fleet. Until then it mainly consisted of transport vessels and liburnians. Since the third century AD, there had developed the *Navis Lusoria* (light flow – i.e., shallow draft – combat ships), and now all the remaining liburnians were replaced by this new type of combat ship. In 306, Constantine moved troops to the Rhine and devastated the home base of the Bructeri just across the Rhine. The river crossings were also improved. In Cologne, he built a wooden bridge over the Rhine which rested on stone pilings.

From AD 310, Constantine was involved in combat with Maxentius and Maximian, co-regents of the Tetrarchy. Maximinian had gone to Massilia (Marseilles). Constantine introduced a fleet to blockade the coast of southern Gaul and block Massilia to prevent the escape of Maximian and launch assaults against his son Maxentius, who was residing in Rome. In Caballadunum (Chalon-sur-Saone, France), Constantine's ships organized a fleet in the Saone estuary and he sailed with it down the Saone and the Rhone. Meanwhile, his legions had taken Massilia. Maximian was forced out in 311 and committed suicide.

In AD 312 Constantine occupied the Italian ports and then set out from southern Gaul with a fleet, augmented with a strong force from Italy, to land marines and occupy the offshore islands and Africa. These large-scale fleet efforts, although unopposed, reveal that there was still considerable strength in Rome's naval forces at this time. The following year, the *classis Germanica* moved back into Germania and was once again so strong that it could aggressively conduct offensive patrols along the Rhine tributaries, ensuring border security.

The reunion of Britain with the Empire (after defeat of Carausius/Allectus) did not end the threat of piracy. Rather, it made new measures necessary and the British fleet acquired greater importance than ever before. Constantius was probably the person responsible for the construction of twelve forts along the southeastern shore of England, the Saxon Shore, which guarded harbours from which fleet detachments apparently operated. Evidence of Roman naval activity occurs sporadically down through Julian's operations in Gaul. Vegetius notes the light camouflaged craft used by the British fleet against the pirates, and the *Notitia Dignitatum* records a distinct type developed from the classic *Sambrica*, affirmed by archaeological evidence from one of the ports, Etaples on the Canche River.

Naval Battle of the Hellespont

Sea power was to play an important part in the campaign of Constantine against Licinius in AD 324, which brought to an end the period of unrest after Diocletian's abdication. In that year, Constantine, a staunch sea-power advocate, was encouraged at the prospect of a successful combined land-sea operation for landing a fleet in his opponent's rear. In preparation for his conflict in the East with his co-regent Licinius, Constantine expanded the naval port in Thessalonica (Greece) in 322. Most units of the Roman fleets were obsolete and in need of repair, and by 321 he had built 200 monoremes, mostly triakonters, but also some pentekonters, allowing him to decommission the numerous polyremes. The new ship types had only a single rank of rowers and were thus equivalents of the Germanic ships of the end of the third century. The triakonters had a total of thirty rowers, the pentekonters fifty.

These new types of monoreme had already been utlized by Carausius against the Frankish and Saxon raiders in the third century. The towering polyreme had had its day, as there were hardly any major battles at sea that would favour the cumbersome craft. Instead, sea warfare now predominantly involved tactical landing operations – raids. The German boats had always been exclusively monoremes, with thirty to thirty-six men at the oars. By AD 323, Constantine, as well as his 200 modern warships, had some 2,000 transports assembled at Piraeus. Many of the ships were from Greece, but most were newly built for the occasion. His opponent had a fleet of 350 warships, mainly older model triremes at anchor in the Dardanelles, prepared for combat in the harbours and bays flanking the Hellespont. Self-confident, Constantine landed with his fleet at the rear of the enemy, but Licinius frustrated this project, and Constantine recalled his fleet and set his army to march overland.

Licinius entrenched himself in Byzantium, and as long as the Dardanelles were closed off by his fleet, he could not be defeated. This was the situation facing the two opposing naval commanders, Amandus on Licinius' side and Flavius Valerius Crispus on Constantine's. Crispus had his van well guarded, backed by several squadrons following an advance force of eighty ships. He faced some 200 triremes of Amandus. The battle took place at the narrowest point of the strait, and although Crispus' fast and manoeuvrable triakonters outmanoeuvred the cumbersome triremes, neither side could gain the upper hand. In the narrow waterways Amandus' numerous triremes were jam-packed and crashed into one another, disabling some and causing others to become tangled. They could neither develop or use their numerical superiority. Crispus' squadrons inflicted considerable losses on the crowded triremes, engaging them with their fast and agile triakonters. However, the sought-after decisive breakthrough failed. Thus Crispus pulled his fleet, with the transports, back to Elaius (Seddulbahir, Turkey) at the western entrance to the Hellepont, at which time Amandus sought protection in the Bay of Kum Kali.

The two fleets met again on the following day. The second clash was fought near the present site of Gallipoli, where so many British and Allied troops perished in the ill-fated amphibious landings of 1915. Amandus had again formed his fleet in order of battle, when he realized that Crispus had strengthened his naval forces in the meantime with pentekonters. Accordingly, Amandus hesitated to begin the fight. The actual outcome of the battle was influenced by the weather. A storm wrecked 130 of Amandus' ships, smashing them against the cliffs on the Asian shore and sinking them along with their embarked land forces. Crispus had suffered no losses from the storm, since his fleet was able to reach shelter in the port of Elaius. Thus depleted, Amandus had to withdraw to the eastern end of the Hellespont to regroup his forces, giving way to Crispus, particularly as the latter had received reinforcements. This naval victory allowed Constantine to move his army across to Asia Minor, using a fleet of light transports to avoid the forces of Martinianus, commander of Licinius' bodyguard. Once Licinius knew of the destruction of his navy, he withdrew his forces from Byzantium. Whether or not he consciously articulated this thought, his actions acknowledged the powerful leverage on military affairs conferred by command of the strategic waterways, and the vulnerabilities incurred by its loss.

Crispus then managed to cross over with significant portions of his army to Calchedon on the opposite Asiatic shore, and augmented his core forces to establish a new army of 130,000 men. He next achieved a surprise troop landing on the shore near the foothills of Hiero Akron (Kavak in Anatolia, Turkey) south-east of Calchedon, an inhospitable and unlikely landing spot due to the rough terrain. Constantine's army then defeated Licinius at the Battle of Chrysopolis. This victory was the final battle in the conflict, Licinius surrendering himself following the battle. Constantine consequently became the sole master of the Roman Empire.

As sole ruler, Constantine founded not only the new capital city named for him (Constantinople), but also Eleutherias harbour on the coast of the Propontis (Sea of Marmora). For this new large harbour, Constantine took 330 vessels from the two old main fleets, Ravenna and Misenum – thus, after a long period of stagnation, an emperor breathed new life into a powerful Roman fleet.

Constantius versus Magnentius: Strategic Employment of the Fleet

The development of Roman naval power did not fail to leave its stamp on Constantine's successors. In the fight against the Franks, beginning in AD 341, Constans utilized Bononia (the old Gesoricum, Boulogne) as the base for his campaign. He similarly utilized this base for a campaign in Britain in 343. The British fleet was not especially employed in the fighting, when the Picts invaded the north again this same year, but when it crossed the Channel in strength with Constans, it was more in the way of a show of force – a demonstration of Roman power. This employment of the fleet is akin to 'showing the flag', most notably in 'gunboat diplomacy' situations which characterized British policing actions in colonial outposts in the late 1800s and US pacification patrols along the Yangtze River in the 1920s.

Meanwhile, Constans' successor, Constantius II, continued in the East the fleet policy of his father by building a new modern port in Seleucia Pierae (Samandag in modern Turkey), the ancient stronghold of the Syrian fleet, and in AD 351, just ten months from laying down the keels, built numerous new vessels and put them into service. Just as Constantine, he was fully aware of the strategic, war-winning potential of the fleet.

Vegetius, writing at the end of the fourth century, attests the disappearance of the old Praetorian fleets in Italy, but comments on the continued activity of the Danube fleet. By the fifth century, only the eastern half of the Empire could field an effective fleet, as it could draw upon the maritime resources of Greece and the Levant. Naval units in the Western Empire were too depleted to be able to carry out much more than patrol duties.

In the land Battle of Mursa on the Drau (Drava at Osijek), Constantius II managed to defeat the Frankish usurper Magnentius, who then fled to Italy. Upon his arrival in Italy, Magnentius apparently left the Ravennate fleet on the east coast unmolested, so Constantius devised a strategy involving the fleet to thwart his opponent's efforts to link up with his main army in the Alps. In AD 352, Constantius took his fleet around the south of Italy and Sicily and landed troops at the Po estuary in Gaul, encircling Magnentius' reserve force from the rear and preventing it from joining the small force already in Italy. There appear to have been further landings in Spain near the Pyrenees, with the object of applying a pincer manoeuvre against Magnentius' isolated forces. This textbook example of a comprehensive strategical landing forced Magnentius to abandon Italy and return to Gaul, where he was defeated in a land battle and committed suicide.

We learn that in the following year, Constantius mounted a naval expedition which recaptured the provinces of Africa, regaining the important harbour of

Carthage, and Hispania from forces loyal to Magnentius, but little is known of the composition of this fleet. Considering the fleet landing operations during this year, over considerable distances in far-flung sea areas, we can perceive very clearly the strategic employment of a Roman war fleet with decisive results. The very fact of such a wide-ranging naval enterprise does speak of the continued value of the fleets, of whatever origin or composition, in the middle of the fourth century to further Rome's domestic and foreign policy.

Chapter Fifteen

Later Fourth Century:
Divided Empire, Divided Fleets

Naval Power in Rome's Battles with the Franks

From AD 355, Constantius II entrusted to his cousin Julian (whom he elevated to the rank of Caesar) the protection of the Rhine frontier against the continuing incursions of the Franks and Alemani. The Roman Germanic fleet was employed by Julian repeatedly in 356 and 357 for Rhine crossings and 'fights on the Main' (the Main River). In 357 and 358, in opposition to the invasion of Lower Germany by the Franks, Julian enclosed an island of the Meuse with the help of his ships.

Naves lusoriae (riverine warships) had completely replaced the river *liburniae* in the fourth century, but were hindered from patrolling by a sheet of solid ice. The Franks were forced to surrender after two months. In AD 359 a squadron of forty river combat ships comprised a crucial segment of the fight against the Alemanni, confederation of Suebian Germanic tribes located on the upper Rhine. Julian undertook a punitive expedition against the Alemanni, who by then were in Alsace, and crossed the Main.

As the Germanic provinces had suffered economically from the incursions of the Germanic invaders, and very large contingents of troops were in the region, Julian built up within ten months a transport fleet of 400 boats, thereby increasing the capacity of the Britannic fleet by 200 per cent.

This fleet began the grain trade from Britain to the Rhine. There the cargo was offloaded and taken aboard by river vessels in areas that had suffered under the Germanic invasions. The sea transport took place without a hitch. This was proof that the Britannic fleet was maintained even at this date on the high seas – in the Channel and the adjacent areas of the North Sea that were subjected to the increasing activities of the Germanic naval forces.

In 360, Lupicinius brought over to Britain, under the protection of the *classis Britannica*, auxiliary troops from Bononia (Boulogne) to Rutipiae (Richborough) to throw back the Scots and Picts who had penetrated Roman territory in northern Britain.

Julian's Parthian Campaign

Proclaimed Emperor in AD 361, Julian was in Constantinople and there built yet another naval base named after him, Port Julius – which was still used by naval forces in the seventh century. He, like his predecessors, appreciated the value of combat-ready naval forces to defend the realm. Already in 361, he had embarked a 3,000-man force on the Pannonian fleet in Raetia (comprising the districts occupied in modern times by eastern and central Switzerland) in his march eastward, and via the Danube brought them to the mouth of the Sava River.

In AD 363, Julian moved successfully against the Persians up to Ctesiphon on the Tigris River, which had previously resisted all efforts to take it; but this time the Emperor had built a fleet (the Euphrates flotilla) of fifty warships and an equal number of pontoons, in addition to 1,100 transport ships. The river fleet, under the command of Constantius Lucillianus, proceeded parallel with the march of the army – more than 60,000-strong – from Samasota along the Euphrates (near Calgan, Turkey). Part of the legions was aboard the fleet transports and kept pace with the army advancing on the river bank. The embarked combat troops, resting aboard the ships, constituted the operational reserve. The cooperation between the land and river forces was excellent. The river flotilla proved valuable in defeating the Persian fortifications erected on islands in the Euphrates. The large number of supply vessels, with food and other materiel on board, took care of the land army's logistic needs. When Julian decided that, having failed to thus far engage the main Persian forces in a major battle, his lines were overextended, he opted to withdraw the advanced legions back to unite with the reserve force.

At first consideration, it is puzzling that the Emperor burned the fleet when he decided to turn back to proceed up the Tigris in order to connect with his second land army. Perhaps this was done so that he would not have to laboriously work the supply/troop vessels back upstream and thus slow the tactical withdrawal/regrouping of his land forces. Perhaps unwise from a strategical standpoint, this decision – as luck would have it – proved felicitous, as Julian was killed in battle shortly thereafter and any intact ships would have fallen into the hands of the Persians.

Campaigns On The Empire's North-Western Fringe

In the West, Flavians Valentian was proclaimed Emperor Valentianus I (AD 364-375) by his troops. In the succession for leadership in the eastern half of the Empire, Emperor Valens (364-378) joined his brother, who now ruled the West. In 364, the Britannic fleet was constantly employed in resisting the persistent and increasingly successful sea-borne attacks of the Picts and Scots. The attacks became progressively menacing until, in 367, Nectarides, the commander of coastal defence in Britain, was killed. In the fourth century, the areas of the Wash and the Solent were exposed to intensified attacks from a Saxon squadron, while the Franks devastated the coasts of Gaul.

In Britain, there was completed – between Norfolk and the Isle of Wight – the so-called Saxon shore, which extended the system of forts harbouring smaller fleets and signal stations under a single commander-in-chief with the title *Comes Litoris Saxonici*. The construction of this system had begun under Carausius in AD 286, but was suspended after the defeat of his attempted usurpation. The continuing attacks of the Scots and the Picts against Roman frontier fortifications in northern Britain necessitated a campaign against them. Theodosius, commander-in-chief (*Magister Militum*) in 368, used the Britannic fleet to bring from Bononia to Rutupiae several legions via the Channel. Assisting the efforts of the legions on land, the fleet was successful in naval battles with the Saxons.

Late Fourth Century: Maritime Policing and Civil Strife

In AD 373, in order to defeat the Berber insurgents in western Mauritania, North Africa (approximately today's Algeria), under one Firmus, Theodosius, father of the future Emperor Theodosius I, led troops which were embarked in Arelate (Arles, France) and sent across the Mediterranean to put down the rebellion. The military details of this operation are lacking, but it demonstrates the use of troop transport to dispatch legions to quell local uprisings.

In AD 374, during the reign of the Emperor Valentianus I, the Visigothic tribes, Qaudi and Jazygians (Iazyges) invaded from the east and penetrated Pannonia, achieving a breakthrough across the Danube River frontier. The Pannonian fleet had little success in their operations against the invaders. Since the Pannonian fleet proved less than effective, there was a reorganization of the Pannonian squadrons, which were subsumed under several authorities.

After Emperor Valentianus was killed in AD 375 fighting against the Visigoths at Adrianopolis, Theodosius I (379-395), son of *Magister militum* Promotus, ascended the throne of the eastern half of the Empire. The Britannic commander of the western Roman forces, Maximus (Maximus Magnus), was proclaimed emperor by his troops in 383 to oppose Theodosius. At that time, there prevailed in the western half, Gratian, a son of Emperor Valentianus I. Emperor Gratian was killed in Gaul in 383 while fleeing the troops of Maximus, who had crossed the Channel with the Britannic fleet. His successor was Emperor Valentinian II (383-392).

In AD 386 the usurper Maximus penetrated to the apportioned territory of the Greutungen Ostrogoths, a *foederatus* (land grant under contract with barbaric warriors who would serve with the legions) in a Roman district on the lower

Danube. There the *Magister militum*, Promotus (Petronius Probus), vanquished a Greutungen Ostrogoth invasion with the Moesian fleet, midstream as they were in the process of crossing the Danube with 3,000 'war canoes'.

While Theodosius I conducted war in the Balkans in AD 388, that same year he sent a fleet against Maximus under the western Emperor Valentinian II to Rome to attack the usurper in Italy. Naval forces of Maximus under the command of Andragathius tried to intercept the fleet before it could land. The attempt failed and actually weakened Maximus' forces in the Alps because troops for the naval forces had to be siphoned off from there. Having failed, Andragathius committed suicide. Valentinian was able to land in Italy, occupying the peninsula without any battles; such battles there were took place only in Sicily. In AD 388, Maximus was captured and killed in Aquileia. These events are evidence that at the end of the fourth century, the Western Roman Empire began to neglect the fleet.

Meanwhile, it became clear that the fleet which Constantine had reinvigorated was increasingly neglected in favour of the ground forces. After the division of the Empire in AD 395 and the capture of Rome by the Goths in 410, the western Roman navy sank into insignificance. Subsequently, the Vandals established themselves as the greatest naval power in the Western Mediterranean.

Chapter Sixteen

Naval Operations at Ebb Tide

Vandal Attacks, Fifth Century

In AD 401, the Visigoths under King Alaric moved to invade Italy but were repelled by an army under Stilicho. Once more, troops were brought from Britannia and other areas to bolster Stilicho's forces, which went on to defeat Alaric twice more. In 408, Alaric and his Visigoths again entered Italy and laid siege to Rome; Honorius withdrew troops from the north but failed to end the usurpation of Constantine, who remained in Britannia and Gaul. Also in 408, Arcadius died, to be succeeded by the infant Thoedosius II as Emperor of the East, where they were themselves beset by problems and unable to lend assistance to the West. In any event, a split having been made, it *de facto* regarded itself as a separate entity by this time.

But in AD 410, the Goths under Alaric took Rome. The western fleet was by this time a non-entity. This erosion of effective Roman sea power, along with overland incursions, led to the rise of the Vandal Empire. Although originating from North Jutland, where they had been farmers, in their new home in Silesia, western Poland and Hungary, they had become horsemen. But the Vandals quickly learned during their stay in Spain how to conduct naval warfare, trained by captive Roman seamen on conquered Roman ships. As early as 425, they conducted piracy on the coasts of the Balearic Islands and Mauritania. In 428, most likely by combined land and sea operations, they took Carthago Nova (Cartagena) and Hispalis (Seville), the last naval base bastions by which the Romans sought to control access to the Mediterranean.

In AD 429, a mobile confederation of the Asding Vandals and a portion of the Alans, numbering some 80,000 in total and led by Genseric, crossed the Strait of Gibraltar from Iulia Traducta (now Algeciras, at the southern promontory of Spain) in order to reach Mauritania and Africa. They met with little resistance from the Mauritanian fleet. The Mauritanian army based at Caesarea (Cherchell, Algeria), which had since 415 successfully operated against the Visigoths, was obviously too weak to prevent the invasion of Mauritania.

In AD 439, the Vandals effected another combined land and sea operation to take the strategically important harbour of Carthage. After sacking Hippo Regius in 430, they established their own kingdom in the area of modern Tunis. Next, with his own and captured ships that he obtained in Carthage, Genseric sealed off the important naval port of Lilybaeum (Marsala in western Sicily) and thus obtained unhindered access to the Western Mediterranean. Valentinian III, unable to stave off this menace, recognized the Vandals as *foederati* in 435 and granted them land lying between Sitifensis in eastern Mauritania and the newly established border of western Africa Proconsularis.

Finally recognizing the real danger of the situation, the East and West Roman wings cooperated, and with the help of the fully intact Byzantine fleet's warships they forced the Vandals to retreat from Sicily. The naval power of the Vandals, however, could not be broken, and the coasts of southern Italy, Sicily and Corsica were constantly ravaged by raids.

The peace between Rome and her new Vandal 'allies' proved ephemeral. Hostilities recommenced on 19 October AD 439, when a combined naval-land operation attacked by the Vandal chieftains Gaiseric and Huneric Carthage and retained possession of this key base, which comprised a strategically significant position in the Western Mediterranean. However, since the legions of Eastern Rome were needed to fight against the Huns, there was a further Vandal invasion of Africa, which consolidated their hold on the Western Mediterranean's southern shore.

In AD 442, Vandal fleets ravaged the coastal towns of Sicily, southern Italy and Corsica. The Vandals then began their devastating raids on grain-rich Sicily, The Sicilian attacks were not merely the result of a desire for booty: they were undertaken to force Rome into granting further territorial concessions. The peace treaty of 442 formalized the Vandal conquests in Africa and their empire in that continent, with Carthage as its capital. Carthage thereby once more became a metropolis upon which a sea empire was based. The Vandals ruled unchallenged in the Western Mediterranean.

Thanks to the superiority of his fleet, the Vandal King Genseric conquered Rome in AD 455, for there was nothing with which to oppose him. In 460, Roman Emperor Maiorianus (Majorian), using the remnants of the two main Italian fleets, attempted to restore Rome's command of the sea. Sailing recklessly into the Bay of Illici (Elche, Spain), 300 vessels of the Roman fleet were destroyed or captured by deputies of Genseric. The planned Roman invasion of Africa was rendered unfeasible due to the loss of the Roman flotilla, and the Vandals were able to extend their raids to Illyria and Greece.

Being as now Eastern Roman territory was affected, they prepared a large-scale operation against the enemy at its base in Carthage. In AD 467, Eastern Emperor Leo I and Western Emperor Anthemius sent an invasion force to drive out the Vandals and reconquer Africa. The Eastern Roman fleet consisted of about 1,200 vessels of all classes, carrying just over 100,000 men, about 70,000 comprising the land force. After taking the island of Sardinia from the Vandals, the army disembarked near Carthage. At this point, a small, newly built fleet of the Western Roman Empire was tasked to secure the islands of the Western Mediterranean. The Eastern contingent formed up in front of the Promunturium Mercurii (Cap Bon), where it joined up with the Western fleet.

Regrettably, the fleet was under the command of Basiliscus. Being as he was the brother of Emperor Leo's wife, nepotism trumped military ability and sound judgment. Basiliscus crowded the ships of the fleet into the harbour until there was hardly any room to manoeuvre, and to compound the error an inadequate watch was set. The Vandals made a surprise night attack with 200 ships, and with the massive use of fire-ships destroyed half the invasion fleet. This led, in AD 474, to the forced recognition of Vandal domination of North Africa, Corsica, Sardinia, Sicily, and the Balearic Islands. This disaster also effectively spelled the end of a Western Roman fleet.

In the middle of the next century, the Emperor Justinian was determined to drive out the barbarian invaders holding the western provinces of the Roman Empire. The obstacles were enormous, and after the disastrous fiasco of AD 467 he needed someone to successfully lead the army in this new invasion. A young general from Thrace named Belisarius had just made a name for himself by defeating a Persian army nearly twice his size. Justinian felt he had found his man.

Chapter Seventeen

Gotterdammerung of the 'Roman' Navy, Rise of the Byzantine Fleet

The Roman Reconquest of North Africa, AD 533-534

While the Romans called the Vandals 'barbarians', they had become somewhat Romanized and had adopted Arian Christianity. Very little is known about the Vandalic language itself, which was of the East Germanic linguistic branch. All that modern historians know about their language is that they were able to speak Latin, which remained the official language of the Vandal administration. But Romanized or not, the Emperor Justinian wanted their lands for himself. They were now proven seafarers, and Justinian appreciated that the Vandals posed a naval and a military challenge.

Finding a general was only the first step. Justinian was responsible for defending an incredibly long border against many enemies. The main enemy at the moment was the Persian Empire. For the first five years of his reign, Justinian reluctantly waged a costly and unprofitable war against the Persians. The victory by Belisarius at Dara in AD 530 (and a huge haul of gold) helped in negotiating (or at least buying) the 'Endless Peace' with the Persians. The Eastern soldiers were now freed up for the invasion of Africa.

Justinian's advisors were solid in their opposition to the campaign. From a military point of view, they felt it was folly to send an invasion fleet of heavy transport ships over 1,000 miles from its home base into enemy-controlled waters, and then to land an outnumbered army (with no reinforcements available) to attack entrenched land forces. In addition, the fleet could only sail in the summer calm of May to November. The autumn and winter storms would leave the army totally cut off. Finance ministers also warned of the huge drain on the treasury, pointing out how the failed attack in AD 467 had nearly bankrupted them.

The Assemblage of the Fleet

The Roman Empire was still the only world power. No other nation had the resources to assemble such a strike force. The logistics alone must have been a nightmare: 36,000 soldiers and sailors, some 6,000 horses, arms, engines, military stores, water and provisions to last for a three-month voyage of over 1,000 miles.

At the harbour of Constantinople, the navy brought together from Egypt, Cilicia and Ionia some 20,000 sailors and 500 transports, ranging in size from 30-500 tons. The proud galleys of old that had made the Mediterranean a Roman lake were long gone. Protecting the fleet were only ninety-two light brigantines. As well as the troops freed up by the peace with Persia, about 10,000 infantry from Thrace and Isauria marched to Constantinople. Another 5,000 excellent cavalry were assigned. There were two additional bodies of Allied troops: 600 Huns and 400 Heruls, all mounted horse archers.

In supreme command of both the navy and the army was Belisarius. Justinian granted Belisarius the title of Autocrator, with almost boundless power to act as if the Emperor himself were present. In June AD 533 the fleet was ready. The Emperor and the Patriarch went in procession down to the docks. Icons waved behind them while marching choirs sang 'Rex gloriae, Domine virtutum' ('King of Glory, Lord of armed hosts'). While the 600 ships were moored in front of the Imperial Palace, the Patriarch offered prayers for the success of the expedition. Most of those who witnessed the sailing felt that they would never return.

Small as the forces looked on paper, this was a major effort by the Empire. Failure could do serious damage to its defence. At the very best, the Eastern Roman army and navy numbered no more than 150,000. The hard core professional battlefield regiments were a much smaller number. The force of 36,000 committed to the invasion amounted to 24 per cent of their armed strength. No more troops could be committed without leaving the huge borders of the Empire defenceless.

Smoothing the Way

Facing the Romans would be a Vandal land force of perhaps 30,000, plus a large fleet. The Emperor recognized that diplomacy was a vital ingredient to a successful invasion. Perhaps a revolution or two would draw Vandal attention and troops from the main attack. He encouraged a rising of pro-Roman factions in Tripolitana with a small military force, and successfully drove out the Vandals. Justinian urged the Vandal governor of Sardinia to rebel, which he did. There was also a dynastic quarrel among Vandals. Gelimer had deposed Hilderic as king three years before, and was keeping him and a few supporters as prisoners. Justinian also used a dispute between the Goths of Italy and the Vandals to his advantage. The Goths granted the Romans permission to dock their invasion fleet in Sicily on the way to Africa.

King Gelimer reacted to the revolutions just as Justinian had hoped. The king dispatched his brother Zano with 5,000 soldiers and 120 galleys to recapture Sardinia. Now there would be no Vandal fleet nearby to attack the Roman troop transports when they were at their most vulnerable, and a large part of the Vandal army would be wasted on a distant island. By making no attempt to recover Tripolitana, Gelimer also ensured that if a Roman army made it to Africa, it would be landing on a somewhat more friendly soil.

The Invasion

The Roman fleet suffered thirst, having been becalmed for sixteen days. An additional 500 men died from disease. Finally, after many weeks, they were able to dock at Caucana on the southern shore of Sicily, where Gothic officers had been ordered to help provision the troops. Intelligence was gathered on the Vandals' movements. Belisarius was urged to speed the operation. The fleet set sail again, passed Malta and finally dropped anchor five days' sail south of Carthage. Before landing, Belisarius held a council or war with some of his generals. They urged that they sail straight for Carthage and surprise it, but Belisarius overruled this view. No one knew the exact location of the Vandal fleet. With the disaster of AD 467 in mind, he felt it was better to get on dry land without delay.

Some three months after their departure from Constantinople, the army and its supplies safely made it to shore. The fleet was formed into a semicircle, with five soldiers stationed on each ship as a guard. The rest of the army built a camp on the shore, 'which they fortified, according to ancient discipline, with a ditch and rampart' (Edward Gibbon, *The History of the Decline and Fall of the Roman Empire*, Volume V. Boston: Little, Brown and Company, 1854, p.106). On the next morning, Belisarius awoke to find neighbouring gardens pillaged. He sharply rebuked the offenders, saying:

> 'When I first accepted the commission of subduing Africa I depended much less on the numbers, or even the bravery of my troops, than on the friendly disposition of the natives, and their immortal hatred of the Vandals. You alone can deprive me of this hope; if you continue to extort by rapine what might be purchased for a little money, such acts of violence will reconcile these implacable enemies, and unite them in a just and holy league against the invaders of their country.' (*The Historians' History of the World: A Comprehensive Narrative of the Rise and Development of Nations as Recorded by over two thousand of the Great Writers of all Ages*, Volume VII, 'The Later Roman Empire', compiled by Henry Smith Williams. London: The History Association, 1904, p.91)

A rigid discipline was enacted, which soon resulted in the natives selling all supplies possible to the Romans.

Belisarius began the ten to twelve day march to Carthage along a road that followed the coast. He sent out 3 miles ahead of the army 300 horse under John the Armenian as advance guard. The contingent of 600 Huns was ordered to march the same distance to the left of the road to protect against a flank attack. The entire fleet was instructed to sail within sight of the land forces to cover the right flank. During the march, a number of towns went over to the Romans without a fight.

Belisarius went on to take the Vandal capital of Carthage after victories at Ad Decimum and Tracamarum: thus did Africa come under the rule of the Eastern Empire.

The Roman fleet next played an important role in the struggle against the Ostrogoths. With only slight numerical superiority in ships of fifty to forty-seven, they achieved victory at Ancona in the Adriatic in AD 551. This success was, moreover, achieved by tactical employment of the ram. Notwithstanding this intense combat, the Ostrogoths retained, at the war's end in 552 a considerable fleet in Spain of 400 dromons.

Further Thoughts on the Ancona Battle

This is usually cited as a naval battle that ended a siege. A large Byzantine army was assembled under the old eunuch general Narses, who marched overland towards northern Italy. According to Procopius, who recorded this war, northern Italy was reasonably secure at this stage. Yet, previously, Belisarius had always been handicapped because this northern route from the western Balkans into northern Italy was blocked due to the invasion of nomadic tribes from north. Narses' rear was by no means secure. Sea communication was still essential for successful execution of his new campaign. Totila, the Ostrogothic king, of course, knew it. He had been challenging Roman dominance at sea, building and acquiring fleets of his own, disrupting Roman sea communication, raiding imperial territories in Greece and elsewhere. But, as Narses was about to shove off, it came down to one naval battle near Ancona (Ancon), also known as the Battle of Sena Gallica (Senigallia) in AD 551. This battle is virtually ignored by modern historians as a mere sideshow, or merely a prelude to the truly decisive final battle in which Totila was killed two years later.

Most Classical scholars and Byzantinists were not interested in naval warfare, and if this Battle of Sena Gallica was a naval engagement of only a modest scale (merely about 100 ships involved), why bother? Only J.B. Bury and W.L. Rodgers dealt with this battle in any meaningful way; more recently, J.A.S. Evans accepted the strategic significance of this battle. The hero of this battle, at least according to Procopius, is a certain 'John', known as the nephew of Vitalian. Together with his colleague Valerian, he commanded the Roman fleet.

This John is a capable but problematic character. During Belisarius' first campaign, John was in charge of a cavalry detachment. After the siege of Rome was lifted, John relentlessly chased the retreating Goths (though he was given a reconnaissance mission) and captured Ariminum (Rimini). This led to a wholesale panic among the Goths – if Belisarius had exploited this situation, he may have ended the war with a total, decisive victory in AD 538. Instead, he was busy with mopping up operations, leaving John besieged in Ariminum and allowing Milan to be destroyed by the counter-attacking Goths. John was perhaps a little hurried and headstrong then. Yet, in 551, John appeared to be a seasoned commander and was fully aware of the larger strategic picture.

When Justinian prepared one last major effort to reclaim Italy, Totila decided to block Ancona to prevent the invasion. He besieged Ancona with forty-seven ships and sent the rest of his fleet, 300 ships strong, to raid the coast of Epirus and the Ionian Islands. Ancona was likely to fall soon, and therefore the Roman commander of Ravenna, Valerian, called upon John, an experienced general who was stationed at Salona (Dalmatia) awaiting the arrival of Narses and his army, to send a relief force. John immediately manned thirty-eight ships with his veterans, and was soon joined by twelve more ships under Valerian himself. The joint fleet set sail for Sena Gallica, some 17 miles north of Ancona.

What was about to happen in the vicinity of Ancona was no mere skirmish: it would determine the outcome of a war. So John, during his pre-battle pep talk to his troops, pointed out that Ancona, which was under Gothic siege, was the last port the Romans controlled. If they lost it, they would lose the last hope of recovering command of the seas and henceforth of bringing in fresh troops to win the war.

What really mattered in warfare was logistics, and in this case, especially naval logistics. Without securing it, the size of Narses' forces did not matter. The Goths, in contrast, seemed to be confident. Their pep talk (again, according to Procopius) shows nothing of strategic rationale. They were feeling totally justified to try to expel Romans from Italy; with one more push, they believed they would win. The size of the opposing naval forces was roughly equal, with both sides deploying about fifty ships. The battle started with a contest of missile firing. The intricate and precise ship manoeuvring skills of old were long gone; most naval battles involved an archery contest. Indeed, Romano-Byzantine warships (dromons) from later centuries show a similar configuration to that of modern combat vessels, with structures like gun turrets in the mid section of the ship erected to provide archers with a secure platform.

After the missile combat phase, in which the Romans blunted the missile assault of the Gothic naval thrust, the ships closed in for a melee. The Roman ability to fight in good formation began to tell. As the Goths had been damaging Roman naval power for the past decade in the absence of strong naval opposition, they did not gain much experience in actual naval combat. The Romans had a similar problem; yet their sailors were better drilled and trained according to accumulated wisdom of naval warfare. In the heat of battle, some Gothic ships drifted off the main body and were easily destroyed, while others sailed too close together and were unable to manoeuvre. In the end, the weary Gothic fleet disintegrated and their ships fled as fast as they could. The Gothic fleet lost cohesion and the Romans seized their chance. Any straggling Gothic ship was rammed and boarded. The main action here involved hand-to-hand combat by boarders. Hard pressed, the Goths gave way; the Romans sensed it and moved in for the kill. The Gothic retreat became a rout, and surviving Gothic ships were abandoned and burned on a beach. The crews and warriors fled inland. They had lost thirty-six ships. It was the last major sea battle fought in the Mediterranean for more than a century.

Procopius concludes this account by implicating that Gothic morale was now broken, even though modern historians are reluctant to take this at face value. Still, it is quite possible that, knowing the strategic picture of the whole war, it dawned on the Goths that the war would go on indefinitely until they were subdued. For all their bravado and optimism, the Goths were war weary. So when the main Roman force of Narses showed up in AD 553, the Goths, and in particular their king Totila, seem to have lost their nerve. Usually such cool customers, now they were fighting like berserk savages who knew nothing about strategy and tactics. They were simply overwhelmed by Narses. Totila fled but died of his wounds (he was possibly hit by a stray arrow).

The Visigothic kingdom was located too far to the west of the Byzantines to be taken, but all the islands of the Mediterranean and the North African coast, along with the Strait of Gibraltar, fell into the hands of Constantinople. This was the last gasp of 'Roman' naval supremacy in the Mediterranean, and the last time it could be called by them *Mare Nostrum* (Our Sea). Until the advent of the Arabs and the raids of the Normans, the Byzantine fleet retained its naval supremacy.

Endgame

We have seen that the rise of the Roman Empire in reality commenced when it won a decisive victory against the Punic navy in the Battle of Mylae. Rome ultimately fell into the hands of Germanic invaders, but 'Rome' connotes by this time only the Western Roman Empire. By the sixth century, it had no fleet. Only Theodoric the Great commenced in AD 526 to reconstruct the naval forces – however, they were no longer under Roman, but rather Germanic rule.

The Eastern Roman navy possessed in their naval base at Constantinople sufficient reserves to compensate for losses suffered. Justinian I (AD 527-565), influenced by a combination of Greek culture and Roman political thought, set out to restore the borders of the old empire. As we have seen, in June 533, his Byzantine fleet, with ninety-two dromons which gained temporary command of the sea, succeeded in landing an invasion force south of Carthage, which eventually fell to Berlisarius.

Even in the struggle against the Ostrogoths the Byzantines played an important role. We have seen how Eastern Roman naval forces, fifty ships strong, played an important part in AD 551 against the Ostrogoths, who had forty-seven ships, in the Byzantine victory at the Battle of Ancona (Sena Gallica, Senigallia). The decisive factor there was likely the tactical employment of the ram. In the last years of the war, the Ostrogoths still possessed a fleet of 400 dromon warships. The Ostrogoth kingdom in Italy was finally overthrown after a twenty-year struggle with the Byzantines in 552. The Visigothic kingdom in Spain persisted, but the Eastern Roman fleet managed to gain control over almost all the African coast, all the islands of the Mediterranean, south-east Spain and the Strait of Gibraltar.

Coda – *Mare Nostrum* to *Mare Aliena*

In most books on naval history, we see a massive gap in the Roman period after the Battle of Actium, which decided the fate of Antony and Cleopatra. *Pax Romana* then broke out under Octavian; no more epic naval battles took place because the Empire successfully removed all naval and maritime threats to civilizations in the Mediterranean basin. The Roman peace meant that the Empire no longer needed a large navy. Roman naval forces at the height of the Empire consisted of small groups performing the tasks of coastguard and police, keeping maritime traffic safe for traders and travellers. And yet, as the grip of Roman power waned from the third century on, the need to rebuild a navy arose.

When Constantine the Great defeated his rivals to become the sole emperor of the Empire and moved the capital from Rome to Byzantium in AD 330, his climactic battle against Maxentius following his 'conversion' to Christianity, having seen a cross over the sun, did not end the civil war. He still had one remaining rival, Licinius, to eliminate, which he achieved by building a navy to control seas around Byzantium, the base of Licinius. His appreciation of the necessity of naval power and its proper employment had been unrivalled since the time of Agrippa in the climactic civil wars of the Republic.

In the fifth century, the need for a strong navy was once again urgent. The Germanic invaders, who were originally land-based bands of warriors and migrants, were learning the art of naval warfare. Their piratical raids now threatened the heartland of the Empire. The Vandals, in particular, invaded and established themselves in Libya by crossing the Strait of Gibraltar. Their kingdom posed a direct threat to Rome itself. The Mediterranean was again the sea of pirates after 400 years of Roman peace. A lack of navy was keenly felt.

In AD 533, the Roman Emperor Justinian made a serious attempt to deal with the Vandal problem. He sent an expeditionary taskforce led by Belisarius, who quickly defeated the Vandals. However, in Italy, a prospect of peacefully reacquiring the whole country from the Goths was foiled. Thus, in 535, Belisarius was sent to conquer Italy and restore the city of Rome to Roman rule. This Gothic War, however, turned out to be a quagmire for Rome. Belisarius easily captured Rome, but was then besieged by the Gothic horde for a whole year. Even though his daring strategic manoeuvres led to the capture of Ravenna, the Gothic capital and the previous seat of the Roman court, the Goths would renew hostilities and recapture the whole of Italy under their new king, Totila. Belisarius had to go back for his second tour of duty, but he would suffer from lack of supplies, reinforcements and morale. The war had devastated Italy, impoverishing local inhabitants, who were no longer disposed favourably towards the Romans. This naturally did not help lift the morale of the Roman leadership. The element of surprise was also gone – in the first campaign, the Goths were not ready for war with the Empire, as they really did not believe that the Romans would actually start war against them, and were also busy fighting the Franks.

Totila, however, obviously learnt Belisarius' tricks and always made moves to pre-empt whatever Belisarius might do. Belisarius could no longer defeat the Goths from a position of numerical inferiority. He appealed again and again to Justinian to send him reinforcements, supplies and money. Money was the most important, as the majority of his troops were paid professionals. When they did not get paid and fed, they could easily switch sides, which Totila readily exploited. The best Belisarius could do was to control the most vital ports for communication between the Empire and Italy to keep Roman prospects alive. The Empire, however, was hard-pressed by other problems. The Balkans was a hotbed of troubles, where waves of invading tribes had to be stopped. 'Justinian's Plague' also broke out in the midst of the Italian campaign in 541, sapping manpower, money and the psychological strength of the Romans.

Totila also appealed to the Persian Empire to intervene. The Persians were at this time the greatest enemy of the Roman Empire. Some modern historians wonder why Justinian bothered to wage war in Italy when Persia was by far the most serious security problem. Fortunately, the Persians did not do much to threaten Rome this time, yet their incursions were enough to divert resources and attention from the West, allowing the situation in Italy to deteriorate. By the end of the 540s, the Romans were just clinging on to some ports on the Adriatic. All remaining Roman forces were hemmed in coastal areas near these ports. Finally Justinian, having recovered from the plague and the loss of his wife Theodora, and sorted out other security problems at least temporarily, resolved to end the war in Italy once and for all by applying a surge strategy which climaxed at the Battle of Ancona described previously.

Thus, after twenty years of struggle, the Empire finally recovered Italy. Yet the end was an anti-climax. Procopius himself at first did not even bother to conclude his account of the war. In retrospect, all was in vain, as Italy would soon be lost to the latest invader, the Lombards; fifty years after the end of this war, the Persians would invade and nearly destroy the Empire; and in the middle of the seventh century, the Arabs would come out with a new religion, Islam, to conquer Egypt and Syria. The Roman Empire would reinvent itself and re-emerge as a regional superpower in the Middle Ages – yet its political and cultural make-ups were so different from those of the Empire that had shaped the Classical world that historians today refuse to call it Roman. We call this new empire Byzantium.

Justinian the Great is often called the last Roman Emperor and Belisarius the last great Roman general. But this minor naval engagement off Ancona is a testimony that the Roman Empire's legacy of military experience was still a great asset for the beleaguered Romans in the East. Worn out by constant conflict and fighting its expeditionary warfare with small task forces of mercenaries, the Roman Empire still boasted the best system of logistics and communication that enabled it to concentrate its material and human resources in order to beat 'barbarians'. This naval battle is further proof that the Empire was still 'Roman' in Justinian's time.

The pressures of maintaining the Western Empire had eventually proved too great for the imperial armies and navies. The hordes of 'barbarians' on the Empire's northern frontiers continuously applied pressure until Rome was sacked by Germanic tribes in AD 410 and 455. By 476, the Western Empire had disintegrated, but by the end of Justinian's reign in 565, Byzantine forces regained control of its eastern bases and the Byzantine Empire would remain for nearly 1,000 years.

One of the main reasons for the longevity of the Eastern Empire was the development about AD 500 of a strong navy. By 700, the imperial navy of the East was once again large enough to be divided into a home fleet and a number of provincial units, as it was in the heyday of the Western Empire. New ship designs and the introduction of 'Greek fire' as a naval weapon contributed to their dominance. The Byzantine navy would remain the strongest in the Eastern Mediterranean until the eleventh century.

By 1100, maritime trade was controlled by the merchants of Genoa, Pisa, Venice and the Republic of Dubrovnik. Again, Italian fleets were masters of the Mediterranean. With the gradual decline of the Byzantine imperial navy, the Ottoman Turks finally overran the Byzantine Empire and captured Constantinople in 1453. They became the unlikely (because, like Rome before the Punic Wars, innately agrarian and land-oriented) dominant Mediterranean sea power, eclipsing that of the Italianate city-states.

Chapter Eighteen

Summing Up: Mahan and Corbett's Notional Critique of Roman Sea Power

Mahan's prefatory critique of the naval aspects of the Second Punic War, discussed in detail in the chapter on that conflict, provides a good idea of how he would have analyzed the sea power of the Roman Empire had he not decided to employ the British Navy of the seventeenth to nineteenth centuries to illustrate his principal thesis. His decision to by-pass the ostensibly more apt First Punic War is explained in his preface to the pages on the Second. No doubt he foreswore more extensive coverage of the ancient period because, as he explained in his introduction to the Second Punic War, the sources were fragmentary and often baffling to a researcher: the scholarship of the 1880s, *pace* Mommsen's fine work, was not yet sophisticated enough and largely ignored naval affairs. Sir Julian Corbett would have similarly found the more nuanced sea-land Roman campaigns of AD 6-600 more apt subjects for his pen than the high-seas clashes had his mission not been so policy-driven.

To make a modern parallel, one would only briefly describe the period from, say 1930-1945, when American 'command of the seas' was being forged, and concentrate on the ensuing period, from 1945 to the present, when it exploited the oceanic domination won in fighting the German Kriegsmarine and Japanese Imperial Navy to build up a flourishing seaborne commerce. In my case, since Mahan had made such a good start in his brief analysis of the Second Punic War, as expanded by Frederick Clark's thesis to embrace maritime strategy and naval presence up to the ascent of Augustus, I reviewed that earlier phase as though under the guidance of the US Naval War College's first instructor.

The beginnings of Rome's maritime awareness had largely been due to the example of its rivals on the Italian peninsula, the Etruscans, who did reap some tangible benefits from their naval assets, a lesson not entirely lost on her land-minded neighbours to the south. While not yet a trading nation herself, Rome certainly could perceive the possibilities inherent in importing and exporting commodities to nations bordering the surrounding seas. The several treaties with Carthage over the period of several generations had tacitly acknowledged Rome's relative impotence on the sea.

Having relied upon the Greek naval associates at the southern end of the Italian boot for assistance in resisting the predations of pirates, Rome found herself quite unprepared for the contretemps with Tarentum and the ensuing invasion by the Epiran forces of Pyrrhus. It was Rome's ally of convenience, Carthage, that exploited her sea command in this conflict, but there were no lessons for Rome at this juncture; the Roman representatives of the people were confident in their solid support of naval-minded associates for this unfamiliar mode of warfare.

In my section on the Second Punic War, I noted how in his preface Mahan attacked the tendency of historians to slight the maritime aspects of human endeavours when writing the annals of nations and of mankind. This was notoriously so in England, where national greatness rested on the use and control of the sea. Citing historians Arnold and Creasy as to how success in arms on land had brought ascendancy, Mahan complained that in neither of these episodes – that is, Hannibal striving against Rome or Napoleon against England – did historians note that 'the mastery of the sea rested with the victor'. In fact, wrote Mahan, Roman sea power obliged Hannibal to undertake a perilous march through Gaul, thereby wasting half his veterans, and enabled the elder Scipio to intercept Hannibal's communications and to return to wage a war on land. Meanwhile, legions passed to and fro by water between Italy and Spain unmolested and unwearied, while Roman sea power sealed off the enemy's approaches by sea, obliging them to come by land. Thus divided, the two Carthaginian armies were separated, and one was destroyed by the combined actions of the Roman generals.

What is more, the Punic Wars showed how abrupt Rome's maritime baptism had been. Up until then, they had been content to rely on naval associates and allies to furnish such sea-based defence as was necessary, and had allocated a few magistrates to administer the skeletal naval force directly operated by Rome. While it should have proven the need to maintain a standing fleet, this lesson was not all that obvious to one who had managed to overcome the world's pre-eminent sea power by simply outlasting her opponent through an exhausting twenty-four-year conflict. Several hundred miles to the east, tyrants who commanded the local waters were busy battling one another and posed no immediate danger to Rome, so she let her fleets rot.

By the time of the wars with the Eastern Mediterranean despots (Macedonian, Syrian and Mithridatic Wars), Rome had belatedly recognized that dependence upon naval-minded associates, while useful, should not be the sole pillar of her naval power; the lapse of shipbuilding and maintenance, and resultant shortage just prior to the urgent major anti-pirate sweep of Pompey the Great, reinforced this lesson. The Civil Wars that led to the establishment of the Augustan Empire were further proof of this dictum.

The fleets of the latter centuries of the Republic were very different from those of the Punic Wars. Since its inception in the late fourth century, Rome's capability on the sea had greatly benefited from the experience of the Greeks and Etruscans. However, we must remember that during the Punic Wars, it was Rome who chiefly manned a large part of its naval squadrons with its own citizens, built its ships with its own money and directed them with a consul or a Roman *praetor*. However, from 200 BC, Rome had reverted to basing its maritime power on its Greek allies, and especially the naval forces of Rhodes, whose training and expertise was unsurpassed.

The allied cities of Ionia, Phoenicia and Syria Pamphylia furnished most of the ships of the Roman squadrons, with the exception of those that Rome had built, which were operated by crews from these cities, so that Greek and Oriental naval technology and experience established themselves increasingly in the Roman navy at the time of the Social War (90-88 BC). As for the commanders of these fleets, who were sometimes Greek, Rome subordinated them to the commanders of the land forces, proof that she had not fully understood the role of a naval force.

These naval expedients did not hinder Mithridates, King of Pontus, during the first war he waged against Rome between 89-85 BC, from seizing control of the Aegean, which led, after his defeat in 84, to the appearance of a permanent fleet for the first time in the history of the Roman navy, finally abandoning the practice of naval disarmament after each victory, which had been a near-fatal habit up to then. This development suggests that naval thought was beginning to emerge, and that the embryo of the imperial navy had commenced, allowing C.G. Starr to say that 'if we ask someone to mention an event that marks the early Roman Imperial navy, this event would certainly be the first war against Mithridates of Rome.'

Another consequence of this development was the establishment by Sulla, probably in 85 BC, of a plan of defence for the coast of Asia Minor. The maritime cities of this region had to build warships and keep them in reserve for future employment in joint objectives. This enabled Rome to maintain control of the sea during the third and final war against Mithridates (83-82). C.G. Starr observes that it was difficult for the Roman state to continue the implementation of a long-term strategic plan due to annual changes of those who were responsible for its execution. This trend continued in 67 when Pompey triumphed in a three-month campaign against the pirates who infested almost all Mediterranean waters. According to Pliny (Natural History, VII, 98), Pompey would have 'given back control of the sea to Rome', which had let its sea power lapse to the point that pirates had the audacity to sink a consular fleet in the port of Ostia (Plutarch, *Pompey*, XXXVIII to XLIV).

At this point, Rome had lethargically though definitively developed an appreciation why control of the surrounding seas was essential and how it should be maintained. From this time on, the Roman navy played a crucial role in the civil wars that brought Augustus to power and thereafter throughout the imperial epoch. The wars against Mithridates and rapid campaign against the pirates had demonstrated the importance of the naval power that had been forgotten since the Punic Wars. F.E. Adcock noted that 'in its most difficult campaign, Pompey relied on naval power and Caesar trusted the sea; in grave situations, the last word was left to the sea.' He was referring to operations around Dyrrachium (Durazzo), where the powerful fleet of Pompey was defeated by Caesarean forces. It has once again been revealed that the exercise of the control of the sea was regarded by the Roman generals as a pledge of victory.

During the Civil War, in the middle of the first century BC, fleets became more and more powerful. Pompey, availing himself of the maritime cities of Asia, managed to assemble a force of about 300 vessels at the beginning of 48; this is Sextus Pompey, son of Pompey the Great, who, having secured the mastery of the Western Mediterranean, ensured the supply of grain to Rome and raided Italian shores to acquire plunder from 42-40 BC.

In 38 BC, the future Augustus, with Agrippa, his military adviser, built a fleet of 400 ships that triumphed over those of Sextus Pompey at Mylae in 37, at Nauloque in 36 and finally at Actium in 31. This armada is the nucleus of the future imperial fleet. Already at this stage we can see the germination of naval-mindedness wherein Octavian, the political and strategic architect, partners with Agrippa, the naval engineer and tactician. The latter invented the harpax, a catapult-launched grapple, and was accordingly honoured for his unique services by being awarded the naval crown by his erstwhile partner, the new Caesar, the first such award ever granted (Livy, CXXIX).

Once Actium was won and Octavian was sole master of the sea, he also captured all of Antony's warships. Gradually, he stopped the production of the largest ship, the quinquereme. Rome had such a firm hold on the sea that it did not need fear an enemy so powerful as to require quinqueremes. Smaller, faster ships were more practical for policing and cheaper to manufacture. For the remainder of their existence, the role of all fleets could be summed up as constituting anti-piracy patrols, transport of proconsuls and legates to their provinces and of military reinforcements, enforcing taxation of river ways and communication with Britannia and other provinces by rivers (as on the Rhine, Rhône, Nile and Danube). Each fleet, however, had its own specific duties to fulfill, depending on the needs of each region.

Upon the institution of the Empire, the army was organized into some twenty-eight legions, mostly stationed on the turbulent borders of the Empire. The fleet, on the other hand, was deliberately sited at the Empire's centre to keep watch on the Mediterranean coasts of Rome's expansive domain. The task was made easier by the fact that the local inhabitants of these coasts no longer possessed threatening navies of their own. The military role of the fleet was to ensure the rapid and safe transport of the armies to threatened areas. Additionally, it served as an important preventative measure against piracy. Unlike the previous century, during which many pirates had been active, the two centuries from Augustus to Septimus Severus (AD 193-211) were characterized by a striking absence of piracy, with the exception of the far west. The trade routes, and particularly the corn supply routes – vitally important for the city of Rome – were of course given special attention by the commanders of the fleets.

Henry Ormerod (*Piracy in the Ancient World*) goes into detail describing the methodology used by those ancient pirates, studying later cases of Mediterranean piracy and comparing them to available sources. They would normally operate within a short distance of a base, rarely attacking ships but going on coastal raids kidnapping civilians for ransom or selling them into slavery in the markets of Delos. Two of the most prominent piratical groups Octavian had to pacify when coming to prominence were the Illyrians, pacified before Actium, and the Cicilians, pacified around 25 BC. Pompey the Great's anti-piracy sweep near the end of the Republic had shown how the way to defeat the pirates was not to try to intercept them at sea and pursue them to their base; the ships of that day could not possibly either provide convoy service to merchant vessels nor blockade pirate coasts. The exercise of sea power in the context of that time meant that the hinterlands, coves, inlets and rocky promontories from which pirates operated would have to be attacked, and the infrastructure supporting the various raiding squadrons eradicated.

As an eminent authority on ancient piracy, Philip de Souza, has observed:

> 'The Romans were aware at this time that the most effective way to deal with pirates was to tackle them on land. This might involve some naval fighting, in order to approach certain bases or strongholds, but the real test of the Romans' determination to ensure the safety of the seas for their friends and allies was their willingness and ability to overcome pirates in their lairs.'

In the years between the reigns of Augustus and Septimius Severus, the fleets were such efficient deterrents of seaborne enemies that there were no reports of pirates except those mentioned above. Augustus himself viewed his achievements at sea with pride, writing in the *Res Gestae* that his fleets reached far corners of the world where no Roman had ever set foot, and defeated enemies both 'on land and at sea'. And indeed he was the foremost patron of sea power, having established the fleets of Ravenna and Misenum in 39 and 22 BC respectively. In addition, he established smaller fleets in Alexandria (to control and tax shipping between the Nile and Mediterranean) and Syria (to secure trade in the East). His early experience with

Sextus Pompey, in which Rome was starving, taught Augustus that a peaceful Mediterranean was crucial to ensure that the imperial organism stays healthy.

Once the imperial fleets were in place, the common perception is that there was little for them to do. However, as demonstrated in the latter half of this book, that was far from the case. The absence of competing maritime powers did not bring about a naval drawdown, such as was done after the Mithridatic Wars.

As can be seen in the chapters detailing the role of the naval forces in securing the provinces against rebellious tribal coalitions, mutinies and treacheries of various legionary commanders, the fleets, as they waxed and waned in response to crises in their sectors, continued to wield 'sea power' in the sense conveyed by the later writings of Alfred Mahan and especially those of Julian Corbett.

Annotated Bibliography

The following bibliography is annotated to reflect the chapters and subjects for which the particular book or article was particularly helpful. I have opted to employ this method in lieu of footnoting, which in this case would unduly bog down the narrative. Where needed, I have indicated direct quotes in the text. Being that I am monolingual, I have relied upon translation software to read excerpts from modern works in languages other than English.

Primary Sources

Cassius Dio, *ROMAN HISTORY*. Loeb Classical Library, 9 volumes, Greek texts and facing English translation: Harvard University Press, 1914–1927. Translation by Earnest Cary.

Livy

Livy, *THE LOEB LIVY* (Loeb Classical Library) London: Heinemann, 1943

In distinct contrast to Polybius, Livy was an academic/bookworm, who had never served as an officer of state or fought a battle, nor did he visit the places he wrote about, or interview eyewitnesses as Polybius had done. However, he did have access to a wide range of sources, including public records and other histories. For his account of the Second Punic War he *consulted* Polybius, but he preferred Polybius' Roman contemporary Coelius Antipater, who was more exciting and romantic, but also generally more 'Roman' than Polybius, giving more attention to the gods, auspices and dreams. Unlike Polybius, Livy does not directly state the ascribed inner thoughts, feelings and nature of his characters, but, in the manner of Shakespeare's soliloquies, he exploits imputed speeches to reveal these traits, and often converts Polybius' explanations into speeches or letters.

Plutarch, *PLUTARCH'S LIVES* (Loeb Classical Library, 1959).

Polybius, *THE HISTORIES OF POLYBIUS*, (Loeb Classical Library edition), online at
<http://penelope.uchicago.edu/Thayer/E/Roman/Texts/Polybius/home.html>

The Histories of Polybius cover 264-146 BC, focussing on the domination of the Romans in the Mediterranean. Polybius is based on eyewitness accounts and official Roman documents, as well as Carthaginian sources now lost to us. As a contemporary, he had the opportunity to interview veterans of these wars. Although a reputable source, caution should be taken as some accounts can be biased. Generally, he should be cross-checked with Livy, although is considered the more reliable in most cases. He took a particular interest in Rome's naval endeavours. His career as a soldier, statesman and diplomat, and his desire for first-hand knowledge, makes him, in general, the more reliable of the two when it came to contemporary affairs.

Tacitus

The Histories and Agricola fill some gaps in the later Republican and early imperial naval operations.

Zonaris

Joannes Zonaris flourished in the twelfth century. He was a Byzantine historian whose world history, *Historical Epitome*, extended from the creation to 1118. He drew on a rich collection of sources, some of which, notably several books of Dio Cassius' *Romaika*, are preserved only through him. For topics where his sources are lost or appear elsewhere in a more truncated form, his testimony and identification of the texts are vital. Zonaras never claimed to be more than a compiler. For Roman history to the destruction of Carthage, he excerpted Plutarch and the first twenty-one books of Cassius Dio, for which he is our only important source. For AD 235-395, covering the period after the histories of Cassius Dio, he is very valuable, in that he has consulted earlier sources now completely lost. Petrus Patricius was his chief source for the period between Severus Alexander and Constantine I. The rest derives from various chronicles, not all of which have been identified. Zonaris is especially important as a source for the period 450–550.

Modern Literature

Bass, George F. (ed.), *A HISTORY OF SEAFARING BASED ON UNDERWATER ARCHAEOLOGY*. NY: Walker and Co./London: Thames and Hudson, 1972.

See references to the chapters focussing on Rome and Byzantium. Although, as noted in the title, the seafaring theme has been treated primarily from the archaeological standpoint – a project made possible by the remarkable advances in underwater archaeology of the two decades prior to publication – there were concise notations regarding the effects of the vessels on maritime campaigns scattered throughout.

Belfiglio, Valentine J., *A STUDY OF ANCIENT ROMAN AMPHIBIOUS AND OFFENSIVE SEA-GROUND TASK FORCE OPERATIONS*. The Edwin Mellen Press, 2001.

While not a comprehensive review of the totality of Roman operations in the 'littorals', as the modern naval parlance calls them, this is a handy precis of a handful of such actions, primarily focussing on those of Julius Caesar. At times the author sounds as if he is writing up a case study for the Marine Corps amphibious landing manual, and, as such, is a bit too glib in applying modern concepts to a period when most naval combat was along the shorelines. However, as noted, this is a useful look at a very neglected topic. The Roman navy itself has been largely overlooked, and certainly its actions at the beachheads have.

Carro, Admiral Domenico, *Rom Aeterna*(website) http://www.romaeterna.org/roma/tabulae_navales_br.html#p2

Through use of online translation software, I was able to study his most important essays and chapters downloaded from the website. It is safe to say that he has revitalized the study of ancient Rome's sea power as a fit subject for modern naval cadets. His enlightening, detailed maps have not only enriched my book, but also helped to frame my narrative.

———, 'Le forze navali, strumento essenziale della grande strategia di Roma', in *L'ESERCITO E LA CULTURA MILITARE DI ROMA ANTICA*, a cura di Simona Carosi e Roberto Libera.

Casson, Lionel, *THE ANCIENT MARINERS: SEAFARERS AND SEA FIGHTERS OF THE MEDITERRANEAN IN ANCIENT TIMES*. NY: Macmillan Co., 1959.

SHIPS AND SEAMANSHIP IN THE ANCIENT WORLD. Princeton UP, 1971.

Very good on ship building, seafaring, mercantile trade, ports and naval infrastructure, especially the *Ships and Seamanship* book. *Ancient Mariners* is superior to the latter book on battles and naval campaigns, but, as is common in books on ancient navies, skimpy on the Roman imperial period. The first mentioned book is written in a breezy, accessible style appealing to a general readership, while the latter is written for the scholar, replete with minute detail and footnoting, with chapters following a thematic rather than a chronological pattern. My sections on maritime commerce and the seagoing qualities of Roman ships, both cargo vessels and warships are heavily indebted to Dr Casson.

Clark, Frederick, *THE INFLUENCE OF SEA POWER ON THE HISTORY OF THE ROMAN REPUBLIC.* Kessinger Publishing, LLC, 10 September 2010. (Original: PhD diss., University of Chicago, 1915, Menasha, Wis.: George Banta Pub. Co., 1915).

Though neglected by many modern historians, this dissertation contains good reviews of the naval wars and campaigns from the Pyrrhic Wars to the Battle of Actium. It is particularly helpful as an early example of applying Mahan to ancient history. He makes frequent reference to the ancient sources, not so much to contemporary studies, although the writings of Mahan were only some twenty-five years old at the time of writing. There were thus few efforts to apply his maxims more broadly, so Clark's pamphlet may be considered a pioneering work.

Custance, Sir Reginald, *WAR AT SEA: MODERN THEORY AND ANCIENT PRACTICE.* Edinburgh and London: William Blackwood & Sons, 1919.

Although the author focusses on the Greco-Persian and Peloponnesian Wars, the way in which he derives lessons for modern (post-First World War) navies is instructive.

Dell, Harry J., 'The Origin and Nature of Illyrian Piracy', *HISTORIA* 16 (Wiesbaden, 1967), pp.344-58.

De Santis, Marc C., *ROME SEIZES THE TRIDENT: THE DEFEAT OF CARTHAGINIAN SEAPOWER AND THE FORGING OF THE ROMAN EMPIRE.* Pen and Sword, 2016.

De Souza, Philip, *PIRACY IN THE GRAECO-ROMAN WORLD.* Cambridge, 1999.

Thematically rather than chronologically organized, a necessary update of the Ormerod study. Good on debunking characterization of various sub-national groups as 'pirates', often being attributable to rhetorical disparagement of the enemy nation with respect to the ancient historian.

Eckstein, Arthur M., Rome Dominates the Mediterranean' in *CHINA GOES TO SEA: MARITIME TRANSFORMATION IN COMPARATIVE HISTORICAL PERSPECTIVE*, by Andrew S. Erickson, Lyle J. Goldstein and Carnes Lord (eds), Naval Institute Press. Annapolis, MD, 2009.

Grant, Peter Kojo Tsiwah, *The Navy in Rome's Rise to Empire: 264-146* BC. Saarbrucken, Germany: Lambert Academic Publishing GmbH & Co. KG,.

Useful for its analytic survey of Roman sea power up to the Third Punic War. This book argues that but for the existence of a navy in the armed forces of Rome, she would have remained merely a hegemon of Italy whose influence and dominion would not have traversed the seas.

Harris, William V., *WAR AND IMPERIALISM IN REPUBLICAN ROME*, *327-70 BC*. Oxford: Clarendon, 1979.

Haywood, J., *DARK AGE NAVAL POWER: A REASSESSMENT OF FRANKISH AND ANGLO-SAXON SEAFARING ACTIVITY*. London: 1991.
Very helpful on the campaigns of the *classis Germanica* in the waning days of the Empire. Makes good use of the archaeological finds of ship hulks and shipbuilding facilities.

Ilari, Virgilio, *ROMAN SEAPOWER: L'EMERSIONE DI UN TEMA STORIOGRAFICO*. 2014 revised edition essay; PDF accessed online at http://www.societaitalianastoriamilitare.org/COLLANA%20SISM/2014%20ILARI.%20Roman%20Seapower.%20Revised%20Edition.pdf
Dr Ilari's essay, like the writings of Admiral Carro, provides a thorough historiographical review of writings on Roman naval matters since the sixteenth century. It was particularly useful on tracing the 'continental' versus 'sea power' dichotomy.

Iliopoulos, Ilias, 'Strategy and Geopolitics of Sea Power Throughout History', *Baltic Security & Defence Review* Volume 11, Issue 2, 2009.
Excellent rundown of the 'continental versus sea power' paradigm through history, mostly modern.

Jane, Fred, HERESIES OF SEA POWER (pp.40-71), 1906.

Kienast, Dietmar. *UNTERSUCHUNGEN ZU DEN KRIEGSFLOTTEN DER ROMISCHEN KAISERZEIT*. Bonn: Rudolf Habelt Verlag, 1966.

Koster, A., and von Nischer, E., 'Das Seekriegswesen bei den Romern', in A. Koster *et al.* (eds), *HEERWESEN UND KRIEGSFUHREN DER GRIECHEN UND ROMER*, 4. Abt., 3. Teil, 2. Bd., of Iwan von Muller and Walter Otto (eds.), *HANDBUCH DER ALTERTHUMSWISSENSCHAFT*. Munich: C.H. Becksche Verlagsbuchhandlung, 1928, pp.609-26.

Kromayer, J., 'Die Entwicklung der römischen Flotte vom Seerauberkriege des Pompeius bis zum Schlacht von Actium', *Philologus* 56, 1897, pp.426-91.

Mahan, A.T., *THE INFLUENCE OF SEA POWER UPON HISTORY, 1660-1783*. Boston: Little, Brown and Company, 1890.

Mason, David, *Roman Britain and the Roman Navy*. Tempus Books, 2003.
Good not only for the *classis Britannia* but for the adjacent theatres (Gaul, Rhine, etc.) as well.

Marsden, Peter, 'Ships of the Roman Period and After in Britain', in George F. Bass (ed.), *A HISTORY OF SEAFARING BASED ON UNDERWATER ARCHAEOLOGY*. NY: Walker and Co./London: Thames and Hudson, 1972, pp.113–32.

Mattingly, Harold, *COINS OF THE ROMAN EMPIRE IN THE BRITISH MUSEUM*. London: Printed on order of the Trustees, 1923.
'The First Age of Roman Coinage', *JRS* 25 (1945), pp.65–76.
——— *et al.* (eds), *THE ROMAN IMPERIAL COINAGE* (9 vols). London: Spink, 1923.
Some of Mattingly's dates for the earliest Roman coins depicting ships have been challenged of late. However, his pioneering works have been useful to me in estimating the appearance of the Roman vessels, as depicted on coins, albeit somewhat crudely.

Meijer, Fik, *A HISTORY OF SEAFARING IN THE CLASSICAL WORLD*. NY: St Martin's Pr., 1986.
A useful supplement to the Casson books on the mercantile networks, routes and wares, as well as the sailing characteristics of the ancient vessels. Some brief, though helpful, commentary on the naval campaigns.

Nedu, Decebal, '*The Beginnings of the Roman Fleet, 509–264 BC*', online at http://www.fift.ugal.ro/revistadeistorie/anale/6/601%20NEDU.pdf

Ormerod, Henry, *PIRACY IN THE ANCIENT WORLD: AN ESSAY IN MEDITERRANEAN HISTORY*. Liverpool University Press, 1924.
Though old and somewhat dated by more recent research, it has some excellent observations on this persistent nuisance. However, his tendency to heavily exemplify with comparisons to piratic episodes from the eighteenth and nineteenth centuries at times overwhelms the ancient examples. Particularly useful on the Pompeian campaign against Cilicia and the pirates' participation in the Mithridatic Wars.

Pagès, Jean, '*Y a-t-il eu une pensée navale romaine?*', online essay at the Euro-Synergies website http://euro-synergies.hautetfort.com/archive/2012/03/02/y-a-t-il-eu-une-pensee-navale-romaine.html
This essay is a good and accessible summary of much of Dr Pagès' other articles on ancient naval science. I found it very useful in applying modern concepts to Rome's naval endeavours throughout my book.

Pargiter, Major R.B., and Eady, Major H.G., *THE ARMY & SEA POWER: A HISTORICAL OUTLINE*. London: Ernest Benn Limited, 1927.

Good for comparisons/contrasts with British overseas expeditions during the *Pax Britannica*.

Pemsel, Helmut, *A HISTORY OF WAR AT SEA: AN ATLAS AND CHRONOLOGY OF CONFLICT AT SEA FROM EARLIEST TIMES TO THE PRESENT.* Naval Institute Press, June 1979.

Pitassi, Michael, *THE NAVIES OF ROME*. Woodbridge: The Boydell Press, 2009.
Pitassi looks specifically at the development of the navies in Rome from 753 BC all the way through to AD 476. He gives a detailed description of how Rome went from barely having a navy to being the exclusive sea power of the Mediterranean. Pitassi uses references from ancient sources such as Polybius and Livy and compares them with modern sources. I have cross-checked my information from other sources with Pitassi to fill in some blanks and to correct any misinterpretation.

Potter, E.B., *SEA POWER: A NAVAL HISTORY*. Annapolis: Naval Institute Press, 1981.

Quirke, Patrick Quinn, *THE BIRTH OF THE ROMAN NAVY*. Canberra: Dickson College, 2011. (https://cliojournal.wikispaces.com/The+Birth+of+the+Roman+Navy).
Submitted as part of The Roman Republic unit at Dickson College, Australia, Semester 1, 1996. It was written in response to the following question: 'Before the First Punic War, the Romans barely had a navy. Explain how the Romans developed and sustained a navy during the course of the First Punic War. Evaluate what, if anything, this explanation reveals about the Romans.'

Reddé, M, *MARE NOSTRUM: LES INFRASTRUCTURES, LE DISPOSITIF ET L'HISTOIRE DE LA MARINE MILITAIRE SOUS L'EMPIRE ROMAIN* (Bibliotheque des ecoles francaises d'Athenes et de Rome). Paris: Diffusion de Boccard, 1986.
Very good on the material and technical aspects (heavily drawn from marine archeology) and the make-up and responsibilities of the various fleets, but skimpy on the strategic direction of the navies. Similar to Rouge but more in-depth.

Rodgers, William Ledyard, *GREEK AND ROMAN NAVAL WARFARE*. Annapolis: US Naval Institute, 1937.
Though Rodgers wrote decades before modern maritime archaeologists like Morison arrived at a logical reconstruction of ancient Greek and Roman

warships, his naval-officer perspective is worthy of study, even though his concepts of the rowing configuration of the heavy 'battleships' of the Late Republic have been superseded. He provides good detail on the battles and campaigns, much of which has survived the test of time.

Rose, J.H., *THE MEDITERRANEAN IN THE ANCIENT WORLD*. London: Cambridge University Press, 1933.
Has some interesting comments on the strategic geography of the 'Middle Sea' as it affected Roman sea power.

Rouge, Jean, *SHIPS AND FLEETS OF THE ANCIENT MEDITERRANEAN*, tr. by Susan Frazer. Middletown CT: Wesleyan UP, 1981 (orig. French 1975).
Valuable for fleet organization, bases, ports, naval infrastructure, ship types and maritime commerce. Not much on the operations of naval warfare *per se*.

Saddington, D.B., '*Classes*. The Evolution of the Roman Imperial Fleets', in Gardiner, Robert, *A COMPANION TO THE ROMAN ARMY*. Blackwell Publishing Ltd, 2007.

Scullard, Howard, *A HISTORY OF THE ROMAN WORLD 753-146 BC*. London: Methuen & Co Ltd, 1961.
Scullard focusses on Rome and Carthage, and section 4 of chapter VII provides a detailed account of Rome's naval offensive in the First Punic War.

Serre, Paul, contre-amiral, *ÉTUDES SUR L'HISTOIRE MILITAIRE ET MARITIME DES GRECS ET DES ROMAINS:SUITE DES MARINES DE L'ANTIQUITÉ ET DU MOYEN ÂGE*. Paris: L. Baudoin, 1888.

Shepard, Arthur McCartney, *SEA POWER IN ANCIENT HISTORY – THE STORY OF THE NAVIES OF CLASSIC GREECE AND ROME*. Boston: Little, Brown, 1924.
Though old, this study makes good use of the sources and provides a serviceable run-down of the naval campaigns and battles up to the end of the Republic. Employing Mahan as a fulcrum, the author gives a layman's rather than a scholar's overview, though evidencing wide reading in the ancient texts.
Mr Shepard writes credulously of ships with ten banks of oars and of ships propelled partly by oars and partly by sail, travelling at a speed of 15 and even 18 knots. Behemoths with characteristics such as these have been debunked by more recent authors.

Starr, Chester G., *THE INFLUENCE OF SEA POWER ON ANCIENT HISTORY*. NY: Oxford UP, 1989.

THE ROMAN IMPERIAL NAVY, 31 BC-AD 324 (2nd ed.). Cambridge, UK: W. Heffer and Sons Ltd., 1960.

'The Myth of the Minoan Thalassocracy', *Historia 3*, 1955, pp.282-91.

My issues with Starr's Influence book have been amply expressed in the text. All told, they are relatively minor, largely due to the purported charge of the book – to debunk Mahan and his nameless disciples' unproven exaggeration of the significance of sea power to ancient states. The synopses of Roman naval wars and campaigns were useful, especially those embedded in the earlier book on the various fleets. Being incorporated in separate biographies of the fleets, I had to extract and meld them to complement my narrative derived from other sources.

Steinby, Christa, *THE ROMAN REPUBLICAN NAVY: FROM THE SIXTH CENTURY TO 167 BC.* Commentationes humanarum litterarum, 123. Helsinki: Societas Scientiarum Fennica, 2007.

Valuable as a supplement to Thiel, who is somewhat dismissive of Roman naval endeavours prior to the First Punic War. Dr Steinby contends that Rome, contrary to Thiel, did appreciate and utilize sea power as early as the period leading up to the Pyrrhic War. She, like Thiel in his countervailing perspective, sometimes makes too creative use of sources and thus exaggerates the Roman duckling's wading efforts.

Stevens, W.O., *A HISTORY OF SEA POWER*. New York: George H. Doran Company, 1920.

Tarn, W.W., *HELLENISTIC MILITARY AND NAVAL DEVELOPMENTS*. Cambridge UP, 1930.

'The Roman Navy', in John E. Sandys (ed.), *A COMPANION TO LATIN STUDIES*. Cambridge UP, 1910, pp.489-501.

'Fleets of the First Punic War', in *Journal of Hellenic Studies*, 1907.

Tarn has some interesting and useful comments on the fleet strengths in the Punic Wars, which had to be checked against more recent estimates. In any event, his line of reasoning helped me in framing other segments of the text.

Thiel, J.H., *A HISTORY OF ROMAN SEA POWER BEFORE THE SECOND PUNIC WAR*. Amsterdam: North-Holland Publishing Co., 1954.

STUDIES ON THE HISTORY OF ROMAN SEA-POWER IN REPUBLICAN TIMES. Amsterdam: North-Holland Publishing Co., 1946.

I have noted my take on Dr Thiel's much-cited 'landlubber' characterization of Rome's attitude and experiences with seafaring – that he was describing a cultural aversion which had to be overcome in order to raise, equip, man and train naval units. This task was done 'holding the nose', as Thiel described it, but with typical Roman engineering thoroughness and expertise. The essence of these two very valuable works is the detailed descriptions and still creditable analyses of Rome's naval activities from her founding to the end of the Republic. Although English is a second language for Thiel, and here and there a few awkward attempts at colloquialisms creep in, he writes in a forthright, assertive style, not hesitating to take a controversial position, but always supporting it with astute reasoning. He has been criticized for a professor's penchant for repeating assertions so as to hammer them home, but I didn't find this disconcerting at all. He does get excited about both the cleverness and the stupidity of the naval contenders, which, again, some reviewers have disliked, but I enjoyed; he doesn't employ hindsight but evaluates in light of the information available at the time.

Even at their most speculative, his comments are stimulating; and without the aid of the inscriptions, coins and papyri which are so useful to historians of Rome in later times, he has reconstituted as well as existing sources permit the strength and distribution, year by year, of the fleets of Rome and her allies and enemies, and has discussed with acumen the influence of naval, military and internal factors on each other and on the general course of events. In doing so, he has gone far toward correcting a common tendency to underestimate the role of naval activities in Roman affairs generally, and especially in Rome's success in subduing the Mediterranean world.

Throckmorton, Peter, 'Romans on the Sea', in George F. Bass (ed.), *A HISTORY OF SEAFARING BASED ON UNDERWATER ARCHAEOLOGY*. NY: Walker and Co./London: Thames and Hudson, 1972.

Vagts, Alfred, *LANDING OPERATIONS: STRATEGY, PSYCHOLOGY, TACTICS, POLITICS, FROM ANTIQUITY TO 1945*. Harrisburg, PA: Military Services Publishing, 1952.
Early chapters dealing with Greek and Roman antiquity. Roman section as usual deals in detail with Caesar's two Britannic invasions, but has good commentary on other amphibious landings of the Late Republic and Late Empire.

Van Doorninck, Frederick, 'Byzantium, Mistress of the Sea: 330-641', in George F. Bass (ed.), *A HISTORY OF SEAFARING BASED ON UNDERWATER ARCHAEOLOGY*. NY: Walker and Co./London: Thames and Hudson, 1972.

Viereck, H.D.L., *DIE ROMISCHE FLOTTE*. Herford, Germany: Koehlers Verlagsgesellschaft, 1975.
I utilized this book by entering selected sections into Googletranslate software on their website. The book was primarily helpful in fleshing out the naval actions

under the emperors up to the late fifth century. Apart from the Pitassi books, there are very few modern references which furnish any detail on the fleets' roles and operations during last five centuries of Rome. Even allowing for the flaws in robotic translation, there are some confusing or plainly erroneous portions of this text which were corrected by cross-checking with other modern sources.

Walbank, F.W., *A HISTORICAL COMMENTARY ON POLYBIUS*, 2 vols. Oxford: Clarendon, 1967.
As would be expected in a discussion of Polybius, the two volumes have important notations on naval matters.

Walling, Herman T., *THE BOARDING BRIDGE OF THE ROMANS: ITS CONSTRUCTION AND ITS FUNCTION IN THE NAVAL TACTICS OF THE FIRST PUNIC WAR*. Groningen, Netherlands: J.B. Wolters, 1956.
This pamphlet is more than the title suggests. It has some valuable discussion on the utility and ultimate discontinuance of the *corvus* during First Punic War. Walling updates, and to some extent corrects, the observations of Thiel on these matters. His later book on the origin and historical evolution of the trireme, while predating my era, was nonetheless helpful as well.

White, A.N. Sherwin, *ROMAN FOREIGN POLICY IN THE EAST*. London: Duckworth, 1984.
I used this as a guide for my summaries of Augustan grand strategical aims guiding naval policies and operations.

Index